Teacher's Edition Contents

Senior Contributing Editor:

Kaye Passmore, Notre Dame Academy, Worcester, Massachusetts

Editorial Consultants:

Leigh Backstrom, North High School, Worcester, Massachusetts

David McIntyre, El Paso Independent School District, El Paso, Texas

Connie Pirtle, Tennessee State Department of Education, Nashville, Tennessee

Barbara Pratt, Richardson Independent School District, Richardson, Texas

Richard Shilale, Holy Name High School, Worcester, Massachusetts

Diana Woodruff, Forest Avenue Elementary School, Hudson, Massachusetts

Faith Zajicek, Temple High School, Temple, Texas

© 2000 Davis Publications, Inc.
Worcester, Massachusetts, U.S.A.

Publisher: Wyatt Wade
Editorial Director: Helen Ronan
Production Editor: Carol Harley
Manufacturing Coordinator: Jenna Sturgis
Copyeditor: Janet Stone
Editorial Assistance: Colleen Strang
Design and Electronic Page Make-up: Tong-Mei Chan
Design Advisor: Douglass Scott

Printed in U.S.A.
Library of Congress Catalog Card Number: 93-74645
ISBN: 87192-468-4
10 9 8 7 6 5 4 3 2 1

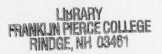

Using Discovering Drawing Effectively

Philosophy of Discovering Drawing

This book was written to provide the drawing student with direction, *not* directions; the weight is on the students to turn general basics of drawing skills into personal expressions. There is no one way to draw. The basics of line, stroke and tone; perspective; proportion; approaches to setting up still lifes; and selection of components in a landscape are identifiable skills that can be, and indeed are, defined in this text, but with the expectation that each student will internalize the basic information and create drawings that are as unique as the individual who drew them.

Organization of Discovering Drawing

Discovering Drawing is intended to provide ideas: to stimulate, prod and excite. Skills and concepts are presented in each chapter along with strategies and suggested exercises to allow students to apply these skills in their own drawings. Basic chapter content, sidebars on materials and techniques, and end-of-chapter activities work together to provide a framework for drawing goals. However, there is flexibility within that framework. For example, sidebars on materials and techniques have application for any subject matter. Use sidebars from any chapter as needed. Chapter activities are intended to be used at any time during the teaching of the chapter. They can

also be adapted to meet needs of students with varying levels of abilities.

Special Features

Chapter Openers Each chapter opener includes an *overview* of content covered in the chapter and concise summary statements of *key chapter points*. *Details* of illustrations in the chapter highlight and convey *visually* the types of skills students will learn in the chapter.

Captions The captions in chapters 1–6 are intended to engage the students in looking at and analysing the artworks in a more thorough way than they might on their own. They can also help you, the teacher, start small group discussions that involve higher-order thinking skills, such as the evaluation of the artwork.

Speaking of Art High-interest anecdotes by and about famous artists provide a fresh, personal look at art.

Artist Biographies Art history is made personal in the biographies of famous artists. Drawing techniques are seen through the eyes of masters of drawing, who struggled with the same problems every drawing student encounters.

Artist Profiles Six contemporary artists whose works appear in this book have written personal statements about their art. These profiles introduce students to what artists do, the materials and procedures they use, purposes that motivate them, and the cultural and social meanings the artists want to convey.

Sidebars Each chapter contains mini-lessons on various tools, materials and drawing techniques. These lessons can be presented at any time during the drawing course.

Think About It Critical thinking skills are highlighted within the instructional content. Each *Think About It* is placed at a strategic point. Some heighten students' awareness of their own mental processes. Some identify thinking skills as goals that are part of the drawing process. Others stimulate student thinking, asking questions that go beyond the content taught in the text.

End-of-chapter Activities A wide range of activities is provided at the end of each chapter. Activities can be completed at any time during the chapter. By reviewing them at the start of the chapter, teachers can select activities for use at appropriate points during the teaching of chapter content. Teachers can also adapt activities as needed to meet different ability levels of students.

Chapters 7 and 8 The material in chapters 7 and 8 could be:
• presented as a cumulative overview of art history at the end of the course.
• integrated into the other chapters with one or two styles of art studied in each chapter.
• used as the framework for a drawing course built around art history. This would work particularly well for an advanced drawing class.

Teaching a Course in Drawing

The Value of Drawing

Drawing provides the foundation for development in the arts. The techniques and tools are immediate. The process enables the artist to make direct statements through selective observation. Drawing is a way to communicate, share thoughts, visualize concepts and give birth to creative and imaginative thoughts. Through constant practice, drawing students strengthen observation skills and stimulate creativity.

The process builds students' confidence in reflecting thoughts and experiences. These experiences will allow the student to think freely, approach problems knowledgeably, develop skills and become more self-reliant.

Last but not least, drawing is a vital way of solving problems. It provides the means of expression for the artist to think quickly, make changes and explore a wide range of possibilities. Drawing is a vehicle used by architects, designers and advertisers to explore new concepts. Drawing allows artists to do more than just record what they see. It enables them to expand their thoughts and dreams.

Creating an Atmosphere for Drawing

For the beginning artist, the act of drawing is far more important than the end product. Experimenting with new directions, styles and media should be an integral part of the learning experience.

In a classroom that stresses the joy in the search and the discovery of graphic expression, students can develop a healthy attitude toward drawing that will serve them well in professional careers. Experimentation and craftsmanship should be equally stressed. Freedom, flexibility, creativity, craftsmanship, content and presentation are all important elements of the drawing process.

Students will benefit from taking the time to explore and reflect without fear of failure. Having the courage to express themselves in their own way is a worthy goal.

Setting Effective Goals

Setting effective goals requires knowing your students' backgrounds, capabilities and aspirations. Students generally have a wide range of abilities. Specific classroom goals should be tailored to meet the needs of all students. While the goal and performance behavior are described in the lesson objectives, teachers may adjust the performance level to their specific classroom situation.

To design an effective curriculum you must also know local and state requirements, and set up goals consistent with them. Goals should be understood by administrators and parents as well.

To develop a sense of direction in your drawing program, let students know precisely what the classroom goals are, the skills required and the methods for attaining those skills. Explain weekly the goals and aspirations of your program. Students should understand how the concepts interrelate to the total program.

Review each assignment as it is completed. Look for the positive attributes, ways to improve and suggestions on how to build upon the skills learned. Encourage students to write brief explanations and evaluations of their work. What did they like about the finished piece? What areas would they like to continue to work on and improve? Letting students analyze and evaluate their work allows them to take responsibility for the direction in their artwork and makes them active learners in drawing. Encourage students to reflect on each exercise as a process rather than a means to an end. The point that drawing is a learning process that students and artists continue all their lives cannot be stressed enough.

Critique Sheets

Critique sheets can be used to help students focus on their own work and become aware of areas needing improvement. They also help them identify and become aware of their own feelings and ideas. The left side of the critique sheet lists the objectives for the assignment. Total possible points for each objective are listed. Students grade themselves according to the extent to which they feel they achieved these objectives. Objective "O", Self-Critique is based upon the questions on the right side of the sheet.

Drawing Critique

Name: _____

Date: _____

Unit: _____

Assignment: _____

Objectives: _____

	Possible Points	Earned Points
A Attitude, participation and completion	_____	_____
B Neatness	_____	_____
C Creativity	_____	_____
D Art Principle	_____	_____
E	_____	_____
F	_____	_____
G	_____	_____
H	_____	_____
I	_____	_____
J	_____	_____
K	_____	_____
L	_____	_____
M	_____	_____
N	_____	_____
O Self-Critique	_____	_____

Total Points Earned _____ _____ _____

Self-Critique

1. Description of artwork: (materials, composition, subject matter, style)

_____

_____

_____

2. My feelings toward this work: (Was I genuinely involved? Does my work show something of my own ideas?)

_____

_____

_____

3. Strengths and weaknesses of my work: _____

_____

_____

4. Problems I encountered: _____

_____

_____

5. Successes I achieved: _____

_____

_____

6. Description of my use of elements and principles in this artwork:

_____

_____

_____

_____

Teaching Procedures

When presenting lessons, make the concepts simple, direct and in a logical progression of activities. Be consistent with developing procedures for assignments. The students should be aware of the philosophy and strategy for the lessons.

Set up a work schedule for projects. Keep your work schedules flexible but be firm. Requiring students to work within set time limits will provide valuable experience for students who pursue future careers in art.

Homework assignments are a valuable part of the drawing program. They reinforce the learning process and allow students to practice and investigate problems independently. Follow up homework assignments with group discussions. Vary the types of homework assignments and the time allotted for completion. Paper preparations, project development and individual research are valid activities. When possible, encourage common goals in assignments in and outside of class. The work should complement each other and promote consistency in the drawing program. Sketchbooks and notebooks can also be important out-of-class components of the course.

Critical Thinking/ Creative Thinking

The creation of images involves inventive problem solving, analytic and synthetic forms of reasoning, and judgment. Every step in art production begins with thought before it ends with executing lines on paper. Drawing is also a *process*, requiring students to continually make decisions, analyze and explore directions while they are creating their artwork.

As students read and discuss the text, respond to the artwork and complete challenges in art production, they are involved in observing, explaining, comparing similarities and differences, predicting and generalizing. These skills contribute to critical thinking and stimulate creative and critical thinking about art and the constant display of visual imagery that is used to disseminate information in our culture.

The Drawing Classroom

The drawing classroom should be well organized, functional, interesting and orderly. The room should provide space for storage of equipment, visual aids, supplies and drawing boards. The materials and equipment should also be properly labeled. Careful attention should be paid to traffic patterns and space in the work areas. Maintain bulletin boards and display areas. Providing space for reading, browsing and reviewing articles can be a positive asset to an art program.

Make sure the artroom includes adequate space for demonstrations and still-life drawing. A strong but flexible lighting system will help greatly. A spray booth is also a necessary item for most rooms for sealing drawings with fixatives.

Safety is an important consideration in the drawing classroom. Precautions must be taken to insure that working with art materials does not lead to student illness or injury. Failure to take necessary precautions may result in litigation if students become ill or are injured in the artroom. While restrictions are necessary, the teacher should be assured that nontoxic materials can usually be substituted for toxic ones with little or no extra cost, and good classroom management will prevent accidents.

Contact The Art and Craft Materials Institute, Inc., 715 Boylston Street, Boston, MA 02116 for a list of art products that are nontoxic and meet standards of quality and performance. Make sure that the artroom has signs on or near all work areas and equipment where injury might occur if students are careless, or should have instruction prior to use of the equipment. Keep a first-aid kit containing antiseptics, bandages and compresses on hand.

Establish a code of behavior conducive to the safety of individuals and their classmates, and enforce it. Keep aisles and exits clear. Do not permit students to work in the artroom without supervision. For a thorough discussion of health and safety hazards associated with specific media and procedures see *Safety in the Artroom* by Charles Qualley (available from Davis Publications, Inc., 50 Portland Street, Worcester, MA 01608).

Motivation

Motivation is the stimulus that sets the creative process in motion in your drawing program. By doing many of the drawing assignments yourself, you will find the projects more meaningful and exciting to teach. If the teacher is excited about the program, the students will be more likely to generate their own enthusiasm.

Because students learn differently, a combination of approaches in introducing lessons often helps build class enthusiasm. Students can be challenged and motivated through:

• the use of demonstrations, videos, slides and lectures to introduce lessons;

• well-prepared assignments that state clear goals, the relevancy of the work and the technical skills to be gained;

• encouragement from peers, parents and the instructor;

• the use of new materials, techniques and fresh subject matter;

• working in different environments;

• workshops presented by guest instructors;

• visits to galleries and museums.

Personal Experiences of Students

Students should use themes and ideas that have relevancy to their daily lives to increase their interest level and personal responses. Students' homes, neighborhoods and schools; planes, automobiles and public transportation; school activities, sports and hobbies are all sources for drawings. Encourage sketching, photography, direct observation and memory to provide subjects, resources, motivation and awareness.

Stimulating Creativity

Motivating students properly can also stimulate creativity. Creativity can be generated by reading poems and stories or listening to music, looking at videos, bringing in unusual objects or having the class illustrate their dreams. Scrap materials, found objects, junk and collections can challenge imaginations.

Creating from Direct Observation

Working from direct observation helps students perceive structure and action around them. Increased perception affects how students see themselves, their friends and their physical environment. Have students draw familiar objects, such as shoes, combs, glasses, musical instruments, tools, jewelry, plants, flowers, and so on.

Art Tools, Materials, Processes

The handling of tools, manipulating of art materials and discovery of new techniques and processes are strong motivational factors in themselves. Introducing new materials and combinations of materials creates new interests, challenges students and encourages them to discover the full potential of materials.

Resource Materials

Films, videotapes and slides can be used to emphasize design concepts, art techniques and processes, major forms of art expression and art history. A bibliography of resource materials appears on page T15. Photographs, reproductions, books and magazines should be conveniently located in the artroom for student reference.

Discussing Art

Communication and discussion of artwork are essential to the learning process. It is essential that drawing students *learn to talk and write about* ideas, concepts, media, styles, artists, subjects, art elements and principles, aesthetics and critical analysis. Communication involves spoken, written and visual forms. To be fully literate, students need to develop skills in all three categories.

Discussions will provide a means for students to learn important art vocabulary. At the same time, in learning to analyze and criticize artwork, students are learning important critical thinking skills. To develop open communication in the classroom:

1. allow students opportunities for class and small-group discussion;

2. encourage all students to participate;

3. have students answer questions posed by their classmates.

Discussions should contribute to students' development in the four content areas of *art history, art criticism, aesthetics* and *art production.*

Art history provides the setting and context during which the artwork was created. An understanding of how the culture and times are reflected in artwork of each period adds important information and meaning to the work. Art history shows how artists have been influenced by previous styles, technology and social change.

Art criticism is analysis and involves critical thinking skills. Students learn how artists manipulate the art elements to achieve effective compositions, and how they use media, procedures and images to communicate ideas. Students who learn to look at art, analyze the composition, offer multiple interpretations of meaning, make critical judgments and talk or write about what they see, think and feel are engaging in art criticism.

Aesthetics refers to our personal responses and sensitivity to works of art. Students come prepared with subjective responses and opinions about art. In discussions of aesthetics, students can reflect upon their sensory experiences and feelings they derived from individual works and develop richer experiences with art in general.

Art production in this text refers to the creation of drawing. The study of art is enhanced through experiences in creating art. Making art can help students understand the technical, visual and creative problems that artists deal with and gives them opportunities to solve such problems in their own work. Art production when integrated with criticism, history and aesthetics will help them understand the power of visual imagery to convey emotions, feelings, concepts and values. Art production is also a means of fostering creative thinking.

Evaluating Drawings

Evaluation is an important aspect of all learning activities, including drawing. Evaluation can take on many different forms but should be based on several considerations. Evaluation should:

1. aid the learning experience;

2. be based on known goals and objectives;

3. consider the artwork from a broad perspective. Consider the learning activities, skills developed, execution, comprehension and problem solving involved in the assignment;

4. recognize that the growth of students is more important than the finished product.

Critiques are a positive way to give students feedback on class assignments. Critiques can evaluate work in progress or can be analyses of finished products. The criticism must be presented in a positive manner which encourages growth and understanding. The discussion should leave students with goals for improvement that build upon previously learned skills.

Critiques should be a regular activity that students can participate in and look forward to as a positive experience. In group critiques, students learn to evaluate their own work as well as that of others. They also begin to see their personal work and style in relation to that of their peers. Whether critiques are given individually or in groups, students should be encouraged to express themselves and even question various responses.

Ongoing meetings with individual students are an important component in the evaluation process. Set up one-on-one meetings with each student on a regular basis. Ask questions, suggest directions, use discussions, provide demonstrations, emphasize ethnicity, provide examples, suggest parameters, and so on. Similarly, a sketchbook which students submit at least once each week in which they express concerns, successes, failures and progress can be used to establish a private dialogue between student and teacher.

Peer interaction is an excellent way for students to exchange information and seek new directions in their work. Elicit student responses to peer work. Encourage students to use ideas they receive from each other's work. Point out that professional artists have always broadened their art styles by sharing their ideas with others.

Portfolios are the heart of the drawing program. Portfolio assessment can be used to see students' progress over a long period. Portfolios are to be evaluated as a *body of work* rather than individual pieces. Allow students to discard or replace weaker attempts at drawing. Have students attach their own written evaluations to pieces. Include students in the evaluation process. Let them monitor their growth in skills, comprehension, analysis and accumulated knowledge.

Exhibiting Drawings

Exhibiting student work is important for several reasons. First and foremost, it helps students understand why art is a form of visual communication. Until someone sees and experiences the artwork, the *communication* process is incomplete. Student displays of art within the school or district are also good public relations material. Such displays encourage student interest in the drawing and art program and develop community support.

Many school art magazines solicit student work. Newspapers may have pages for students or welcome examples of topical art. Local companies may allot window space for the general public. Exchange of student art among regional schools is another possibility. Involve students in local, state and national competitions, which give students a chance to work towards something and are a vehicle for gaining some recognition. Have students actively search for ways to publish their work.

Portfolio Tips

Mats and mounts may be any size. Just remember their function is not only to preserve the artwork, but also to show it off to its best advantage. Therefore, keep the mats large enough to make the piece look good. For most works, a mat about three inches wide works well. Some art shows have rules concerning the size and color of mats. Usually the mat is the same width all around the work of art. However, often the lower margin of the mat is cut to be a little wider than the top and sides. The reason for this is to compensate for an optical illusion created when works hang vertically. A lower margin of identical size to the top and sides appears smaller. If you anticipate that an artwork will be preserved for years, use only acid-free mounting boards and tape.

To cut a mat that is three inches wide on all sides:
• Measure the drawing or artwork.
• To determine the overall size of the mat, subtract one inch from each of the artwork's dimensions. Then add six inches (twice the width of the mat margins) to each dimension. Note the size of this rectangle.
• Cut a mat board this size with a paper cutter.
• Using a ruler and pencil, lightly draw a box three inches inside of the outer edges.
• With a metal ruler and utility knife cut out this box. Be sure to protect your work surface with a piece of heavy cardboard.
• Position your artwork in the mat. Tack it with a few small pieces of tape. Check the position.
• Tape completely around the whole piece of art on the back of the mat.
• Tape a piece of mat board, posterboard, or foam core over the back of the mat and artwork.

Matting and Mounting Supplies
mounting board: mat board or
    posterboard
tape
metal rulers
pencils
cardboard to protect work surface
utility or X-acto knives or a mat
    cutting system

Bibliography

Books About Drawing

Albert, Greg, ed. *Basic Figure Drawing Techniques*. Cincinnati: North Light Books, 1994.

Angelo, Sandra. *Exploring Colored Pencil*. Worcester, MA: Davis Publications, Inc., 1999.

Betti, Claudia, and Teel Sale. *Drawing: A Contemporary Approach*. Orlando: Harcourt Brace Jovanovich, 1998.

Beverly, Robert and Terence Coyle Hale. *Anatomy Lessons from the Great Masters*. New York: Watson-Guptill Publications, 1977.

Blake, Wendon. *Figure Drawing Step by Step*. Mineola, NY: Dover Publications, 1998.

———. (drawings by Ferdinand Petri). *Starting to Draw*. New York: Watson-Guptill Publications, 1981.

Borgeson, Bet. *Basic Colored Pencil Techniques*. Cincinnati: North Light Books, 1997.

———. *The Colored Pencil*. New York: Watson-Guptill Publications, 1995.

Brommer, Gerald F. and Joseph Gatto. *Careers in Art: An Illustrated Guide*. Worcester, MA: Davis Publications, Inc., 1999.

Brommer, Gerald F. *Exploring Drawing*. Worcester, MA: Davis Publications, Inc., 1988.

Calle, Paul. *The Pencil*. Cincinnati: Writer's Digest Books, 1985.

Camhy, Sherry Wallerstein. *Art of the Pencil: A Revolutionary Look at Drawing, Painting, and the Pencil*. New York: Watson-Guptill Publications, 1997.

Civardi, Giovanni. *Drawing the Female Nude*. New York: Sterling Publishing Co., 1995.

Doyle, Michael. *Color Drawing: A Marker-Colored Pencil Approach*. New York: John Wiley and Sons, 1997.

Edwards, Betty. *Drawing on the Right Side of the Brain*. Los Angeles: J. P. Tarcher, Inc., 1989.

———. *Drawing on the Artist Within*. New York: Simon and Schuster, 1987.

Enstice, Wayne, and Melody Peters. *Drawing: Space, Form and Expression*. Englewood Cliffs, NJ: Prentice-Hall, Inc., 1995.

Fellows, Miranda. *100 Keys to Great Pastel Painting*. Cincinnati: North Light Books, 1994.

Gatto, Joseph. *Drawing Media and Techniques*. Worcester, MA: Davis Publications, Inc., 1986.

Goldstein, Nathan. *The Art of Responsive Drawing*. Englewood Cliffs, NJ: Prentice-Hall, Inc., 1998.

———. *Figure Drawing*. Englewood Cliffs, NJ: Prentice-Hall, Inc., 1999.

Graves, Douglas R. *Drawing Portraits*. New York: Watson-Guptill Publishers, 1983.

———. *Life Drawing in Charcoal*. Mineola, NY: Dover Publications, 1994.

Guptill, Arthur L. *Rendering in Pen and Ink*. New York: Watson-Guptill Publications, 1997.

Hanks, Kurt, and Belliston, Larry. *Draw! A Visual Approach to Thinking, Learning and Communicating*. Los Altos, California: William Kaufmann, Inc., 1990.

———. *Rapid Viz: A New Method for the Rapid Visualization of Ideas*. Menlo Park, CA: Crisp Publications, Inc., 1992.

Harrison, Hazel. *How to Paint and Draw: A Complete Course on Practical and Creative Techniques*. Brookline, MA: Hermes House, 1998.

———. *Pastels: Art School: Step-By-Step*. New York: Anness Publishing, Ltd., 1998.

Kaupelis, Robert. *Learning to Draw: A Creative Approach to Drawing*. New York: Watson-Guptill Publications, 1989.

Lohan, Frank J. *The Drawing Handbook*. New York: NTC Publishing Group, 1993.

Larson, Karl V. *See & Draw*. Worcester, MA: Davis Publications, Inc., 1993.

Martin, Judy. *The Encyclopedia of Colored Pencil Techniques*. Philadelphia: Running Press, 1997.

Mayer, Ralph. *The Artist's Handbook of Materials and Techniques*. New York: The Viking Penguin Press, Inc., 1991.

Mendelowitz, Daniel M., and Duane A. Wakeham. *A Guide to Drawing*. 5th ed. Orlando: Harcourt Brace, 1997.

Michelangelo Buonarroti. *Michelangelo Life Drawings*. Mineola, NY: Dover Publications, 1980.

Mugnaini, Joseph. *Expressive Drawing: A Schematic Approach*. Worcester, MA: Davis Publications, Inc., 1988.

Nice, Claudia. *Sketching Your Favorite Subjects in Pen and Ink*. Cincinnati: North Light Books, 1993.

Noad, Timothy. *Mastering Calligraphy*. Godalming, Surrey, UK: Combe Books, 1995.

Parramón, Jose Maria. *The Basics of Artistic Drawing*. Hauppauge, NY: Barrons Educational Series, Inc., 1994.

Petrie, Ferdinand. *Drawing Landscapes in Pencil*. New York: Watson-Guptill Publishers, 1992.

Pogany, Will. *The Art of Drawing*. Lanham, MD: Madison Books, 1996.

Roukes, Nicholas. *Art Synectics*. Worcester, MA: Davis Publications, Inc., 1984.

———. *Design Synectics*. Worcester, MA: Davis Publications, Inc,. 1988.

Sarnoff, Bob. *Cartoons and Comics: Ideas and Techniques*. Worcester, MA: Davis Publications, Inc., 1989.

Shadrin, Richard L. *Design and Drawing: An Applied Approach*. Worcester, MA: Davis Publications, Inc., 1993.

Sheaks, Barclay. *Drawing Figures and Faces*. Worcester, MA: Davis Publications, Inc., 1987.

Smagula, Howard J. *Creative Drawing*. Carmel, IN: Brown and Benchmark, 1993.

Winter, Roger. *On Drawing*. San Diego: Collegiate Press, 1991.

Woolwich, Madlyn-Ann C. *The Art of Pastel Portraiture*. New York: Watson-Guptill Publishers, 1996.

Books About Artists

Allara, Pamela and Alice Neel. *Pictures of People: Alice Neel's American Portrait Gallery*. Waltham, MA: Brandeis Univ., 1998.

Boggs, Jean Sutherland, Susan F. Rossen, and Edgar Degas. *Degas*. Chicago: Art Institute of Chicago Museum, 1996.

Broude, Norma. *Georges Seurat*. New York: Rizzoli, 1992.

Burchfield, Charles. *Charles Burchfield's Journals: The Poetry of Place*. New York: SUNY, 1992.

Clark, Kenneth. *Leonardo da Vinci*. New York: Penguin, 1993.

Escher, M.C. and J.L. Locher, ed. *M.C. Escher: His Life and Complete Graphic Work*. New York: Harry N. Abrams, 1992.

Goff, Robert. *The Essential Salvador Dali*. New York: Harry N. Abrams, 1998.

Guerman, Mikhail. *Antoine Watteau*. New York: Harry N. Abrams, 1981.

Hall, Douglas. *Klee*. San Francisco: Chronicle Books, 1994.

Helms, Cynthia Newman. *Diego Rivera: A Retrospective*. New York: W.W. Norton, 1998.

Hulton, Pontus, ed. *Marcel Duchamp: Work and Life*. Boston: MIT Press, 1993.

Kramer, Linda. *The Graphic Works of Philip Pearlstein 1978-1994*. Springfield, MO: Springfield Art Museum, 1995.

Loyrette, Henri. *Degas: The Man and His Art*. New York: Harry N. Abrams, 1993.

Miró, Joan, Elsa Haas, trans. and Jose Maria Faerna, ed. *Miró*. New York: Abradale Press, 1995.

Munz, Ludwig and Bob Haak. *Rembrandt*. New York: Harry N. Abrams, 1990.

Picasso, Pablo. *The Artist and His Model: 180 Drawings*. Mineola, NY: Dover Publications, 1994.

Roffo, Stefano, ed. *Pierre Auguste Renoir*. New York: Gramercy Books, 1994.

Schneider, Angela, ed. *Alberto Giacometti: Sculptures, Paintings, Drawings*. New York: te Neues Publishing Co., 1997.

Solway, Arthur. *Claes Oldenburg: Multiples in Retrospect, 1964-1990*. New York: Rizzoli, 1991.

Venn, Beth, Adam D. Weinberg, Andrew Wyeth, and Michael G. Kammen. *Unknown Terrain: The Landscapes of Andrew Wyeth*. New York: Whitney Museum of Art, 1998.

Waldman, Diane. *Roy Lichtenstein*. New York: Solomon R. Guggenheim Museum, 1994.

Whitney, Wheelock and Theodore Gericault. *Gericault in Italy*. New Haven: Yale Univ. Press, 1997.

Art History and Art Appreciation Books

Brommer, Gerald E. *Discovering Art History*, 3rd ed. Worcester, MA: Davis Publications, Inc., 1997.

Eitner, Lorenz E. *An Outline of 19th Century European Painting from David through Cezanne*. New York: HarperCollins, 1997.

Gilbert, Rita. *Living with Art*, 5th ed. New York: McGraw-Hill, 1998.

Grieder, Terence. *Artist and Audience*, 2nd ed. Madison, WI: Brown and Benchmark Publishers, 1996.

Janson, H. W. *History of Art*, 5th ed. New York: Harry N. Abrams, 1997.

Preble, Duane; Preble, Sarah; and Frank, Patrick. *Artforms*, 6th ed. Reading, MA: Addison Wesley Longman, Inc., 1999.

Rose, Barbara. *American Painting: The Twentieth Century*. New York: Rizzoli, 1986.

Stokstad, Marilyn. *Art History*, rev. ed. New York: Harry N. Abrams, 1999.

Strickland, Carol. *The Annotated Mona Lisa: A Crash Course in Art History from Prehistoric to Post-Modern*. Kansas City: Andrews and McMeel, 1996.

Tansey, Richard G. and Fred S. Kleiner. *Gardner's Art Through the Ages*. 10th ed. Orlando: Harcourt Brace, 1995.

Welton, Jude. *Eyewitness Art: Impressionism*. New York: DK Publishing, 1993.

West, Shearer, ed. *The Bulfinch Guide to Art History*. Boston: Little, Brown and Company, 1996.

Zelanski, Paul, and Fisher, Mary Pat. *The Art of Seeing*, 4th ed. Paramus, NJ: Prentice Hall Inc., 1999.

Audiovisual/Multimedia Resources

Alarion Press, P.O. Box 1882, Boulder, CO 80306
(800) 523-9177

American Library Color Slide Co., Inc., P.O. Box 4414, Grand Central Sta., New York, NY 10163
(800) 633-3307

Art Image Publications, Inc., 61 Main St., Champlain, NY 12919
(518) 298-5432

Art Video Productions, 6225 Shoup Ave. #106, Woodland Hills, CA 91365
(818) 884-6278

Canadian Film Institute, 303 Richmond Rd., Ottawa, ON K1Z 6X3

Canadian Filmmakers Distribution Centre, 37 Hanna Ave., Suite 220, Toronto, ON M6K 1W8 Canada
(416) 588-0725

Carousel Films, Inc., 1501 Broadway, Suite 1503, New York, NY 10036

Crystal Productions, 1812 Johns Dr., Glenview, IL 60025
(847) 657-8144

Davis Art Slides, 50 Portland St., Worcester, MA 01608
(800) 533-2847
www.davis-art.com

Facets Video, 1517 W. Fullerton Ave., Chicago, IL 60614
(800) 331-6197

Films for the Humanities and Sciences, P.O. Box 2053, Princeton, NJ 08543
(800) 257-5216
www.films.com

Films Incorporated, 5547 N. Ravenswood Ave., Chicago, IL 60640
(800) 323-4222
www.publicmedia.com

International Film Bureau, 332 S. Michigan Ave., Chicago, IL 60604
(312) 427-4545

Media for the Arts, 360 Thames Street, Suite 2N, Newport, Rhode Island 02840
(800) 554-6008
www.art-history.com

Museum at Large, 20 West 22nd St., #1401, New York, NY 10019
(212) 691-2977

Museum of Modern Art, 11 West 53rd St., New York, NY 10019

National Gallery of Art Extension Service, Washington, DC 20565

National Museum of African Art, Smithsonian Institution, 9500 Independence Ave. SW, Washington, DC 20560
(202) 357-4600

Pyramid Media, P.O. Box 1048, Santa Monica, CA 90406
(800) 421-2304
www.pyramidmedia.com

Reading and O'Reilly Inc., 2 Kensett Ave., Wilton, CT 06897
(800) 458-4274

Universal Color Slide Co., Inc., 8450 S. Tamiami Tr., Sarasota, FL 34238
(800) 487-0250

Video Ed Productions, Inc., 4301 East-West Highway, Hyattsville, MD 20782
(301) 927-7474

Discovering Drawing

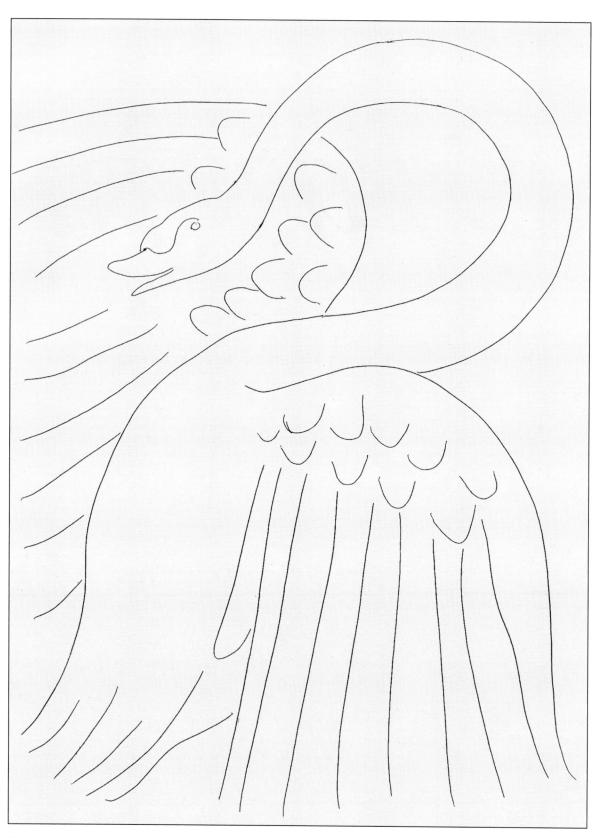

Henri Matisse, *Swan*, 1930-32. Etching, 13" x 9 3/4" (33 x 25 cm). Collection, The Museum of Modern Art, New York (Mrs. John D. Rockefeller, Jr., Purchase Fund).

DISCOVERING
Drawing

Ted Rose

Davis Publications, Inc.   *Worcester, Massachusetts*

The Author

Ted Rose has twenty years of high school and
university teaching experience. His students have
won national, regional, and state competitions.
These awards include First Place prizes in both
the Mississippi and Texas Collegiate Competitions
and a Gold Medal in Scholastic Magazine's Art
Competition in New York. Ted has taught in the
Tennessee Governor's School for the Arts and
The Tennessee Arts Academy and is active in
numerous art education organizations.

He has also worked as a full-time artist, and
has over 100 works in corporate collections and
twenty-one solo exhibits in seven states and four
foreign countries. His artwork is represented in
galleries in Tennessee, Texas, Missouri,
Mississippi, and Georgia.

Ted currently serves as Director of Fine and
Performing Arts at David Lipscomb University in
Nashville, Tennessee. He holds a Master of Fine
Arts degree from the University of Tennessee at
Knoxville and a Master of Education degree from
Edinboro University, Edinboro, Pennsylvania. He
lives with his wife Kathy, son Mason, and daugh-
ter Anna in Nashville, Tennessee.

© 2000 Davis Publications, Inc.
Worcester, Massachusetts, U.S.A.

Cover: Student work by Aleksandra Otwinowska.
Untitled, 1995. Mixed media, 18" x 12" (45.7 x
30.5 cm). Plano Senior High School, Plano,
Texas.

Senior Art Education Consultant:

Kaye Passmore, Notre Dame Academy,
Worcester, Massachusetts

Editorial Consultants:

Leigh Backstrom, North High School,
Worcester, Massachusetts

David McIntyre, El Paso Independent School
District, El Paso, Texas

Connie Pirtle, Tennessee State Department of
Education, Nashville, Tennessee

Barbara Pratt, Richardson Independent School
District, Richardson, Texas

Richard Shilale, Holy Name High School,
Worcester, Massachusetts

Diana Woodruff, Forest Avenue Elementary
School, Hudson, Massachusetts

Faith Zajicek, Temple High School,
Temple, Texas

Managing Editor: Wyatt Wade
Associate Editor: Claire Mowbray Golding
Production Editor: Nancy Burnett
Production: Steve Vogelsang
Copyeditor: Janet Stone
Editorial Assistance: Holly Hanson, Amee Bergin,
Denise Nephew
Design and Electronic Page Make-up: Tong-Mei
Chan, Cathleen Damplo, Constance Jacobson,
Douglass Scott, WGBH Design
Design Advisor: Karen Durlach

Printed in U.S.A.
Library of Congress Catalog Card Number:
93–074646
ISBN: 87192–281–9
00 01 02 03 04 / 10 9 8 7 6

Contents

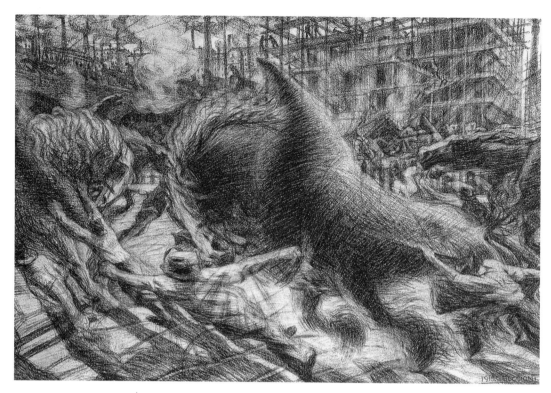

Umberto Boccioni, study for *The City Rises*, 1910. Crayon, chalk and charcoal, 23 1/8" x 34 1/8" (23.1 x 34.1 cm). The Museum of Modern Art, New York. Mrs. Solomon Guggenheim Fund.

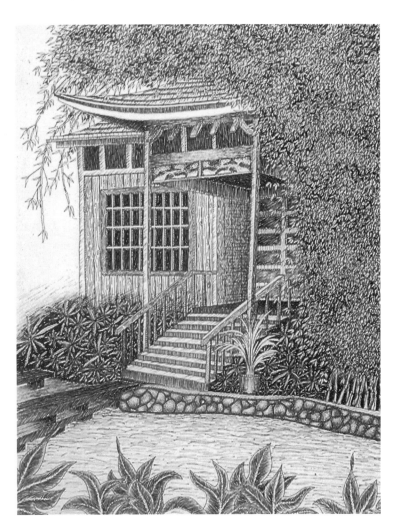

Student work by Kyung-Eui Kim, Honolulu, Hawaii.

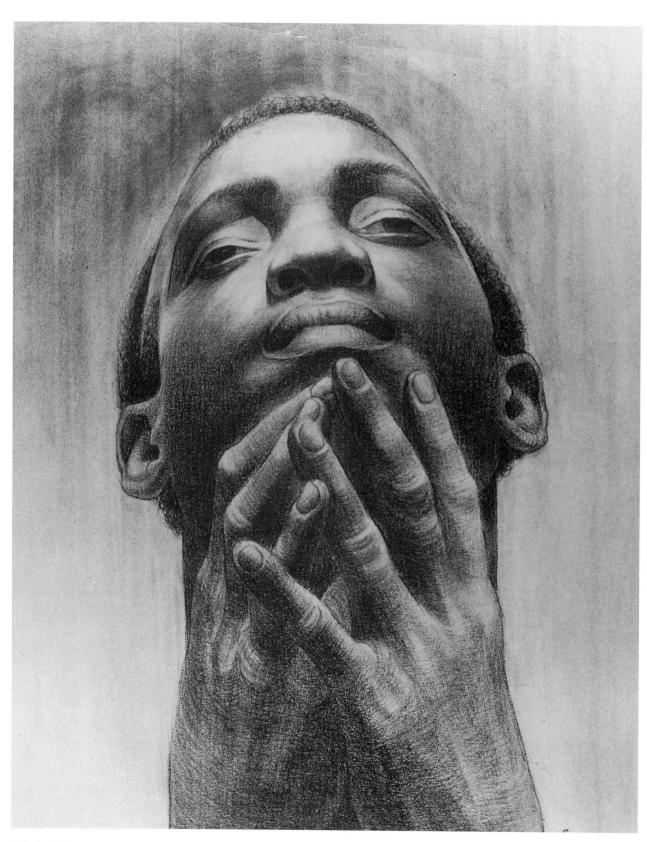

Charles White, *I Believe*. One of a series of drawings used on the "Harry Bellafonte Special" television program, NBC, 1960. Original in the collection of Mr. and Mrs. Harry Bellafonte. Courtesy Heritage Gallery, Los Angeles.

Part I
Visualizing

Chapter 1
Goals of Drawing

Objectives

Students will be able to
- Understand that drawing is a form of communication. (Aesthetics)
- Understand that drawing is a skill that may be developed by trial and error. (Art production)
- Discuss practical uses of drawing in today's world.
- Understand that there is no right or wrong way to draw. (Aesthetics)
- Begin to draw regularly in a sketchbook. (Art production)

Vocabulary

sketch
sketchbook
thumbnail sketches
doodling

Chapter Overview

This chapter provides a foundation for the process of drawing that students will learn in this book. Drawing is defined as a method of communication, a means of developing important personal insights, and a process that requires time, practice, and trial and error.

Lesson 1

pages 2–7   45 minutes

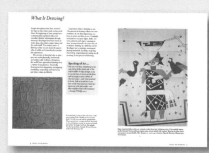

pages 4–5

Teach

Direct students to study the drawings on pages 4 and 5. Encourage them to imagine what these artists were trying to communicate. As students consider how prehistoric people communicated through their drawings, suggest that they read "Cave Drawings," page 196. Compare the medium and subjects of the *Room of the Bison* drawing to the rock carvings on page 4.

Studio Experience

After discussing artistic styles and symbols on pages 4–7, have students design and draw stylistic symbols that represent their interests and activities. Students may introduce themselves to the class by explaining the meanings of their symbols.

Materials

paper
pencils or markers

Lesson 2

pages 8–11   45 minutes

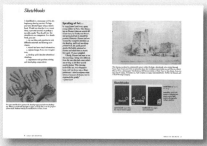

pages 8–9

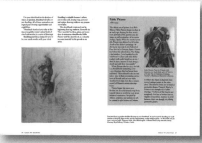

pages 10–11

Teach

- Introduce students to the process of keeping a sketchbook/journal. You may want to refer them to the drawing on page 9 by Seth Eastman, a soldier in the U.S. Army who kept a sketchbook. Sketches from Leonardo da Vinci's notebooks offer other good examples.
- Motivate students to begin regularly drawing and writing in their sketchbooks. Set up guidelines for using sketchbooks in this course. Sketchbooks can be personal diaries and not intended to be shared with others; they can be used for homework assignments and rough drafts; they can also be periodically passed in to allow you to evaluate students' progress.

• Assign students one of the sketchbook activities on page 19. Remind them to examine the text illustrations that correlate to their activity, and discuss how they might begin this drawing.

Studio Experience

Allow students to create a distinctive cover featuring their name for their sketchbook. Encourage them to make their name easy to read in this design so that anyone can tell at a glance whose book it is. They may draw their design either on a page-size adhesive label or a sheet of paper which may be glued to the front of the sketch book. Adhering a sheet of self-sticking laminating film over their drawing will make the cover quite durable.

Materials

drawing media such as markers
   and colored pencils
drawing paper and glue or
   page-size adhesive labels
self-sticking laminating film

Lesson 3
pages 12–17   45 minutes

Teach

• After students have read page 12, discuss how to develop good drawing habits and set up suitable work spaces. Ask students to list some of the materials they will need as they begin to draw. For example, they will probably need some type of drawing board or hard smooth surface under their

paper. When they draw in their sketchbooks, they will need drawing media such as those described on pages 22 and 23. If they are using pencil or charcoal, they will probably want to use one of the erasers shown on page 90. If they are drawing outside, they may need tape to keep their paper from blowing.

• Compare and contrast some of the styles and directions that the artists whose work appears in this chapter have taken. How are the styles different? Which art elements are stressed in each?

Studio Experience

Have the class read and discuss the biography of William Blake (page 16). Then assign students activity b about illustrating a dream, on page 19.

Materials

drawing media such a pencils or
   markers
sketchbooks or drawing paper

Lesson 4
page 19   45 minutes

Reteach

Review with students the ideas from this chapter, that drawing is a form of communication with many different ways to visualize a message. Refer students to the Matisse drawing on page ii. Ask them to find other drawings in this chapter which are most like this one. Which are most different?

Activities

Instruct students to complete one of the activities. Choose an activity based on the level of your students' skills. In the Style activity, in which students draw compositions in the style of three different artists, students might use markers, pastels, charcoal, pencils, or oil pastels. If students draw on the scratchboard, stress that their designs may be abstract or non-representational.

Assess

• In a class discussion, ask students why people draw. They should indicate an understanding of drawing as a form of communication. Ask them to list some practical uses of drawing in their world. (Aesthetics)

• Review the drawings in this chapter. Ask students which ones appeal to them and why. Encourage a response from everyone in the class so that the students will understand that there is no right or wrong way to draw. There are many different types of drawing styles. (Aesthetics)

• Review the drawings in the students' sketchbooks to determine that they are beginning to draw regularly in them. (Art production)

• Look for experimentation in their works. Do students understand that drawing is a skill that may be developed by trial and error? (Art production)

Chapter Warm-up
Introduce students to the drawing process by asking them to talk about what drawing means to them. What positive or negative experiences have they had? Establish that drawing involves special skills, which they will learn about in this book, but more importantly, it involves individual responses. Each student will learn at a different rate, through different methods, and with varying results.

Higher-Order Thinking Skills
Ask students to give their own answers to the question, What is drawing? Is drawing a method of self-discovery? Is it a universal language? Point out that looking is not necessarily seeing, nor is seeing necessarily understanding. Encourage students to articulate what they learn about themselves and the world through the process of drawing.

Context
The Dutch artist Piet Mondrian is most famous for his white canvases with primary colors arranged on grids, such as *Broadway Boogie Woogie* on page 150. He drew this chrysanthemum early in his career. Mondrian spent years gradually abstracting and simplifying his drawings in an attempt to achieve harmony in his compositions.

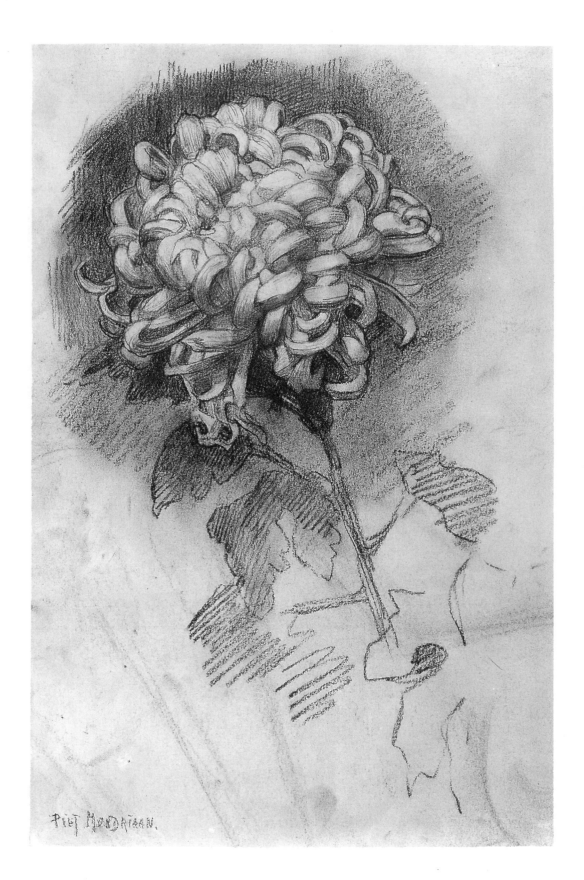

1 Goals of Drawing

Drawing is both a mental and physical act. The physical aspect—what your hand records—is a reflection of what your eyes see and your mind thinks. Drawing is a type of language all its own. Throughout this book, you will be exploring drawing as a form of communication.

In this chapter, you will explore the interrelationship of drawing to everyday life. There are many types of drawing, some of which have practical uses in the business world. Other types of drawing are expressions of a culture. How do you see drawing in your own life?

This chapter explains the importance of using a sketchbook and gives you some suggestions on how to use it as a tool for drawing.

In the last section of the chapter are some guidelines you can follow to make your drawings—and the drawing experience—meaningful and satisfying.

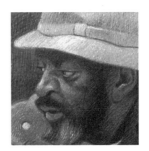

Vocabulary
sketch
sketchbook
thumbnail
   sketches
doodling

Extension
Give some examples of drawing done accidentally or intentionally on nontraditional materials (marks on carpenter's wood, diagrams for math or science class, doodling on notebooks, carvings on benches or light posts, graffiti signs and messages, etc.). Discuss how these relate to drawing. (They are a form of visual communication.)

Inquiry
To expand students' understanding of the varied art forms from all over the world, ask students to select artists with ethnic backgrounds similar to theirs. Have them provide some information about the artists and their work.

Key Chapter Points

- Drawing is communicating.
- Drawing is a skill that anyone can develop.
- Drawing has a practical value in today's world.
- There is no right or wrong way to draw.
- The best way to learn is by trial and error.

When you draw something, you make it important. The way you draw it shows others what it means to you. What do you think this flower meant to the artist? Why did it catch his eye? Piet Mondrian, *Chrysanthemum*, 1906. Pencil, 14 1/4" x 9 5/8" (36 x 25 cm). The Museum of Modern Art, New York. Gift of Mr. and Mrs. Armand P. Bartos.

What Is Drawing?

Higher-Order Thinking Skills

Encourage students to write brief reflections about each artwork they create, examining their thought processes as well as their feelings about the final result. Stress that drawing involves analytical and evaluative skills, not just creativity. What problems did they encounter and solve as they drew? How would they apply their experiences to their next drawing?

Context

See Georgia O'Keeffe's charcoal drawings on pages 18 and 31.

People throughout time have searched for ways to leave their mark on this earth. Since the beginning of time, people have communicated significant ideas and recorded valuable information through drawings. Drawings have been found on rocks, skins, clay, fabric, paper, bones and the earth itself. The unique aspect of drawing is that we can creatively express what is within and immediately translate life experiences.

The process of drawing helps us interpret our world physically, emotionally and aesthetically. Cultures throughout the world have approached drawing from a variety of perspectives. Essentially, drawing involves imagining, investigating, translating, responding and expressing our ideas, values and beliefs.

Learning to draw is learning to see. The process of drawing reflects our own evolution. In our first experiences, we learn to touch and then to see. Gradually, we learn how to sense lights, darks, textures, patterns and edges. Learning to draw involves basically the same type of evolution. Drawing is a skill that can be developed just as reading, counting or playing basketball. Looking, analyzing, discovering, responding and acting are all necessary in the process of drawing.

Speaking of Art...

"Did you ever have something to say and feel as if the whole side of the wall wouldn't be big enough to say it on and then sit down on the floor and try to get it onto a sheet of charcoal paper—and when you had it down, look at it and try to put into words what you have been trying to say with just marks—and then wonder what it all is anyway."
—*Georgia O'Keeffe,*1915

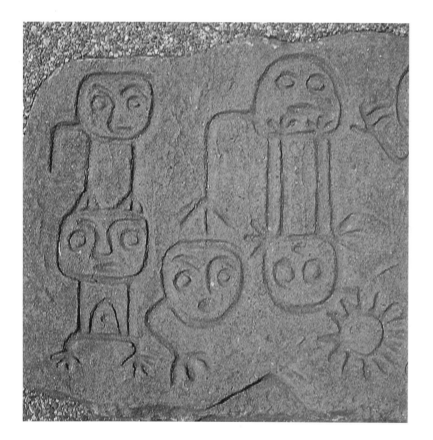

If you had only a rock to draw with, how would your drawings look? Would you try to create detail? Would you work only in straight lines? These ancient rock carvings may have been used to record important events, or to serve as boundary markers or magical symbols. Petroglyphs. Nootka, Sproat Lake, Canada. Werner Forman Archive/Art Resource, NY.

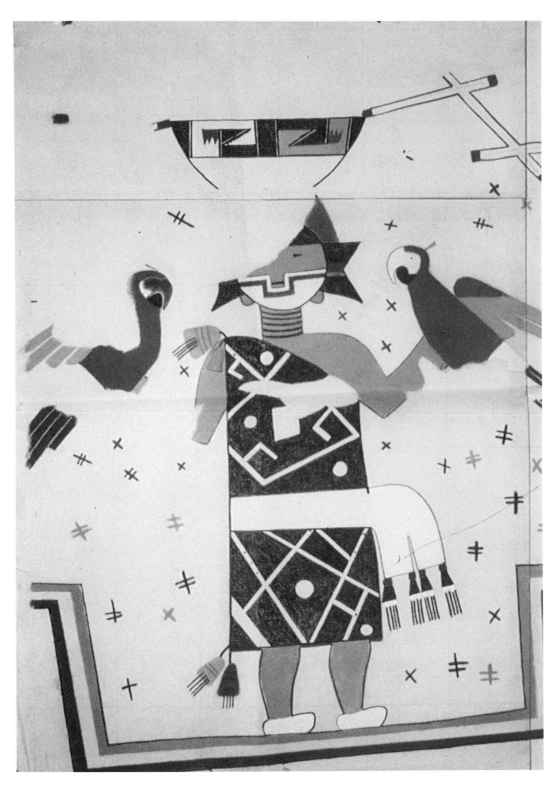

Many American Indian tribes use symbols to show how they feel about events. What symbols appear in this drawing? How would you express some of your beliefs with symbols? Drawing of a kiva mural from pottery mound, Pueblo, New Mexico, ca. 1350-1450. Courtesy Maxwell Museum, Albuquerque, New Mexico.

Drawing As Language

In the same way that a poem or a piece of music expresses a person's thoughts and feelings in a tangible form, a drawing is a way for you to express yourself through a visual format.

The process of drawing enables you to see more accurately by studying the objects around you. If you have ever drawn an object, you already understand this concept. Consider how the drawing process has made you more aware and more sensitive to the world around you.

Just as each of us has our own unique style of handwriting, an artist should strive to have a unique style of expression. Experiment with ideas and search for your own special style of drawing. Explore new directions in your art. Use ideas from other artists and from other times and build upon them.

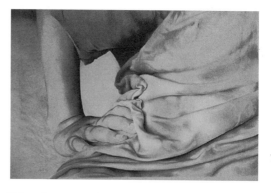

What drawing style will you develop? Will it be realistic, like this artwork, showing every detail as clearly as the eye sees it? Susan Avishai, 1993. Colored pencil. Courtesy of the artist.

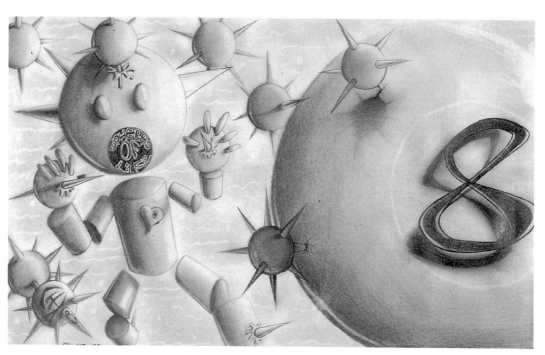

How will you express your ideas in your drawing? Will you find new ways to describe ordinary objects through drawing? Student work by Rafael Vasquez, El Paso, Texas.

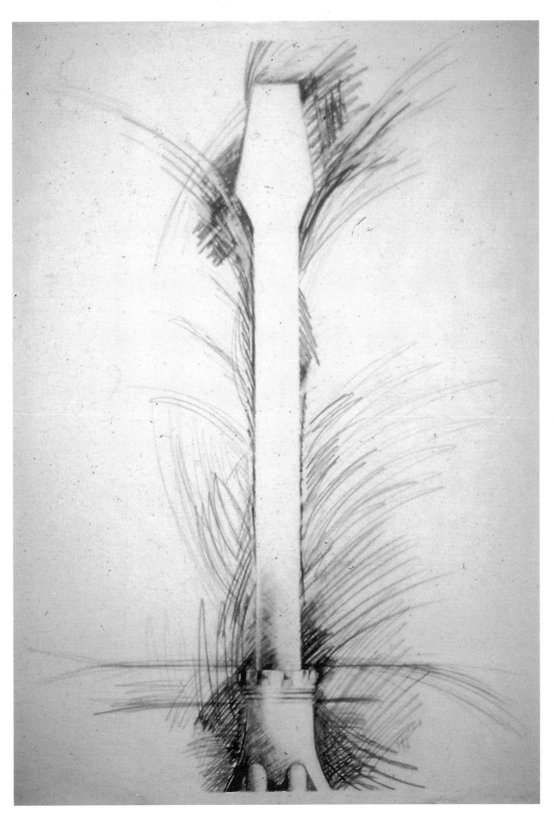

What kind of subject matter will you explore through drawing? Will you draw what you imagine? Student work by Geoffrey Broderick, Santa Fe, New Mexico.

Sketchbooks

Teaching Tip
Sketchbooks can be used to establish an ongoing dialogue with each student about his or her progress. You may want to have students pass in their sketchbooks on a regular basis. Set up a dialogue sheet in each sketchbook. Tell students to write weekly comments they would like to share with you. Respond to these comments, suggest areas you feel the student might explore, offer encouragement, etc., on the sheet, and return to the student.

A sketchbook is a necessary tool for the beginning drawing student. Perhaps you have already begun using a sketchbook. Would you describe it as a visual diary, a personal journal, or perhaps a movable studio? You should view the sketchbook as a companion. In a sketchbook, you can:

1. try out ideas and experiment with different materials and drawing techniques;

2. record and save visual information;

3. capture images from your imagination;

4. develop quick sketches (thumbnail sketches);

5. experiment with problem solving and developing compositions.

Speaking of Art...

In 1944, James Lord was a gutsy young soldier in Paris. After knocking on Picasso's door on several different visits, he finally met Picasso and persuaded him to sketch his portrait. However, Picasso had not focused his complete attention on the drawing, and Lord was disappointed with the quick pencil sketch. He boldly returned to Picasso and asked him to sketch him again. Picasso complied.

"Clearly, Picasso had seen in me that morning a being very different from the one who had come unbidden to ring at his door several months before. This drawing looked like me, was adequately large, and was in no way a disappointment. I tried to express some awkward manner of thanks, but he dismissed this gently."
—*James Lord*

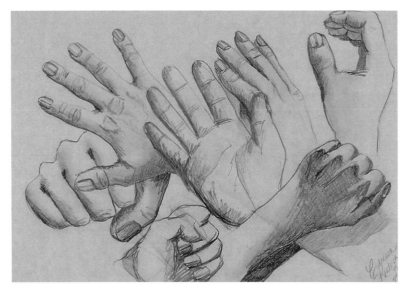

Use your sketchbook to practice the drawing topics you find most challenging. When you look back through its pages, you'll be able to see the progress you've made. Student work by Carissa Renteria, El Paso, Texas.

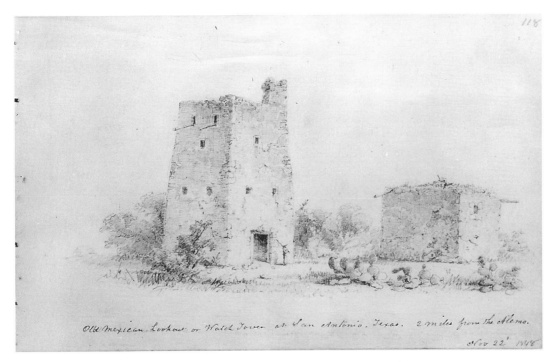

This drawing was done by a nineteenth century soldier who kept a sketchbook as he traveled through Texas. If you found yourself in an unfamiliar place, how would you record what you saw? How is a sketch different from a photograph? Seth Eastman, *Old Mexican Lookout or Watch Tower at San Antonio, Texas, two miles from the Alamo*, November 22, 1848. Graphite on paper, from sketchbook. McNay Art Museum, gift of Pearl Brewing Company.

Interdisciplinary Connection

American History—
• Have students research the time and place Seth Eastman sketched this scene. It was drawn in Texas in 1848, three years after Texas had been annexed to the United States.

• Sketchbooks played an important role in the exploration of the American West during the early 1800s. Artists were part of the exploration parties. Encourage students to research the works of Titan Ramsay Peale or Samuel Seymour, who both were part of the Yellowstone Expedition led by Major Stephen Long in 1820, or the portraits of Native Americans made by George Catlin or Karl Bodmer.

Context

Seth Eastman was originally from Maine. In 1829 he graduated from West Point, where he later taught drawing. He became known for his paintings of Sioux tribal life, eventually illustrating Henry Schoolcraft's *Indian Tribes of the United States* and painting commissions for Congress.

Sketchbooks

useful sizes: 9" x 12", 11" x 14"

materials: pencil, ink, markers, ballpoint pen, conté crayon, light washes, photographs, collage, graphite

spiral-bound: opens flat, has easy-to-remove pages

hardbound: two pages, more permanent

Extension

Encourage students to keep a sketchbook of a journey (even the trip from home to school). Often cars move too fast to draw a complete scene, but students should be able to sketch general impressions of trees, buildings, and other features of the area. Later these sketches may be combined into a landscape drawing or painting.

Context

A sketch from one of Leonardo da Vinci's notebooks is on page 200. Leonardo drew figures, cadavers, plants, and natural phenomena in order to study nature and understand how things work. He sketched ideas for inventions and wrote his notes in mirror-image Renaissance Italian. In 1994 computer entrepreneur Bill Gates paid over $30 million for a Leonardo notebook, *Codex Leicester*.

Inquiry

Students may research sketches from Leonardo da Vinci's notebooks on the Internet and in books. The CD-ROM *Leonardo da Vinci* published by Corbis features the *Codex Leicester*.

Use your sketchbook to do sketches of major art projects, thumbnail sketches or just doodling. All of these approaches can expand your drawing opportunities and capabilities.

Thumbnail sketches have value in letting you quickly record various kinds of visual information in a series of drawings.

Doodling provides a chance for you to let your marks wander with your mind.

Doodling is valuable because it allows you to relax and develop very personal and unique drawings without any preconceived plan.

The sketchbook is not used just by beginning drawing students. Leonardo da Vinci recorded his ideas, plans and inventions in numerous sketchbooks. Pablo Picasso used his sketchbook as a valuable resource material for his growth as an artist.

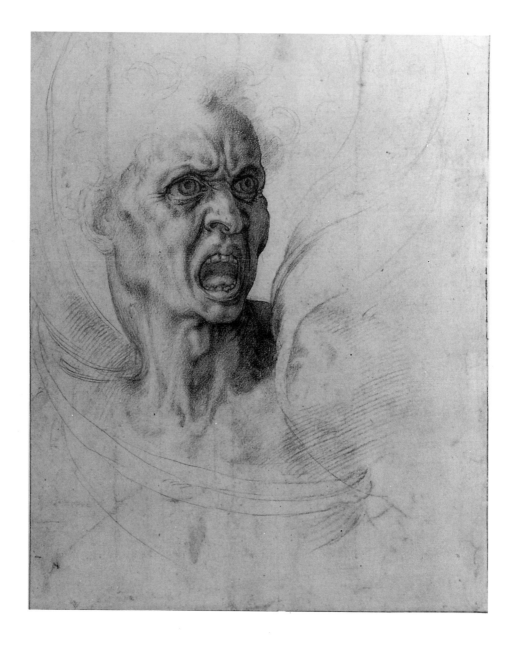

Pablo Picasso

1881–1973

The oldest son of painter Jose Ruiz Blasco, Pablo Picasso began to draw at an early age. Among his first works were portraits of his parents and his sister, as well as sketches of his native Malaga, Spain. When he was ten years old, Picasso was allowed to fill in the details of his father's paintings. At eleven, he was sent to the School of Fine Arts in La Coruna, Spain. Picasso said about his school days, "For being a bad student, I was banished to the 'calaboose'—a bare cell with white-washed walls and a bench to sit on. I liked it there, because I took along a sketch pad and drew incessantly."

When Picasso died in 1973, he left 175 sketchbooks containing over 7,000 drawings that had never been exhibited. Those sketchbooks are not only a type of diary containing caricatures of friends and cartoon-style sketches from trips, but also a unique record of Picasso's artistic development.

Picasso began his career as a Realist, but he soon turned away from natural vision to search for new possibilities of expression. Inspired by African sculpture and prehistoric art, he created a style known as Cubism,

Higher-Order Thinking Skills
Encourage students to compare the two portraits on pages 10 and 11. How are they alike and different? What is the emotion in each? How did each artist depict this emotion?

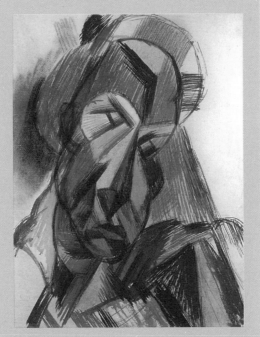

Pablo Picasso, *Head of a Woman*, 1909. Gouache over black chalk, 24" x 19" (61.8 x 47.8 cm). The Art Institute of Chicago, Charles L. Hutchinson Memorial Collection.

in which the object is depicted from several vantage points at the same time. The natural forms are reduced to geometric shapes. Picasso's *Head of a Woman* is an example of a Cubist drawing. The form of the head is not completely lost but is broken into an angular composition. Instead of facial features, there are sharply cut, tilting geometric planes.

You don't have to produce finished drawings in your sketchbook. It can be used for doodling, for small sketches of ideas for larger works, and for concentrating—as this artist has done—on the details you are most concerned with. Unknown artist, after Michelangelo, *A Damned Soul*. Early sixteenth century. Courtesy Royal Library, Windsor Castle.

Establishing Attitudes and Directions

Design Extension
Have students write a list of fifty objects that they might draw. Develop a class list of possible subjects. Discuss how they could combine five of these objects into an imaginative drawing.

Establish a healthy attitude when approaching drawing. Try to approach every drawing as if it will be the best drawing you have ever done. This is a positive and aggressive direction. Equally important is working with the subject matter with a positive attitude.

Developing good work habits is another essential part of the drawing process. Good work habits include being prepared with the proper materials, equipment and lighting. Set up a comfortable working space. Drawings often fail not because of technical ability, but from poor work habits or lack of planning.

As you experiment in drawing, learn from your mistakes. What are your strengths and weaknesses in your technical abilities and observational skills? Look at each drawing you complete as a learning experience, not as a success or a failure. Incorporate new information you are learning in the drawing process into your next drawing to overcome what you think are your weaknesses.

Today's technologies have provided more media that can be used for art than ever before. Become familiar with these media. Go to art museums and galleries to see how other artists are developing new directions in art. Throughout this book, you will have opportunities to learn how to use the current materials that are available for drawing.

You may discover that by developing your own style, philosophy and form of expression in drawing, you may find yourself as well.

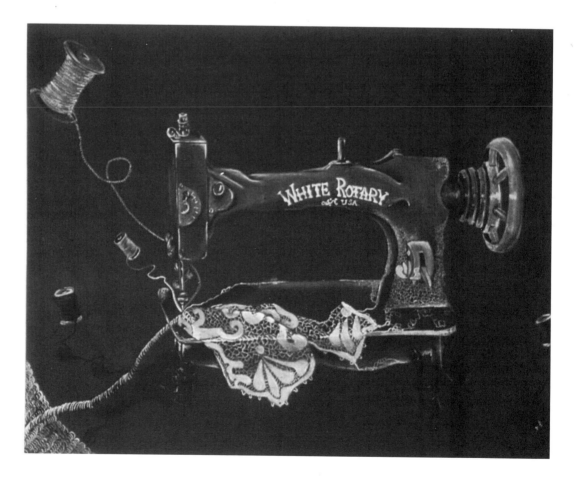

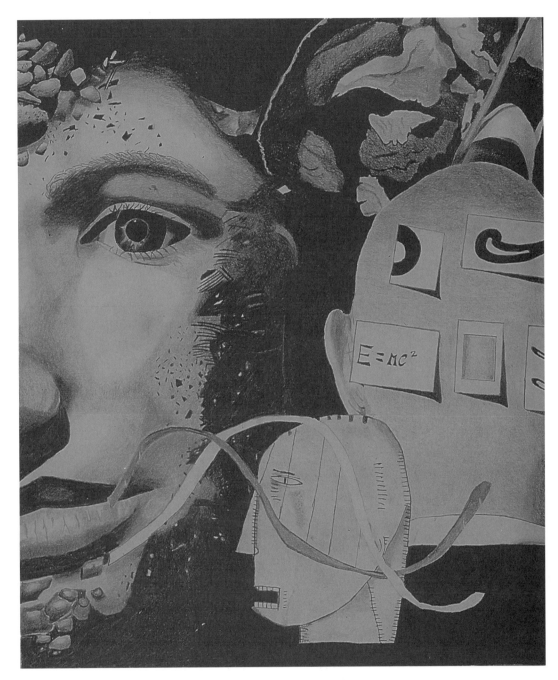

It might seem difficult at first to find ideas for your drawings. Start by jotting down things you think about during the day—your math homework, a video game, the weather. You may find that your thoughts bring new images to your mind. Student work by Stephen Gist, Temple, Texas.

Have you ever tried drawing in white on black paper? Or with a feather dipped in ink? Can you make a drawing with the sole of your shoe? Sometimes you'll get surprising results from an unusual medium or technique. Student work by Ginger Urick, East Detroit, Michigan.

The Role of Drawing Today

Higher-Order Thinking Skills

• Display slides of artworks from different cultures. Discuss and demonstrate how an understanding of art history can enrich the viewer's understanding of an artwork.

• Direct students to the statement by artist Joanna Kao on page 235. Discuss her statement and work in terms of the six guidelines on these pages.

• Select a contemporary piece of art. Have students explain how it is a reflection of the time in which it was created. How are students' drawings also a reflection of their times?

• By comparing Yetti Frenkel's portrait of two men with a portrait drawing by Ingres on page 17, students may understand how art can reflect the society in which it is produced. Ask students to develop a list of characteristics that indicate in which century each work was created. Of course they will notice the clothes and setting, but encourage them to also consider the pose and attitude of the subjects.

Consider how art has enriched your life. Have you drawn pictures of friends and family or scenery? Perhaps you have photographed them. What makes you want to record what you see? Why is the process of drawing an important method of communication?

In a unique way, drawing promotes human understanding, achievement and self-improvement. Drawing serves as a means of making lives fuller and richer, enriching whole societies and cultures.

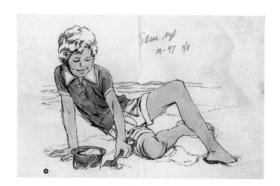

Fashion designers use drawing to show others their ideas.

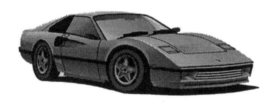

Graphic artists produce illustrations for many different clients. This illustration was created on a computer for an advertisement. Courtesy Commercial Graphics, Worcester, Massachusetts.

Our society benefits from a better educated and aesthetically aware public. One measure of the strength of a culture is its art, through which the culture expresses its values and beliefs. Through art, we gain understanding and valuable knowledge of cultures past and present.

On a practical level, drawing provides a means of solving problems and developing ideas. Drawing is a quick, flexible and direct method for putting together information. Designers use the sketching process to visualize ideas and concepts for new products. Fashion designers use drawings to develop ideas for jewelry. Graphic designers create logos, symbols and layouts for the corporate world. Illustrators, architects and cartoonists all use drawing as a vehicle for visual and creative thinking and to communicate their ideas.

All of these areas require an understanding of basic drawing and visual communication skills.

Perhaps you have already grasped how your drawings reflect your personal responses to life. Can you also understand how your drawings relate to your culture? Your drawings have value. They express not only your feelings, but also some of the feelings that are unique to your time in history. Be willing to examine the direction and value of your work. Here are some guidelines to help you grow as an artist.

1. Create artwork that expresses your personal philosophy. What do you think about? What do you feel is important? Do you wish for a peaceful world? A world without pollution, without illness, without poverty? How might your drawings reflect what you feel?

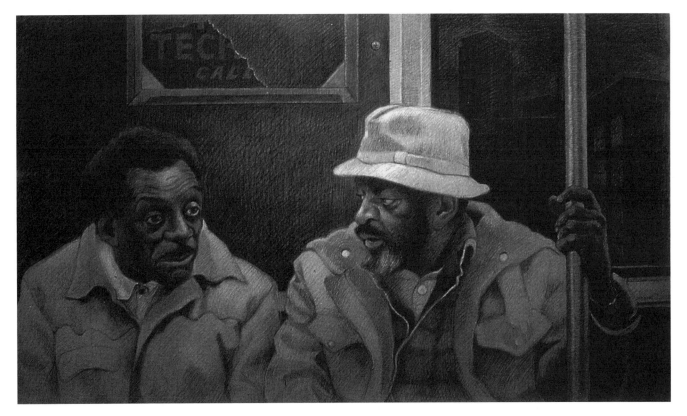

People-watching is good preparation for sensitive drawing. How do people's faces look on a bus or train, or when they're telling a joke or yawning? Yetti Frenkel, *Orange Line #1*, 1987. Pastel and conté, 32" x 54" (81 x 137 cm). Courtesy of the artist.

2. Produce drawings that have originality. All artists get ideas from other artwork, or from things they have seen, but they add ideas or techniques that are completely their own. Listen to your imagination: where does it take you? How would you like to change the things you see? Apply ideas like those to your drawings.

3. Develop drawings that use a variety of approaches, themes and subject matter. The more you explore new ways of doing things, the more confident you'll become. Confidence will allow you to take risks and seek new challenges.

4. Produce drawings that communicate important ideas and challenge the viewer to see a subject in a new way. You have

insights that no one else has; you see things as no one else does. When you draw, try to remember that other people don't necessarily think the way you do—about anything. That may inspire you to tell them, through your drawings, how you view life, the world, yourself.

5. Create artwork that reflects our current society but demonstrates a thorough understanding of a previous culture's achievements in art.

6. Develop an in-depth understanding of other artists' styles and work in order to develop your own individual approach to drawing.

William Blake

1757-1827

William Blake's passion for art began with his fascination with drawing. As a child, he was constantly sketching from nature and copying copper prints. He was also an avid reader. Stories from the Bible, Shakespeare and Milton fascinated the young artist and inspired his first poems and pictures. It was the world beyond empirical evidence that always appealed to him the most.

At age fourteen Blake began his apprenticeship to James Basire, a London engraver. After seven years of learning his craft, Blake became a certified printmaker himself. He became an engraver of other artists' works, as well as a creative artist in his own right.

In 1779, Blake decided to continue his education at the London Royal Art Academy. Although he enjoyed his classes in figure drawing, Blake was more interested in drawing from imagination rather than from life. Blake believed that "the artist has to put before the viewer forms and poses which hitherto have existed only in the darkness and confusion of an irrational mind or one beset with uncontrolled passions."

Blake often claimed that his fantastic imagery originated in his visions. Once he told his neighbor that a ghost of a flea appeared to him. As his friend watched, Blake began to draw the monster. It had a tongue like a lizard and its head was covered with green and gold skin. In its hand was a cup to hold blood.

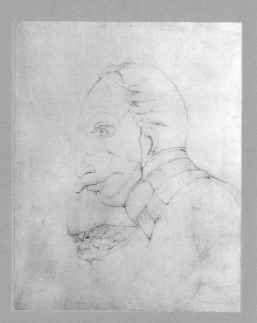

Blake is known for his watercolor illustrations. This sketch shows his fascination with other-worldly images. William Blake, *The Head of a Ghost of a Flea*, 1819. On paper, 7" x 6" (19 x 15 cm). The Tate Gallery, London. Art Resource, NY.

Speaking of Art...

Jean-Auguste Ingres was one of Jacques Louis David's students. In 1801, he won the French Academy's Prix de Rome, a scholarship to study art in Rome. He remained in Italy after his year of study and supported his family by drawing pencil portraits. Before he began a painted portrait, he would make hundreds of pencil sketches. In 1824, he returned to Paris, where he lead the French Academy for over forty years.

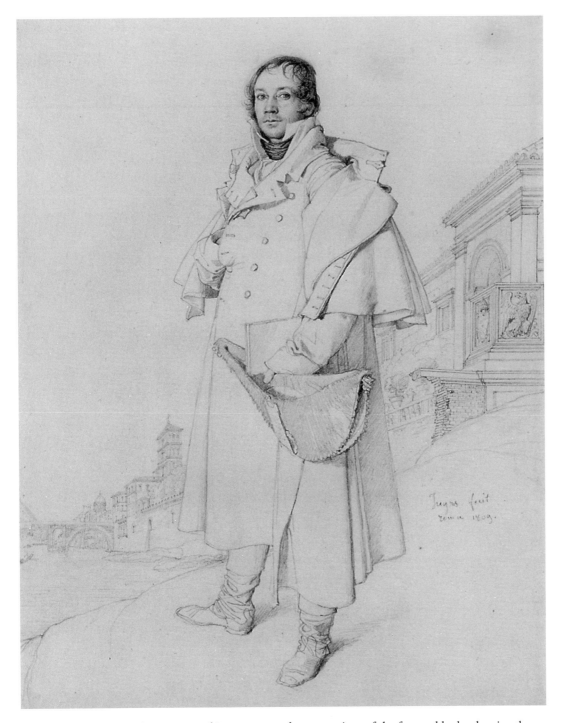

Context

During his stay in Rome, Ingres drew many pencil portraits of the French who were there during the French occupation. He used sharp-pointed graphite pencils to lightly outline the costumes but incorporated darker tones to accentuate the facial features and hair. With the fall of Napoleon and the French government in Rome, he came under financial strain, and drew occasional visiting foreigners for income.

Extension

Bring in other examples of Ingres' portraits for the class to see. Call students' attention to his use of line to create fine details and textures.

Drawing effective portraits means working to master the proportions of the face and body, showing the folds of clothing and the textures of skin and hair, and capturing small personal details. Jean-Auguste-Dominique Ingres, *Charles François Mallet, Civil Engineer*, 1809. Graphite on cream wove paper, 11" x 8" (26.8 x 21.1 cm). The Art Institute of Chicago, Charles Deering Collection.

Summary

Context
O'Keeffe sent this drawing and some others to her friend Anita Pollitzer who showed them to Alfred Stieglitz, owner of the art gallery 291. He described these drawings as "the purest, finest, sincerest things that have entered 291 in a long while."

You have learned in this chapter how drawing can be a language all its own. Drawing is communicating. It is a language which can cross all boundaries around the world and still be enjoyed and understood. As you progress through this book, consider how drawing is an integral part of our society.

Successful drawing, like any other art form, depends a great deal on establishing a positive attitude. Learning how to plan and seek directions in your drawing is critical to getting good results. Learning how to express your concerns and emotions in a complex and ever-changing world can be a joy and a challenge.

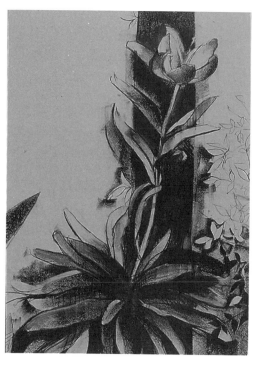

Your best drawings will probably be of things you care about or find visually interesting. If they don't come out as you'd imagined them, try again. It takes time and practice to develop good drawing skills. Melissa Gill, *Untitled*, 1993. Charcoal on paper. Courtesy of the artist.

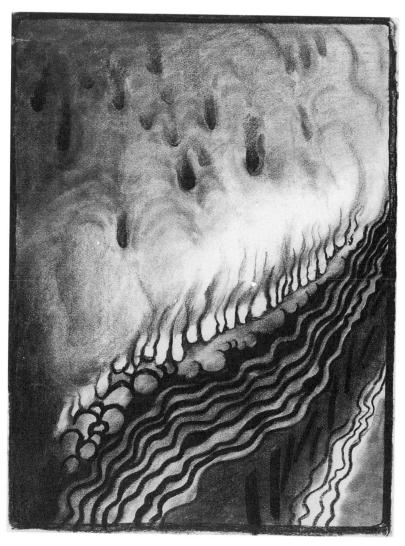

Some drawings suggest feelings rather than show you things you've already seen. What feeling does this drawing give you? Georgia O'Keeffe, *Special No. 9*, 1915. Charcoal on paper, 25" x 19 1/8" (64 x 49 cm). The Menil Collection, Houston. Photograph: Paul Hester.

Activities

Sketchbooks

a Select a subject that interests you and develop it in ten different ways. Begin with a simple contour drawing. Try different techniques such as blending, crosshatching and stippling to add value. Try drawing the subject from a different viewpoint. Draw the subject as though it were fading away. Search for new creative methods as you complete this exercise. see page 62

b Write down a dream you have had. Record as many details as you can remember. How did you feel during your dream? Illustrate your dream. Try to capture the mood. see page 16

c Select an object. Imagine how it would look if it were collapsed, melted, exploded or in some other unusual state. Draw one of your mental images. see pages 185 and 186

d Select a familiar object or item of food. Create a series of sequential sketches in which the object gradually transforms into something else. see page 212

Style

Compare and contrast the work of three artists who have very different styles. In a short essay, identify the main characteristics of each style. What makes each style different from the others?

Create your own composition. How would each of the artists approach it? Try drawing your composition in each of the three styles.

Images and the Written Word

Make a list of descriptive words in a journal. Record quotations you have heard or read that have made an impression on you. Are there specific details of experiences, dreams, sights and sounds that you could record in your journal? Use your journal writing as a source for drawings in your sketchbook. Think of how you can create a visual representation of written expression. see page 187

Design Elements in the Environment

Can you find design elements and principles of art in your everyday environment? Consider the shapes and patterns in buildings, the colors and lines in automobiles, as well as the designs you find in the natural world. Each day for a week, record some images and patterns you see. At the end of the week, write a paragraph about what you have seen. Reflect on how important these elements are to your everyday life. Consider how your life would be affected without their presence.

Careers

Research a career in art that interests you. How are drawing skills used in that career? If possible, visit a workplace and talk to an employee. Write a brief report about this career. Include a job description, training required, responsibilities, opportunities and salary.

Drawing on Scratchboard

Using a scratchboard that has not been inked, randomly paint colored inks over its surface. You may want to leave a few places white. When the colored ink has dried, cover the scratchboard with black ink. Let the ink dry. Now draw a design on the scratchboard. see page 26

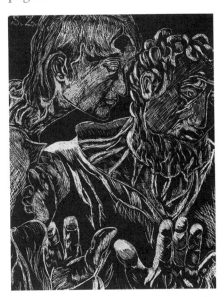

Student work by Sebastian Zapisek.

Chapter 2
Establishing a Composition

Objectives
Students will be able to
  • Define and analyze the elements of design: line, shape, texture, value, and color. (Art criticism)
  • Define and analyze the principles of art: balance, emphasis, harmony, variety, movement, and proportion. (Art criticism)
  • Define the terms simulated and actual texture and support your definitions with examples. (Art criticism)
  • Demonstrate an understanding of values by creating a value scale with a gradation of values. (Art production)
  • Experiment with creating a range of values in their own drawings. (Art production)
  • Create artworks that demonstrate their understanding of art elements and principles. (Art production)
  • Perceive and discuss how various artists, including Käthe Kollwitz, have utilized art principles and values in their work. (Art history/cultures)
  • Use their knowledge of art elements and principles to make aesthetic judgments about artworks, including their own art. (Aesthetics)

Vocabulary
line	emphasis
shape	harmony
texture	variety
value	movement
color	proportion
balance	

Chapter Overview
This chapter explains the elements of design and the principles of art. Students explore ways to use the elements and principles to establish unity in a composition. Students also learn how to apply this art vocabulary to analyze illustrations.

Lesson 1
pages 20–25   45 minutes

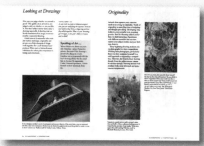

pages 24–25

Teach
  • Have students study the drawings on pages 24 and 25. Discuss which of the media on the preceding pages might have been used to create these works.
  • When considering creativity, stress that drawing from life is much more creative and original than copying an existing drawing or photograph.

Studio Experience
Allow students to experiment with at least five of the different drawing media described on pages 22 and 23. Provide different kinds of papers and blending tools. Encourage students to make thick and thin lines, shading from dark to light values, and drawing

dots and crosshatching. Which media work best on which papers? For example, some pencils will not sink into the surface of some papers while many inks will spread and blot on construction paper. Which media and papers seem most appropriate for fine details and which for large, soft blending areas of values? Experiment with erasing the different media.

Materials
assorted drawing media—pen and
  ink, markers, pencils, charcoal,
  charcoal pencils, graphite
  pencils, crayons, oil pastels
assorted papers—white drawing
  paper, bond paper, construction
  paper, charcoal paper, watercolor paper, illustration board
rubbing and blending tools such
  as erasers and stumps

Lesson 2
pages 26–28   45 minutes

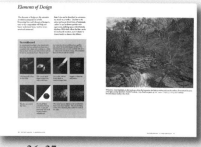

pages 26–27

Teach
  • Ask students to describe some of the lines on page 27. Have them contrast these lines with those in the drawing of the dust-pan on page 24. (The lines on

page 27 are much more organic and flowing than the mechanical lines on page 24.)

• Call students' attention to the varying width of the lines on pages 28 and 29. They should notice how lines form shapes on page 29.

Studio Experience
Have students create different types of lines on inked scratch-board. Demonstrate how to use the scratching tools shown on page 26. Encourage them to try several of these techniques to create light and dark values using varying widths of line.

Materials
8" x 10" inked scratchboard
scratching tools such as sgraffito
   nibs or scrapers in pen holders,
   X-acto knives, large needles,
   or scribers
rulers

Lesson 3
pages 30–31   45 minutes

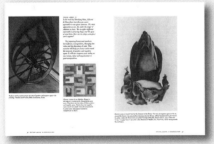

pages 30–31

Teach
Explain the difference between negative and positive space. The spaces between the spokes in the wheel on page 30 are examples of negative space. Discuss the positive and negative spaces in O'Keeffe's *Banana Flower*.

Studio Experience
Call students' attention to the positive and negative space in the student letter design on page 30. Point out how some of the negative space is light and some is dark. Have students draw one of their initials large (about 3" x 3") on a sheet of tracing paper. After they are satisfied with their design, have them blacken the back of the letter with pencil and transfer it several times onto a piece of drawing paper to form a pattern, as in the student design on page 30. Tell students to darken the positive and negative spaces to create a varying, interesting design.

Materials
9" x 12" tracing paper
9" x 12" drawing paper
pencil

Lesson 4
pages 32–33   45 minutes

Teach
Introduce the concept of texture by pointing out a variety of actual textures in the classroom that students may touch, such as bricks, glass, rough walls, tile floors, denim, heater grates, silky fabrics, shoe soles, and rough sweaters. Direct students to study the simulated textures in the illustrations. How did the artists create an illusion of texture?

Studio Experience
Instruct students to create a sampler of textures with pencil rubbings. Demonstrate laying a thin piece of paper over a textured surface such as a coin and rubbing with the broad side of a soft lead pencil. Students should plan to make about thirty rubbings in order have a collection of at least twenty-four. They may rub things all over the art studio. Either provide a collection of textured objects for them to rub or send them outside and around the school grounds to collect textures. Samples can range in size from a few square inches to about a half sheet of typing paper. Have students glue their rubbings to a large sheet of paper.

As an extension, suggest that they create a shape collage with rubbings.

Teaching Tip
The paper must be thin for this to work. Use photocopy paper or even tracing paper.

Materials
collection of textured objects
   such as coins, combs, leaves,
   keys, expired credit cards,
   burlap, heavy lace, and shells
photocopy paper or tracing paper,
   6 to 8 sheets per student
soft lead pencils
construction paper, 12" x 18"
scissors
glue

Lesson 5
pages 34–36   45 minutes

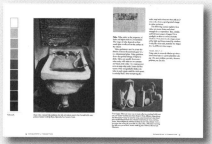

pages 34–35

Teach
Explain that value refers to the darks and lights in an artwork. Study the wide range of values in the illustrations on these pages. Can students identify light, dark, and medium values in each illustration? Direct the class to the biography of Kollwitz on page 36. Have students analyze this self-portrait and another on page 138. How did she use light and dark values for dramatic effect?

Studio Experience
Have students create a value scale such as the one on page 34 using charcoal or pencil. Tell them to draw six 1" squares in a row. Next, have them leave the first box white and gradually darken them until the last box is black.

Another way to create a value scale is to draw five boxes on gray paper, making the first box white with pastel or conté crayon and the last box black with charcoal. Make the middle box a gray value halfway between black and white. Then fill in the second and fourth boxes with middle values between the gray in the center box and the white in the first square and then the gray in the center and the black in the last square. As a challenge this may be extended to nine boxes; students fill in medium values between each of the original five.

Lesson 6
page 37   45 minutes

Teach
• To explain the color terms hue, value, complementary, analogous, primary, secondary, neutral, warm, and cool, refer students to the color wheels on pages 154 and 155. Using an assorted color set of pastel sticks, have students demonstrate their understanding of these terms by selecting a complementary color scheme, then a set of three analogous colors, then two neutral colors, and finally a warm and cool set of colors. Check their selections as they set out the pastel sticks to form the various color schemes.

• Have the students work in pairs to describe the color in Degas' *Rehearsal on the Stage* (page 165). List their descriptions on the board. Compare the range of values in the color and black-and-white versions.

Studio Experience
Call students' attention to the color value scale on page 155 and then the drawing media pictured on page 158. Using a white and a color pastel, have students create a color value scale. Then they may draw simple shapes such as circles and shade them using a range of light to dark values to indicate their three-dimensional form.

Materials
colored, blendable drawing media
    such as pastels
white drawing paper
assortment of rounded objects

Lesson 7
pages 38–43   45 minutes

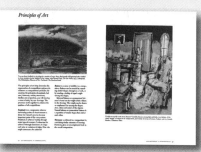

pages 40–41

Teach
• As a class, read page 38. Encourage students to explain why the artists made *Texas Plates* horizontal, and *Delmonico Building* vertical. How do the main shapes impact the composition? Imagine the effect if the artist had made the horizontal one vertical and vice versa.

• Display the charts listing the elements of design and art principles from the Chapter Warm-up. Remind students that art principles have to do with how the art elements are arranged in a composition. Teach students that contrast of values, colors, or textures is often used to emphasize one part of a composition. Ask students what Curry emphasized in *The Line Storm*. They may notice the light-valued lightning streaks against the dark clouds, and how these lines seem to point toward the hay wagon. Look back at the illustrations on pages 38 and 39 to discover how these artists emphasized their center of interest.

• Explain to students that balance has to do with the relative weight of objects in the composition to each other. Tell them to imagine a vertical line through the middle of Andy Warhol's *Marilyn* on page 219. The composition on both sides of this line would be identical, making this a formal or symmetrical composition. O'Keeffe's *Banana Flower* on page 31 is an example of an almost symmetrical composition. Ask students to imagine dividing the student art on page 41 in half vertically. These two halves are very different; this is an example of an informal or asymmetrical arrangement. Direct students to find other examples of asymmetrical balance in the book.

• After reading about harmony, call students' attention to how the artists created harmony in the illustrations on these pages. Curry used the same type of lines throughout to create an overall harmony.

• Introduce the terms variety, movement, rhythm, proportion, and unity. Divide the class into groups of three or four students. Assign each group one or two of the eight art principles to define and explain to the rest of the class. To support their explanation,

each group should find an image in this book to use as a clear example of their art principle.

Lesson 8
pages 44–45   45 minutes

Reteach

• Display the charts listing the art elements and principles. Review with students the meaning of each term. Ask students to cite an example of each of these elements and principles in works in this chapter or in posters in the class.

• Assign an activity on page 45. The Leaf Composition activity is particularly easy for beginning drawing students. After students arrange leaves to create a center of interest, balance, repetition, and rhythm, they draw their composition. They may also add color.

Assess

• Students should list and define the art elements and principles. Have them select pieces of their artwork and describe how they used the elements of design and principles of art in these works. Students may complete this assignment in a class discussion or as a written assignment. (Art criticism/Aesthetics)

• In a class discussion, review with students the difference between simulated and actual texture. Have each student give examples of simulated and actual texture. (Art production)

• Have students discuss how Kollwitz and another artist in this

chapter utilized art principles and values in their work. Which element and principle is most important in each of these artist's works? You may want to assign this activity as a written assignment. (Art history/Aesthetics)

• Have students collect the artworks they produced for this chapter and arrange them into a portfolio. (Portfolios may be as simple as a piece of craft paper folded over their art with their name in large letters on the front.) If possible, hold a conference with each student to assess how well he or she met the requirements of each activity.

Did the student demonstrate an understanding of black to white values by creating a value scale with a gradation of values? (Art production)

Did he or she experiment with creating a range of values in the drawings? (Art production)

Did the student create artworks that demonstrate an understanding of art elements and principles? (Art production)

• To determine whether students can analyze their own artworks in terms of elements of design and principles of art, ask them which pieces of their art are especially effective examples of some of the art principles and elements. For example, did they create a rounded form effectively using of a wide range of values? Is their letter design a very good example of negative space? Which of their artworks do they like best and why? (Aesthetics)

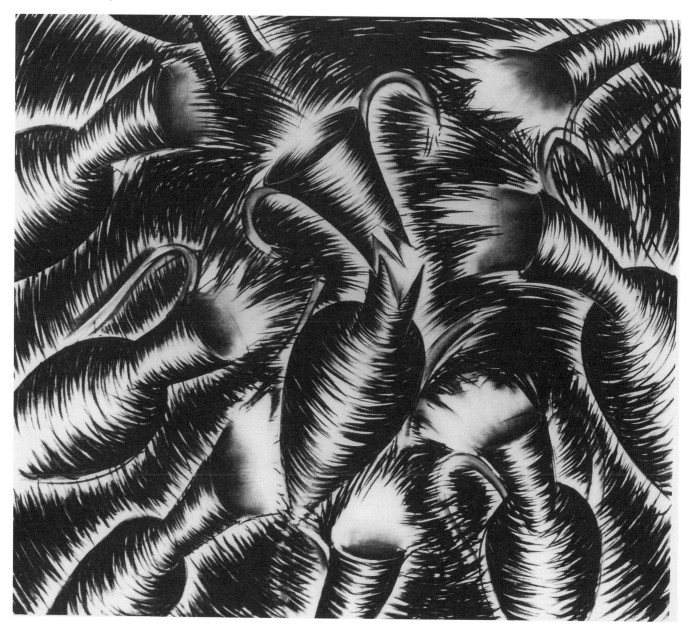

Strong, confident lines and stark contrasts give this drawing a feeling of intense energy. What unifies it? Is it balanced? Have you ever imagined giving everyday objects lives of their own? Susan Chrysler White, *Untitled 2*, 1981. Dayglow, gouache, charcoal, 48" x 42 1/2" (121.9 x 108 cm). Courtesy Stedman Art Gallery/Rutgers-Camden Collection of Art.

2 Establishing a Composition

This chapter covers the basic vocabulary of art, the fundamentals on which artworks are created. The vocabulary may not be new to you. You have probably used these terms to describe many things in your environment. Apply what you already know as you discover how the vocabulary is used in the context of art.

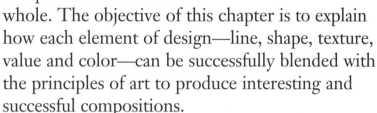

This chapter explores the principles of art that enable the artist to organize the elements of a composition into a unified whole. The objective of this chapter is to explain how each element of design—line, shape, texture, value and color—can be successfully blended with the principles of art to produce interesting and successful compositions.

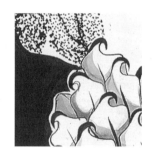

The principles of art include balance, emphasis, harmony, variety, movement and proportion. Any successful composition includes at least some of them. These fundamental principles can also help you analyze an artwork and discover the idea or concept the artist has attempted to communicate.

Vocabulary
line
shape
texture
value
color
balance
emphasis
harmony
variety
movement
proportion

Higher-Order Thinking Skills
Ask advanced students to identify important principles of art in the drawing on page 20. Which is most emphasized? (movement) What two elements of design are represented? (line and value)

Key Chapter Points

- The elements of design are line, shape, texture, value and color.
- The principles of art are balance, emphasis, harmony, variety, movement and proportion.
- Texture is simulated in a drawing.
- Value is the gradation of shades between black and white.
- Unity is a principle of design that relates to a sense of wholeness in a composition.

Glossary of Drawing Materials

Pen and Ink

1. broad tip marker
2. fine tip marker
3. brush tip marker
4. chisel tip calligraphy pen
5. extra fine point marker
6. 0.5 mm point felt pen
7. technical drawing pen with interchangeable nibs
8. fountain pen
9. pen holder and nibs
10. black drawing ink
11. reed pen
12. bamboo brush
13. bamboo brush
14. Sumi-ink ink stick and grinding stone

Charcoal

1. stick charcoal
2. stick charcoal
3. compressed charcoal square
4. compressed charcoal round
5. charcoal pencil extra soft
6. charcoal pencil medium/2B
7. charcoal pencil hard/HB
8. powdered charcoal

Graphite

1. flat sketching pencil 6B
2. ebony pencil
3. sketching pencil 4B
4. drawing pencil 9B
5. drawing pencil HB
6. drawing pencil H
7. drawing pencil 8H
8. graphite woodless pencil
9. graphite stick 4B

Conté/Grease

1. crayon
2. oil pastel
3. conté stick
4. conté pencil white
5. conté pencil black 2B
6. conté pencil black 3B
7. china marker
8. lithographic crayon

Rubbing and Blending Tools

1. rolled paper stump
2. tortillon
3. rolled paper stump
4. chamois
5. erasers
6. cotton balls
7. cotton swabs

Pen and Ink

The earliest pens were reed pens made from bamboo cane, and quill pens from feathers. Today artists have a wide range of pens available to use, from those that need to be dipped in ink to those that carry their own supply of ink in the barrel in refillable or disposable cartridges.

Ballpoint pens, fountain pens with a refillable or disposable cartridge and felt-tipped markers are good tools for continuous line drawing of consistent thickness, since they carry their own ink supply. The best and most expensive tool with a continuous flow of ink is the technical drawing pen. Technical pens are refillable and are available with a variety of interchangeable nibs that produce lines that range from thin (.13 mm nib) to thick (2.00 mm nib).

The blackest and most permanent ink is India ink. It has been in use since about 2,500 BC. The solid form (Sumi-e sticks) is ground on a grinding stone and mixed with water, generally used for washes. Liquid India ink is used with reed pens, quills and brushes. Additional types of ink are those for fountain pens and technical pens.

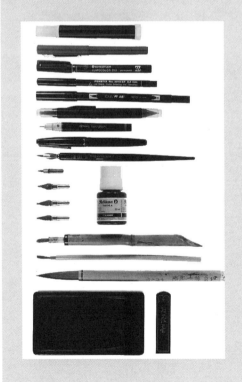

Charcoal

Charcoal was used as a drawing medium by the Greeks and Romans, by artists in the Middle Ages and Renaissance and is still used today. Until the sixteenth century, when fixatives were discovered, charcoal drawings could not be kept. Charcoal can be erased with kneaded rubber erasers and worked with a chamois, rolled paper stumps, cotton swabs and fingertips.

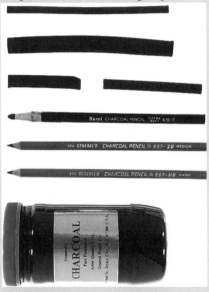

The two types of charcoal are stick and compressed. Stick charcoal is carbonized wood or vines and can be purchased in varying thicknesses. Compressed charcoal is ground carbon mixed with clay or binding substances. Compressed charcoal produces a richer, blacker line than stick charcoal and is more difficult to erase. Charcoal pencils are compressed charcoal encased in wood, in a variety of gradations such as extra soft, soft, medium, hard. Letters and numbers may indicate the gradation, such as H (hard), 2B (soft).

Powdered or dust charcoal can be purchased in jars or made by scraping the stick form down with a knife. Charcoal powder is worked with stumps or fingertips.

Charcoal's thickness and the difficulty in keeping the point sharp make it a medium suited to large, free drawing rather than small, precise work. Since charcoal smudges easily, finished drawings must be fixed to preserve them.

Graphite

Graphite, the most commonly used drawing material, comes in stick and pencil form and in a great variety of hardnesses (from 8B, the softest, to 9H, the hardest). Graphite pencils are generally called lead pencils, although they are actually made of graphite mixed with clay. Soft lead pencils contain less clay and produce a darker line, while hard pencils contain more clay and produce a lighter line. Graphite has a shiny, metallic quality and even at its darkest is not a true black.

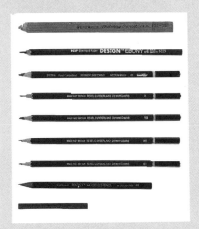

Conté/Grease

Conté is a finely textured, semihard, oily material in pencil and stick forms, in several degrees of hardness. It comes in colors, including sanguine, sepia, white and black. Conté is smoother and more permanent than charcoal.

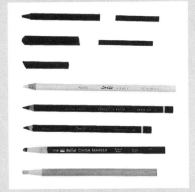

Lithographic crayons (made for drawing on lithographic stones for printmaking) and oil pastels are greasier than conté. Lithographic crayons come in several degrees of hardness. China pencils, similar to lithographic crayons, may be used on concrete for preliminary drawings for murals.

Wax crayons are inexpensive, round or square, wrapped in paper or unwrapped. Remove the wrapper to use the sides for broad strokes.

Rubbing and Blending Tools

Stumps/tortillons for rubbing and blending are made of tightly rolled paper, felt or chamois. Use pointed ends for rubbing small areas, blunt ends for larger areas. Tear away a layer to get a clean point. You can make your own by tightly rolling a triangle of paper.

Alternative tools for rubbing and blending are cotton swabs for small areas and cottons balls for large. Chamois is a soft leather used for smoothing areas of charcoal and pastel drawing.

The fingertips and lower palm of your hand can also be used for rubbing and blending.

Blending with erasers is discussed on page 90.

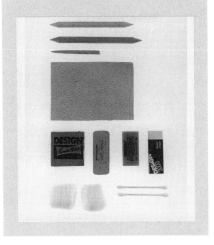

Computers

There are many paint/drawing software programs available. Most offer a choice of tools such as pencil, brush, airbrush to create lines of varying texture and thickness; a choice of closed or open shapes, with thick or thin borders; and a variety of patterns that can be used to fill shapes to show shading and texture. The drawing may be done using a stylus on a graphics tablet or a mouse. Scanners can be used to transfer photographs to the computer screen where they can be manipulated, distorted or replicated.

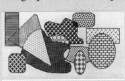
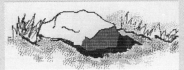

The great advantage to using a computer as a drawing tool is that you can save your drawings at different stages of development and recall them later.

Looking at Drawings

Higher-Order Thinking Skills
Ask students to define what they think makes a good work of art. You may want to list their criteria on the chalkboard. Encourage students to consider such criteria as: good design, harmonious relationships among parts, craftsmanship, the aesthetic response the work provokes, whether it was intended to be seen as a work of art. Then have them work in small groups to pick works of art in this book that illustrate and support their definitions.

Extension
Have students discuss how artists have helped them look at familiar objects in a different way. You may want to provide examples of well-known works, such as flowers by Georgia O'Keeffe and soup cans by Andy Warhol, etc.

Inquiry
Assign students to research the art of Cimabue and Giotto and write a description of a work by each artist. Encourage them to notice how important drawing was in each work.

How can you judge whether an artwork is good? The quality of an artwork is not judged solely on whether or not you like it. Nor does subject matter alone make a drawing successful. A drawing that is a literal translation of an image is not necessarily a successful drawing.

Good artwork is successful when subject matter, technique, originality and proper use of the elements of design work together for a well-balanced composition. When each of these elements reinforces the others, the composition is strong and structured.

THINK ABOUT IT
As you work to create a balanced composition, you are analyzing the separate elements and synthesizing them, or figuring out how they all fit together. Thus, as your drawings get stronger, so does your ability to reason and to think!

Speaking of Art ...
When Giotto was about ten years old, Cimabue, a great Florentine painter, discovered him drawing a picture of a sheep on a rock. Cimabue was so impressed with the boy's drawing ability that he asked him to become his apprentice. Under Cimabue's guidance, Giotto learned to draw accurately from life.

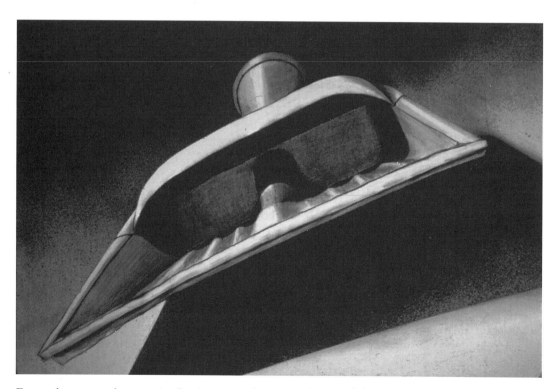

Even a dustpan can have an air of excitement and mystery about it, if the artist finds a way to communicate his or her own excitement. Notice how the dustpan's angled position and deep shadows make it seem to move toward you. Student work by Gladys Cosby, Abilene, Texas.

Originality

Artwork that captures your attention tends to be strong in originality. Think of originality as something that is intriguing and thought-provoking. Developing originality in your artworks is an on-going process. Start by choosing subject matter that you find interesting. Experiment with different materials that can best express your subject matter and your feelings about it.

Many beginning drawing students rely on photographs for their compositions. Working from photographs, particularly those you have composed yourself, is a valid approach to organizing a composition. However, the benefits from drawing directly from the subject matter cannot be stressed enough. Working directly will produce fresh, more informed and spontaneous compositions.

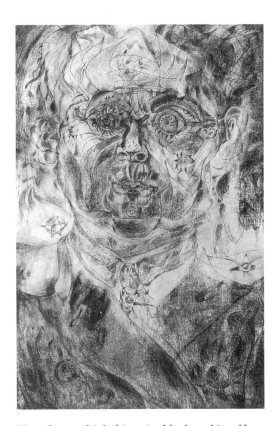

How do you think this artist felt about himself the day he drew this self-portrait? Do you think it shows originality? What face would you like to show to those around you? How would you reveal your personality? Joan Miró, *Self-Portrait, I*, 1937. Pencil, crayon and oil on canvas, 57 1/2" x 38 1/4" (146.1 x 97.2 cm). The Museum of Modern Art, New York. James Thrall Soby Bequest.

Higher-Order Thinking Skills
Discuss ways in which the images on this page are thought-provoking. (subject matter, points of view, execution, scale, lighting) Have students turn to pages 186–190 to view additional examples of originality in art.

Design Extension
Have students make a class drawing. Tell one student to draw an object on one part of a large sheet of paper, then cover it with a piece of paper and pass the sheet on to the next student. Each succeeding student should draw another object on the large sheet. The result will be a drawing composed of many objects, some of which won't fit together. Is the end result strong in originality? Does it work as a whole?

Context
Surrealist artist Joan Miró was born in the Catalan region in Spain in 1893. Miró expressed his deep feelings about World War II in a series of self-portraits, which he described as an attempt to escape. In these self-portraits, he developed a set of symbols (earth, man, stars, and woman) which he repeated often in his later artworks.

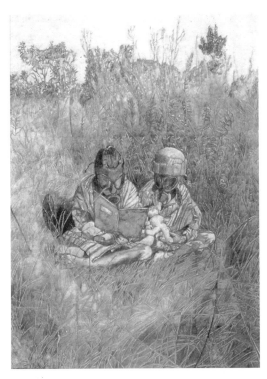

Surprise is a good way to catch a viewer's attention and hold it. Here, a pleasant-looking scene is soured by the presence of gas masks. What message is the artist sending? Student work by Elizabeth Buscemi, Livonia, New York.

Elements of Design

The elements of design are the armature on which a composition is built. Examining how each element of design is used in the composition will help you better understand how a work is structured and composed.

Line Line can be described as a continuous mark on a surface. The line is the oldest and most direct form of communication. It can be drawn quickly with expression, defining space with dramatic rhythms. With little effort the line can be drawn heavily to show more volume or drawn faintly to denote the delicate.

Teaching Tip
Explain that an armature is like a skeleton that provides structure. For example, music is based on the armature of notes, chords, and bars. Language is based on the armature of sentences and paragraphs. In the same way, the elements of design are the structure for an artwork. As students learn about the elements of design (line, shape, texture, value, color), encourage them to see how each element is related to the whole.

Design Extension
Line drawings are a good way for beginning artists to capture the basics of a subject, not the details. Give students some opportunities to draw quick studies and experiment with capturing the most they can of a subject with the minimum amount of lines. They should not be concerned with accuracy at this point.

Computer Connection
Encourage students to experiment with drawing on the computer. They should draw both straight lines and organic curved ones, and draw and fill in some shapes.

Context
Another example of Jack Beal's use of line can be seen on page 137.

Scratchboard

In scratchboard drawings, a clay-coated cardboard that has been painted with black ink is scratched with a sharp tool, resulting in a white line on black. Almost any kind of sharp tool can be used to scratch the board. The most common scratchers for scratchboard are sgraffito nibs, which fit into drawing pen holders. Pre-inked scratchboards now are available with silver or colors under the black coating. The scratched lines on these boards are colored.

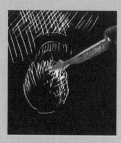

This sharp nib is best for fine lines.

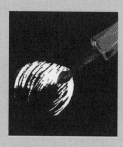

This curved spade-shaped scraper can make wider lines.

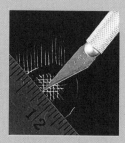

Try a ruler with an X-acto knife to scratch straight lines.

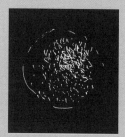

Stipples or dots can add texture.

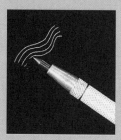

Needles can scratch fine lines.

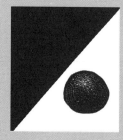

Pre-inked black scratchboard is easy to use, or you can paint India ink on all or part of white scratchboard.

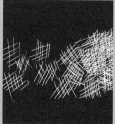

The values become lighter as the crosshatched lines come closer together. The crosshatching on the left is freehand, but a ruler was used on the right.

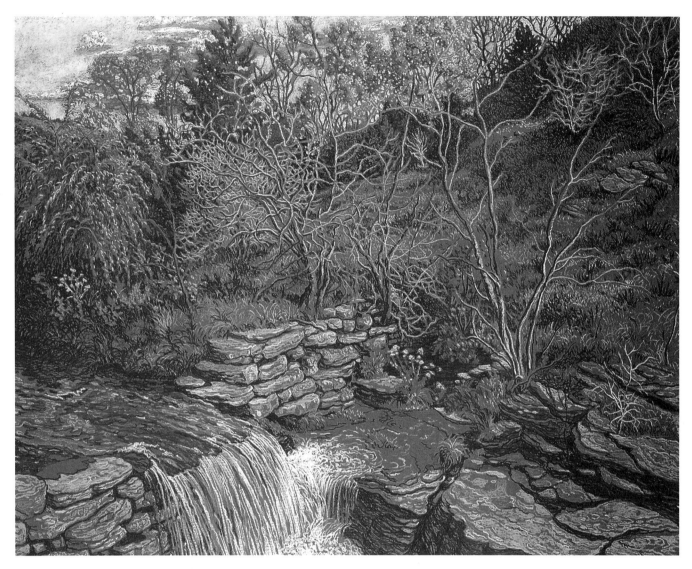

White lines create highlights in this landscape, giving the impression that light is striking only certain surfaces. From which direction is the light coming? Jack Beal, *Untitled Landscape*, 1979. Pastel on paper, 47 1/2" x 47 1/2" (120.7 x 120.7 cm). Courtesy Frumkin/Adams Gallery, New York.

Developing a line composition which causes the flat surface of the paper to appear three-dimensional is one way to explore the line as an element of design. Try repeating lines to create a pattern and then varying the thickness of the lines. Focus on getting a sense of how a composition is organized. Can you see the value of using repetition and variation in your lines?

Shape The closing of a line creates a shape. A shape is two-dimensional with a recognizable boundary. The shape of an object in a drawing is often called the figure and the surrounding space is called the ground. The relationship between the figure and the ground is called the figure-ground relationship.

Figure and ground are often referred to as positive and negative space. The positive space is created by solid objects in the composition. The negative space is the area around the solid objects.

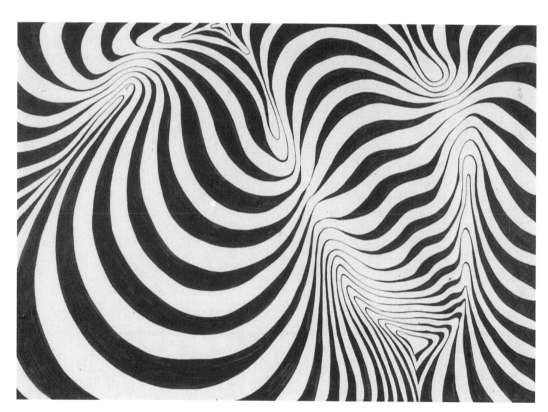

Varying line width helps create movement. In this work, notice how repeated lines and varied widths also create the illusion of three-dimensionality. Student work by Geinene Haynes, Nashville, Tennessee.

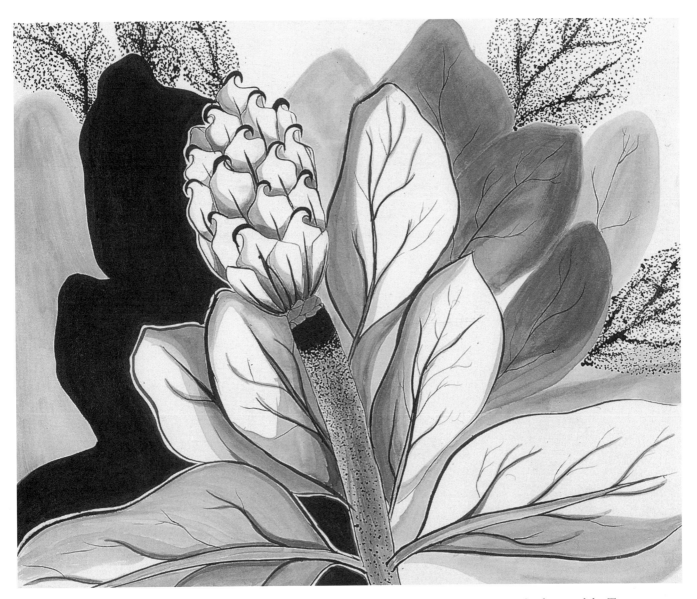

The solid areas of ink in this drawing make the negative space stand out more than the positive space. Student work by Tara White, Temple, Texas.

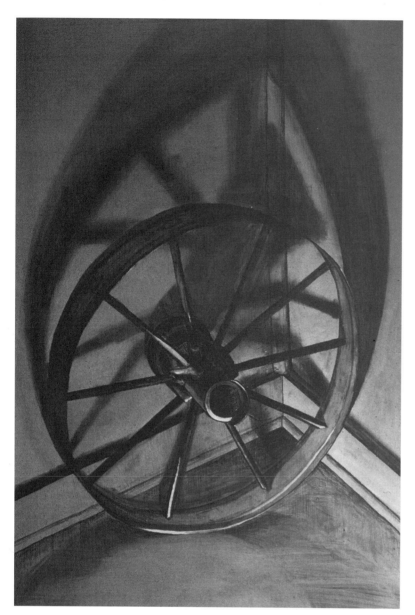

THINK ABOUT IT
In his book Six Thinking Hats, *Edward de Bono shows that there are many approaches to any given situation. The more approaches we use, the wider the range of solutions we have. Try to explore different approaches to drawing shapes and the space around them. How can the shapes and spaces work together?*

Try repeating letters and numbers throughout a composition, changing the value and the direction of each. This exercise will help you better understand the concept of positive and negative space. It will also improve your ability to use variety, value and organization in your composition.

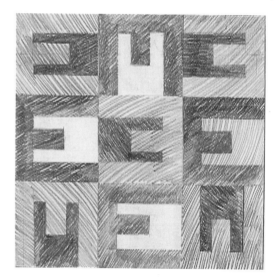

Shadows can be used to create two sets of positive and negative space relationships. Student work by Jim Hale, Commerce, Texas.

Choose a letter of the alphabet. Repeat it throughout a composition, changing the position of the letter and the values of both positive and negative space. Notice how the negative space stands out clearly from the composition in some cases, and appears neutral or insignificant in others.

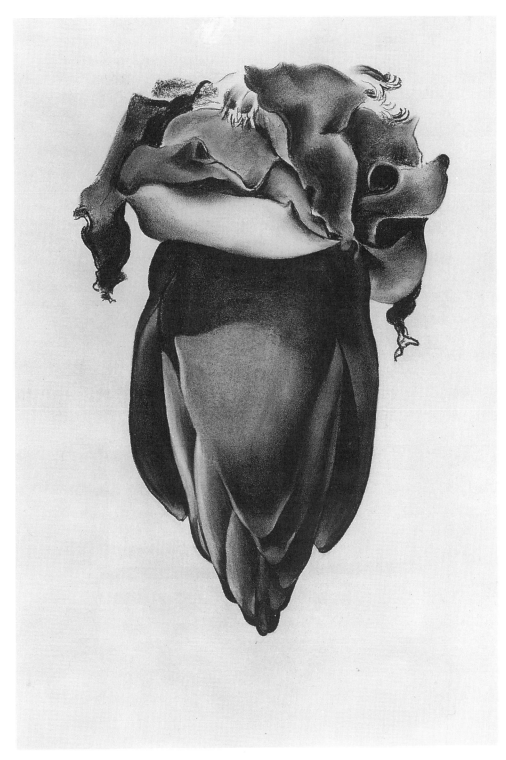

Higher-Order Thinking Skills
Have students identify positive and negative space in the drawings on these pages. To help students better understand how positive and negative space work together, have them reverse the positive and negative space in one of the drawings and redraw it.

Extensions
• Have students keep their drawings of a letter. Use them for further discussion in Chapter 3, in which figure-ground relationships are explored more fully.

• Remind students of the Georgia O'Keeffe drawing on page 18. As students study the negative space in these examples, read them the O'Keeffe quote on page 65 about negative space.

• Students may draw the negative space around chairs as described in the Positive and Negative Space activity on page 45.

Positive space is created here by the blossom of the flower. You can see negative space in the air around the flower. Can you see how showing only the flower, without background or the rest of the plant, makes the flower look powerful? Georgia O'Keeffe, *Banana Flower*, 1933. Charcoal, 21 3/4" x 14 3/4" (55.2 x 37.5 cm). The Museum of Modern Art, New York. Given Anonymously (by exchange).

Design Extensions

• Bring to class some small objects with different textures, such as a bristled brush, a piece of carpet, or foam sponge. Put the objects one at a time in a small bag. Have students reach in and touch the object, then write one or two words that describe it. Finally, have them draw it. Encourage them to use many different kinds of line—dots, strokes, crosshatching—to describe textures visually.

• Have students experiment with different drawing tools to explore texture. Students can invent textures by using media such as pen, brush, glue, and wax crayon.

• Suggest that students use rubbings to create a collage. Have them make a whole series of rubbings of various textures such as coins, soles of tennis shoes, bricks, leaves, and combs. Students may cut the rubbings into shapes and glue them to a piece of paper in an interesting design. They may want to add lines with markers.

• Create texture rubbing designs as described in the Texture Rubbing activity on page 45.

Texture Texture refers to the sense of touch. This element describes the surface quality of an object. For example, rust on metal is a texture you can see and feel; the grain in a piece of wood is a texture you can see. Texture can add valuable visual information and create intrigue in drawing.

A drawing that suggests or duplicates various kinds of textures in a composition has simulated texture. A drawing that actually includes pieces of paper, cloth, wood or other materials has actual texture.

To develop a feeling for various textures, try making a rubbing. Lay a piece of typing paper on top of a textured surface and rub a soft lead pencil back and forth across it. The image that comes up will give you an accurate transfer of the object's surface. To fully explore a range of textures, collect up to one hundred rubbings that are three to four inches square. Select the best twenty-four rubbings and glue them on a large sheet of paper. Choose rubbings based on uniqueness, strength of image, and range of value.

Did this exercise make you more aware of surface textures? Notice the different marking systems you created in each rubbing. The rubbings are a way to record visual information. You can use this information to learn to draw simulated texture.

THINK ABOUT IT
Making a rubbing that records visual information is a simple task that can bring you one step further to the more complex task of drawing simulated texture. Learning to transfer what you have learned in one task to a new, more challenging task is a valuable thinking skill.

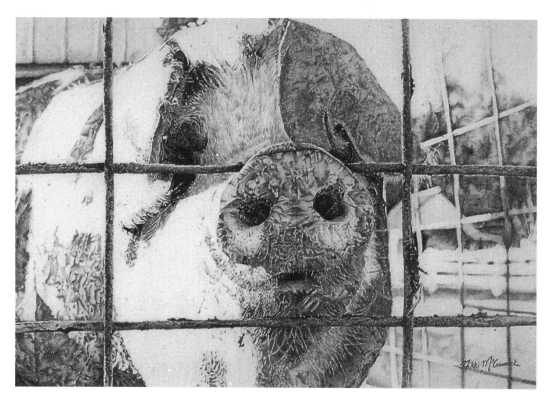

Can you feel the bristles on this pig's chin? Notice how the bristly areas are scattered throughout the composition, rather than used all over the pig's body. How does that help create visual interest? Student work by Nicole McCormick, Indianapolis, Indiana.

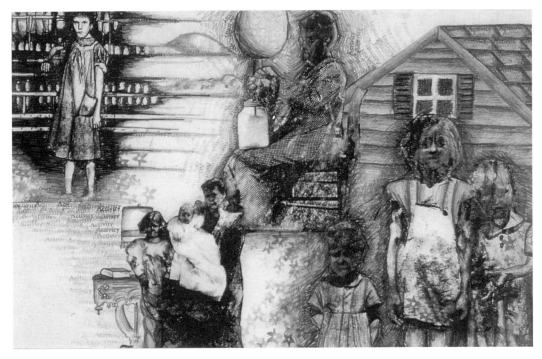

How would you describe the textures in this composition? Rough? Gritty? Oily? Worn smooth? Student work by Megan Boehm, Macedonia, Ohio.

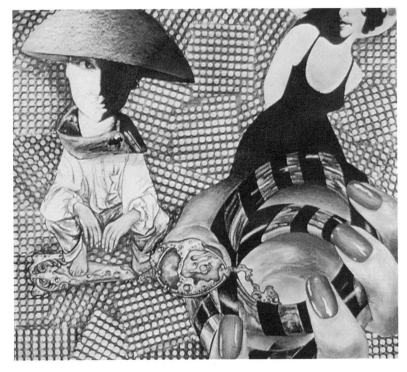

Smooth, solid areas are placed next to patterned ones in this montage. Student work by Katy Kaufman, York, Pennsylvania.

Value scale.

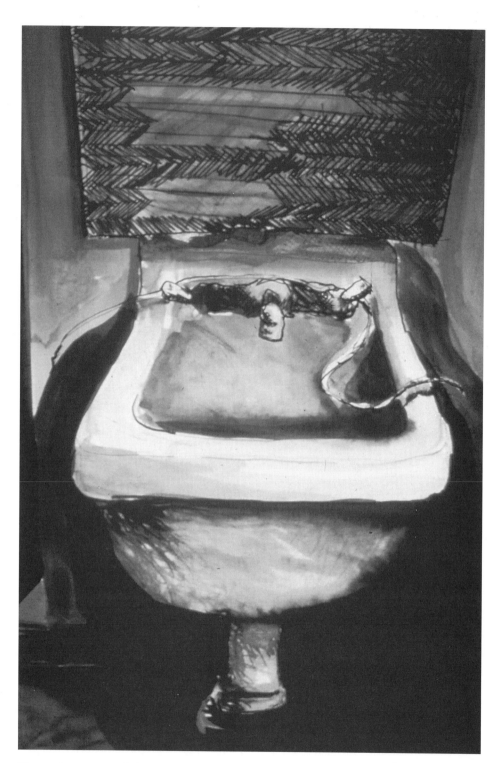

Sharp value contrasts help emphasize the sink and make it seem to leap forward in the composition. Student work by Bryan Lipscomb, San Antonio, Texas.

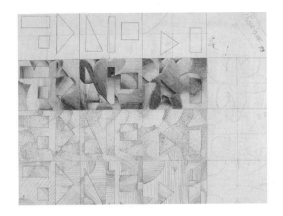

Value Value refers to the properties of darks and lights used in a composition. The range of value depends on how much light is reflected on the surface of the objects.

Value gradation is used to create the illusion of three-dimensional space on a two-dimensional plane. Value gradation shows the gradual change of lights to darks. Values are usually shown on a value scale, with white at one extreme and black at the other. Try creating your own six-step value scale. Leave the first square white and gradually darken the value in each square until the sixth square is entirely black. After completing the scale, step back at least ten feet and see if your scale shows a good gradual change in value gradation.

The following exercise explores how value can create drama and visual strength in a composition. Tear, wrinkle and fold some pieces of paper. Use a spotlight on them to create dramatic shadows. Next, draw in the shapes created by light and those created by shadows. Using the value scale, translate the shapes into six different value ranges.

THINK ABOUT IT
Using value to create the illusion of a three-dimensional object is a form of problem solving. The more problems you solve, the more problems you can solve.

Design Extensions
• A value scale illustrates extreme light to dark as a progression through the gray scale in any number of equal parts. Have students use charcoal to create a sphere that progresses in value from white to black. Try the same exercise on black paper using white chalk.

• Shine a bright light on a collection of white objects such as Styrofoam™ shapes and eggs. Call students' attention to the dark, medium, and light values before they draw it with white conté crayon and black charcoal on a medium-value gray paper.

• Students may experiment creating values in a composition by doing the Value activity on page 45.

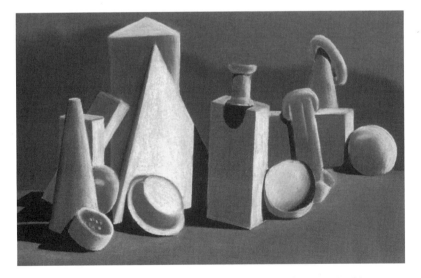

Top of page: There are many ways to create value in a drawing. In this exercise, the student used the same basic shapes in three different compositions. He then created a range of values by using tones (second row), dots (third row) and hatching (bottom row). Student work by Oscar Tovar, El Paso, Texas. Above: Brightly lit still lifes can help you see value changes. Notice how areas that receive the most light are clean white, while those receiving less light are gray or black. Student work by Jaime Behrens, Rosemount, Minnesota.

Käthe Kollwitz

1867–1945

The art of Käthe Kollwitz, a German printmaker and sculptor, is usually discussed in connection with the art movement called German Expressionism. For Käthe Kollwitz, like many of her contemporaries, art became a way of dealing with social and political issues. Unemployed workers, strikes and political assassinations were frequent themes in her works.

World War I brought new imagery into her art. Mourning parents and corpses dominated her famous series of woodcuts entitled *War*. Through art, Käthe Kollwitz expressed her grief over the loss of her son Peter, who was killed in battle.

Following Hitler's rise to power in 1933, she was expelled from the Art Academy of Berlin, where she had taught in the Graphic Arts Department. Unable to teach and no longer allowed to exhibit her works, she withdrew from public life. However, she did not stop creating. She died in 1945, leaving a large collection of prints and drawings, as well as numerous self-portraits, she had drawn over the years.

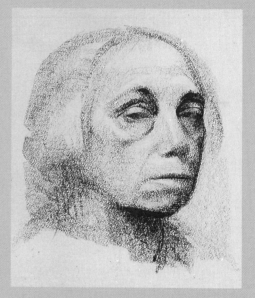

Käthe Kollwitz, *Self-Portrait*, 1919–20. Lithographic crayon, pen and ink. Courtesy The Galerie St. Etienne, New York.

The lithograph is an example of skillful use of value. Kollwitz marked the features of her face with the pointed end of the crayon. She used the flat side of the crayon to indicate areas of light and shadow with broad, sculpting strokes. The image that emerges is a sincere likeness of the aging artist. The portrait reveals a face full of dignity but also marked by weariness and sadness.

Color Color can be effectively used in drawings. You can draw with colored pencils, pastel chalks and even wax crayons. Although color is not essential in drawings, it can provide additional character, interest and effects in a composition. The function and structure of color should be understood by all beginning art students.

The following characteristics of color can be beneficial in understanding how color functions.

1. Light is the presence of all color.

2. Objects in space reflect different wavelengths of light to create color.

3. White is the presence of all light.

4. Black is the absence of all light.

5. The spectrum of color as you view a color wheel is the diffusion of the wavelengths of light.

The following terms are essential in developing an understanding of the concepts of color.

1. *Hue* is the common name of a color on the color wheel (See page 154).

2. *Value* conveys the lightness and darkness of a color.

3. *Complementary colors* are colors that are opposite each other on the color wheel.

4. *Analogous colors* are colors that are next to each other on the color wheel.

5. *Primary colors* are red, yellow and blue. These three colors in the spectrum cannot be produced by mixing pigments.

6. *Secondary colors* are green, orange and violet. They are created by mixing any two primary colors.

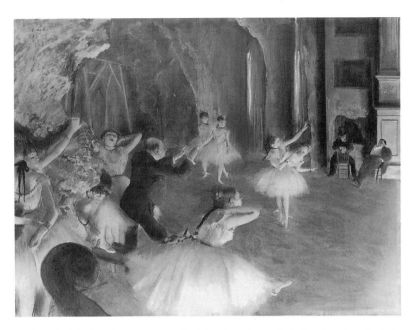

Although this drawing was created with colored pastels, it has depth and vitality in black-and-white as well. Here you can see that its wide range of values gives the composition visual interest. Turn to page 165 to see it in color. Do you think the work is more effective—that is, catches your attention, makes you want to look more closely—in color or in black-and-white? Why? Edgar Hilaire Germain Degas, *Rehearsal on the Stage*, nineteenth century. Pastel, 21" x 28 1/2" (53.3 x 72.3 cm). The Metropolitan Museum of Art, New York, Bequest of Mrs. H. O. Havemeyer, 1929. The H. O. Havemeyer Collection.

7. *Neutrals* are white, gray and black.

8. Colors can be divided into *cool colors* and *warm colors*. Cool colors are greens, blues and violets. Warm colors are yellows, oranges and reds.

For more about color in drawing, see the section on color in Chapter 6.

THINK ABOUT IT
Of all the visual elements, color is the most fascinating. Explore the many different color schemes. Analyze and evaluate the many options open to you. Then, narrow all these possibilities into the one you wish to use.

Design Extension
Explain that intensity has to do with the brightness or dullness of a color. Colors may be made less intense by blending them with their complementary color. After students have studied the intensity chart on page 155, they may create their own intensity chart using two complementary colors.

Context
Refer students to page 207 to see a sketch of a ballet dancer by Degas. In order to get the movements just right, Degas often constructed wax models of his subjects and then drew from these.

Dividing the Picture Plane

Higher-Order Thinking Skills

• Make sure students understand the difference between horizontal and vertical. Analyze vertical and horizontal compositions throughout the book. (For example, look at *Twelve Views of Landscape* on page 92.) How does each composition affect the impact of the picture? What happens to the picture if you change its format from vertical to horizontal and vice versa?

• You may want to use your own or a student's work in progress to demonstrate how to break down and plan a composition on the picture plane. As you demonstrate, provide suggestions for evaluating the composition:

   —Is there a balance between positive and negative space throughout?

   —Does the division of space fit the subject well?

   —Do the main lines lead the viewer's eye around the composition?

Before you begin drawing on a surface, think first about how you will compose on the picture plane. Never skip the crucial step of planning your composition in your rush to draw an image.

THINK ABOUT IT

Facing a blank drawing space forces you to use higher-order thinking skills. You can't avoid complex thinking in the visual arts!

The picture plane is the illusionary flat surface on stretched canvas, illustration board or drawing paper on which you will create a drawing. A picture plane that is predominantly vertical tends to be more dynamic and grand in scale. The picture plane that is horizontal reflects a more stable and restful attitude.

Understanding how compositional structure interacts with your subject matter is a very important consideration in making your drawing. First consider your subject matter, which has its own shape. How will that shape impact your composition? How will you arrange and interpret the visual information?

Dividing your picture plane can help you see what is happening structurally in your drawing. Break the composition into equal parts to see how the positive forms and negative spaces have to be handled. Recall the elements of design covered at the beginning of this chapter. How will you incorporate these elements into your drawing?

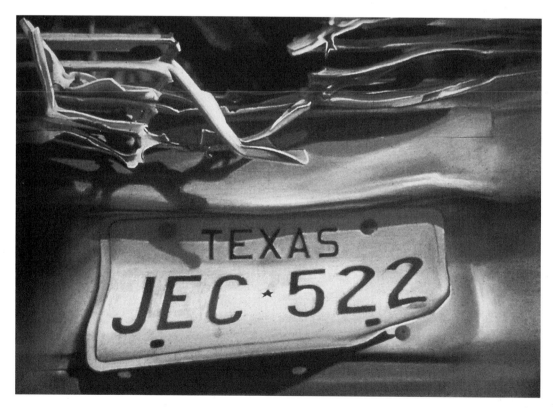

Horizontal compositions can seem calmer than vertical ones. But this artist creates some tension and mystery by showing us only part of what may—or may not—be a car. Why do you think he chose to show only this section? Author, *Texas Plates*, 1983. Charcoal, 18" x 24" (45.7 x 61 cm). Private collection, Nashville, Tennessee.

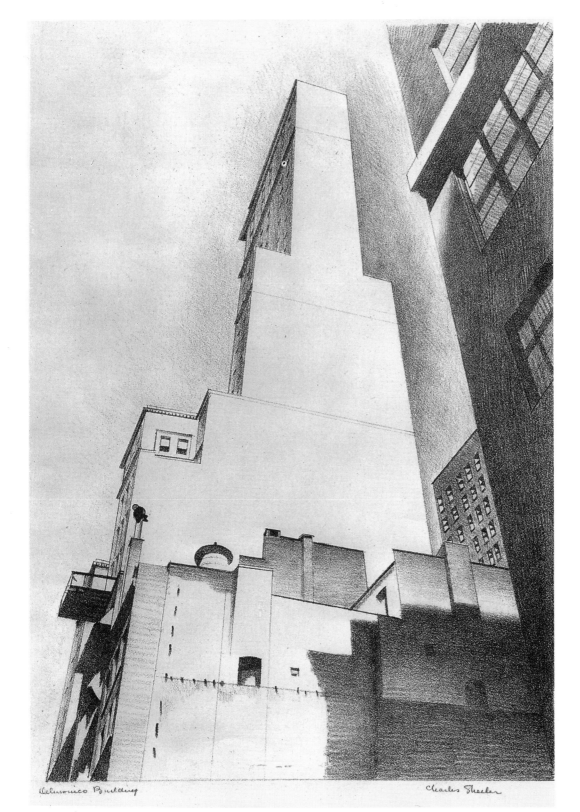

Delmonico Building *Charles Sheeler*

Context
Charles Sheeler was an American photographer and painter born in Philadelphia and educated at the Pennsylvania Academy of Fine Art. In the 1920s and 1930s he painted and photographed very unemotional, detached American urban scenes. For another example of Sheeler's work, turn to page 103.

Design Extension
To explore the different feel between vertical and horizontal compositions, students could make two compositions—a horizontal one using various thicknesses of horizontal lines, and a vertical one using various widths of vertical lines. Suggest that they title their works based on the mood created by the vertical and horizontal composition.

If you've ever looked straight up into the sky in a city full of skyscrapers, you'll know how dizzy it can make you feel, and how far away the sky seems. Here, the artist gives the building stature by allowing it to take up all but a fraction of the vertical paper. Its whiteness makes it look pure and dazzling. Charles Sheeler, *Delmonico Building*. Lithograph, printed in black, 9 3/4" x 6 11/16" (24.8 x 17 cm). Collection, The Musuem of Modern Art, New York. Gift of Abby Aldrich Rockefeller.

Principles of Art

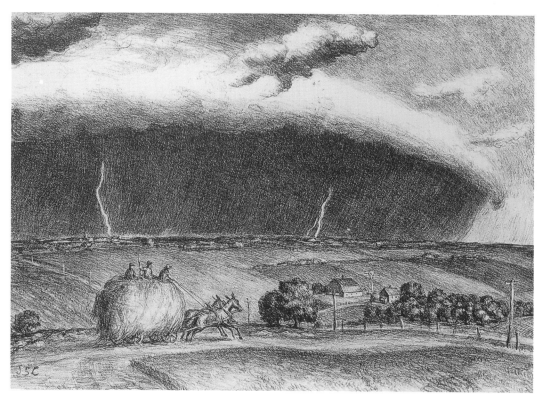

You can show emphasis in drawings in a number of ways. Here, dark clouds and lightning bolts combine to focus attention on the brightly-lit hay wagon. John Steuart Curry, *The Line Storm*, 1933. Lithograph. The Philadelphia Museum of Art. Purchased: The Harrison Fund.

The principles of art help determine the organization of compositions and provide solutions to compositional problems. By studying the principles of emphasis, balance, harmony, variety, movement, rhythm and proportion, you will develop a sense of unity in your drawings. The processes work together to enhance the qualities of all compositions.

Emphasis in a composition refers to developing points of visual interest to direct the viewer's eyes to the most important parts of the composition. Emphasis is achieved mainly through some type of contrast. Contrast can be achieved through dominance in shape and value or variation of edges. How else might dominance be achieved?

Balance is a sense of stability in a composition. Balance can be created by repeating similar shapes throughout a work, or by creating a feeling of equal weight among the shapes.

Informal balance or asymmetrical balance is based on the weight of the objects in the drawing. The weight can be shown or emphasized by varying the shapes, sizes, values and colors of the objects. Formal balance or symmetrical balance is a repetition of similar shapes that mirror each other.

Harmony is achieved in a composition by combining similar elements of drawing. Harmony gives an uncomplicated look to the overall composition.

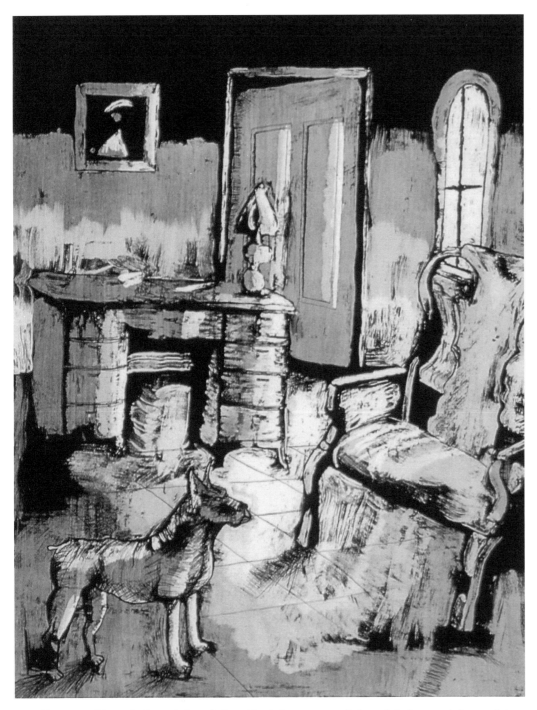

Would you say this work shows balance? Consider balance among light and dark areas, balance of the visual "weight" of objects in the composition, and balance from top to bottom. Student work by Camilla Fancher, Columbus, Ohio.

Cooperative Learning (continued from page 41)
Principles shown in the image on this page:

unity: line weight
balance: gas tank and phone booth
variety: in shapes
emphasis: door in center

Interdisciplinary Connection
Music—Ask the music teacher to explain to your class how art principal terms are used in music. For example, rhythm and movement have almost identical meanings. Play selections of music to demonstrate these terms.

Extension
To help students better understand movement in compositions, assign the Analyzing Movement activity on page 45.

Variety refers to differences and can provide complexity to the composition. Variety is achieved by using different or contrasting values, shapes and textures in a composition to create interest and uniqueness. Variety can act as a counterbalance to harmony in a drawing. Variety helps an artwork from being boring.

Movement adds energy and excitement to a composition. It is a way of recording and showing action in a drawing. Movement also directs the viewer's eye through the work. Drawings that successfully use movement have a feeling of strong direction.

Rhythm is a type of movement in a drawing. It can be conveyed by repetition of shapes or colors. Alternating areas of darks and lights can also produce a sense of rhythm.

Proportion refers to relationships in size between objects or between the parts of a single object. Proportion also reflects the size relationships of the parts to the whole drawing. Proportion gives the artist a way to stress or emphasize areas by enlarging, distorting or exaggerating them to create strong visual effects.

Unity is achieved when all the parts of the composition relate to each other. Unity gives the drawing a feeling of oneness. It gives a sense of strength that keeps the work from being confusing.

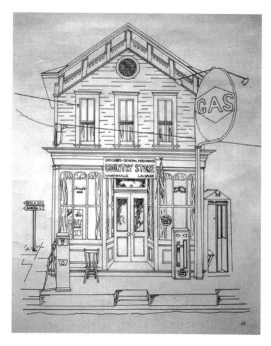

Is there much movement in this drawing? How about harmony? How many of the principles of design can you use to describe it? Notice how the artist's use of line gives the image a simple, clean look. Student work by Ron Bastyr, Slippery Rock, Pennsylvania.

Learning to combine and use the elements and principles of design takes time. Analyze your own drawings to see how well you have incorporated these elements. Try the following methods to help you evaluate your work.

1. Divide your composition into four equal quarters, and analyze how well the positive and negative space is varied.

2. Look at how well the edges in your composition are varied.

3. Examine carefully how well your range of value carries from a distance. Is the overall design visually exciting from a variety of distances?

4. Make sure you have a focal point and enough variety in your composition to hold the viewer's attention.

5. Try to have a variety of textures or surface qualities in your drawings.

6. If color is used, make sure the color scheme is effectively used and blended into the composition.

7. Reexamine any areas in the composition that appear to be confusing or misdirected. Consider ways to bring unity to the composition.

THINK ABOUT IT
To develop a sense for unity in your drawing, think about what you did and how you did it. How can you apply what you learned to your next drawing?

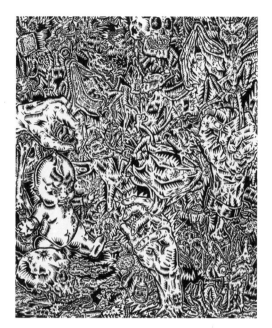

Far from being boring or static, this work gives you so much to look at that you might not know where to start. What sort of mood do you think the artist was in when he created it? Student work by David Berger, Cincinnati, Ohio.

Cooperative Learning (continued from page 42)
Principles shown in the images on this page:

Berger work
variety and movement: jagged lines, explosive
emphasis: baby, hand pointing to baby
unity: texture

Bailey work
rhythm: line
unified: line
variety: shape (open to closed)
balance: asymmetrical

Cooperative Learning
To demonstrate the different art principles, have groups of four to five students arrange themselves into living tableaus. Photograph their tableaus. One student may be the director, another the photographer, one the recorder to write their comments, and one the cheerleader who makes sure that everybody participates. If you are lacking cameras, students may sketch their composition.

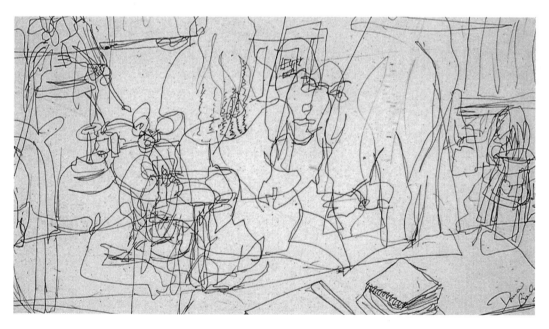

Could this drawing have been made from one very nervous, continuous line? Try something similar yourself. Does your drawing show as much movement as this one does? Student work by Donna Bailey, Adel, Iowa.

Summary

The elements of design and the principles of art provide the fundamental foundation for good drawing compositions. This chapter has helped you examine the properties of design that serve as a foundation for successful compositions.

Too many beginning students become fascinated with capturing the likeness of an object rather than thinking of the overall composition. Understanding how to incorporate the elements of design and principles of art in drawing is essential for your growth as an artist. Once you become comfortable with these elements, you will begin to apply them almost intuitively in your drawing. Consistently improving the design qualities in your drawings will help you produce powerful compositions.

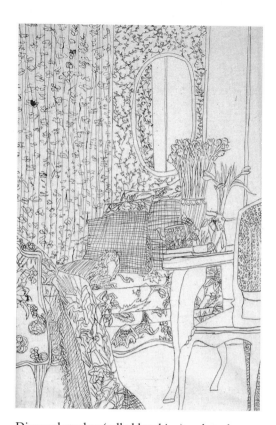

Diagonal strokes (called hatching) and strokes that cross each other (crosshatching) are the only ways this artist created shadow areas. Is there much variation in line width here? Student work by Carmen DePina, Brockton, Massachusetts.

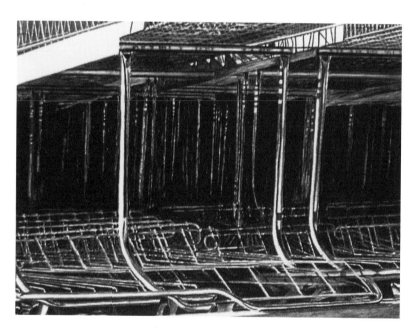

The lines in this work are lighter and more open in the foreground, darker and denser in the background. Is the same true in an actual forest? Has the artist given you enough visual information to tell what this urban forest is made of? Linda Murray, *The Urban Forest Marches On*. Carbon pencil, 22 1/2" x 30" (57 x 76 cm). Courtesy of the artist.

Activities

Pattern Drawing

Draw outlines of shapes to create a composition. Then create at least five different patterns, and fill in the outlines with these patterns.

Texture Rubbings

Use a pencil on white paper to draw outlines of several different objects. Leaving the objects white, fill in the background, or negative space around the objects, with texture rubbings. Experiment with wax crayons or ebony pencils. Create as many different black textures as you can. see pages 172 and 173

Leaf Composition

Arrange fall leaves on a piece of paper, considering design: emphasis, balance, repetition, line and rhythm. Lightly draw the leaves. Add color with pencils or watercolors.

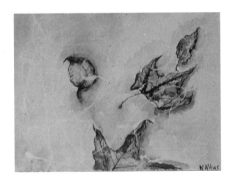

Student work by Nicole Nicas.

Positive and Negative Space

Stack chairs or stools on top of one another to create an interesting arrangement. Use markers to color in the negative spaces between and around the chairs. Do not draw outlines of the chairs. Instead, concentrate on accurately developing the negative spaces.

Analyzing Movement

Look at some traditional drawings and paintings by artists such as Degas, Homer, Constable and David. On photocopies of these works circle the center of interest in red, trace the movement of the eye through the picture in blue, and mark any recurring rhythms in green. see page 165

Art Criticism

Select a famous artwork that genuinely appeals to you. What one thing do you notice when you look at this artwork? Does it convey a particular mood? What qualities in the work contribute to that mood? Label four columns in your journal *description*, *analysis*, *interpretation* and *judgment*. Spend no more than fifteen minutes filling in the columns with a description of what you see, the elements and principles used in the work, what you think the work means, and your feelings and personal response to the work.

Value

Create a line design on a piece of paper by drawing lines that begin on one side of the paper and go off the other side of the paper. Use curved or angled lines to create an interesting design with a center of interest. Allow lines to cross each other, dividing the paper into small sections. Choose one section to shade. Include values from black to totally white.

Continue shading adjacent sections. However, in these adjacent areas, make the black of the first section adjacent to the white of the next section. Continue shading in this manner so that black will always be adjacent to white, and middle values will be next to each other.

Drawing with Music

Wassily Kandinsky said, "Art is music. Music is art." Listen to a piece of music. Create a composition that reflects feelings and thoughts you experienced as you listened to it. You might create an abstract composition based on the expressive qualities of lines, shapes and colors. Or you could create a realistic drawing of something in your life that the music reminded you of.

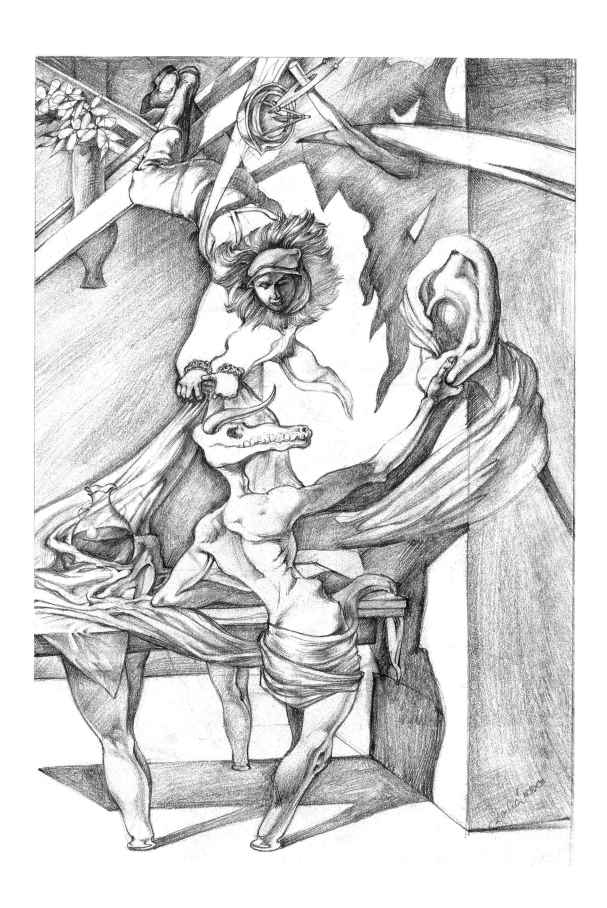

Part 2
The Process
of Drawing

Student work by Boris Zakic, Yugoslavia.

Chapter 3
Drawing from Objects

Objectives
Students will be able to
- Define still life as an arrangement of inanimate objects to draw. (Art criticism)
- Demonstrate their understanding of value as the relative lightness or darkness of a color or shade in drawings of single objects and still lifes. (Art production)
- Understand figure-ground as the relationship between images and background. (Art criticism)
- Use a variety of line types in their drawings. (Art production)
- Create compositions which indicate an awareness of figure-ground relationships and negative space. (Art production)
- Understand that positive space refers to objects, and that negative space refers to space around the objects. (Art criticism)
- Perceive and discuss how various artists including Janet Fish and van Gogh have used light and dark tones and figure-ground relationships in their art. (Art history)
- Develop and use aesthetic judgments based on their knowledge of value, figure-ground relationships, and positive and negative spaces as they consider their own art and that of others. (Aesthetics)

Vocabulary
line, stroke, and tone
value
figure-ground relationship
positive space
negative space
modeling
overlapping
transparency
hatching

Chapter Overview
Chapter 3 provides several approaches to still-life drawing. Still-life drawings are taught in terms of developing a marking system based on line, stroke, and tone; using value effectively in a composition; dealing with form in a drawing; and organizing lighting in a composition.

Lesson 1
pages 48–55   45 minutes

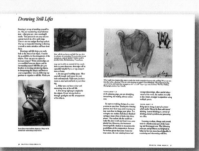

pages 50–51

Teach
After students have read pages 50–55, have them examine the drawings to determine which of the media on pages 54 and 55 the artists used to create the draw-ings. How was the artist holding his or her drawing tool for most of the strokes in each drawing? In some the artist was using the broad side of the charcoal and in others the fine tip of the tool.

Studio Experience
Set out a selection of hard and soft charcoals and conté crayons for each student to experiment with. Demonstrate how to make strokes, lines, and tones with each media. Encourage students to use a range of tones and then try blending and erasing some of their marks to discover which ones smudge and erase most easily. Refer the students back to the O'Keeffe charcoal drawing on page 18. Encourage them to use a wide variety of tones in their drawings as O'Keeffe did. Suggest that they try combining all their random experimentation lines and strokes into an abstract composition. Students may spray their artwork in a **well-ventilated** area with fixative to preserve it.

Materials
charcoal and conté crayons of various hardness
kneaded erasers
blending tools: tortillons or stumps, paper towels or chamois, cotton balls
18" x 24" newsprint, 2 sheets per student

Lesson 2
pages 56–57   45 minutes

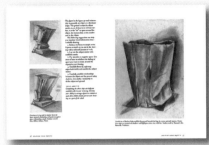

pages 56–57

Teach

• Call students' attention to the illustrations of the bags. Ask them where the light is coming from. Where are the darkest and lightest values? Where are the middle values? Note how there are no heavy outlines around the sides of the bag, but the planes are defined by contrasts of areas of light and dark. Review with students the meaning of figure (the object) and ground (what the object stands on and the air surrounding the object).

• Set a paper bag in a bright spotlight so that the bag casts a shadow. Explain to students that as they sketch the bag, they should think about the figure-ground relationship. That means the bag should not appear to float in the air, but sit firmly on a surface, which is usually indicated by shadows.

Studio Experience

Demonstrate how to lightly sketch or block out a bag on paper. Emphasize that students should fill their picture plane and work quickly to block in the large major areas of shadow, before beginning any details. Be certain that all students have a close unobstructed view of the spotlighted bag. In large classes, bags may be set in several places around the room. Students who draw quickly should draw a second view of the bag from another angle. Students may preserve their completed drawings with workable fixative (sprayed only in well-ventilated area).

Materials

charcoal of varying hardness or
   compression
newsprint or charcoal paper
kneaded erasers
workable fixative
blending tools
spotlight

Lesson 3
pages 58–59   45 minutes

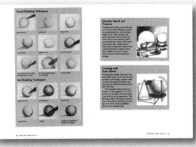

pages 58–59

Teach

• Discuss the various modeling (shading) techniques shown on page 58. Have students analyze the Watteau drawing on page 203 and the one by Hopper on page 211 to discover which of these techniques these artists used.

• Call students' attention to the drawing examples on page 59. In this lesson they will experiment with both ways of drawing. Can they see how different shapes in the top illustration seem to have been drawn more quickly than others?

Studio Experience

Encourage students to make shapes with quick, swinging strokes such as the ovals in the illustration, and slowing down to draw some of the more precise shapes. Point out how some strokes are made with heavier lines while others are much lighter. Play music with a variety of rhythms and encourage students to draw in time to the music.

Studio Experience

Assign students to draw a series of geometric forms. After five minutes, have them change hands and keep drawing. Do this several times. They should notice how the direction of their modeling or shading strokes changes as they switch hands.

Materials (for both studio experiences)

ebony drawing pencils
12" x 18" white drawing paper, 2 to 3 pieces per student

Lesson 4

pages 60–61   45 minutes

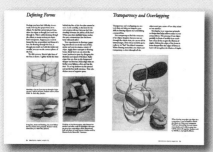

pages 60–61

Teach

After students have studied the drawings on these pages and noted how each drawing was originally drawn transparently, use one or both of the following studio experiences to demonstrate drawing transparently. Students will probably be able to complete one of these studio experiences in a class period. Some students will understand how to draw the box almost intuitively, but for others, depending on their skill and experience, you might want to introduce this "drawing through" method of sketching a box in the next chapter after they have studied linear perspective.

Studio Experience

Set a hollow box in a bright light. Demonstrate to students how to lightly "draw through" the shape of the object. Encourage them to draw the object large, filling their page. After they have lightly sketched in the main shape, they should step back from their drawing and double check their shapes and proportions. At this point, when they have light sketch lines but before they have begun to add values, it's easy to correct major shapes. When they are satisfied with the shape of the box, they should begin to add tones. Remind them to add shadows to the surface on which the box is resting and in the background. They may preserve their completed drawing with workable fixative.

Studio Experience

Set an object such as a shoe, a shell, or a toy animal in a bright light. Discuss with students the many different angles or views from which they could draw this object. They could look at it from several sides, the top, and the bottom. Demonstrate how they may draw in one view, and then lightly sketch in another view overlapping the first one. Direct them to draw at least three overlapping views. Encourage them to draw large, overlapping their objects near the center of the page. Remind them to consider the figure-ground relationships as they draw in each view, noticing how the positive shapes of the object also create negative shapes with the edge of the picture plane.

Materials (for both studio experiences)

charcoal or ebony pencils
18" x 24" drawing paper
erasers
workable fixative
spotlight

Lesson 5
pages 62–65   45 minutes

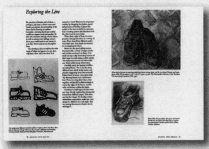
pages 62–63

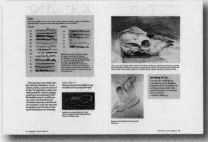
pages 64–65

Teach
Explain that the way lines are drawn in a composition will play an important role in establishing the mood or character of an art-work. Lead students in studying the drawings on these pages to note the thick, thin, wiggly, and gently curving lines in each of the drawings. Notice how many different ways the same subject—shoes—are drawn on these pages and the role that line plays in each drawing. Ask students to describe the owners of the shoes on pages 63, 64, and 65.

Studio Experience
Have students take off their shoes and draw them, or collect a variety of old shoes for them to draw. They should draw their shoe several times using a differ-ent type of line in each drawing. Encourage them to experiment drawing with a variety of media as illustrated on page 64.

First, they should do a blind contour drawing with a continu-ous line. Looking only at their subject (their shoe), they should draw it with one continuous line. Tell them not to look at their paper or take their pencil off the paper once they begin drawing.

In their second drawing, they should try a modified blind con-tour drawing, looking at their paper occasionally to see where their pencil is, but pausing in their drawing as they take this peek. When they are drawing, they should look only at their subject.

Next, they may draw the shoe with quick sketchy lines, then with heavy dark lines, and finally with the broad flat edge of their pencil. They may also try drawing the shoes with experimental media (such as twigs dipped in ink), as listed in the chart on page 64.

Lead students in drawing a pair of shoes in a variety of arrange-ments from different views. In each of their drawings they should continue to experiment with a variety of line types.

Materials
drawing media: pencils, charcoal pencils, twigs and ink, markers
12" x 18" drawing paper
erasers
workable fixative

Lesson 6
pages 66–69   45 minutes

Teach
Call students' attention to the illustrations on pages 67–69. Ask how they can tell that one piece of paper is in front of another. Stress that shadows and value variations suggest the texture, form, and space in these compositions. Then call their attention to the compo-sition in these drawings, noting how the forms fill the picture plane and also how their shapes create negative shapes with the edge of the composition.

Studio Experience
After students have looked over the illustrations of the paper sculpture projects and drawings on this page, teach them how to begin building a small paper sculpture with interesting nega-tive spaces.

Students should divide a piece of paper into four quadrants by drawing a horizontal and a vertical line. Then they should draw a few dark lines, as in the illustration, indicating where they will locate paper in their composition. Next have students tear or cut a sheet of paper into strips of varying widths which they arrange on the dark lines. They should bend and crease these strips to create some vertical or arching forms. Add a few drops of glue or tape to keep the sculpture stable while it is being drawn. Place the sculptures in bright light and draw them with pencils or ink washes.

Materials
12" x 18" drawing paper, 3 pieces
    per student
glue or tape
pencils
rulers
spotlight
optional: ink wash supplies,
    watercolor brushes, india ink,
    water, small water containers

Lesson 7
page 70–75   45 minutes

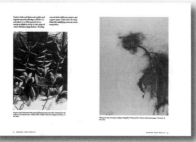

pages 72–73

Teach
Students should notice the contrasts of light and dark values in the drawings on these pages. As they read about Janet Fish on page 71, they should look back at her painting on page 48. Call their attention to the strong contrasts of lights and darks.

Studio Experience
Set a plant in a bright light so it creates interesting shadows. (In larger classes locate several plants around the room.) First, students should make a blind contour drawing of the plant as a study. Then, they may draw a modified contour drawing of plant, adding dark shadows.

Materials
pencils
18" x 24" white drawing paper
erasers

Lesson 8
pages 76–77   45 minutes

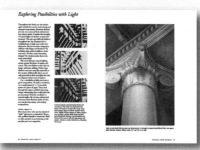

pages 76–77

Teach
Call students' attention to the drawings of shadows on page 76, noting how shadows in themselves may make interesting compositions. Then study the drawing of the column on page 77 to see how shadows define forms on architectural drawings.

Studio Experience
Before the class begins this drawing, scout the school during the time of day that the class meets for interesting shadows formed by architectural elements. Take the class to that part of the school to draw the shadows using pencil or marker. Students will probably need a stiff board under their paper as they draw.

Materials
12" x 18" or 18" x 24" drawing
    paper
pencils or black markers
drawing board (stiff board to
    place under drawing paper)
erasers
optional: masking tape to hold
    paper to board

Lesson 9
page 78–79   45 minutes

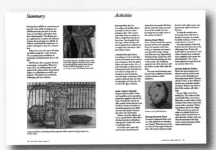

pages 78–79

Reteach

• Review with students the still lifes in this chapter as well as the ones that they have drawn. Remind them what they have learned about figure-ground relationships, and line, stroke, and tone in this chapter.

• Assign one of the activities on page 79. The timed drawings in Shading Simple Objects will build skills by focusing students' attention on one object for a brief period of time. Inside a Fruit or Vegetable and Drawing Reflective Surfaces activities will help them develop an awareness of surface textures and value ranges.

Assess

• Ask students to define still life, figure-ground relationship, and positive and negative space. (Art criticism)

• Discuss with students their understanding of value. Ask them to select examples from this chapter that feature light and dark values. They should mention the work of Janet Fish. (Art criticism)

• Working in small groups, have students select one of the artworks in this chapter and explain the figure-ground relationship. They should also identify the positive and negative spaces in this composition. (Art criticism)

• Assign students to select works they created in this chapter that demonstrate effective use of light, dark, and medium values; a variety of line types; figure-ground relationships; and negative space. They should label which of these concepts each piece represents. Select several pieces to preserve by matting or mounting to display in a class or school art exhibit. (Aesthetics)

• Look through a portfolio of each student's artwork created during this chapter to determine whether the student developed an understanding and effective use of values, a variety of line types, figure-ground relationships, and positive and negative spaces. Do you and the student agree which works demonstrated the most effective use of these concepts? Discuss any differences of opinion about the artworks with the student. (Art production/criticism)

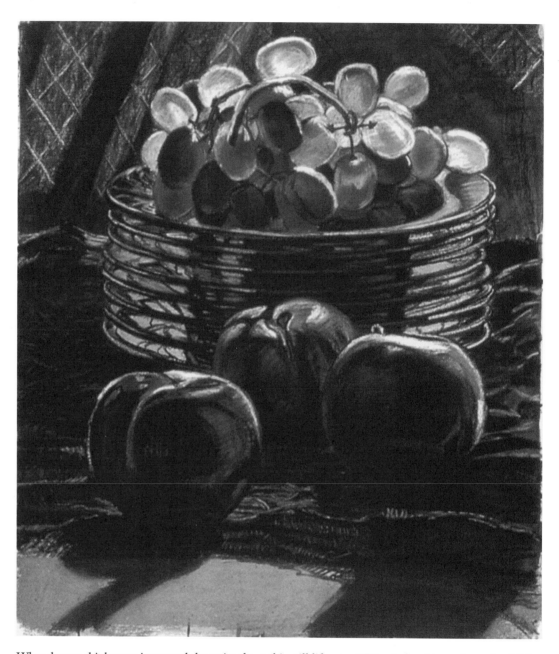

What do you think most interested the artist about this still life setup? Was it the objects themselves? The way the light made them look? Janet Fish, *Green Grapes*, 1979. Pastel on paper, 28 1/2" x 25 1/4" (72.4 x 64.1 cm). Photograph courtesy of the artist.

3 Drawing from Objects

Throughout time, artists have used still lifes as a way to learn to see and to draw from objects. The term *still life* refers to an arrangement of stationary objects used by the artist for a composition. Still lifes allow the artist to study and draw the arrangements for varied lengths of time with controlled lighting.

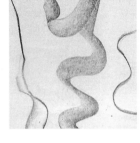

In this chapter, you will learn how to arrange objects and plan an interesting composition. You will learn to simplify visual information and interpret it. The goal of this chapter is to teach you to approach still lifes with direction and confidence.

To draw still lifes, you need to learn the basics of value, modeling and overlapping. You will learn to use line, stroke and tone to create edges, structure and shadows. This chapter concludes by giving you some possibilities for exploring light in your varied environment.

Vocabulary
line, stroke and tone
value
figure–ground relationship
positive space
negative space
modeling
overlapping
transparency
hatching

Design Extensions
• To consider more about how we see and draw, students may draw a picture upside down as described in the Drawing What You See activity on page 79.

• To further develop observational skills, arrange transparent objects such as bottles and glasses on a windowsill for the students to draw. Or, students may draw reflective surfaces as described in the last activity on page 79.

Key Chapter Points

- A still life is an arrangement of inanimate objects to draw.
- Value is the relative lightness or darkness of a color or shade.
- Figure-ground refers to the relationship between images and background.
- Positive space refers to objects or enclosed areas. Negative space refers to space around the objects.

Drawing Still Lifes

Drawing is a way of teaching yourself to see. You are transferring visual information—what you see—into meaningful marks. This process is not easy, and you cannot learn it in a few quick steps. There is no one unique drawing method. The key to successful drawing is allowing yourself to make mistakes and learn from them.

Drawing a still life helps you really look at the form of an object. Consider the possibilities in the arrangement of the objects. How can you use spaces in between objects? What relationships can you establish between objects and the surrounding space? Still lifes give you freedom in moving and placing objects, in interpreting the shapes and forms in your composition. Use the following suggestions to organize a still life. While you

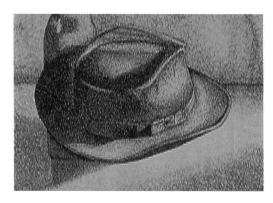

How well do you know your hat? Can you draw its softness, its worn places? Can you make it look mysterious, comical, devilish? Student work by Jennifer Little, Mechanicsburg, Pennsylvania.

may not be able to control all the conditions in your classroom, these tips will be especially helpful if you set up compositions at home.

1. Set up a good working space. Allow yourself enough work space for your tools and materials. Make sure you have room to step back and look at your drawing.

2. Make sure you have a clear and interesting view of the still life.

3. Use strong lighting to emphasize the objects. Create strong shadows through spotlights and the arrangement of the objects.

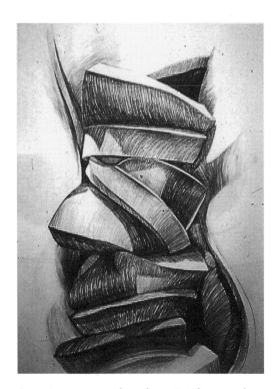

Sometimes even random shapes in a heap can be turned into interesting compositions.

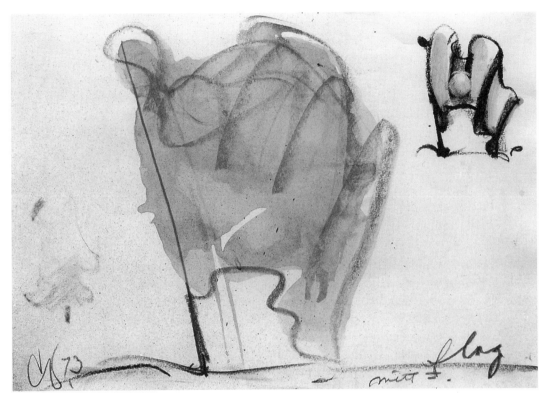

What might have inspired this artist to make the visual connection between mitt and flag? Was it an accident that led to a drawing? Was the artist thinking on paper? Claes Oldenburg, *Mitt Compared to Flag*, 1973. Crayon and watercolor on paper, 9 1/2" x 13 7/8" (24.1 x 35.2 cm). Courtesy The Pace Gallery. Photograph courtesy Leo Castelli.

THINK ABOUT IT
In the planning stage, you are identifying, interpreting and making abstract connections.

Be open to making changes in a composition as you draw. During the drawing process, new ideas may come to you; you may even *have* to change your plans. For example, one student had almost finished carving a stone when it broke into three pieces. The student felt she could not make the piece work and that it was completely lost. However, the instructor encouraged the student to reexamine the possibilities of the composition. Because the broken pieces had come from one large stone, the new existing forms had strong relationships. After careful observation of the work, the student was able to do a better, stronger composition using multiple pieces.

THINK ABOUT IT
Being open to change is part of a process which author Edward de Bono calls lateral thinking. Lateral thinking is a process of thinking around a problem and generating new ideas.

Learning to adapt, change and rework areas is a fundamental part of the learning and drawing process. The following concepts and problems are designed to help you become more knowledgeable in examining and discovering still lifes.

Line, Stroke and Tone

Extension
Review the work with line that students completed in Chapter 2. Look through the book for examples of line, stroke, and tone as well.

Design Extensions
• Encourage students to try drawing balls and rounded forms with a flat side of the charcoal or conté crayon, using a circular motion, to add a three dimensional quality to their drawings.

• Students may draw the outside and inside of fruit as described on page 79 in the Inside a Fruit or Vegetable activity. After they have completed their drawings, they may eat their subject matter.

Line, stroke and tone are tools of a marking system that enable the artist to approach any drawing with a wider range of techniques.

The **line** helps establish the edges found in the composition. Make this mark by using the corner edge of a charcoal, graphite or conté stick. You can also control the line's *weight* (thickness), *speed* (does the line make sharp, jagged movements or lazy, slow ones?) and *sharpness* (is it a crisp, lean line or a fuzzy, blurry one?).

The **stroke** is a heavy line that gives weight, structure and strength to the drawing. Make this mark by using the blunt end of the charcoal or conté stick. The stroke effectively accomplishes the same results as a line, but with more emphasis.

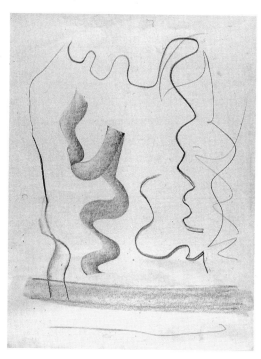

Experimenting with line, stroke and tone will help you become familiar with the effects you can create.

Tone allows you to establish negative space (the space around objects) and shadows quickly. By laying the charcoal or conté stick on its side and pulling it across the paper, you can develop large areas of tone. Tone can help you create the shadows that make an object look three-dimensional. Using shading to make objects look three-dimensional is called *modeling*.

Each of these marks can be varied in pressure, weight, speed and rhythm to capture the essence of the subject matter. Paper bags are a good subject to use in developing line, tone and stroke. The bags provide sharp creases, varied edges and deep shadows for making the necessary variety of marks.

Now that you have some understanding of line, stroke and tone, a review of negative space and figure-ground relationships may be helpful. If you're having trouble remembering the difference between negative and positive space, try imagining a furnished room without a ceiling. Imagine pouring three tons of JELL-O™ into the room. Where the JELL-O™ gels is the *negative space*; the furniture or other objects in the room can be considered the *positive space*.

THINK ABOUT IT
Working with positive and negative space is similar to fitting together the pieces of a puzzle. Every piece is important; all the pieces work together.

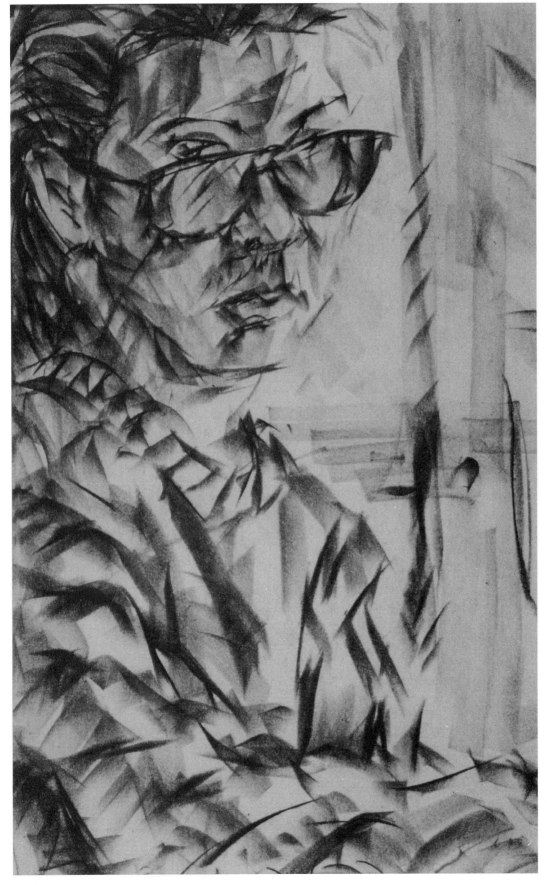

Interdisciplinary Connections
Music, English—To spur discussion and under-standing of line, you may want to use these suggested activities:

• Play different types of music and have students draw lines that match the music.

• Have students match different types of lines with descriptive words, such as aggressive, peaceful, grouchy, etc.

• Ask volunteers to write on the chalkboard onomatopoeic words or made-up words that suggest visual imagery, such as inky-binky, va-va-boom, etc. Have students draw lines to accompany these words.

• Have students repeat the exercises using different media.

Discuss students' results.

Higher-Order Thinking Skills
Ask students to describe how the artist used tone in this drawing.

This artist used the side of her drawing tool to create a portrait almost entirely of tone. What mood does the work project? Student work by Shawn Alexander, Elmont, New York.

Charcoal, Conté and Graphite

Charcoal is a dry drawing material that has been used since prehistoric times. It comes in a variety of forms: vine, compressed charcoal, charcoal pencil and powdered charcoal.

Vine charcoal is thin, soft and delicate. It is available in six-inch lengths, different thicknesses and different degrees of softness (or blackness). It can be easily smudged, smoothed or erased. Drawings must be sprayed with a workable fixative to avoid unwanted smudging and keep the image intact. Vine charcoal works best on rough textured paper.

Compressed charcoal is made from ground-up powdered charcoal that has been compressed into sticks with a binding medium. The sticks are available in square or round shapes. Compressed charcoal, like pencils, is numbered to designate the degree of softness (or blackness) and is graded from oo (very soft) through 5 (hard).

Charcoal pencils are thin sticks of compressed carbon encased in wood. Pencils have four standard degrees of hardness: 6B (extra soft), 4B (soft), 2B (medium) and HB (hard). Charcoal pencils are clean and very convenient to use. They are more suitable for smaller, detailed types of artwork.

Powdered charcoal may be sprinkled onto the desired surface and then erased or rubbed to shade areas and create special effects.

Conté crayons are available in five colors as well as black, gray and white. They are manufactured in three degrees of hardness: HB, B and 2B. Conté crayons create a smooth hard texture that is not powdery. The point, edge and side can be used to create interesting effects and build up tones gradually.

Graphic sticks are three-inch-long square sticks made of graphite and clay. The degrees of hardness range from 2B, 4B and 6B.

Fixative is a matte or glossy aerosol spray that is used to protect charcoal, pencil and pastel drawings from smudging. *Workable fixative* means that the drawing may be worked on even after it has been fixed. **WARNING: Do not use fixative spray except in a well-ventilated area or outside. It can be harmful to your health.**

Newsprint is an inexpensive paper made of wood pulp. Newsprint is available in rough or smooth textures and in pads up to 24" x 36".

Chamois is a small, soft leather cloth used to blend and smooth pastels or charcoal.

Charcoal paper is highly textured paper designed to hold dry pigment.

Teaching Tip
Charcoal may be the best medium for students to work with initially. Students tend to strive for details when they use pencils. Encourage students to work quickly and not be concerned with detail at this point. Once students are familiar with drawing still lifes, they can move on to pastels and pencils.

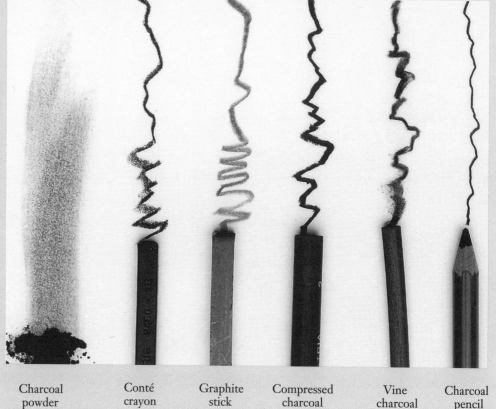

| Charcoal powder | Conté crayon | Graphite stick | Compressed charcoal | Vine charcoal | Charcoal pencil |

Techniques

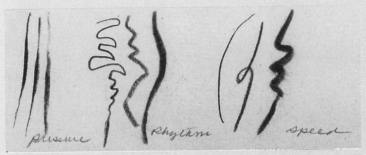

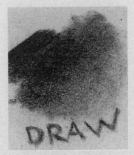

These lines illustrate changes in pressure, rhythm and speed.

Use a stump or tortillon to draw with or smooth and soften areas.

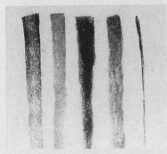

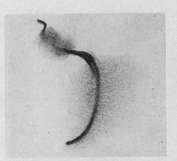

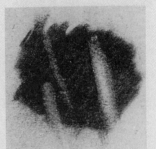

Line, stroke, tone

Use your finger, a paper towel or a chamois to smudge and blur areas.

Use tissue, cotton or a kneaded eraser to soften, clean and create highlights.

Supplies

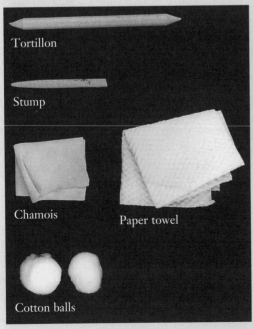

Tortillon

Stump

Chamois

Paper towel

Cotton balls

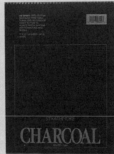

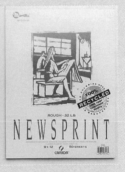

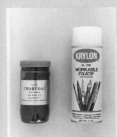

Charcoal paper
Newsprint
Powdered charcoal
Workable fixative

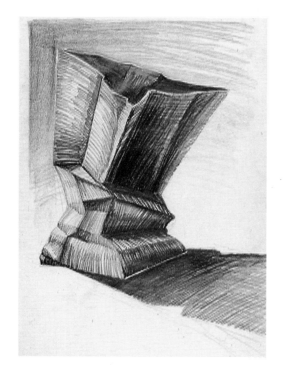

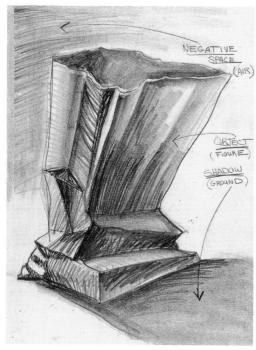

Drawings of a bag and its shadow show the
figure-ground relationship and positive/negative
space relationships clearly. Student work by
Gina Miller, Abilene, Texas.

The *figure* in the figure-ground relationship is generally an object or a dominant
shape. The *ground* is what the object
stands on, or, if there is no obvious surface, it is the "air" or space around the
object, the horizon line, or the shadow
cast by the object.

The following suggestions can help
you translate visual information into a
workable drawing.

1. Reduce the forms to simple terms.
Express as much as you can in the drawing with a minimal amount of work.

2. Lay out the subject matter with
confident marks.

3. Pay attention to negative space. Use
areas of tone to reinforce the feeling of
space you want to create around the
objects in your drawing.

4. Establish forms by exploring
edges both inside and outside the subject
matter.

5. Carefully establish relationships
between the object and the ground using
shadows. Use marks consistently to
define object and ground.

THINK ABOUT IT
*Completing the above steps can help you
establish order in your drawing. Develop
your ability to arrange objects in relation to
each other; think of each part in your drawing as a part of the whole.*

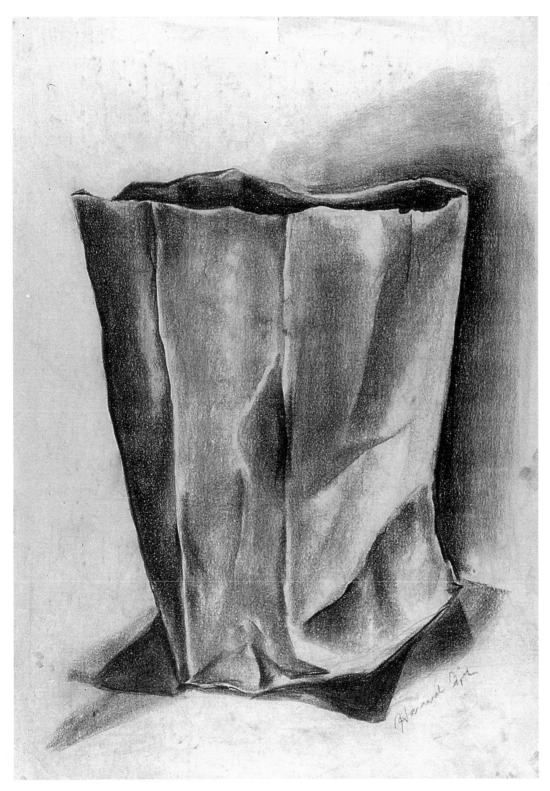

Extension
Review students' drawings of a letter they completed in Chapter 2, in which they experimented with positive and negative space. In that exercise, they used value to differentiate between positive and negative space. Now, they are learning to use tone to establish positive and negative space and create a sense of volume.

Design Extension
For another challenge, students may draw their book bags, backpacks, and purses.

Careful use of shadows helps establish the ground beneath the bag, its creases and dark interior. Notice how edges are created with shadows and highlights rather than with line. Student work by Hannah Cofer, Knoxville, Tennessee.

Pencil Modeling Techniques

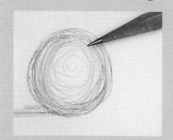

gesture sketch

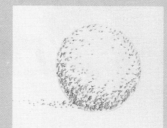

straight lines

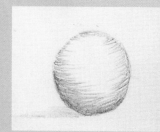

contour lines

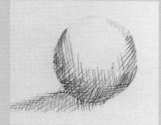

crosshatching

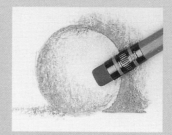

stipples or dots

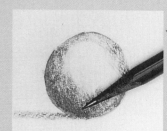

side of the pencil

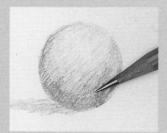

back and forth marks, which gradually build up darker

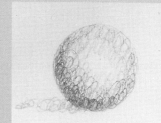

side of the pencil; blended, eraser highlight

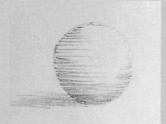

round scribbles

Ink Modeling Techniques

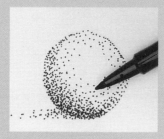

stipples or dots

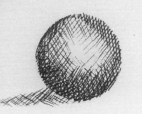

crosshatching

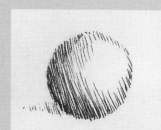

straight lines

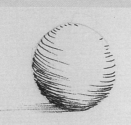

contour lines

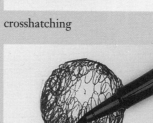

scribbles

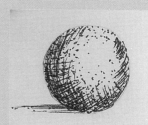

combined crosshatching, scribbles and stipples

Rhythm, Speed and Pressure

Changing the rhythm, speed and pressure of your mark-making is essential in creating interest in your drawing. Suppose you could translate your marks into music. If you made each mark with the same rhythm, speed and pressure, the marks would sound monotonous, like a single note of music. Just as songs have varied notes, a good composition requires varied lines, strokes and tones to create space, variation and compositional intrigue.

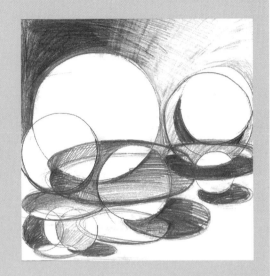

Interdisciplinary Connection

Psychology—As students experiment drawing with both of their hands, they will probably begin to question some of the reasons and implications of being right- or left-handed. In Western cultures five to twelve percent of the population is left-handed. Assign students to research studies on left brain–right brain theories. They should discover that often the right hemisphere of the brain controls speech in left-handed persons. This is reverse of most right-handed people.

Drawing with Both Hands

Drawing lines, strokes and tones with both hands is one way to increase your sensitivity and develop a greater range of marks. By using both hands, you prevent your marks from going all the same direction.

The immediate response by most students to this suggestion is "I can't." In fact, you can draw with both hands if you practice and are persistent. This drawing method will help you develop speed. You will also benefit by becoming aware of the many possibilities there are for making marks.

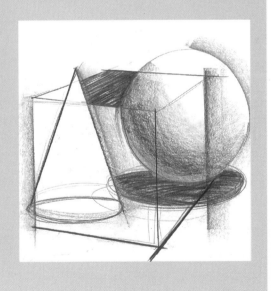

Defining Forms

Perhaps you have had difficulty in correctly drawing the proportions of an object. To find the correct proportions, draw the object as though you could see through it. This is called *drawing through* the object; it means making an object look transparent. Suppose you want to locate the true proportions and shape of a box. By drawing through the box, as though you could see both the inside and outside, you can see the correct planes of the box.

Try this exercise. Sketch light lines of the box as shown. Lightly sketch the lines

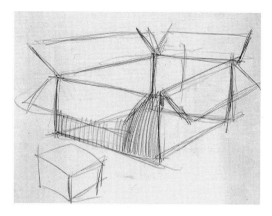

Sketching a box as if you can see through it helps you get a feel for its forms. Student work by Oona Elliot, St. Ann's Bay, Jamaica.

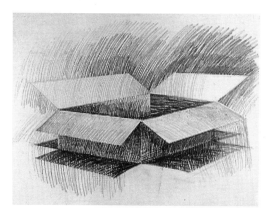

Using line, stroke and hatching, the artist defines the box's forms more precisely. Student work by Oona Eliot, St. Ann's Bay, Jamaica.

behind the face of the box that cannot be seen. Look carefully at the lines for the correct proportions. Can you find relationships between the planes of the box? When you draw multiple boxes, notice the space relationships that the boxes have with each other.

Your experiments in drawing a paper bag introduced you to the uses of line, stroke and tone to create a variety of edges. Apply these concepts to drawing boxes. Study how you can show the boxes' position in space by changing the thickness and speed of the lines. Make edges that are close to the foreground sharper and heavier. Make edges that are farther away lighter, softer and less distinct. To set up shadows on the ground and on the box itself, use tone. Tone also defines areas of negative space.

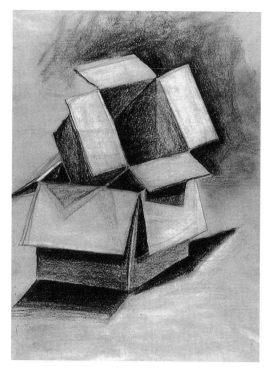

Working on box-brown paper, with charcoal for shadows and white chalk for highlights, this artist has given her composition a three-dimensional look and plenty of visual interest. Student work by Hannah Cofer, Knoxville, Tennessee.

Transparency and Overlapping

Transparency and overlapping are two tools that can help you improve your skills in drawing objects and establishing a composition.

Use *transparency* to find the structure of an object. Imagine that you can see through the object, that you can see all its internal edges. Draw those invisible parts; really try to "feel" the object's structure. When drawing more than one object, use transparency to draw through all the objects and get a sense of how they relate to one another.

Overlapping is an important principle in design that helps achieve unity in your compositions. The placing of one object partially in front of another is an excellent visual device to give the illusion of depth. Making the edges of the forms in front sharper than the edges of forms in back will strengthen the illusion of depth.

Design Extensions
• Cut a hole in the side of a box. Have students try drawing the box and hole at different angles. Do they see how the shape of the hole changes as the position of the box is changed?

• Advanced students may benefit from more challenging exercises. Give them a variety of boxes, such as pizza or candy boxes. Tell students to place one box inside a plastic bag. Have them draw both the box and the plastic bag as well.

Teaching Tip
Before students go on to the next section of this chapter, you may want to begin collecting shoes and bones to use as subject matter for drawing exercises. A biology teacher may be helpful in securing bones.

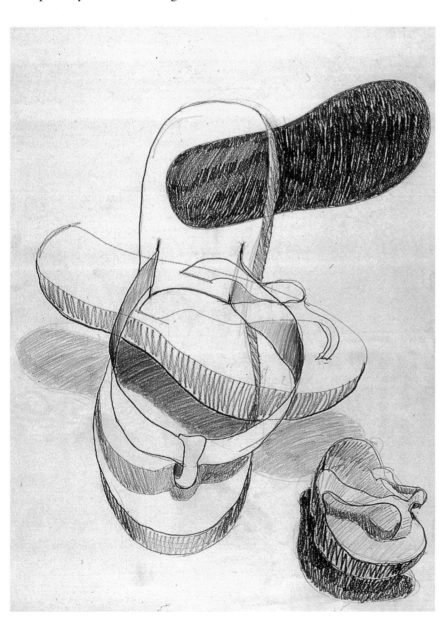

When drawing more than one object in a composition, it can be helpful to sketch the objects as if they were transparent. You'll see relationships between objects more clearly, and be able to sense how well the shapes fit together. Student work by Bill Meyer, Springfield, Illinois.

Exploring the Line

Higher-Order Thinking Skills
Reinforce the horizontal/vertical orientation that students learned in Chapter 2. Check that students are developing a sensitivity to the placement of objects on the page by asking them to compare the two shoe compositions on page 63.

Do you have a favorite pair of shoes—perhaps a pair that is almost worn out? Could you capture the personality of the shoes just by drawing an outline? Certainly a coloring-book type outline would not suggest much personality. To draw the character and age of your shoes, as well as express your feelings toward them, you would need to use variety in your line. You'd need to use descriptive lines.

Try drawing a shoe to explore the wide range of edges and spaces you can draw with lines. How old is the shoe? Is it creased or worn? Illustrate its unique personality by changing the rhythm, speed and pressure of the line. Capture the weight of the shoe to define its structure. Use a marking system that describes both the object and its personality.

Then, draw a pair of shoes in a composition. Arrange the shoes in a variety of ways. Draw them from different angles. Vary their sizes. Add depth and interest by overlapping the shoes.

Bones are also good subject matter. Bones provide a variety of edges, cracks and crevices not found on shoes. Cow skulls are especially interesting because of their large size and unique surface cracks. The numerous caverns and holes make cow skulls unlike many other bones.

Carefully study the features of different animal bones. Try to see the many different lines visible in the bones, and practice suggesting those lines yourself. Edges found in bones vary a great deal. Try drawing bones with a continuous line. Then, try using short lines, close together and parallel (called *hatching*) to create the edges of the bones, and the value and texture within the bones.

Continue to build upon the line work you have already explored by drawing the bones from different angles. This time, overlap the images. To develop a more interesting composition, make sure each image is a different size and angle. Also try varying the amount of space that is overlapped.

Try using many different materials and line weights to draw your shoe. How does its character change when you draw it with a different tool? Student work by Jennifer Pratt and Nick Palumbo, Worcester, Massachusetts.

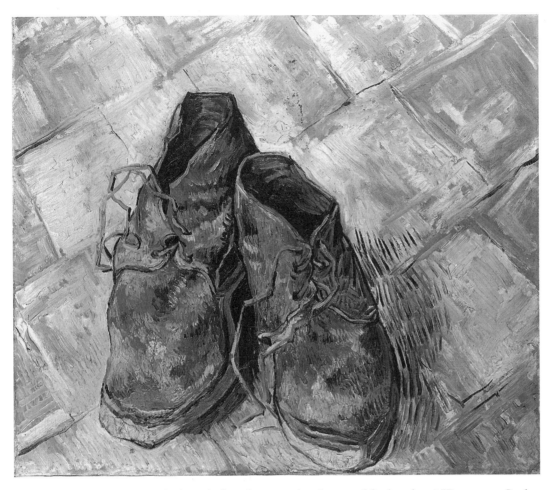

What kind of person do you think might have been wearing these, and for how long? Vincent van Gogh, *Shoes*, 1888. Oil on canvas, 17 3/8" x 20 7/8" (44.1 x 53 cm). The Metropolitan Museum of Art, Purchase, The Annenberg Foundation Gift, 1992.

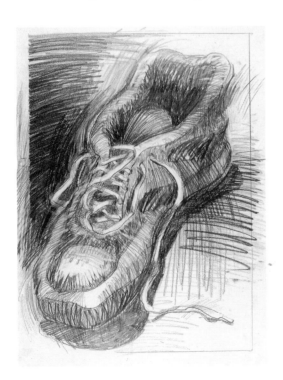

What kind of "personality" does your shoe have? Would you use active lines like these to express that personality? Student work by Karl Selden, Dothan, Alabama.

Design Extensions
• Students may translate one of their line drawings into wire. By bending 14-gauge aluminum sculpture wire with their hands, they can easily form wire sculptures. Wire cutters are also necessary for this project.

• Encourage students to experiment drawing shoes and bones with various experimental media and techniques such as those in the chart. They may try drawing with twigs and feathers dipped in india ink, and then draw with a pencil or marker taped to a long stick.

Inquiry
Assign students to find reproductions of wire sculptures by Alexander Calder. Figures such as his *Circus, Sow, and Cow* may inspire them as they create their own wire sculptures.

Cooperative Learning
Divide the class into learning groups of four to five students each. Have each group select a theme such as animals, shoes, the circus, or tools. They should draw objects for their theme and then create wire sculptures from these drawings. Each group should create a large sculpture or assemblage of their individual sculptures.

Line

Line is a mark made by using a tool, such as a pen or pencil, and pushing, pulling and dragging it across the surface. Lines can be made with many different tools and methods.

Materials

(a)
(b)
(c)
(d)
(e)
(f)
(g)
(h)
(i)
(j)
(k)
(l)
(m)

Methods

(n)
(o)
(p)
(q)
(r)
(s)

Materials: (a) twigs; (b) feathers;(c) finger: (d) markers; (e) airbrush; (f) charcoal (g) calligraphy pens; (h) pencils (all types); (i) 3 pencils tied together; (j) cardboard edges (k) crayons; (l) string dipped in ink; (m) brushes. **Methods:** (n) draw at arm's length; (o) draw with opposite hand; (p) draw with two hands; (q) draw with eyes closed; (r) draw with pencil taped to 4-foot stick; (s) draw with pencil in fist.

When drawing a more complex bone, like a fish bone, remember to vary the direction, rhythm, speed and pressure of the line. One beginning art student intuitively grasped this concept by applying something he learned playing football! He found that when he varied his running speed on the football field, his movements became less predictable and more productive. In the same way, when he varied the speed of his lines in drawing, his lines became more interesting.

THINK ABOUT IT
Making connections between different areas and subjects can bring unexpected results!

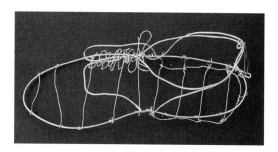

Another way to explore lines is to "draw" with wire. Student work by Patrick Terrien, Worcester, Massachusetts.

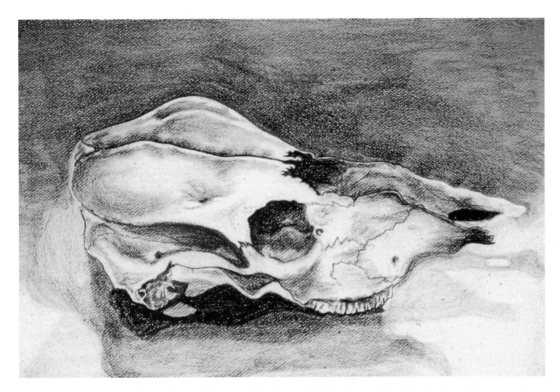

The crevices and irregular surfaces of bones make them a challenging subject for drawing. Try capturing the overall shape of a skull or bone with one continuous line. Then, as this artist did, use line, stroke and tone to create a more detailed composition. Student work by Marquita Stearman, Commerce, Texas.

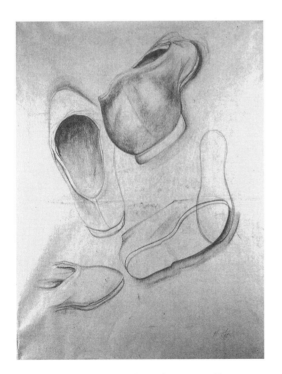

Speaking of Art...

"I was the sort of child that ate around the hole in the doughnut, saving the hole for last and best. So, not having changed much, when I painted the bones, I was most interested in the holes."
—*Georgia O'Keeffe,* 1915

Student work by Hannah Cofer, Knoxville, Tennessee.

Organizing Space

Design Extension

The main objective of the paper sculpture still life assignment is to interrelate the elements of design in two- and three-dimensional design. The same qualities that make a sculpture successful are also found in a two-dimensional work. The only difference is the sculpture deals with more space.

To help students understand how these relationships can be combined, have them construct a paper sculpture. It should be designed so that all of the lengths, widths, and edges of the paper vary. Placement of the paper should also be varied. The positive and negative space should be arranged as interestingly as possible. Setting up a strong spotlight will add drama to the composition. The next step involves sketching the sculpture from various angles to explore the possibilities for a final composition. The final composition should be selected for its strong design qualities.

The project should help students see the possibilities for using design concepts in both drawing and sculpture.

There is an important relationship between space and design. Learning how to plan the entire composition before you begin drawing is an essential step in the drawing process.

Here is one easy method to set up a composition of a still life. Place a sheet of paper flat on the table. Draw two pencil lines that divide the paper into four equal parts. Next, take a second sheet of paper and tear it into many pieces of various sizes and edges. Place the torn paper on the four squares. Be sure the positive and negative space in each square differs from that in the other squares. Shine a spotlight on the still life. Look at it from any angle. Is the composition dynamic and challenging?

THINK ABOUT IT
This activity involves the thinking skills of identifying, analyzing and interpreting. Think of how you can apply what you learned in this exercise to your own compositions.

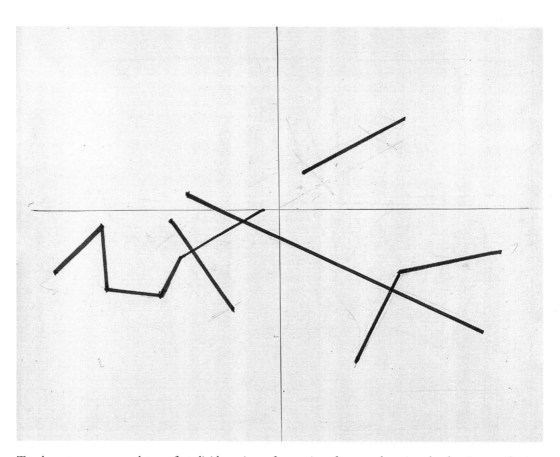

To plan a torn paper sculpture, first divide a piece of paper into four equal sections by drawing one horizontal and one vertical line. Then draw simple lines to show the positive and negative space within each section. Make sure the use of space is different in every section.

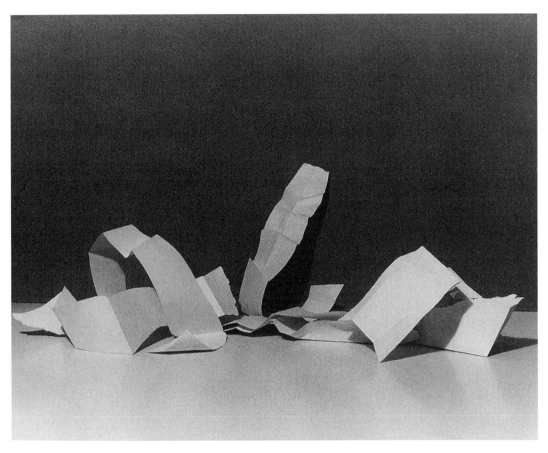

Design Extension
Refer students to page 167 to see Chipman Laman's painting of crumpled paper, *Old Mail*.

Extension
Encourage students to try adding ink washes to some of their pencil drawings. To create washes, pour a little ink into small containers. Then add a brush full of ink into another small container of water. Repeat this so you have two washes of different values. As students begin painting and dipping their brushes back and forth into the ink and different washes the darkness of these will change.

Using your simple line drawing as a guide, construct a torn paper sculpture. Is positive and negative space still different in every section? Are interesting highlights and shadows created when you shine a bright light on your sculpture?

Unification of Space

Washes unify a drawing, develop contrast, produce patterns and create form. Try pen-and-ink washes on Bristol, railroad or illustration board. Experiment with heavy drawing paper, charcoal, bond, mimeograph or craft papers.

Try watermedia washes on watercolor, charcoal or heavy drawing papers. Experiment with tagboard, oatmeal and bond papers.

Hint: To wipe out or blot wash areas, use a paper towel.

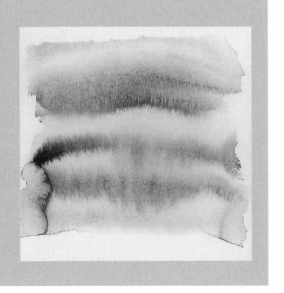

Design Extension
Students should try
drawing other types of
crumpled papers and
fabrics such as notebook
paper, tissues, burlap,
and striped fabric. Lightly
crumple the fabric or
paper and set it in a
heap in a bright light.
Call students' attention
to how the lines in the
paper and fabric go in
different directions. By
drawing in the printed
lines, they will begin to
replicate the contours of
the form. Encourage
them to use a range of
light, dark, and medium
values to indicate the
three-dimensional form.

Refer students to Susan
Avishai's *Study in Blue*
on page 237 and *Terra
Cotta Silk* on page 78.
These are both detailed
studies of fabric.

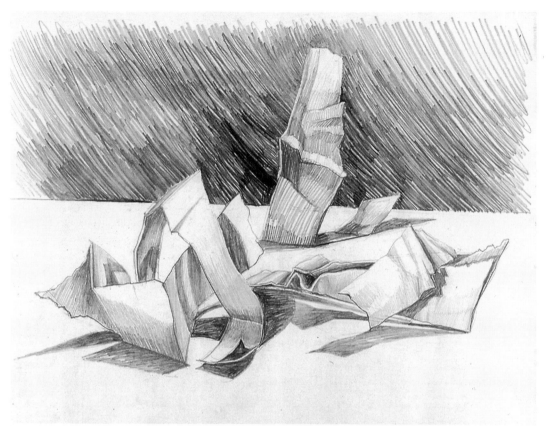

Your drawing from the paper sculpture should make use of line, stroke and tone to create edges, establish forms and suggest three-dimensionality. Have you used a wide range of values? Student work by Ramona Sartoro, Gulfport, Mississippi.

Paper Sculpture Still Life

What makes a sculpture successful? Does a sculpture share the same design concepts of a drawing? To find answers to these questions, construct a paper sculpture and use the work as the basis for a still-life drawing. This experience is an excellent way to learn about space and form. It will also help you understand the similarities and differences between two- and three-dimensional work.

A Paper Wall Relief

Create a paper wall relief from paper strips woven together. Use the various elements of design to create interest. Layering the paper at different heights will cast unusual shadows and increase the relief's complexities and sculptural qualities. Use a strong light source to cast shadows. Notice how important shadows are in a sculpture. How do they create interest? Explore overlapping. Practice "pushing and pulling space"—making objects farther away recede; making objects closer to the viewer come forward. To do this, make background objects look grayer and softer than foreground objects. Give foreground objects sharp edges, and stronger darks and lights.

Inquiry
Students may research the very realistic, almost trompe-l'oeil, drawings of nineteenth-century American painters William Michael Harnett and John Frederick Peto, who delighted in painting crumpled papers such as old letters, fading photos, and torn business cards tacked to rough walls.

Design Extension
The paper wall relief assignment is designed to teach students to push and pull space. The relief should be constructed of strips of paper that have different edges and lengths. The strips of paper may be taped, stapled, or glued to a sheet of illustration board.

The strips may be folded, twisted, or interwoven to provide a variety of shadows within the composition. The shadows help create depth: areas with darker values recede (are "pushed back"); areas with lighter values come forward (are "pulled") and appear sharper.

This process gives the drawing a powerful feeling in terms of space.

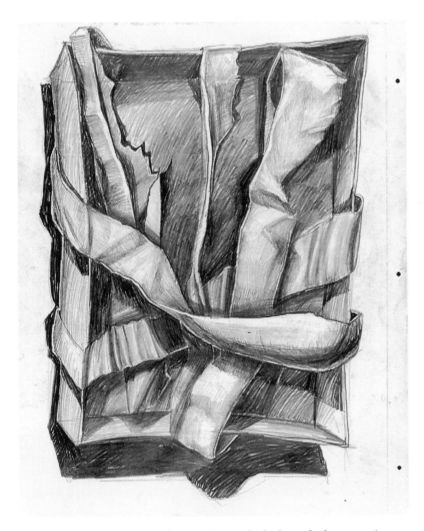

Can you tell which areas are closest to you and which are farthest away in this wall relief? How has the artist suggested distance? Student work by Ramona Sartoro, Gulfport, Mississippi.

Interrelating Darks and Lights

Higher-Order Thinking Skills

Use Freckelton's work to reinforce the importance of planning a composition before drawing it. By squinting at the drawing, students should begin to see patterns of light and dark. Ask students to analyze how the artist planned where the lights and darks would fall in the foreground and background.

Understanding how to interrelate darks and lights in a composition is an important drawing concept. Many beginning drawing students isolate their subject matter by confining their darks to just the form or background. This isolation causes the subject matter and its environment to appear unrelated. To avoid this problem and make objects visually interesting, look for lights that are found inside the subject matter and lights found in the ground. Then, develop the composition by filling in the dark areas within the forms and the surrounding space. Be sure to develop shadows and negative areas of space to accent the highlights found in the composition.

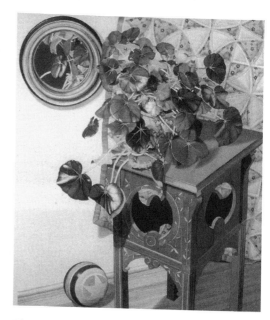

Plants are a good subject to use when studying the relationship between darks and lights in a composition. The play of light on leaves, interesting shadows and the plant's many layers give the artist much to work with. Sondra Freckelton, *Ball and Begonia*, 1993. Watercolor, 38 1/2" x 33" (97.8 x 83.8 cm). Courtesy Maxwell Davidson Gallery.

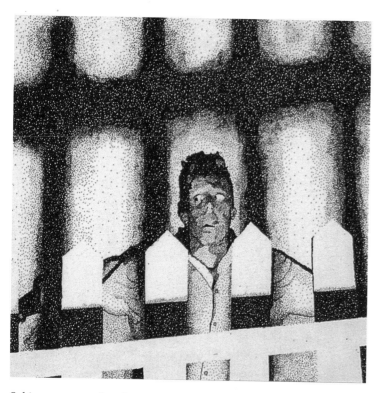

Subject matter and environment are closely related—perhaps a bit too closely for the subject's comfort?—in this comic/horrific ink drawing. How has the artist used dark areas to create an obvious focus? Student work by Pamela Zernia, Kenosha, Wisconsin.

Janet Fish

1938 –

Still life painting has a long tradition in the history of art. The most famous still life compositions come from seventeenth century Holland. Executed in warm, rich colors, the Dutch paintings convey the beauty of ripe fruit, richly ornamented fabrics and gold-trimmed goblets. Still lifes remain a popular subject with Realists like Janet Fish, who paints contemporary household objects. A simple glass bowl of fruit placed on a sunbathed table is a modern version of an old theme.

Although Janet Fish is a Realist, her art is more about perception than representation of objects. She has a special interest in depicting the properties of light as it moves through glass goblets and creates intricate designs on casually arranged fruit and candy. Reflections and shadows significantly enrich the visual texture of her paintings and drawings.

The treatment of light is important in conveying the mood of an artwork. In *Green Grapes* (see page 48), homely objects bathed in patterns of light and shadow provide a sense of joy and serenity. Janet Fish captures in her art something that is easily missed in reality—moments of beauty of common things.

Context
Janet Fish was born into a family of Boston artists in 1938. She studied sculpture at Smith College and then later at Yale. In a time when most of the art world was caught up in abstraction, Fish began painting realistically, trying to capture the beauty in ordinary objects. She was particularly interested in how light reflects on glass surfaces. See her *Green Grapes* still life on page 48.

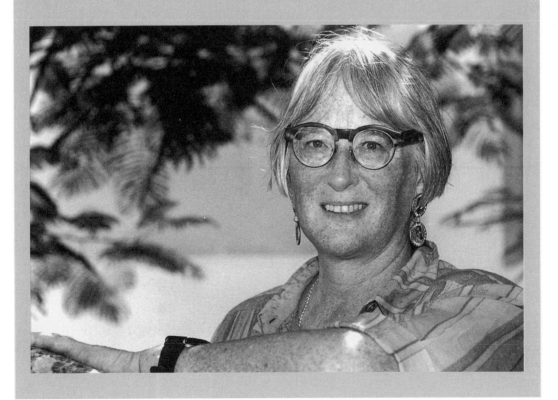

Design Extension
Students may try
drawing a light plant
with white conté crayon
on dark paper. They
may also draw on gray
paper using both white
conté crayon and black
charcoal pencil.

Context
Chiaroscuro is the
Italian term referring to
the contrasts of lights
and darks. Explain to
students that Melissa
Gill's drawing on this
page is a good example
of chiaroscuro. Can
they find other examples
in this chapter? (Janet
Fish's *Green Grapes*,
page 48)

Explore darks and lights and positive and negative space by drawing a still life of a dark plant on a white ground. Use a strong spotlight to create a wide range of values and interesting shadows. Develop areas of darks within the positive and negative space. Notice how the darks define the underlying structure of the composition.

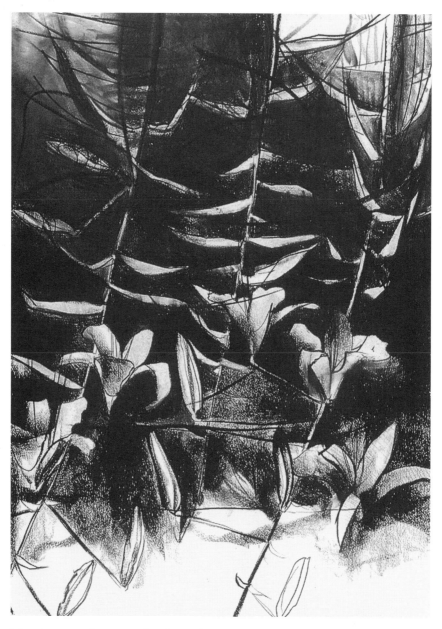

Negative space dominates this charcoal drawing. Its strong value contrasts give the image power and presence. Melissa Gill, *Untitled*. Charcoal on paper. Courtesy of the artist.

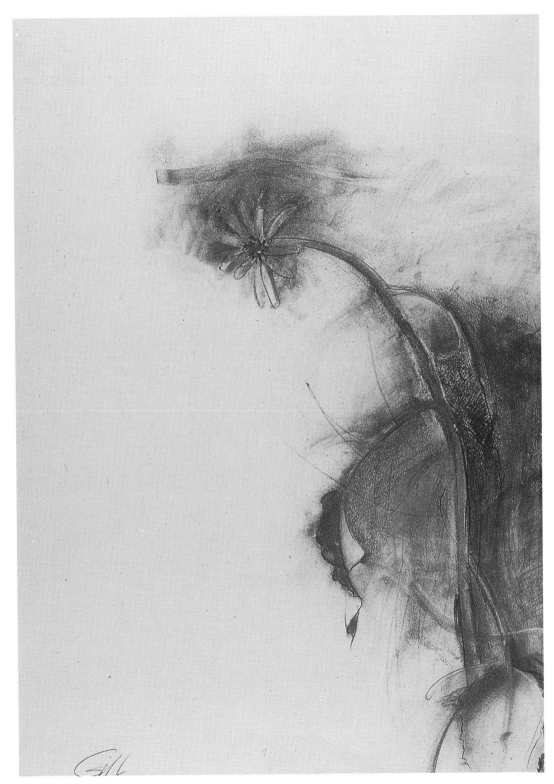

What gives this drawing its feeling of fragility? Melissa Gill, *Untitled*. Charcoal on paper. Courtesy of the artist.

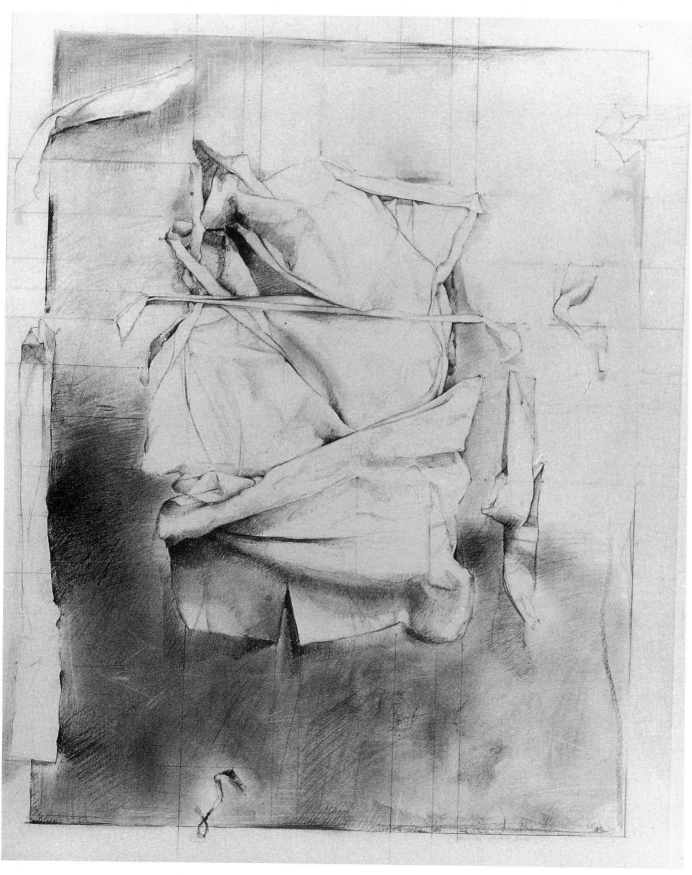

In this drawing, the artist explored a variety of values to suggest the wrinkles and folds in fabric and paper. Stephen Posen, *Untitled*, 1973. Graphite on paper, 40" x 32" (101.6 x 81.3 cm). Collection of Louis and Susan Meisel.

When developing darks and lights, work the entire composition equally rather than trying to finish one part of the drawing at a time. Push and pull the dark and light areas in order to develop a relationship between the forms and the surrounding space. Layer values over the forms to achieve a rich sense of depth.

Carefully study the value changes in a single shadow. Be sure to include these changes in the drawing. Be sensitive to variations in the shadow edges.

Gradually build value throughout a composition to find the correct relationship within the composition. Use a full range of value changes to achieve as much contrast as possible. Dramatic variation in value and intriguing arrangement of composition create strong impressions.

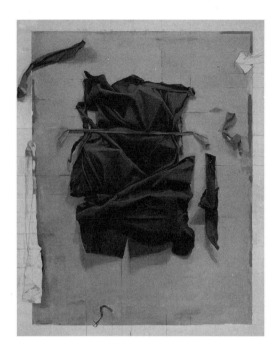

The painting based on the drawing (opposite) uses a narrower range of dark values to suggest folds. Which work do you think is more interesting? Stephen Posen, *Untitled*, 1973. Oil, acrylic, graphite on canvas, 40" x 32" (101.6 x 81.3 cm). Collection of Louis and Susan Meisel.

Value

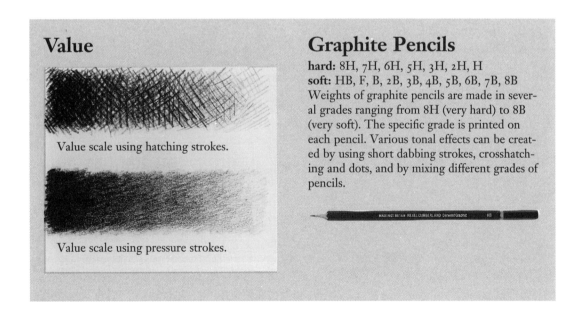

Value scale using hatching strokes.

Value scale using pressure strokes.

Graphite Pencils

hard: 8H, 7H, 6H, 5H, 3H, 2H, H
soft: HB, F, B, 2B, 3B, 4B, 5B, 6B, 7B, 8B
Weights of graphite pencils are made in several grades ranging from 8H (very hard) to 8B (very soft). The specific grade is printed on each pencil. Various tonal effects can be created by using short dabbing strokes, crosshatching and dots, and by mixing different grades of pencils.

Exploring Possibilities with Light

Throughout this book, you are encouraged to look for ways to create strong and unusual compositions. Dramatic shadows provide one source of fresh and interesting subject matter. Consider the interplay of natural light and shadow in your environment. The sun casts different shadows throughout the day. Compare how a building looks at high noon and in late afternoon. Do you see some unique possibilities with shapes and shadows? Try isolating areas, such as windows, doors and stairs. Do they create interesting designs? Do shadows make them even more interesting?

The most dramatic natural lighting occurs around the hours of sunrise and sunset. The cast shadows at this time are longer and more striking. Notice long shadows cast over areas like stairwells or fire escapes. Subjects like these are not only powerful in darks and lights but also are elegant in their sense of pattern.

Use a viewfinder to help you locate a good composition. To make a viewfinder, cut a small square (2" x 2") out of the center of a piece of paper. Then, look through the square and find interesting design relationships that would otherwise go unnoticed. Hold the viewfinder at unusual angles. By viewing architectural structures from dramatic points of view, you can develop unique and exciting compositions.

THINK ABOUT IT
How do you know when you have found the "right" approach to a composition? Do you solve problems logically or intuitively? Build on what you learn in each drawing to help you plan your next composition.

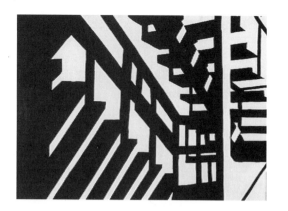

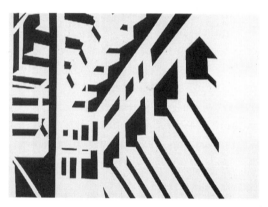

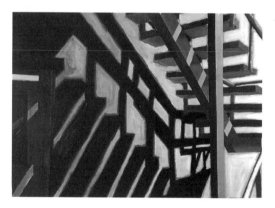

Look for patterns and interesting shadows all around you. This artist was attracted by the shapes and shadows around a fire escape. Top: Here positive shapes are black, negative shapes white. Middle: Positive shapes are white, negative ones are black, and the whole image has been turned backward. Bottom: A more realistic rendering of the scene is still rich with pattern and shadow. Student work by Chad Brown, Memphis, Tennessee.

Extension
Use a Polaroid™ camera to isolate architectural details at different times of day, or have students bring in pictures.

Higher-Order Thinking Skills
Viewpoint is important in this illustration. Turn a drawing upside down and squint. How does the image change?

Light reveals details that you may not always notice. A strongly lit subject viewed from below can appear quite dramatic. Author, *Column*, 1989. 28" x 40" (51 x 102 cm).

Summary

Drawing from still lifes is a natural way to learn the basics of the drawing process. Still lifes can train your eyes to see the shapes of real objects and explore their three-dimensionality. This chapter gave you opportunities to explore the elements of shape, form and space in a still life. In addition, you learned the importance of positive and negative space in a composition.

Reflect for a moment on your developing skills in using line, stroke and tone. Are you gaining more confidence in translating visual information from a still life?

Still lifes also allow you great freedom in arranging a composition. When you isolate areas, use striking shadows and approach the subject matter from unusual angles, you will produce powerful compositions. This makes your work fresh, challenging and more creative.

Design Extension

Lead students in arranging a huge class still life in the center of the classroom. Incorporate several spotlights to shine on or within this arrangement. Encourage students to select a viewpoint and portion of the still life that they would like to draw. They may use viewfinders to find their composition, which should fill their page.

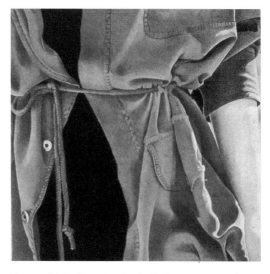

From which direction is the light coming in this work? Why might the artist have chosen to show us only this part of her subject? Susan Avishai, *Terra Cotta Silk*. Colored pencil, 15 3/8" x 15 3/8" (39.1 x 39.1 cm). Courtesy of the artist.

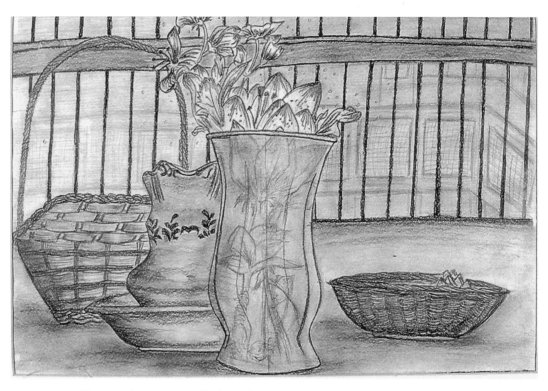

Strong vertical lines in the background help unify this still life. Student work by Joo-Hyun Lee, El Paso, Texas.

Activities

Drawing What You See

In working with familiar objects and subject matter, we often attempt to draw what we *know* rather than what we actually *see*. Select a simple line drawing you have done. Turn it upside down and copy it. (Your drawing will also be upside down.) Concentrate on angles, lines and shapes rather than subject matter.

A Partial View of an Insect

Use reference books to find illustrations of common insects such as ants, mosquitoes, flies and spiders. Select one insect to draw. Use a 2-inch viewfinder to isolate one area of the insect's body. Draw that section only on a large scale, as though you were viewing the insect through a microscope. With pencil or charcoal, draw the body by using light and dark value. Do not draw the figure with line.

Inside a Fruit or Vegetable

Bring in different kinds of fruits and vegetables, such as pumpkins, grapefruits, eggplants and red cabbages. Examine the outsides of these organic forms; then cut them in half to examine the insides. Is the inside appearance very different from the outside? Compare the colors, line and textures.

Choose one of the objects and create a pencil sketch. Then fill in the lines and colors with prismacolor pencil. Consider the values of individual colors.

If you have time, repeat the exercise, this time drawing the object from the outside. Did drawing the inside first make you more aware of the outside? Are you becoming more visually aware of the surfaces of objects?

Shading Simple Objects

Draw a series of timed five-minute sketches of fruits and vegetables. Every five minutes, trade fruits with your classmates and create a new charcoal drawing, making each fruit seem very important by drawing it large. Concentrate first on the form and shading and then on the texture. Try shading by using the side of the charcoal. Add the shadow on the table under the fruit.

The same timed technique may be used with a collection of bottles and jars to learn to shade reflections.

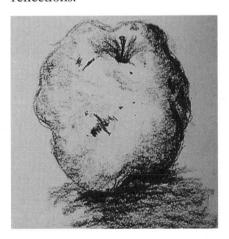

Student work by Kelly Budzyma.

Drawing Geometric Forms

Construct a geometric form such as a cube, pyramid or octahedron out of paper. Then tape your form to a base of white paper so that the form will remain stationary. Light the form with a light source coming from the right or the left of the form.

To make the exercise more interesting, look at the form as though it were part of a surreal, dreamlike landscape. Perhaps you see the layout as a desert.

Pay close attention to the dark shadows that the form casts on the white paper base. To draw the shadow effects, use pencil or conté values. Consider how crosshatching or stippling could capture the textural qualities. Try to draw sharp contrasts between the shadows and the white areas. see page 35

Drawing Reflective Surfaces

Metal cans and containers have reflective surfaces which can be used to create challenging and interesting compositions. Set up a still life of three or four different-sized tin cans and other metallic containers. Remove any labels so that all the surfaces will reflect light.

Set up a light source from behind you. The surfaces of the cans should reflect areas of very light value as well as dark. Do the containers have ribs or seams that create surface variations? Notice any shadows cast by the objects.

Take some time to study the shape of a cylinder before you begin to draw. Consider how to draw the inner volume of the can. Does the intensity of the light source create contrasting, darker values inside the can? see page 48

Chapter 4
Structures and Landscapes

Objectives
Students will be able to
- Identify one-, two-, and three-point perspective in artworks. (Art criticism)
- Create drawings that use perspective to give an illusion of depth. (Art production)
- Perceive and appreciate how artists including Vincent van Gogh, Leonardo da Vinci, Salvador Dali, and M.C. Escher used perspective in their art. (Aesthetics/Art history)
- Understand and appreciate how non-Western cultures indicate depth in their two-dimensional artworks. (Art history/Aesthetics)
- Understand that a landscape drawing shows the natural environment while a cityscape shows architecture and a human-made environment. (Art criticism)
- Perceive and appreciate how artists including Andrew Wyeth, Rembrandt van Rijn, Charles Sheeler, and Robert Cottingham composed their landscapes and cityscapes. (Art history/Art criticism)
- Create their own landscape and cityscape drawings with a consideration of viewpoint, emphasis, and a variety of textures. (Art production)
- Perceive and appreciate how artists include reflections in their artworks. (Art criticism/ Art history)
- Create their own drawings of reflective objects. (Art production)
- Develop and use aesthetic judgments based on their knowledge of perspective and landscape and cityscape composition. (Aesthetics)

Vocabulary
perspective
vanishing point
horizon line
exaggeration
foreshortening
distortion
foreground
middle ground
background

Chapter Overview
Chapter 4 explores the world beyond the still life. Students learn to indicate depth using linear perspective. Students first explore drawing objects from nature accurately, using detail and texture, before they attempt a landscape drawing. Students also learn to draw an urban landscape, learning to look for interesting angles and viewpoints, and using shadows to create interesting compositions.

Lesson 1
pages 80–83   45 minutes

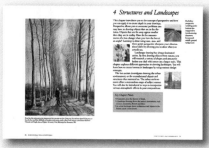

pages 80–81

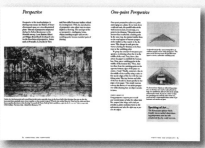

pages 82–83

Teach
- As students study the converging perspective lines in Leonardo da Vinci's drawing on page 82, explain that this type of perspective drawing began in the 1400s during the Italian Renaissance. Call students' attention to the much simpler perspective drawings on page 83. Notice how parallel lines seem to meet at the same point. Lead them in drawing a very simple one-point perspective, such as railroad tracks. On the board draw a horizontal line labeling it horizon line. Put a dot on the line and label it vanishing point (VP). Now draw the parallel lines of

the track converging to this point. Next do the same thing with a box, first drawing the front side and then vanishing the sides back to the vanishing point.

• Hold a cardboard box low and explain that this box is below the horizon line; so, we see the top or inside of the box. Hold the box up at eye level, noting how neither the top or bottom is visible. Then lift it up above eye level (the horizon line), pointing out that now the bottom of the box may be seen.

Studio Experience

Give each student a small box to move and observe. Students should draw a one-point perspective view of a box in a road similar to the drawing on page 83. Then have students use rulers to draw a series of boxes above, below, and even with the horizon line. They should also draw boxes to each side of the vanishing point.

Materials

small boxes, such as 2" x 2" slide boxes
pencils
12" x 18" white drawing paper
pink pearl erasers
rulers

Lesson 2
pages 84–85   45 minutes

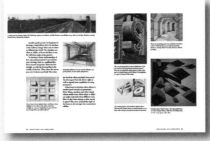

pages 84–85

Teach

• Call students' attention to the converging parallel lines in the drawings of halls on pages 84, 85, and 93. Ask students to identify the sets of parallel lines in these drawings. Next, identify parallel lines in the art studio such as the top of the walls, the baseboard, and the upper and lower window frames. Explain how they would converge if they were drawn on a flat surface.

• After students have looked at the drawings of three-dimensional letters on pages 85, 106, and 107, suggest that they try drawing the letters of their own names in three dimensions. This could be done either in or out of class.

Studio Experience

• Arrange for students to sketch in a hall, corridor, long porch, alley, or narrow room. Have them draw the corridor freehand, calling attention to relative proportions and angles within the composition. Or, introduce how to use a grid to draw a scene. (Using a grid is similar to the technique used by Renaissance artists, who made their grids by stretching string through a wooden frame.) Each student should very lightly draw a grid of 2" squares on a sheet of paper before beginning to draw their composition. Demonstrate how they may use a transparent grid to sight the proportions and placement of objects within a setting. For example, if a door is two squares high in the transparent grid, then they would draw it two squares high on their paper.

• Students can also actually draw the scene on Plexiglas with an erasable marker as they look through the sheet. (In essence, they are tracing reality.) Students should later copy this drawing in pencil onto their paper. Tape the sheet to a window or easel while drawing.

• Point out the dark and light areas in the scene. Ask how they can tell where one plane joins another. Usually the walls, ceiling, and floor will each be a different value.

Materials
pencils
erasers
12" x 18" white drawing paper
drawing board
tape
rulers
optional: transparent acetate
   grid marked with 1" squares,
   1 per student
   overhead marking pen

Lesson 3
pages 86–87   45 minutes

Teach
• After demonstrating how
to draw a box using two-point
perspective, allow students to
experiment drawing boxes above
and below the horizon line. If
they did not draw a spotlighted
box as described on page 60, they
should do that now.

• After students have studied
the two-point perspective drawings of buildings on these pages,
they may draw either a city block
or a large building such as their
school.

Studio Experience
Take students to an area where
they will have a view of a corner
of a large building or a block of
buildings. Teach students to draw
the building(s) using the two-
point perspective techniques that

they just learned. If the drawing
will take more than a class period,
the students should photograph
their views in case they cannot
return to the exact spot during the
next class.

Materials
pencil
18" x 24" white drawing paper
drawing board
erasers
tape
rulers

Lesson 4
pages 88–91   45 minutes

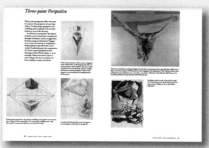

pages 88–89

Teach
• Explain that artists create
foreshortening when they draw
and compress a form so that it
seems to extend or project into
space. Have them study drawings
of human bodies such as in Dali's
Christ in Perspective on page 89,
the top view of the man in
the chair on page 91, Mantegna's
Dead Christ on page 114, and
Michelangelo's figure on page
201.

• To explain three-point
perspective, point out to students
where the three vanishing points
are in the drawings on page 88.
Have them explain the three-
point perspective view in Sheeler's
Delmonico Building (page 39) and
Land of Lincoln (page 91).

• Go over the characteristics
of some of the erasers on page 90.

Studio Experience
Demonstrate to students how to
create a three-point perspective
building by drawing a horizon
line, adding two vanishing points
to the horizon line and one more
either at the top or bottom of
their page. Refer them to the
lower-right illustration on page
88. Suggest that they draw
several buildings using three-
point perspective. Encourage them
to experiment with the different
types of erasers as they soften
edges to create an illusion of
distance.

Materials
pencils
18" x 24" white drawing paper
rulers
erasers—pink pearl, kneaded,
   gum, and/or vinyl

Lesson 5
pages 92–95   45 minutes

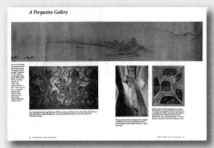

pages 92–93

Teach

• Explain that artists of non-Western cultures follow different conventions to indicate depth on a flat surface. Distant objects are often higher on the picture plane and overlapped. In these examples, only the Japanese drawing on page 94 uses anything close to linear perspective, but parallel lines really do not converge as in the Western system.

• Have students contrast the Chinese and Mixtec styles, noting how the Chinese drawing is subtle with blurring of some features, but every detail is starkly outlined in the Mixtec art. How is space indicated in each work?

Studio Experience

Have students select one of the non-Western cultures on pages 92–95 and draw a school scene in a similar style. Make certain they understand how to indicate depth. Remind them that these drawings will not be realistic as in the Western tradition. The uses of perspective will be different from the techniques they have learned in this chapter.

Materials

drawing media such as pencils,
  ink, and markers
12" x 18" white drawing paper
erasers

Lesson 6
pages 96–97   45 minutes

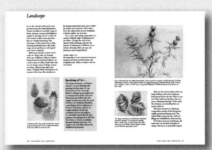

pages 96–97

Teach

Supplement the nature studies on these pages by bringing in pine cones, shells, sand dollars, starfish, bones, flowers, seed pods, pot plants, branches, leaves, and insects for students to draw. Before they begin their drawings, have students discuss the unique texture, design, and shape of each of the objects.

Studio Experience

Using pencil, pen, markers, and twigs dipped in ink have students draw nature objects from several different angles. Try blind and modified contour line drawings, quick sketches, and shaded studies with a wide range of values to indicate forms.

Materials

drawing media such as pencils,
  pens, markers, twigs, ink
18" x 24" drawing paper
erasers

Lesson 7
pages 98–101   45 minutes

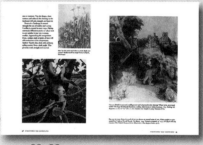

pages 98–99

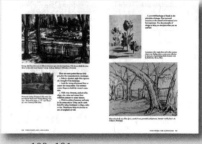

pages 100–101

Teach

Have students answer the questions in the captions. Ask them how each artist has created emphasis and how they used the four points on page 100 in their landscapes.

Studio Experience

If possible, take the students outside to draw; or, have students draw a view from the windows. Using viewfinders to find an outdoor composition with a center of interest, students should sketch a landscape. Encourage them to sketch their whole picture before returning to details of individual objects. They should include a foreground, middle ground, and background, choosing one part of the picture to emphasize.

If they draw outside, have them photograph their scenes in case they need more than one class period to complete their work.

Materials

pencils
12" x 18" drawing paper
erasers
viewfinders
tape (to keep paper from blowing)
optional: camera and film

Lesson 8
pages 102–107   45 minutes

Teach

• As students study the illustrations on pages 102 and 103, ask for a weather report for each scene. Point out the important role the atmosphere plays in each work.

• Ask whether the foreground, middle ground, or background is emphasized in each work on pages 104 and 105. Point out how each artist made a decision to either focus on a large or a small area in their surroundings. In which ones does texture seem especially important?

• Call students' attention to the different media Robert Cottingham used in the two works on page 106 and 107. Go over the eight points for drawing urban scenes on page 106 before students begin their own drawings.

Studio Experience

Take students someplace where they will have a variety of human-made objects or buildings to draw. This could be the school parking lot, an area with trash and junk, a grain elevator, a playground, or a bridge. Encourage students to use viewfinders to find an unusual view of an everyday subject. Have them photograph their scene if they do not complete the drawing in one class period.

Materials

drawing media such as pencils,
   markers, or pen and ink
18" x 24" drawing paper
erasers
tape
drawing board
optional: camera and film

Lesson 9
pages 108–111   45 minutes

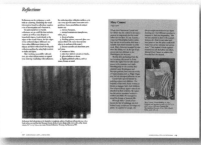
pages 108–109

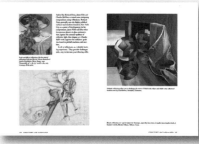
pages 110–111

Teach

After students have noticed how each artist handled the reflections in the drawings on pages 108–111, allow students to draw a still life which includes reflective objects.

Studio Experience

Arrange a still life that includes a mirror, drapery, and household objects. Mirror tiles are good for this, but you can also use a shiny hubcap or reflective Christmas ornaments. Before students begin to sketch, discuss the reflections and how students will indicate these in their drawings. Emphasize how important value contrasts will be in these drawings. They should also consider their composition, making their objects fill or extend past their picture plane. They should lightly block in their whole picture before beginning to concentrate on details in individual objects.

Materials
drawing media such as charcoal
   or pencils
18" x 24" white drawing paper
mirror or other reflective object
   and other still life objects
erasers
fixative (if charcoal is used)

Lesson 10
pages 112–113   45 minutes

Reteach
• Review one-, two-, and three-point perspectives with the class by looking back at the illustrations on pages 80–91. Go over how other cultures indicate depth. Review some of the important points of developing a landscape such as choosing an unusual viewpoint and emphasizing some part of the composition.

• Instruct students to complete an activity on page 113. The Cars with Attitudes activity will give them a chance to incorporate their skills in perspective into a creative piece of art, as well as learn how to simplify and abstract a subject.

• Display the class landscape drawings and discuss how students arranged their compositions. What is emphasized in each? Did they create textures? In which pieces is there a foreground, middle ground, and background? Did any students blur the edges to create atmospheric perspective in the background? Are there effective value contrasts in the drawings?

Assess
• Ask students to identify one-, two-, and three-point perspective in artworks in this book. (Art criticism)

• Have students explain how some non-Western cultures indicate depth in their two-dimensional artworks. (Art history/Aesthetics)

• To determine that students recognize the difference between landscapes and cityscapes, have them identify examples of each. (Art criticism)

• Divide the class into four groups and assign each group to study and report on how Vincent van Gogh, Leonardo da Vinci, Salvador Dali, or M.C. Escher used perspective and created depth in their art. Have them share their conclusions with the class. (Aesthetics/Art history)

• Challenge students to analyze the compositions of the landscapes and cityscapes of Andrew Wyeth, Rembrandt van Rijn, Charles Sheeler, and Robert Cottingham. They should especially consider how these artists used space, emphasis, and value in their compositions. (Art history/Art criticism)

• Suggest that students select, from the pieces they created, those they consider the most and the least effective. Have them support their selections with reasons. Go over their work together to see if you agree. (Aesthetics)

• Check their drawings to determine that they created drawings using perspective to give an illusion of depth; landscapes and cityscapes utilizing emphasis and a variety of textures; and drawings of reflective objects which capture value contrasts. (Art production)

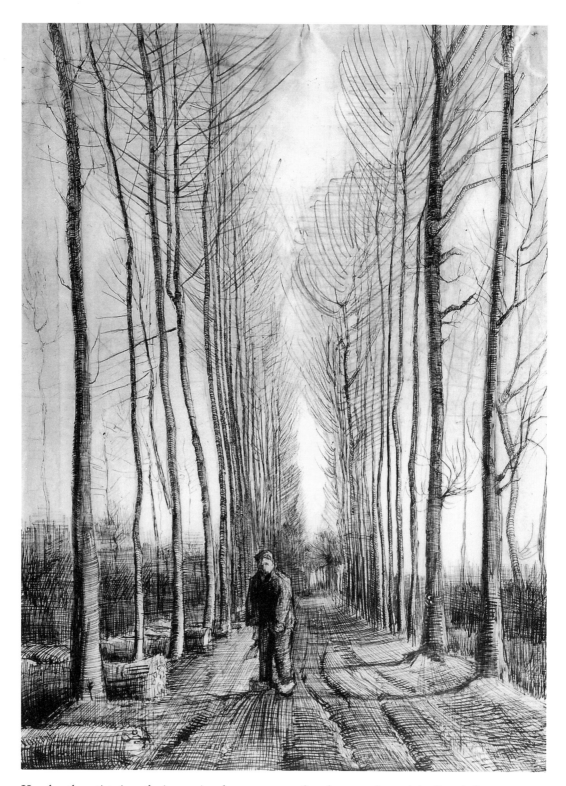

How has the artist given the impression that you can see for a long way beyond the figure? Can you see how he has used line skillfully to broaden some areas, make others look narrow, and create shadows? Vincent van Gogh, *Lane of Poplars*, 1884. 21 1/4 x 15 1/2" (54 x 39.4 cm). Collection V.W. van Gogh. Courtesy Foto Marburg/Art Resource, NY.

4 Structures and Landscapes

This chapter introduces you to the concept of perspective and how you can apply it to create depth in your drawings. Perspective allows you to overcome problems you may have in drawing objects that are in the distance. Objects that are far away appear smaller than they are in reality. How do the measurements of a box change when you view the box at an angle? Learning to draw using one-, two- and

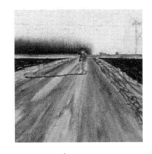

three-point perspective sharpens your observational skills by allowing you to draw what you *actually* see.

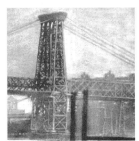

Landscape drawing has always fascinated artists. By first drawing objects from nature, you will research a variety of shapes and structures before you deal with nature on a larger scale. This chapter explores different approaches to drawing landscapes. You will learn how to create interest in landscapes by using various design concepts.

The last section investigates drawing the urban environment, or the manufactured objects and structures that surround us. The urban environment offers a tremendous range of subject matter. You will also be introduced to ways to incorporate various atmospheric effects in your compositions.

Vocabulary
perspective
vanishing point
horizon line
exaggeration
foreshortening
distortion
foreground
middle ground
background

Inquiry
Monet, as well as van Gogh, painted a series of poplars. Assign students to research Monet's paintings of poplars and compare Monet's arrangement of the trees to van Gogh's.

Context
Van Gogh felt that the person in a landscape was the most important part of the picture. He said, "Well—first comes the figure; I personally cannot understand the rest without it, and it is the figure that creates the atmosphere." See page 206 for another van Gogh landscape featuring one-point perspective and a figure.

Key Chapter Points
- Perspective gives the illusion of depth.
- A landscape drawing shows the natural environment, such as trees, mountains, flowers and lakes.
- An urban landscape shows architecture and objects in the human-made environment.

Perspective

Perspective is the visual technique in drawing that creates the illusion of three-dimensional space on a two-dimensional plane. The use of perspective originated during the Italian Renaissance in the fifteenth century. Leon Battista Alberti and Filippo Brunelleschi developed rules for the foundation of perspective. Artists such as Donatello, Leonardo da Vinci and Piero della Francesca further refined the development. With the introduction of perspective came other ways to create depth in a drawing. The concepts of linear perspective, overlapping forms, objects receding in space and use of a vanishing point became essential parts of drawing.

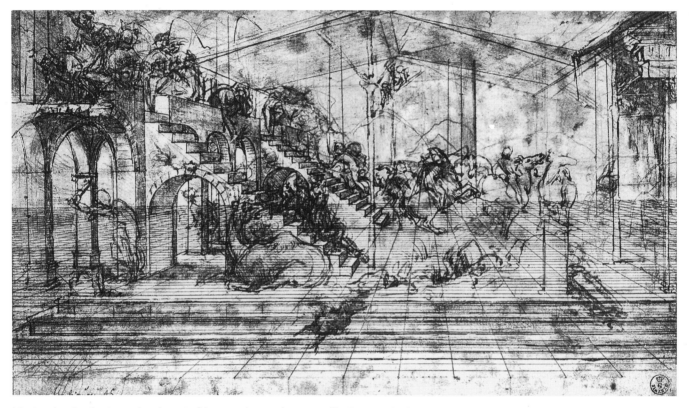

Notice the fine horizontal and vertical lines in this study, especially those in the lower half of the drawing. Can you see that the horizontal lines gradually move closer together as they recede in space? What do the vertical lines do? How has the artist used these lines as guides elsewhere in the drawing? Leonardo da Vinci, *Study of Stairs and Horses*, 1481-82. 6 1/2 x 11 1/2" (16.5 x 29.2 cm). Uffizi Gallery, Florence, Italy. Alinari/Art Resource, NY.

One-point Perspective

One-point perspective refers to a point converging on a plane. If you look down a railroad track, the parallel sides of the track seem to meet, or converge, at a point in the distance. This point on the horizon line is called the *vanishing point*. In the same way, the painted marker lines on the road appear to become progressively smaller as they recede in the distance. This change in scale gives the viewer a feeling for distance as the lines meet at the vanishing point.

To grasp the concept of one-point perspective, try drawing a box that is in the middle of the road. First, draw a line across the paper to establish the horizon line. Next, put a vanishing point in the middle of the horizon line. Then, draw two lines from the vanishing point to the opposite bottom edges of the paper to create a "road." Finally, construct a box in the middle of the road by using a ruler to line up the edges of the box with the vanishing point. The top, bottom and sides of the box should be drawn parallel to the edges of the paper. This simple exercise conveys the theory of one-point perspective while showing how an object recedes in space.

THINK ABOUT IT
Using perspective requires you to recall your mental picture of what the subject looks like, compare that image with what you actually see, form conclusions based on this information and select the right way to present the subject.

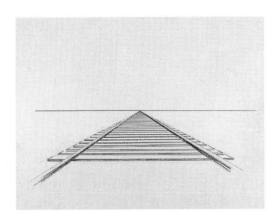

A railroad track in flat, open countryside is an excellent example of one-point perspective. The point on the horizon where the parallel tracks appear to meet is called the vanishing point.

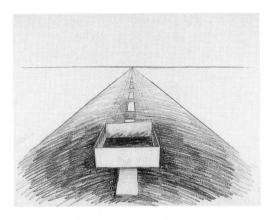

To discover how objects are affected by perspective, use the lines of a road or railroad track to help you establish the sides of a box in the middle of that road or track. If you use a ruler to align the vanishing point with the sides of the box, you'll see how a right-angled shape seems to get narrower as it recedes in space.

Speaking of Art...
The Renaissance painter Paolo Uccello was so excited about drawing perspectives that his wife complained that he would not rest.

Extension
Show students a reproduction of Leonardo da Vinci's *The Last Supper*. Point out the one-point perspective and how most of the major lines seem to converge on Jesus' head.

Inquiry
Have students create a poster about a Renaissance artist who used linear perspective in his compositions. They may research artists such as Masaccio, Uccello, Piero della Francesca, and Mantegna. They should include examples of the artist's use of linear perspective and information about the artist's life.

Interdisciplinary Connection
Mathematics—Review with students the definition of parallel lines as defined in geometry, two lines that never meet. Compare this to the art theorem that parallel lines converge to the same vanishing point.

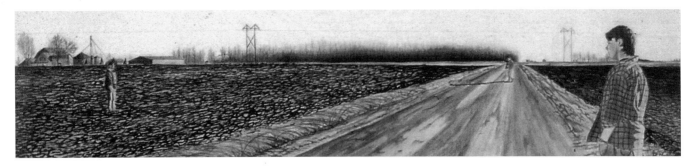

A wide, narrow format makes this landscape appear even flatter, and the horizon even farther away, than it is in fact. Student work by David Hicks, Russiaville, Indiana.

Interdisciplinary Connection

Mathematics—Discuss with students how using the grid is a way to establish proportions within their drawings. By changing the ratio of the size of the squares on their acetate grid to that on their paper, they may change the size of their completed drawing. For example, if the grid on their acetate is marked in 1" squares and the grid on their paper is 2" squares, their completed drawing will be twice the size of what they see through the grid. If their paper is marked in 3" squares, images will be three times larger.

Extension

Point out the one-point perspective in the photograph on page 221. Suggest that students extend the sides of the street to their vanishing point. For another example of one-point perspective, see Linda Murray's *The Urban Forest Line* on page 188.

Another good exercise for beginners is drawing a long hallway. How do the lines of the hallway change when you see them at different eye levels? Try standing on a chair or ladder, or lie on the floor to see the differing angles of perspective.

To develop a better understanding of how one-point perspective can enhance your drawing, look at a cardboard box from several viewpoints. Draw the box straight on with the horizon line in the middle of the box. Then, draw the box as you view it above your head. How does

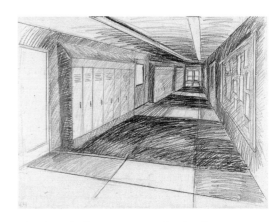

Sketching hallways in your school will give you good practice in one-point perspective.

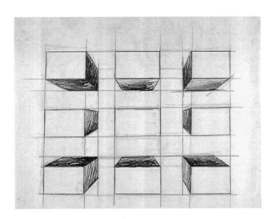

Draw boxes from slightly above and below, from slightly to one side or the other, and from straight on. Are you beginning to get a feel for how perspective can affect objects?

the box look when you look down on it? Try drawing it from the left or right as well to expand your capabilities in using perspective.

Using boxes to develop other objects is another good exercise in perspective. Draw letters, numbers and other simple objects inside boxes. Draw them at different angles and make them different sizes. How do the forms change as they recede in space? The more unusual the angle of the boxes is, the stronger the composition will be.

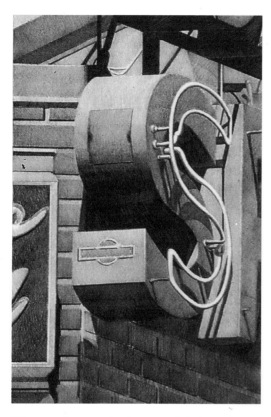

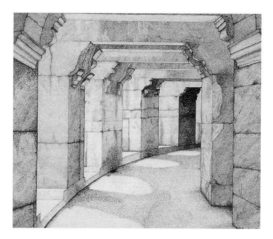

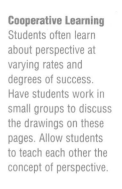

Here the vanishing point has vanished around the corner. What leads your eye into the picture? Student work by Mark Ferencik, Durham, North Carolina.

The use of perspective is more subtle here. Can you see how the large letter recedes in space? Why do you think the artist chose to show only part of a much larger word? Robert Cottingham, *S*, 1992. Courtesy of the artist.

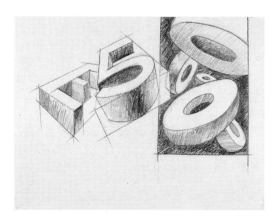

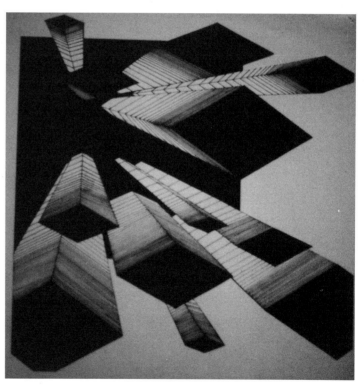

Try making letters and numbers appear three-dimensional. Setting them at unusual angles or on their sides will give you good perspective practice.

Getting dizzy? Don't worry—it's only perspective at work. Ronnie Naizer, *Help Me, I'm Falling*. Ink, 20 1/2" x 15" (52.1 x 38.1 cm).

Two-point Perspective

Teaching Tip
Demonstrate two-point perspective step by step by drawing the horizon line, then two points on horizon, then the front corner of box, etc. Have students follow along with you.

Extensions
• Bring in architectural renderings so that the class may discover how perspective is used in this field. Local architects, house plan magazines, and brochures for new subdivisions are possible sources for these drawings.

• For other examples of two-point perspective see the pickup truck in *Paul's Corner Cushion* on page 225 and the student drawing on page 189.

Design Extension
Students may draw the outside of their home as a sketchbook assignment. If they live in an apartment building, they should draw the building.

To draw a box from a three-quarter viewpoint, you need to use two-point perspective. In two-point perspective, there are two vanishing points on the horizon. To draw a box realistically in two-point perspective, simply draw lines from the two vanishing points to establish the sides of the box.

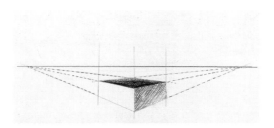

Two-point perspective makes use of two vanishing points rather than one, and allows you to depict more complex objects and scenes.

Try to draw a city block in two-point perspective. This exercise will challenge your creativity and technical ability. Architecture poses interesting problems for the artist. How will you approach the subject matter? Can you draw the street where you live? Can you draw your street, your city block, your neighborhood as it may have looked in 1900? Do some research; find some old photographs of your area, and note how things have changed since they were taken. Then, imagine what a photograph taken in 2900 AD might show. Draw what you imagine.

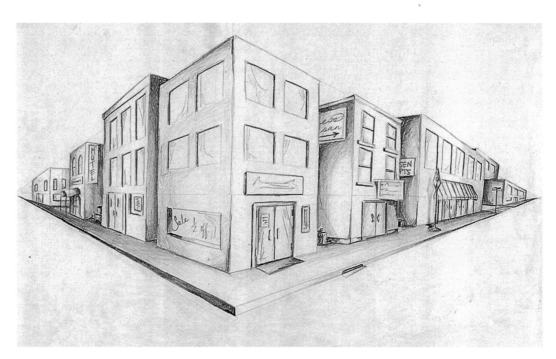

What do streets in cities or towns near you look like? Is the architecture like this? Using two-point perspective, you can draw a familiar street corner—and then change it to suit your own tastes. Don't forget to note where sunlight or moonlight is coming from, to create shadows and highlights. Student work by Geinene Haynes, Nashville, Tennessee.

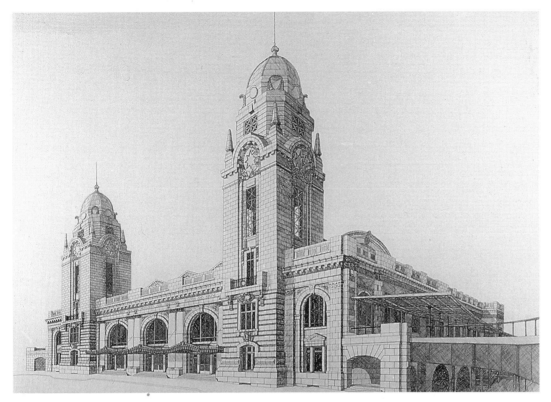

Although the train station is presently unused and falling down, this artist found old photographs and restored it, through drawing, to its former glory. Student work by Todd Cahill, Grafton, Massachusetts.

Design Extensions
• Have students glue a photocopy of a building photographed in two-point perspective to a piece of paper. Tell them to extend the picture beyond its original boundaries by drawing their own additions, using the vanishing points. (See below for a cooperative learning variation.)

• Assign A Furnished Room activity on page 113, which offers a creative way to perfect linear perspective skills.

Cooperative Learning
Project slides of a building onto a large sheet of paper. Have students work as a group to extend the lines of the building to their vanishing points and draw additions to the scene.

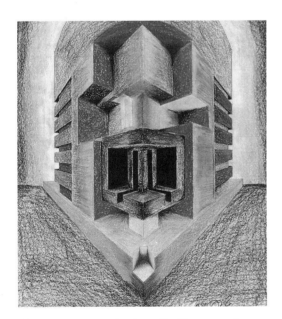

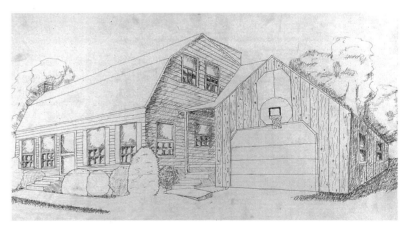

Selective use of detail gives this simple line drawing depth and feeling. Student work by Jen Townsend, Grafton, Massachusetts.

Two-point perspective is applicable to any shape, not merely buildings and boxes. Abstract and nonobjective works, too, can be given three-dimensional qualities through its use. Student work by Ernesto Arriola, El Paso, Texas.

Three-point Perspective

Extensions

• For other examples of three-point perspective see *Help Me, I'm Falling* on page 85.

• An early famous example of foreshortening is the huge painting of *The Battle of San Romano* by Italian Renaissance artist Paolo Uccello. (See Speaking of Art on page 83.) Not only did he try to represent receding fields in the background, but he also drew horses and men so they seemed to come in and out of the picture. Show a reproduction of this painting to students to discuss the foreshortening, the sense of distance, and the energy of a battle.

Three-point perspective allows the artist to enhance the perspective of very long objects. In three-point perspective, the vanishing point is placed at the extreme bottom or top of the drawing.

In addition to perspective, the illusion of depth can be created and strengthened through techniques, such as exaggeration, foreshortening and distortion. Exaggeration means overstating or magnifying— making things larger than they are in reality. Foreshortening is the compression of a form's natural proportions (See Mantegna's *Dead Christ*, chapter 5, as an example). Distortion occurs when an artist changes the size or position of a form, making it appear unrealistic.

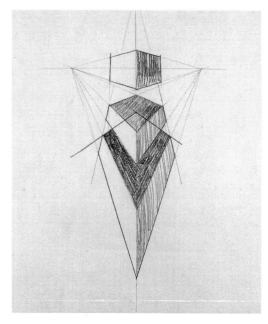

Three-point perspective allows you to exaggerate forms. Notice how, in this diagram, the side vanishing points are close together, the lower vanishing point is far down the page, and the resulting box form is extremely elongated. What would happen if you moved the side vanishing points farther apart?

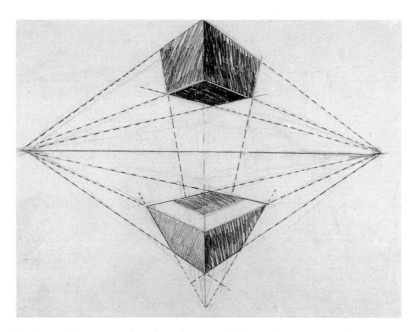

In three-point perspective, the primary vanishing point appears at the extreme top or bottom of the composition. Two secondary vanishing points—like those used in two-point perspective—are used at the sides.

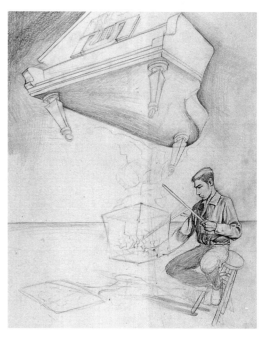

A pencil work showing three-point perspective. Its counterpart in ink is shown on page 89.

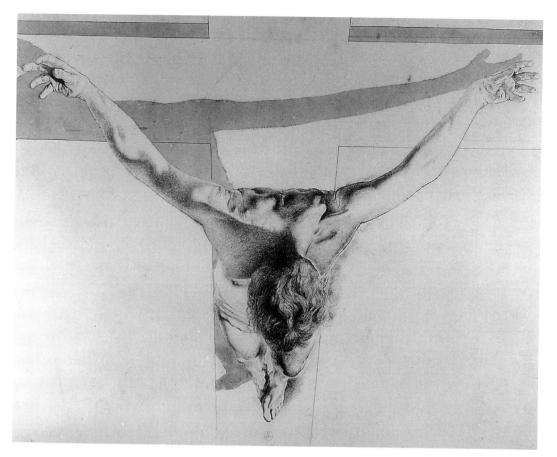

When you foreshorten an object or figure, you change its proportions. How does this figure differ from a figure seen from straight on? What has the artist exaggerated or emphasized? Why? Salvador Dali, *Christ in Perpective*, 1950. Sanguine, 30" x 40" (76.2 x 101.6 cm). Collection of the Salvador Dali Museum, St. Petersburg, Florida. ©1993 Salvador Dali Museum, Inc.

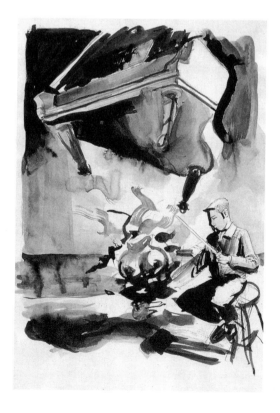

A similiar version, in ink, of the work on page 88. Which shows more detail? Which has more visual energy? Student work by Boris Zakic, Yugoslavia.

Inquiry
Assign students to find examples of foreshortening by Michelangelo in the Sistine Chapel. His detractors thought that because he was a sculptor, not a painter, he would have trouble drawing the foreshortened figures that would be necessary for a ceiling painting.

Context
Salvador Dali (1904–89) was a Spanish artist and a leading Surrealist. He used perspective in his precise, academic style to create a feeling of unrest in his dream-like, nightmarish scenes.

Design Extensions
• Challenge students to draw an upper corner of the art studio, their bedroom, or a kitchen. Remind them that parallel lines converge and to use value variations to indicate where walls and ceiling meet.

• The Ant's View activity on page 113 will provide students an opportunity to creatively draw three-point perspective.

Erasers

The basic function of an eraser is to eradicate undesirable marks. An eraser can also be used as a "drawing tool" to soften, blur or blend areas. In shaded areas, the eraser can be manipulated to create lines and highlights. There are four basic types of erasers.

Art gum is a block-shaped, dry rubber eraser that is especially good for removing pencil and charcoal. It can be used on all papers without harming or smearing the surface. It crumbles easily, and you must be careful the small bits of eraser do not cause unwanted smudging.

A *kneaded eraser* is soft, flat and extremely pliable. It absorbs erased material easily and must be systematically kneaded with the fingers to expose a clean surface. The eraser can be shaped into different forms to soften areas, erase details or create highlights. It is a versatile material that will not damage the surface of the paper.

A *vinyl eraser* is a newly developed elongated eraser that is excellent for removing marks on paper or film. It is made with a low abrasive material that does minimal damage to the surface of the paper.

A *pink pearl eraser* is wedge-shaped, firm and beveled on both ends. Its sharp edges and flat surfaces are very effective for blending and softening lines and shadow areas. It can be used on all drawing surfaces but does not clean as thoroughly as the other three types.

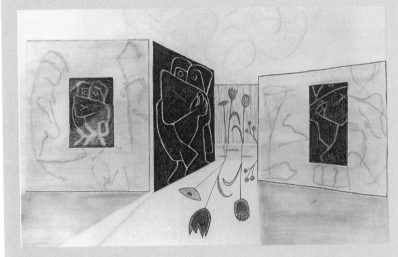

Esther Pullen, *Parcel for Paul.* Pencil on paper. Courtesy of the artist.

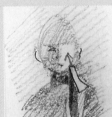

Create highlights

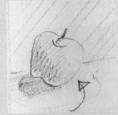

Lighten and soften; change value

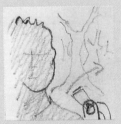

Smudge to create distance or depth

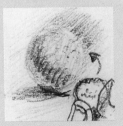

Create texture, distort, blend

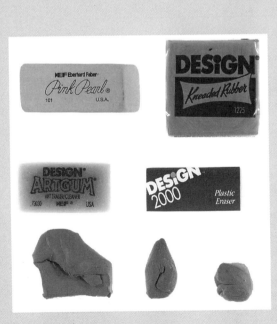

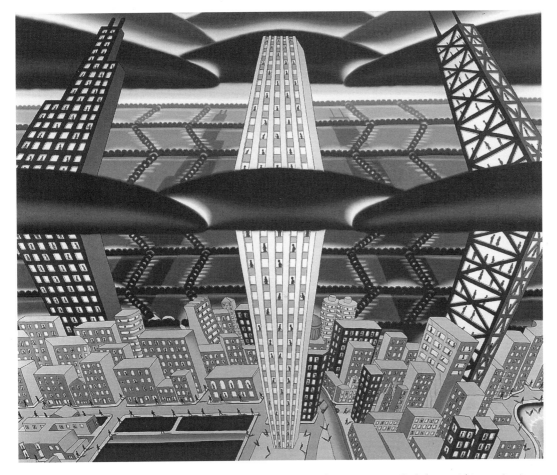

Extension
Refer students to the drawing by Charles Sheeler on page 103. Discuss it in terms of three-point perspective. Students can experience three-point perspective by standing at the base of a tall building or grain elevator and looking up.

Design Extension
Refer students to the Escher print on page 93. Notice how this view is inside a box and then out into another world. Students might create their own view of a world by cutting holes in a box, drawing the inside of the box, and then drawing what they imagine to be outside this box.

Look carefully at this work, especially at the small, lower buildings. Can you find the vanishing points? How has the artist played with the rules of perspective? Roger Brown, *Land of Lincoln*, 1978. Oil on canvas, 71 1/2" x 84" (181.6 x 213.4 cm). Courtesy Phyllis Kind Gallery, NY.

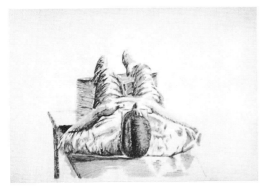

Does this drawing show exaggeration, foreshortening or distortion? Student work by Nicole Pupillo, Worcester, Massachusetts.

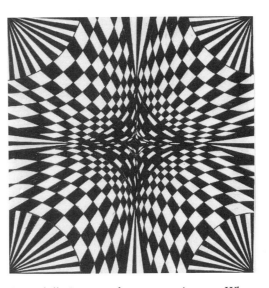

Optical illusions can show perspective, too. What kind of perspective has this artist used? Student work by Keira Olivas, El Paso, Texas.

A Perspective Gallery

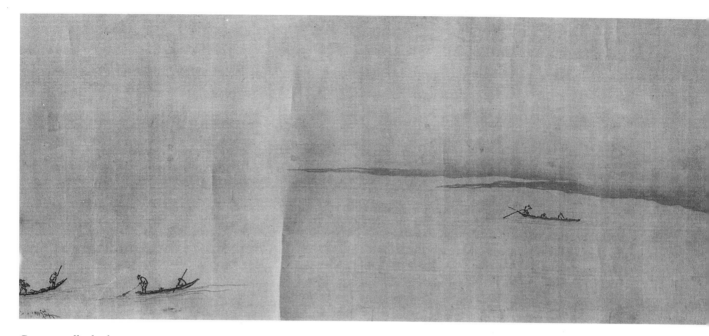

Can you tell whether the mountains in this landscape are in the foreground or background? Would you say this work has much depth or little depth? Why? *Twelve Views of Landscape*, Chinese, ca. 1180–1224. Handscroll, ink on silk, 10 3/4" x 99 3/4" (27.3 x 253.4 cm). Courtesy The Nelson-Atkins Museum of Art, Kansas City, Missouri (Purchase: Nelson Trust).

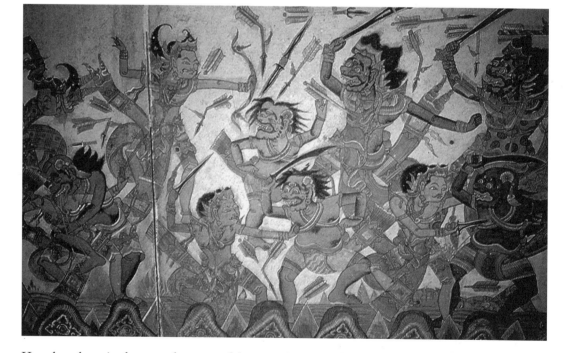

How does the artist show you that some of these warriors are in front of the others? *Scenes from the Kerta Gosa Hall of Justice Ceiling*, Klungkung. Courtesy Ronald Sheridan/Ancient Art and Architecture Collection, London.

Extension
Refer students to another example of Chinese art on page 199.

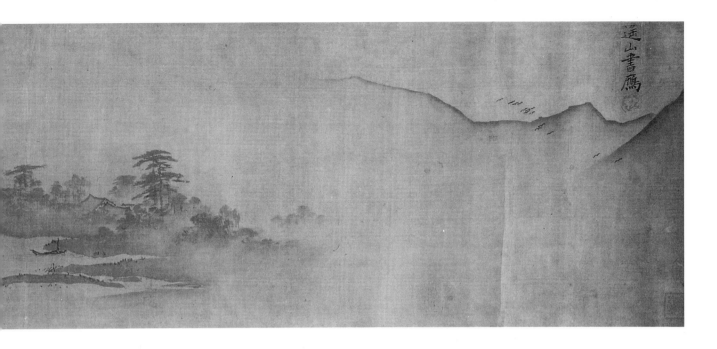

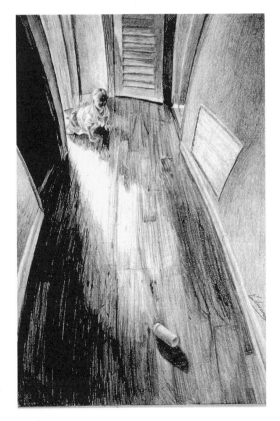

How does this artist's use of perspective and light contribute to the work's somewhat mysterious mood? Student work by Ryan Edwards, St. James, New York.

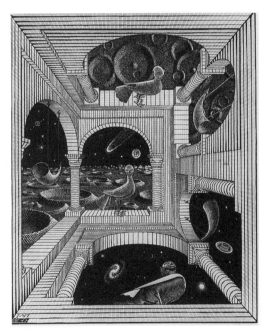

Escher is known for his unusual uses of perspective. Where is the ground? Where is the sky? Are we looking in a window, down from the ceiling or up from the floor? Maurits Cornelis Escher, *Other World*, 1947. Wood engraving. 20 1/2 x 16 3/4" (52 x 42.5 cm). Courtesy Art Resource, NY.

Computer Connection
Draw shapes using
oval and rectangle tools.
Using placement, size,
and overlapping, create
an illusion of depth.

**Higher-Order
Thinking Skills**
Impressionist artists of
the nineteenth century
were influenced by the
way Japanese artists
organized their composi-
tions and indicated
space. Compare how
Mary Cassatt indicated
depth in her print on
page 109 with *Minister
Kibi's Trip to China*.

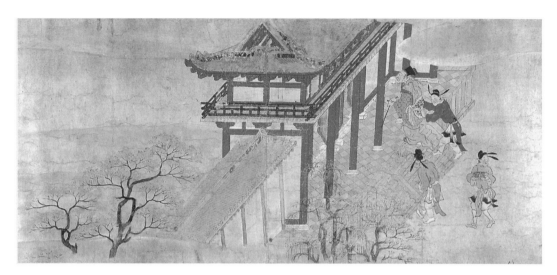

In many non-Western cultures, realistic use of perspective is not important. How would you describe the use of perspective in this work? *Minister Kibi's Trip to China* (detail), Japan, Heian period, 12th century. Ink and color on paper, 12.7" x 961.4" (32.2 x 2442 cm). Courtesy Museum of Fine Arts, Boston. Willima Sturgis Bigelow Collection by Exchange.

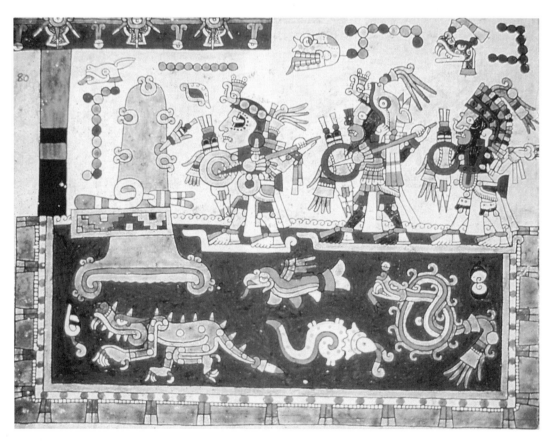

Do you think this artist was interested in showing you the warriors' environment? What makes you think so? *Warrior Leaders Canoe on Lake*, Pre-Columbian, Mixtec. Courtesy Ronald Sheridan/Ancient Art and Architecture Collection, London.

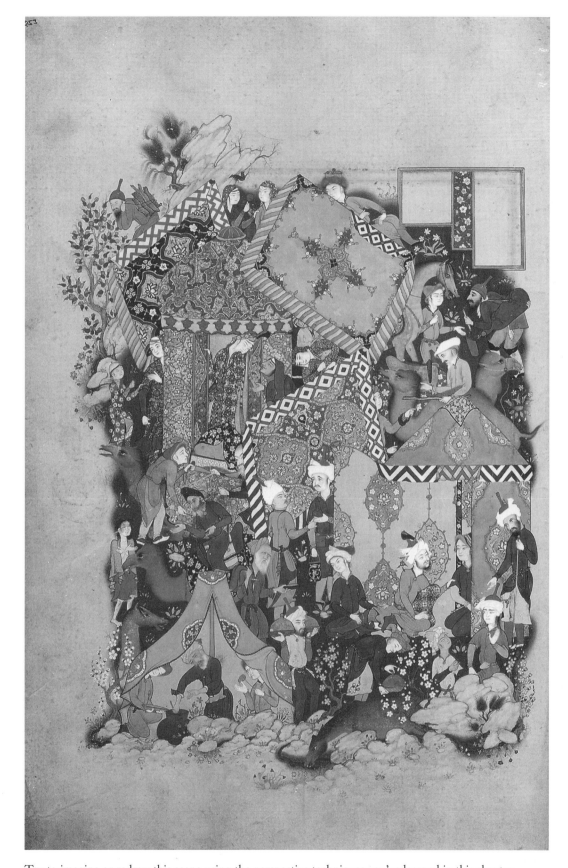

Design Extension
Students may create a collage to indicate depth. They should cut photographs and textures from magazines and arrange them on a paper to create an illusion of depth.

Try to imagine or redraw this scene using the perspective techniques you've learned in this chapter. What would be visible? *Persian Manuscript Illumination*. Courtesy of the Freer Gallery of Art, Smithsonian Institution, Washington, D.C. 46.12–253b.

Landscape

Design Extension
Encourage students to study the fine detail in Dürer's *The piece of turf* on page 202. Students may make a similar drawing by cutting a hole about the size of a playing card in a piece of cardboard and setting this view-finder right over their "piece of turf." They may draw just what they see in the frame.

Interdisciplinary Connection
Biology—In a sketchbook or journal students may draw and describe a small ecological community such as a square yard under a tree. They should sketch the plants in this area regularly over the course of the school year to record their changes.

Extension
Examples of van Gogh's work appear on pages 63, 80, and 206. Sometimes his art was quiet and calm, but at other times it vibrated with swirling lines and brilliant colors. Find other works by van Gogh and compare the tranquillity and energy to the ones in the book.

In art, the natural world can be your greatest source for visual information. Nature provides an incredible range of forms, patterns, textures and designs to explore in drawing. Go for a walk and look around. Collect ideas and items that are visually interesting. Take advantage of what nature has to offer. Studying individual forms, like rocks, twigs, leaves and flowers, will expand your visual vocabulary.

Before you attempt to draw a landscape on a large scale, try drawing close-ups of different objects in nature. Experiment drawing found objects; use a wide variety of media. Each object has its own unique sense of design, texture and shape. Observe the object and select a medium which best captures the essence of the form. Pay attention to

developing marks that carve out or reflect the texture and structure of the object. Draw the object from several viewpoints to better explore the structure.

For a more interesting composition, be creative with the angle of placement of the object. Change the scale of the objects in the drawings, and vary the amount of refinement in different areas within a drawing. How can you add interest to your compositions?

THINK ABOUT IT
Drawing objects in the natural environment sharpens your powers of observation and strengthens your ability to compare and contrast objects.

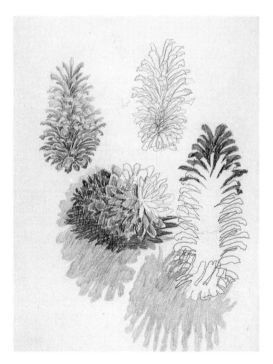

Studying and drawing small natural forms at close range is good practice. Try to capture the object from many different points of view.

Speaking of Art …

Van Gogh produced a prodigious amount—10,000 drawings and paintings in nine years. At one point in his career, van Gogh showed a change in perception and an enhancement of line and color. Historians now believe that the change in style was partly the result of illness. Dr. Shahram Khoshbin, a neurologist and art authority at Harvard University, studied van Gogh's medical records and concluded that he had epilepsy. Dr. Khoshbin found that his own patients with epilepsy have told him that before a seizure, everything becomes detailed and clear. Van Gogh wrote and talked about this heightened perception.

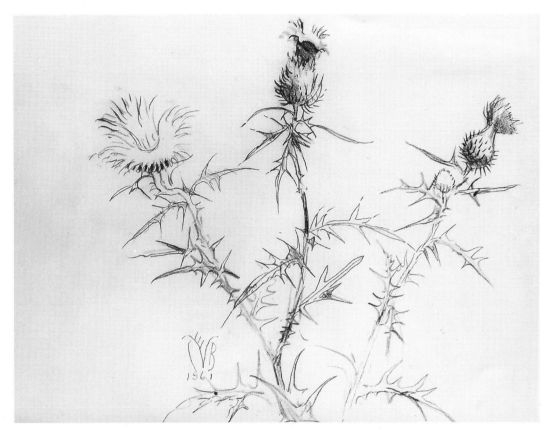

Line, stroke and tone are visible in this sketch. Can you see how creating a detailed drawing of a thistle might help you draw a whole field of thistles in a larger landscape? Charles Burchfield, *Study of Thistle*, 1961. Crayon, 13 1/4" x 18 7/8" (33.7 x 47.9 cm). Collection of Whitney Museum of American Art, New York.

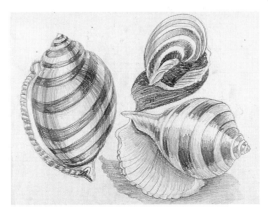

The shapes and textures of shells have fascinated artists for centuries. As you practice drawing objects, think: How are these shapes like other shapes I've seen? What do these shapes remind me of? What do they mean to me?

After you have drawn objects close up, begin looking at the entire landscape, from the ground to the sky. What do you see? How could you interpret what you see in a landscape drawing? What makes the landscape so compelling that you want to draw it?

The basic structure of a landscape composition consists of the foreground, middle ground and background. The relationships among the sky, earth and foliage are established by these sections.

To develop harmony in landscape, the artist must use the basic principles of design. One key to a successful composi-

Extensions
• See Watteau's *Study of a Tree in a Landscape* on page 203. Point out how he has emphasized the foreground with darker values, details, and size and created a very light, indistinct background.

• Demonstrate how to emphasize one part of a landscape as described in the Shifting Intensity activity on page 113. This activity could be a sketchbook assignment.

• To introduce the variety in landscape drawing, display slides of landscapes by artists from different centuries and cultures.

Higher-Order Thinking Skills
Ask students: from what viewpoint was the Wyeth image taken? What is in the foreground, middle ground, and background of the landscapes on pages 98 and 99? How has each artist added interest to the landscapes?

tion is variation. Vary the shapes, sizes, textures and values in the drawing so the landscape will gain strength and interest.

Drama in a landscape is created through the use of conflict and variety. Conflict is created in many ways. Placing extremely different textures or values next to one another is one way to create conflict. Approaching the composition from a unique angle or point of view will add excitement to the composition. Andrew Wyeth often deals with ordinary subject matter from a fresh angle. This gives his work strength and interest.

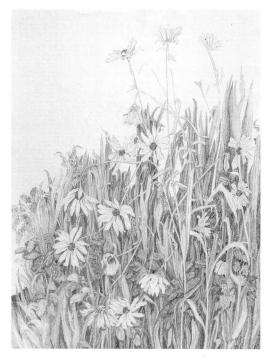

How has this artist used value to create depth and texture? Student work by Angie Evans, Gulfport, Mississippi.

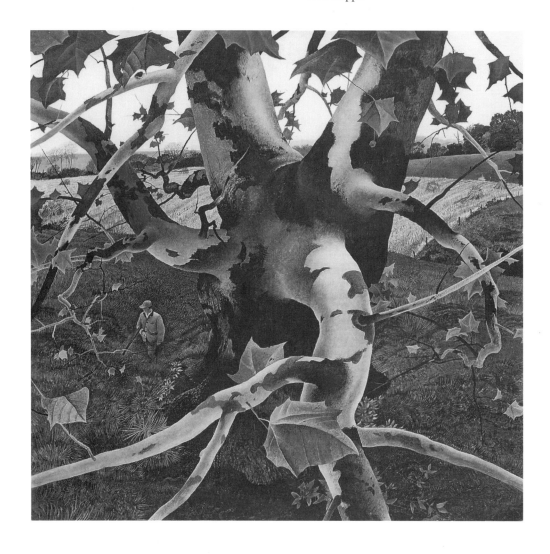

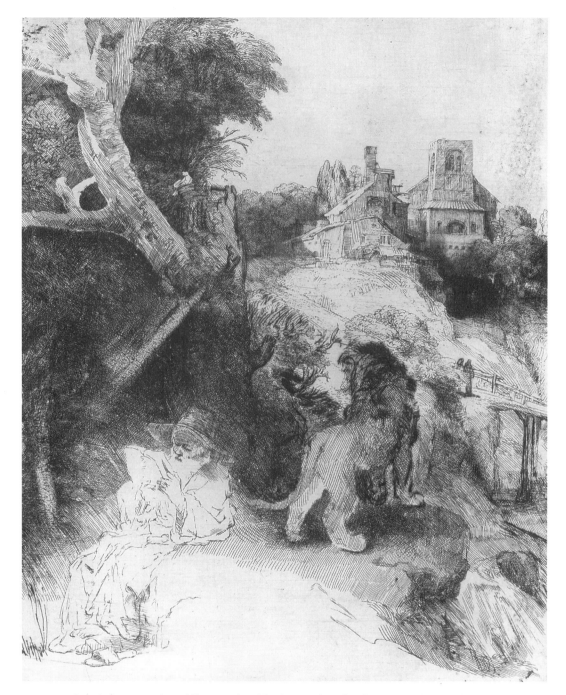

Can you identify foreground, middleground and background in this drawing? Where is the most detail visible? The least? Rembrandt Harmensz van Rijn, *Saint Jerome in Italian Landscape*, 1653. Etching and drypoint, 10 1/4" x 8 1/4" (26 x 21 cm). Courtesy Los Angeles County Museum of Art.

One way to create drama in a work of art is to choose an unusual point of view. Whose might be represented here? Andrew Newell Wyeth, *The Hunter*, 1943. Tempera on panel, 33" x 33 7/8" (83.8 x 86 cm). Courtesy The Toledo Museum of Art. Elizabeth C. Mau Bequest Fund. 46.25.

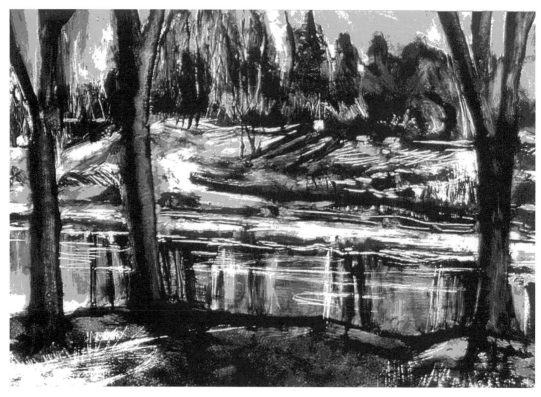

Strong, dark lines that move in different directions give this drawing drama. Why do you think the artist chose to show this scene? Student work by Anthony Balistreri, Milwaukee, Wisconsin.

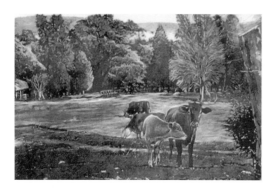

Notice the variety of textures in this work. Can you find the focal point? Thomas Riesing, *Cows*, 1991. Charcoal on paper, 27 1/2" x 39" (69.9 x 99.1 cm). Courtesy of the artist.

Here are some points that can help you plan the composition of a landscape.

1. Select a dynamic angle that captures the strength of the landscape.

2. Look for strong directional lines to accent the composition. Use variation within shapes to hold the viewer's atten- tion.

3. Make sure elements, such as color, shape, size, value and texture have sufficient contrast to create interest.

4. Work to achieve harmony and unity in the composition. Unity can be estab- lished by using dominance in shape, color or size. Dominance helps to develop an area of emphasis as well.

A powerful landscape is based on the principles of design. Your personal response to the natural environment is no less important. Use the principles of design to help you interpret what you see and feel.

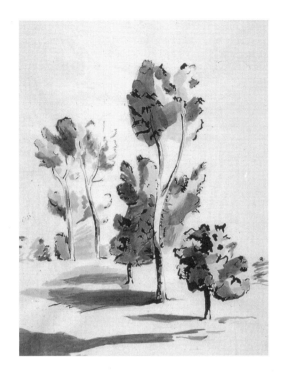

Sometimes a few simple lines and washes communicate your feelings about a scene more effectively than a lot of painstaking detail. Student work by Kirk Lieb, Akron, Ohio.

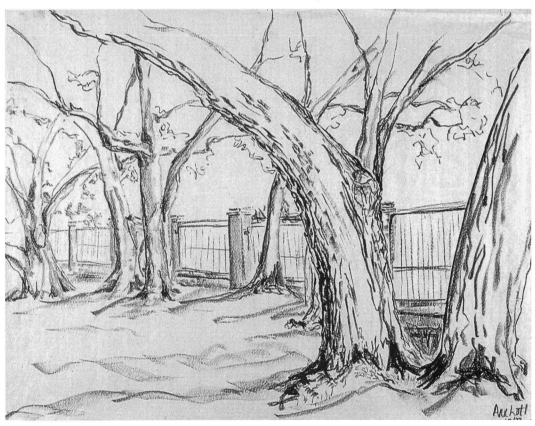

This artist's lively use of line gives a stand of trees personality and presence. Student work by Ann Lott, Gulfport, Mississippi.

Urban Environment

Teaching Tip

Urban landscapes may
be more easily drawn
as details, instead of the
more broad view of a
landscape in nature.
Closer views encourage
scrutiny of detail. Urban
landscapes may include
cotton gins, feed towers,
or other elements of
industry. One popular
landscape may be the
mall.

An urban landscape is based on elements in our human-made environment. In our surrounding world, it is difficult to turn around and not see highways, buildings, planes, cars or other influences of people.

In the 1930s, Charles Sheeler began capturing unique aspects of our industrial environment by developing close-up views of steam engines, machinery and buildings. His compositions emphasized strong design qualities from refreshingly different points of view.

Spend time walking around the manu-factured environment to explore all the various possibilities you can use in a com-position. Urban environments are full of visual interest. Junkyards, docks, bicycles, fire escapes, fences, cars, trucks, gasoline stations and diners are just a few possibil-ities you can explore.

Look for areas in the urban environ-ment that have visual complexities that create interest. Search out compositions that are refreshingly different and chal-lenging.

How does a deserted street look in early morning? at night? Study the urban environment you want to draw during different times of the day. Notice how changes in light throw different areas into shadow. How do shadows play on walls of buildings and streets at a corner or an intersection?

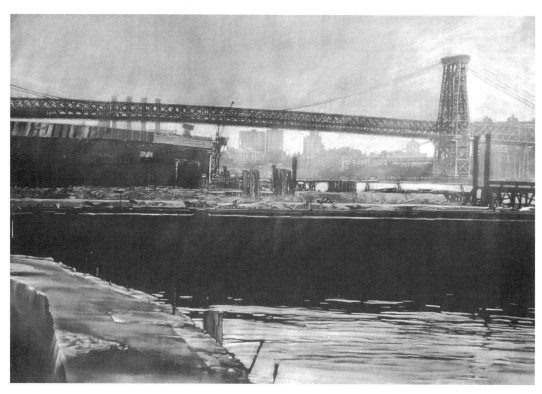

How has the artist shown you that some buildings are in the far distance here? Thomas Riesing, *Williamsburg Bridge, East River*. Charcoal on paper, 42 1/2" x 62" (108 x 157.5 cm). Courtesy of the artist.

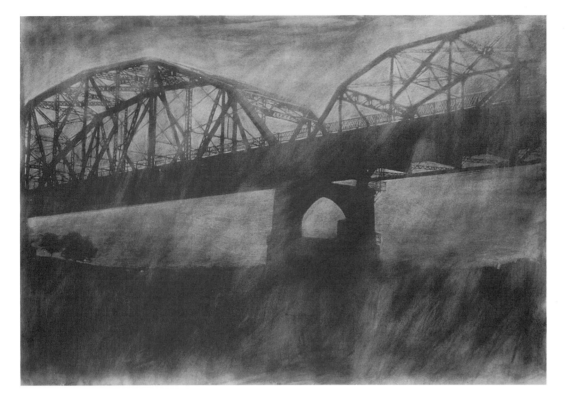

Try showing your urban landscape at several times of the year, in bad weather, at dusk or midnight. Thomas Riesing, *View From NE: Alcoa Highway Bridge*, 1985. Charcoal on paper, 42 1/2" x 62" (108 x 157.5 cm). Courtesy of the artist.

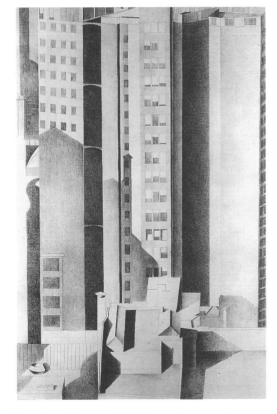

In spite of the use of shadows and perspective, these buildings look flat. What creates that effect? Do you think that's what the artist intended? Charles Sheeler, *New York*, 1920. Pencil, 19.9" x 13" (50.5 x 33 cm). Courtesy The Art Institute of Chicago.

At the same time, look for atmospheric qualities that may add interest to your subject matter. Fog, rain, snow or darkness can often provide intrigue and character.

THINK ABOUT IT
Before you can interpret and evaluate something, you first need to see it.

Design Extension
Encourage students to
draw freeway and high-
way overpasses from a
safe viewpoint. Usually
these are composed
of many interesting
negative spaces.

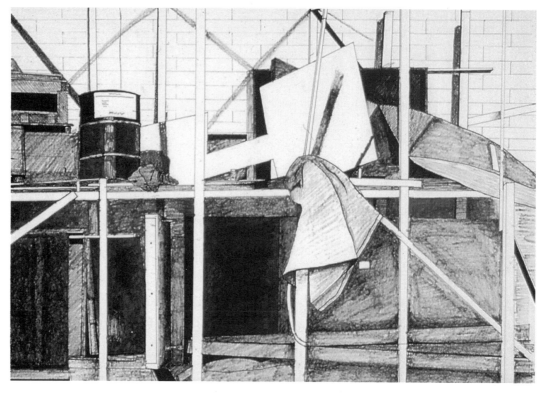

Can you find a repeated pattern here? How does it help unify this composition? Student work by Todd Alcorn, Delta, Ohio.

Use a viewfinder to
find compositions
that other people
might not notice.
Sometimes objects
that are damaged or
rusty have more visu-
al interest than those
that are intact.
Student work by
Christopher
Borkowski, Parma,
Ohio.

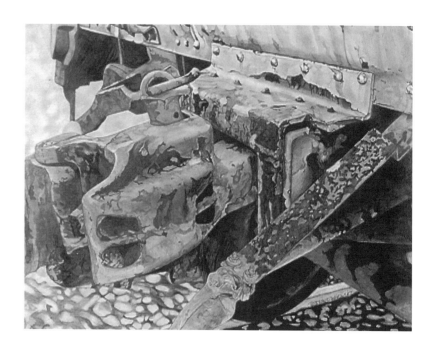

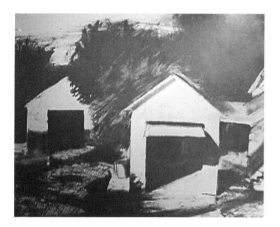

Try to look at the scenes around you with new eyes, even though you see them every day. Does your neighborhood look exactly the same in the morning as it does in the afternoon? Student work by Ron Milhoan, Knoxville, Tennessee.

Inquiry
The Ash Can School was a group of American artists who specialized in painting realistic urban scenes during the very early years of the twentieth century. Robert Henri, William Glackens, George Luks, John Sloan, and George Bellows were part of this group who rebelled against academic art and painted real scenes of city life. Assign students to research one of these artists and then share information about his life and art with the class.

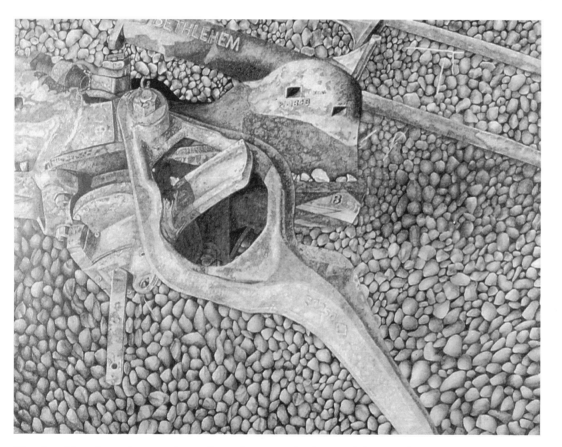

How has this artist made unusual use of negative space? Student work by Janet Zavodsky, Parma, Ohio.

Robert Cottingham
grew up in Brooklyn.
One of his most exciting
childhood memories
was his first visit to
Times Square. He is
best known for his
paintings and prints of
city storefronts, signs,
movie marquees, and
even a monumental
alphabet. He isolates
words, letters, and sym-
bols from their original
meanings as he
simplifies his subjects
into their essential com-
positions of shapes and
bold color. For more
information about
Robert Cottingham's
Photo-Realism, students
should read pages 224
and 225.

Always look for subject matter you can respond to in the drawing. Your personal interest in the subject matter always makes the drawing more exciting and will be reflected in the end product.

Here are a few suggestions to help you draw the urban environment.

1. Select an environment that provides the best view and strong relationships among the foreground, middle ground and background.

2. Develop exciting, unusual angles and perspectives of the subject matter.

3. Emphasize directional movement and rhythm within the composition.

4. Lay in large areas of shapes and lightly capture the essence of the whole composition.

5. Build up areas of darks, gradually solidifying the shapes and shadows.

6. Use atmospheric perspective. (*Atmospheric perspective* is the illusion, produced in drawing or painting, that objects farther away from the viewer are hazier and less distinct than objects close up.) You can create atmospheric perspective by fading forms and softening their edges as they recede in space.

7. Give forms in the foreground stronger contrast. Use crisper, sharper edges and colors.

8. Develop a strong sense of lighting. Make sure the shadows reinforce the forms.

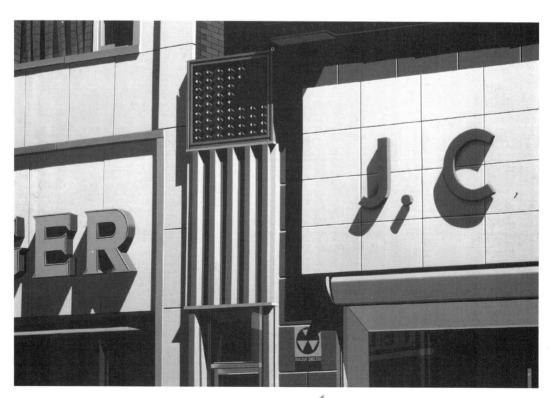

Above and opposite: In the drawing of this scene, the artist uses hatching and crosshatching to create shadows and define forms. The painting uses flat areas of color. The painting's edges are much sharper than those in the drawing. Which medium do you think works best to give you the "flavor" of a city street? Why? Opposite: Robert Cottingham, *J.C.*, 1982. Graphite on Vellum, 13" x 20" (33 x 50.8 cm). Above: Robert Cottingham, *J.C.*, 1982. Acrylic on canvas, 21" x 31" (53.3 x 78.7 cm). Both works courtesy of the artist.

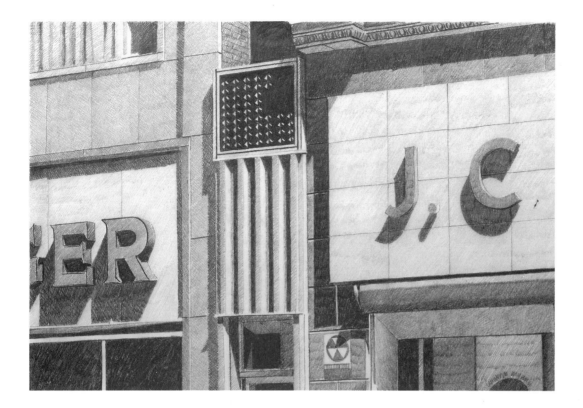

Design Extension
Encourage students to
draw a close-up detail
of a sign associated with
a building. Suggest that
they crop their subject,
filling the picture frame
as Cottingham did.

Extension
For an unusual view of
a scene students may
look down on a subject
from an upper story of
a building.

Be sensitive to capturing the time of
day, blowing wind, season of the year or
other elements of nature which can create
interest in the composition. Working
early in the morning or late in the
evening will provide the best long shadows and richest colors. Remember to
work for an unusual point of view in the
composition. Try using a stepladder or
get low on the ground to find a different
point of view. Select a view that offers
freshness and vitality.

Reflections

Extensions
• Display photographs or slides that contain reflections. Discuss how polarization of light affects reflections in nature. Point out that reflections can emphasize distortion.

• Notice how important reflections are in the Photo-Realism art on pages 224 and 225.

Design Extension
As a sketchbook assignment students may draw some of the reflective surfaces suggested in the second column on this page.

Context
For another drawing by Seurat, see page 205. Georges Seurat is best known for his Pointillism paintings composed with a myriad of tiny dots of color. However, he preceded each of these major works with a series of drawings of his subject.

Reflections can be intriguing to work with in a drawing. Recording the visual information found in reflections requires a lot of investigation and observation.

To understand how to handle reflections, set up a still life that includes a mirror as well as some drapery or household objects. Look closely at the edges of the actual objects. Are the edges of the reflected objects different? Are there other differences between the objects and their reflections? Develop the reflective qualities by using high contrast in darks and lights.

After working successfully with mirrors, try other subject matter to expand your drawing vocabulary with reflections.

By exploring other reflective surfaces, you can come up with some innovative compositions. Some possibilities in subject matter are:
1. chrome bumpers,
2. musical instruments (saxophones, tubas, etc.),
3. sheets of mylar,
4. drinking glasses, vases and glass containers filled with water (incorporate objects in and out of the water),
5. kitchen utensils and aluminum pots and pans,
6. streams or lakes,
7. side-view mirrors on cars or trucks,
8. glass windows or doors,
9. highly polished surfaces, such as stone, bronze or steel.

Reflections don't always have to be detailed or completely realistic. Could you tell that this was a river bank before you read the title? Georges Seurat, *Bords de rivière (Banks of the river)*, 1883–1884. Conté crayon, 8.8" x 11.9" (22.4 x 30.2 cm). Private Collection. Courtesy Art Resource, NY.

Mary Cassatt

1844–1926

When Mary Stevenson Cassatt told her father that she wished to become a painter, he responded that he would rather see her dead. To Mr. Cassatt, a respected Philadelphia banker, painting was not an occupation that even a sensible man would consider as a life work. Mary, however, managed to convince her father, and at the age of seventeen she was admitted to the Philadelphia Art Academy.

Shortly after graduating from the Art Academy, she moved to Paris, where she copied her favorite masterpieces at the museums and made sketching trips to the country. She admired many Renaissance and Baroque painters, but it was the works of Impressionists such as Edgar Degas that had the strongest influence on her.

Cassatt had a special interest in painting women and children. The majority of her work shows women at leisure or engaged with their children. Her subjects always appear natural and absorbed in their activities. By capturing the private moments between a mother and child, she managed to reveal the beauty of domestic life.

Although Mary Cassatt is best known for her oil paintings, she left behind many exceptional drawings and prints. As a painter of people, she always sought perfection in her figure drawing and tried different exercises to improve it. Said one biographer, "She was not satisfied to draw with a pencil. Instead, she chose to use metal and steel point so that the plate could hold every trace of her mistakes and corrections." This method, which required tremendous self-discipline and effort, allowed Mary Cassatt to achieve the beautiful line she desired.

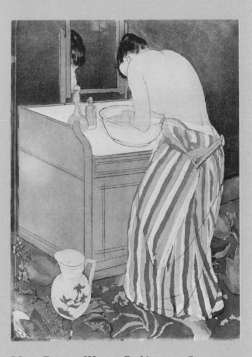

Mary Cassatt, *Woman Bathing*, ca. 1891. Drypoint and aquatint in color, 14 5/16" x 10 9/16" (36.4 x 26.8 cm). Courtesy the Metropolitan Museum of Art, Gift of Paul J. Sachs, 1916. (16.2.2).

Context

• After viewing a huge exhibition of Japanese *ukiyo-e* prints in 1890, Mary Cassatt was inspired to create her own series of prints showing women in their domestic routines. Her work is similar to that of Japanese artist Kitagawa Utamaro (1753–1806). Both Cassatt and Utamaro often depict women in everyday activities, such as arranging their hair. Bring Japanese prints to class so that students may discover the similarities between Cassatt's work and the Japanese art.

• See one of Mary Cassatt's prints of a mother and child on page 207.

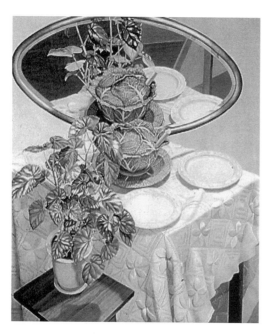

Look carefully at reflections. Do the objects'
reflections look just like the objects themselves?
Sondra Freckleton, *Mirror Image*, 1992.
Watercolor, 46" x 38 3/4" (116.8 x 98.4 cm).
Courtesy of the artist.

Artists like Richard Estes, Janet Fish and
Charles Bell have created some intriguing
compositions using reflections. Richard
Estes generally uses the highly polished
surfaces and windows found in New York
City as a point of development for his
compositions. Janet Fish's still lifes often
incorporate glasses or glass containers
that capture the unusual qualities of
reflective light (See chapter 3.). Charles
Bell's work explores the reflective qualities found in pinball machines and mar-
bles.

Look at reflections as a valuable learning experience. They provide challenges
and a way to increase your drawing skills.

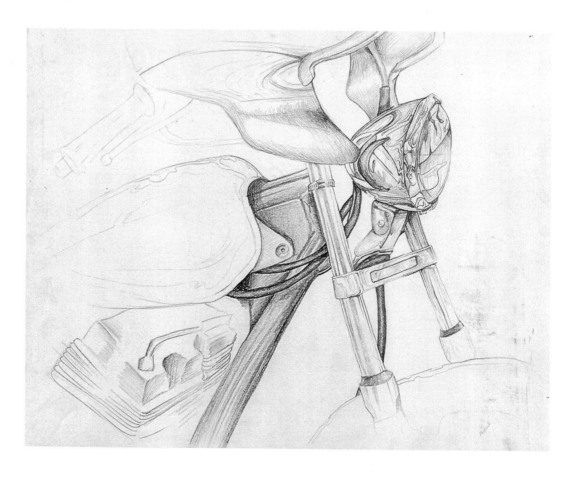

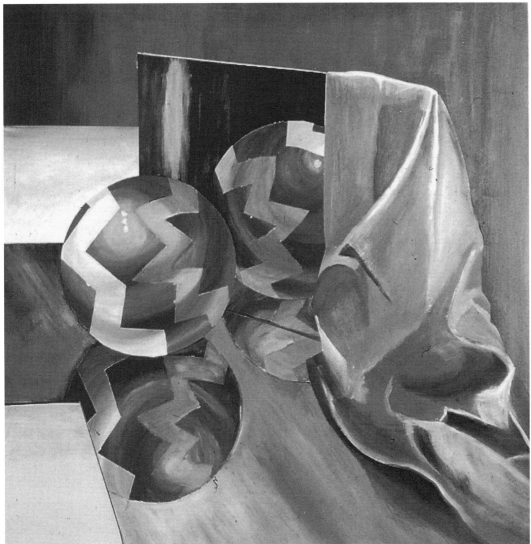

Interdisciplinary Connection

Physics—Polarized light is composed of orderly arranged light waves, as compared to regular light with waves going in many directions. Light may become polarized as it passes through filters, such as water and other reflective surfaces. This is one reason why reflections are sometimes slightly darker than the original subject. Have students research polarization and the reflection of light waves in a physics textbook.

Multiple reflections allow you to challenge the viewer: Which is the object and which is the reflection? Student work by Chad Brown, Memphis, Tennessee.

Bicycle reflections are a good subject for drawings, especially since there is usually one around to look at. Student work by Michael Adkins, Abilene, Texas.

Summary

Higher-Order Thinking Skills
Challenge students to compare the mood created in the drawings of the vehicles on pages 38, 225, and 234. What is each artist saying about this piece of transportation? How does the artist's style affect the message?

This chapter has introduced you to a wide range of drawing skills and possibilities for compositional exploration. You have learned to successfully incorporate perspective into your drawings. You have also gained experience in working with objects found in nature. This investigation has given you a chance to confront various textures, shapes and structures that nature so richly provides.

By building upon these experiences you have learned how to approach drawing landscapes and our urban environment.

As an artist, you need to challenge yourself constantly to grow and explore new directions in drawing. Working with a diverse range of subject matter will increase your ability to think visually. Handling a variety of subject mater, techniques and compositions will promote your drawing skills.

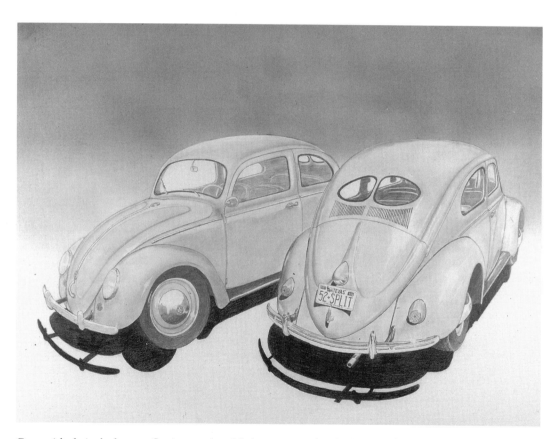

Cars, with their shadows, reflections and molded curves, can be challenging subject matter for drawings. Try contrasting a clean vehicle with a dusty or muddy one, or imagine the view from above or from underneath. What personalities do cars have? Student work by Humberto Pina, Goodrich, Texas.

Activities

Shifting Intensity
Draw a small landscape with a clear foreground, middleground and background. In this first drawing, use value contrasts to emphasize the foreground. Draw the same landscape two more times, emphasizing middleground in the second drawing and background in the third. Compare the three drawings. Which is most effective? Can you say why?

Analyzing Landscapes
Find a variety of landscape paintings, drawings and photographs from magazines, newspapers and other sources (cards or postcards from museums, advertising supplements, old books that can be cut up). Try to find as many as twelve different examples. Bring them into class and discuss them with your classmates. Which landscapes show romantic views of nature? Which show nature realistically? When people appear in them, are they shown large, as if they are important, or very small in relation to natural forms? How many different styles of landscape could you find?

Cars With Attitudes
Contour drawings of cars can be used as the basis for a series of drawings and abstractions.

First, make a contour drawing of a car. Color the drawing with felt-tip pens, colored pencils or watercolors. Now think carefully about the car. Is it fast, slow, hot, a wreck, stodgy? Write a description of the car. What is its attitude?

Draw and paint the car again, but change it to show its atttitude. Exaggerate features, show several sides or views at the same time. Distort it. Abstract it so that it is recognizable as a car, but not completely realistic.

In a third drawing, just show the mood of the car. The drawing should be nonobjective, so the viewer should not actually be able to see a car in the drawing. Think: What kinds of lines would you use to show speed? What lines would suggest a junkyard car? An old, beaten-up truck?

Creating Texture with Colored Pencils
Use colored pencils to create texture in a landscape or cityscape. Colored pencils allow you to "layer" colors to produce complex blendings. Experiment with letting the pencil strokes show, instead of blending the soft colors together

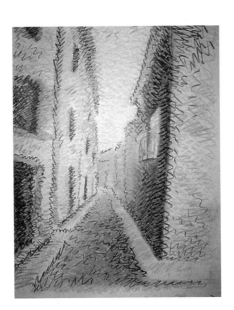

Student work by Stephen Doyle.

to create a smooth surface. Explore the uses of value and shading as you create texture. see pages 162 and 164

A Furnished Room
Use a large sheet of drawing paper and a pencil. Using two vanishing points, draw a room that is open to the viewer. Furnish it with at least ten objects that are also drawn in perspective. This room may be a kitchen, a spaceship, your dream bedroom, an office or a living room. Some ideas for objects are furniture such as beds, chairs, tables, televisions and bookshelves. You may add windows, rugs, books, wall posters—whatever you'd like to see in a room.

Usually this project works best if you draw a transparent box very lightly first. Plan your furnishings first on tracing paper.

Ant's View
On a piece of illustration board, with pen and ink or marker, draw a room from an ant's view. This room might be the artroom, the cafeteria or the gymnasium. Get down low on the floor with a viewfinder to find an interesting composition. Think like an ant. What looks big? What is little? What is dangerous? With a pencil, plan out your composition on paper first. If you go to another part of the school, you might photograph your view, to help you when you cannot get to that spot.

Chapter 5
Anatomy and the Figure

Objectives
Students will be able to:
- Create gesture, contour, and negative shape drawings of human figures in a variety of media. (Art production)
- Draw figures with lifelike human proportions. (Art production)
- Demonstrate an understanding of skeletal anatomy in their figure drawings. (Art production)
- Create portraits and self-portraits that indicate an understanding of human facial proportions. (Art production)
- Create figurative compositions which bear evidence of thoughtful placement of figures in relation to other objects within the piece of art. (Art criticism/Art production)
- Perceive and appreciate figure and portrait drawings by various artists including Philip Pearlstein. (Art history/Aesthetics)
- Understand that portraits may capture not only a person's likeness but also the person's emotions. (Aesthetics)

Vocabulary
gesture drawing
contour drawing
proportions
outline

Chapter Overview
This chapter introduces students to figure drawing. Students explore the skeleton to gain a basic understanding of human anatomy and proportion. Next, students approach the figure through gesture, contour, and full figure drawing. The chapter concludes by helping students understand how to approach portrait drawing.

Lesson 1
pages 114–119   45 minutes

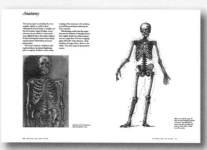

pages 116–117

Teach
Using a skeleton—either one borrowed from the biology department or the illustrations of a skeleton on pages 117 and 118—point out significant features about the skeletal anatomy. For example, call attention to the zygomatic arch, or cheekbone, on both the skeleton and then someone's face. Note how deep the eye sockets are and that they are located in the middle of the skull, not the forehead. Count how many vertebrae are in the neck. Notice how thin the clavicle or collar bone is. Who in the class has broken their collar bone? How do the scapulae (shoulder blades) connect to the humerus (long bone in the upper arm)? Note that the elbow joint is about at the waist or just above the pelvic bone. Comment on how many bones and joints are in the hand and how much movement this allows.

Studio Experience
On sheets of brown wrapping paper that are slightly larger than the height of the students, have students sketch the skeleton. Use pencil first to establish the proportions, then sketch with black charcoal and white chalk to model and shade the bones. (See the Cooperative Learning suggestion on page 117.)

Materials
brown wrapping paper, about 6'
   per student
white chalk
black charcoal
pencil
eraser
fixative

Lesson 2
pages 120–123   45 minutes

Teach
Explain that many artists begin a figure drawing by capturing the overall movement of their subject with a light gesture drawing and then gradually adding more details. The quick gesture drawing helps the artist draw figures that seem more animated or less stiff.

Studio Experience
Allow students to use a variety of drawing media such as those on page 121 to create a series of gesture drawings. Students should take turns posing. They should be clearly visible to the whole class. Poses should be brief, lasting only thirty to sixty seconds. Suggest

stop-action poses from activities that the students know well such as gymnastics, sports, and dance. You might include props such as hockey sticks and baseball bats. Have the models face a different direction in each pose so that each student artist will have an opportunity to draw a variety of views.

After students have caught on to this technique, have two students pose in interactive positions such as playing London Bridge or ballroom dancing. The folds in the student models' clothes will indicate the underlying body structure and movement. Point these out as students begin to draw.

Materials
various drawing media such as charcoal, pencils, markers, and crayons
18" x 24" newsprint paper, 6 to 10 sheets per student

Lesson 3
pages 124–127   45 minutes

Teach
After students have viewed the drawings on these pages, lead them in creating a series of contour drawings. Explain that contour shows bulk and form while outline only shows the outside edges of an object or figure.

Studio Experience
Demonstrate how to create a blind contour drawing by looking only at the subject that you are drawing, not the paper, and keeping the pencil on the paper for the whole

drawing. Students might begin by drawing several views of their own hand before beginning full figure contour drawings. Be sure the whole class can clearly see the student models. Have the models stand, sit, and lie down, facing a different direction for each 5- to 10-minute pose.

Remind students that this is not a race. Usually the most interesting blind contours are those where the artist has taken the time to notice every lump, bump, wrinkle, and fold in the subject.

Materials
18" x 24" newsprint or drawing paper
drawing media such as markers, pencils, or charcoal pencils

Lesson 4
pages 128–129   45 minutes

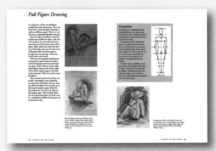

pages 128–129

Teach
• Introduce students to body proportions by calling their attention to where various body parts are in relationship to each other. Note that the elbow is near the waist, the wrist at the top of the legs, and fingertips in the middle of the thigh. The hand is about the size of the face.

• Pose a student in a spot where everyone can see him or her. Demonstrate how to measure the size of the head by sighting with a pencil. With one eye locate the top of the pencil at the top of the model's head and your thumb at the model's chin. Using that measurement, count how many heads tall the body is. Note that the waist is usually three heads down. Refer students to the drawing on page 129. As the class takes their own measures, compare how many heads each student finds the model to be. Emphasize that the head measurement begins at the top of the skull, not the top of the hair. Often hair stands up inches above the skull.

Studio Experience
Stand a student model on a table or other place where the whole class can easily see the entire figure. Students should lightly sketch the figure, marking the proportions as in the diagram on page 129. Repeat this process with several different student models.

Materials
charcoal pencil or pencil
18" x 24" newsprint or drawing paper
erasers

Studio Experience
After students have read page 128, lead them in drawing the positive spaces in several seated student poses. Then have students reverse the process by drawing the nega-

tive spaces in a series of poses. Finally, concentrating on both the positive and negative space, have them draw a figure. Encourage students to use viewfinders to locate the negative spaces between the figures and the edge of the composition.

Materials
charcoal
18" x 24" newsprint or drawing
  paper

Lesson 5
pages 130–133   45 minutes

Teach
Explain that in this lesson students will focus on drawing hands and feet, details which are sometimes passed over in quick sketches. Direct students' attention to the studies on these pages.

Studio Experience
Guide students in drawing a series of blind (not looking at the paper while drawing) and modified blind (peeking at the paper every once in a while) contour drawings. They may wish to add shading and contouring as in the student drawings on pages 130 and 131.

After they have completed the hand drawing, encourage them to take off their shoes to draw views of their feet.

Materials
charcoal or pencil
18" x 24" newsprint or drawing
  paper

Lesson 6
pages 134–137   45 minutes

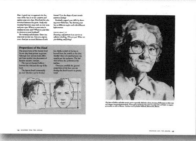
pages 134–135

Teach
• Teach students to measure facial proportions on themselves and other students. They should note that there is the same distance from the middle of the eyes to the top of the skull as from the bottom of the chin to the middle of the eyes. Point out where the nose is in relation to the eyebrows and mouth.

• While looking at a student model lead the class in creating a diagram similar to the one on page 134. Demonstrate drawing a three-quarter view as in the portrait on page 135.

Studio Experience
Shine a spotlight on a student model's face so that one half of the face is in shadow. Students should create a series of 10- to 15-minute sketches. Begin with shorter time lengths and gradually extend the length of each pose. Students should quickly sketch in the whole face, checking the proportions, and then add the details. After each pose, have the artists move over one or two places to get a different view. (This is usually

easier than changing the spotlight and having the model face a different direction for each pose. It also breaks the monotony of repeating a similar activity, provides students with a chance to back away from their drawings to check proportions, and lets them notice other students' work.)

Materials
charcoal or sanguine conté crayon
18" x 24" newsprint, drawing
  paper, or charcoal paper
erasers

Lesson 7
pages 138–139   45 minutes

Teach
• Tell students to read the suggestions for self-portraits and study the examples on these pages before beginning the studio activity.

• Have students consider what props they might include in their self-portrait to give a clue to their personality.

Studio Experience
Provide each student with a mirror. Suggest that they turn their head slightly sideways instead of looking straight into the mirror. Arrange the lighting so that their faces have shadows. (You might use flashlights, spotlights, or even turn off the room lights so that the only source of light is from windows on one side of the room.) Each student should draw a self-portrait using charcoal, pencil, or conté crayon.

Materials

mirrors (These may be mirror tiles backed by cardboard; cover the edges with duct tape for safety.)

drawing media, such as pencils, charcoal, or sanguine conté crayon

18" x 24" drawing paper or charcoal paper

Lesson 8
pages 140–143   45 minutes

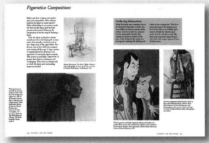

pages 140–141

Teach

• In each drawing on these pages note the lines that connect the figure to the edge of the composition. Call attention to the Giacometti drawing, which is similar to how students will begin their figurative compositions. Point out how Giacometti arranged his mother in a lattice of lines.

• Discuss the suggestions for using a system of organizational lines on page 142. Ask students to explain this concept of structural lines in their own words.

Studio Experience

Have students draw a figure in a setting, using a series of organizational lines to determine the placement of this figure in their composition. Students may draw themselves, friends, or family in a real or imaginary location. Suggest that they review the ways to indicate depth that they learned in Chapter 4.

Materials

drawing media, such as pencils, charcoal, conté crayon, or ink

18" x 24" paper (type will vary depending on media selected)

Lesson 9
pages 144–147   45 minutes

Reteach

• In a class discussion have students compare and contrast the images on pages 144 and 145. Discuss the mood, drawing technique, organizational lines, and other elements that contribute to each composition. Notice how the negative space is arranged in each of these drawings.

• Introduce one of the activities on page 147. Students may work together to complete a huge figure in the Drawing the Figure on a Grid activity. The Figure and Elements of Design activity would also provide a culminating project for figure drawing.

Assess

• Assign students to select their most successful gesture, contour, and negative space drawings of human figures, portraits, and self-portraits, as well as their figurative compositions, to include in their portfolio. Suggest that they place the drawings that they feel are most successful on top of the stack. Review the portfolios, checking for these areas:

—Is there evidence that students understand skeletal anatomy in their figure drawings? (Art production)

—Did students create gesture, contour, and negative drawings of human figures in a variety of media? (Art production)

—Check the portraits and self-portraits for realistic human facial proportions. (Art production)

—The figurative compositions should show evidence of thoughtful placement of figures in relation to other objects within the piece of art. (Art criticism/Art production)

—Are figures drawn with lifelike human proportions? (Art production)

• Reteach any areas of weakness or misunderstanding. Give students a chance to rework drawings.

• Review with students some of the figurative artists that they studied in this chapter. Ask them to write a description of one of their drawings, explaining how the artist captured not only the person's likeness but also the person's emotions. What do they appreciate about this particular piece of art? (Art history/Aesthetics)

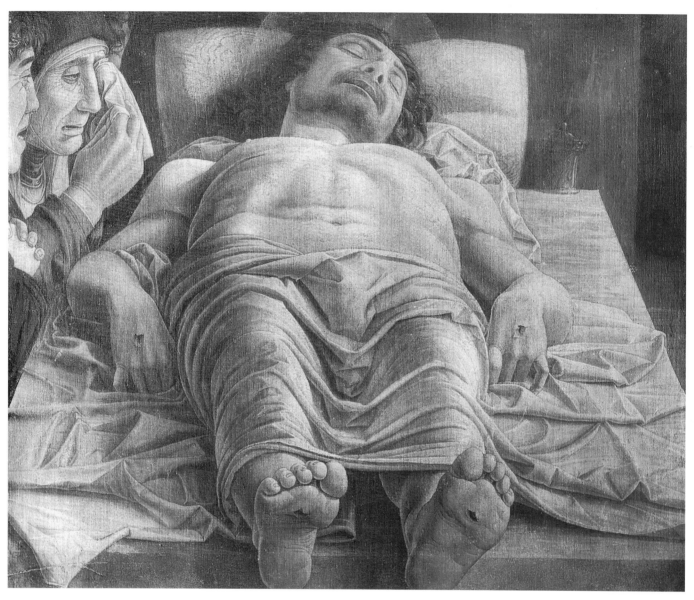

Foreshortening, discussed in Chapter 4, is an important skill to master in figure drawing. Try to see the shapes of the body as *shapes*, rather than as familiar forms like arms and legs. Can you imagine why the artist wanted to portray his subject from this angle? Mantegna, *The Dead Christ*, late fifteenth century. 26 3/4 x 21 7/8" (68 x 81 cm). Pinacoteca Dibrera, Milan, Italy. Courtesy Alinari/Art Resource, NY.

Chapter Warm-up

• Explain that in this chapter students will learn to draw figures in many different ways—from quick studies of the whole body to slow careful portraits. With students, look through the book to see the wide variety of styles used to draw the body.

• Call their attention to Mantegna's *The Dead Christ* and discuss the questions in the caption.

• Introduce the idea of bones and joints. Discuss how these affect the structure of the human body and conse-quently how it is drawn. Have everyone put their hands on their hips, noticing that their arms bend at the elbow joints. Draw two semicircles ( ) on the board. Explain that if our arms had bendable wire in them, they might look like this. (You can also demonstrate this using pipe cleaners or plastic-coated wire.) Draw two acute angles on the board. Explain to students that because our arms have joints, they are more like this < > than like semi-circles.

5 Anatomy and the Figure

This chapter introduces you to drawing figures and portraits. Drawing the human form is one of the most interesting and challenging tasks for an artist. Before you can draw a figure, you need an understanding of the structure of the human skeleton. You also need

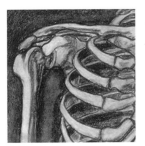

an understanding of proportions of the human form. In exercises that isolate specific body parts, you will learn the overall proportions of the human figure as well as sharpen your observational and drawing skills.

Human beings, of course, are more than just skeletons. Learning to capture the characteristics and emotions of a figure requires skill in observation and interpretation. In gesture drawing, you will learn how to draw quickly, with just a few lines, to capture a figure's general characteristics, form, weight and movement.

Contour drawing is a method that allows you to use line to explore both the outside and inside edges of a form. Several methods of contour drawing are presented in this chapter.

Once you have learned the basics of contour drawing, you will learn how line, stroke and tone can be used to draw a figure meaningfully and with speed.

Finally, you will learn to put all of the skills taught in this chapter together to draw portraits and figurative compositions. You will also learn how to arrange a figure within a composition.

Vocabulary
gesture drawing
contour drawing
proportions
outline

Extension
Foreshortening is defined on page 88. Salvador Dali's foreshortened *Christ in Perspective* on page 89 may be compared with Mantegna's foreshortened Christ. Challenge students to find the foreshortening in Michelangelo's figure on page 201.

Higher-Order Thinking Skills
Give students three minutes to write five words that come to mind when looking at *The Dead Christ*. Or, have students write a detailed description of it. Ask students: What are the most striking features of this image? How did Mantegna fit a human figure into a square shape? (by use of foreshortening) Did he draw the figure accurately? Was distortion his goal?

Key Chapter Points

- An understanding of the human skeleton and anatomy is the starting point for drawing a figure.
- Gesture drawing is a method of drawing simple lines to capture a figure and pose quickly.
- Contour drawing defines the edges of a form to suggest three dimensions.
- The human figure is proportional.
- A portrait captures both likeness and emotions.
- Placement of a figure and its relationship to other objects in the drawing must be carefully considered in developing the composition.

Anatomy

The human figure is probably the most complex subject on earth to draw. Although the human body is complex and has an awesome range of edges, curves and mass, do you think it is necessarily more *difficult* to draw than other subjects? Perhaps drawing the human form simply requires keener observation and more perseverance.

The body is built on a skeleton, making the skeleton the logical beginning point to explore. Without a clear understanding of the structure of the skeleton, you will have problems in drawing the body correctly.

The drawings on the next few pages illustrate the skeleton. Using light pencil lines, lightly sketch one entire composition on a large sheet of brown wrapping paper. Draw the entire skeleton—skull, vertebrae, rib cage, pelvis—down to the ankles. Take time to get the proportions correct.

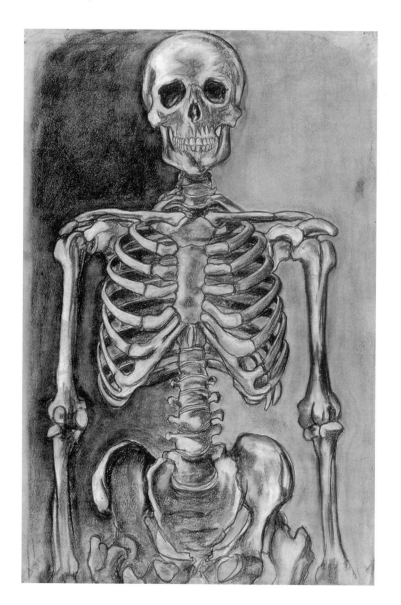

Student work by Humberto Pina, Goodrich, Texas.

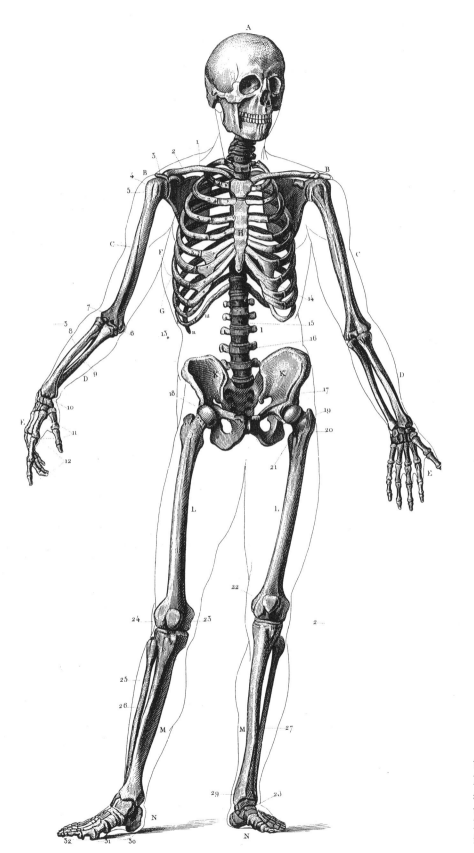

Stress that the parts of a body are proportional and best seen in a skeleton. If possible, borrow a skeleton from the science lab. Use string as a measuring tool to compare lengths of bones and proportions. For example, point out how the position of the jaw relates to the base of the brain.

Teaching Tip
Photocopy the skeleton drawings on these pages for your students to use as references and resources.

Cooperative Learning
Have students work in pairs. Have one student trace the outline of the other on a large sheet of paper to establish figure proportion. Then have the two students draw a skeleton inside the outline.

What is your body made of? How do your bones fit together and move? A careful look at what's beneath your skin will help you draw what's visible from the outside.

From the side you can
see how full and curved
the rib cage is, and how
the spine curves gently
as it moves from skull to
pelvis.

From the back you'll
notice the large plates
that form the shoulder
blades, and the bumpy
joints of elbows, shoul-
ders and spine.

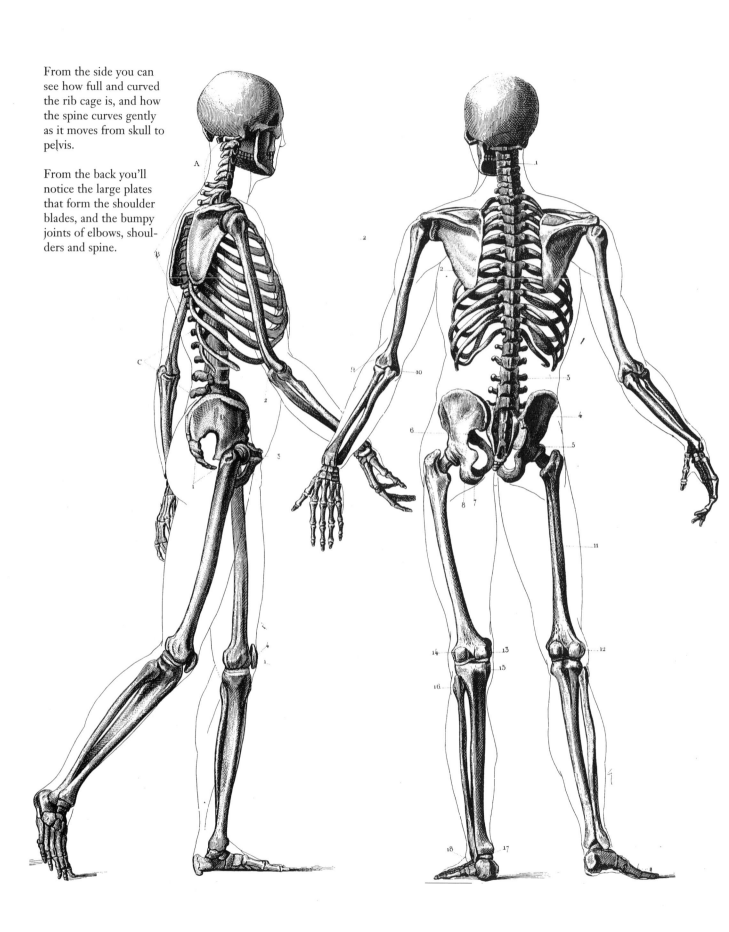

When you are satisfied with the whole image, use black charcoal and white chalk to develop the sketch. Develop sharp edges and high contrast on the bones that are closest to you. Use gray on bones that are farther away. Using a wide range of value and a variety of edges will give the skeleton a good sense of space and depth. You will also be creating a stronger sense of structure in your composition.

The skull is another good area to practice drawing. Use marks to develop and carve out the structure of the skull. Vary the edges to add interest. This practice will be of great benefit when you begin to draw figures and portraits.

THINK ABOUT IT

To better understand an object, you can observe it, describe it or illustrate it. Using all three methods may bring the best results.

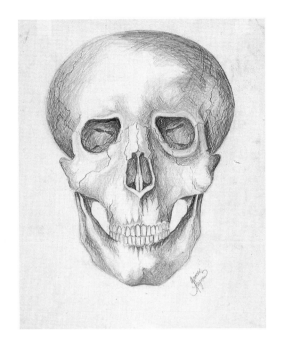

Student work by Geinene Haynes, Nashville, Tennessee.

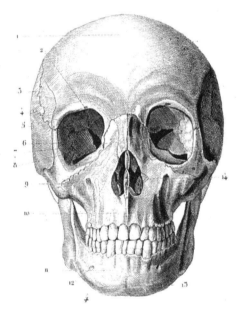

Notice how many teeth show in a skull, as opposed to a face covered with skin.

Gesture Drawing

Teaching Tip
Students may feel
uncomfortable initially
in drawing and posing
for each other. Allow
students some practice
sessions to get them
accustomed to looking
at each other.

**Interdisciplinary
Connection**
Physical Education—
Students may capture
the movements involved
in sports and exercise
with gesture drawings.
Visit a physical educa-
tion class to draw
subjects that are playing
and exercising.

Can you convey movement in a drawing? Suppose you wanted to draw someone jumping or running. How would you capture the movement of the figure? A quick sketch, or gesture drawing, can capture and express the sense of movement. Gesture drawing can do more than show movement. The goal of gesture drawing is to capture the figure's weight, mass and movement with a few lines. The drawings should contain a great deal of information with just a few sketchy lines.

Do not confuse gesture drawing with outlining or contour drawings. An outline shows the outer edges of a pose. Contour drawing shows the fullness of a form. Gesture drawing, however, refers to quickly drawn lines that define the basic characteristics of a pose. Use the following suggestions to experiment with gesture drawing. Try to complete your drawing in one or two minutes.

1. Don't try to be totally accurate. Just try to capture the overall sense of movement of the pose.

2. Draw quickly without first thinking how to draw. Just do it.

3. Don't deal only with edges of the figure. Work inside and outside the edges of the figure with rhythmic lines.

4. Look for lines that convey the weight of the figure.

5. Try to express the feeling of the pose.

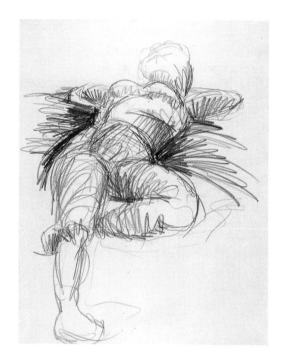

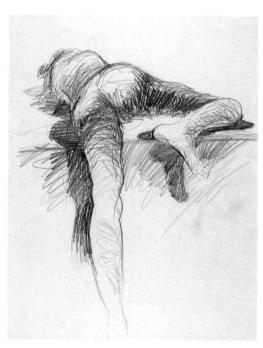

Gesture drawings use loose, casual strokes to capture a pose or an attitude. They're not intended to be realistic or completely accurate, but they should give the viewer a sense of what you see. Try to reveal movement or the amount of tension the body shows.

Newsprint Tablets

Newsprint tablets provide an economical paper for quick sketches and studies. Newsprint comes in smooth and slightly rough (toothed) textures. The newsprint with a tooth is better for charcoals, pastels and chalks. Carbon pencil does not usually make a very dark mark on newsprint. Felt-tip markers work well on newsprint, although they sometimes bleed through the paper. If this happens, tear a sheet from the tablet and use it as a blotter under each page as you draw.

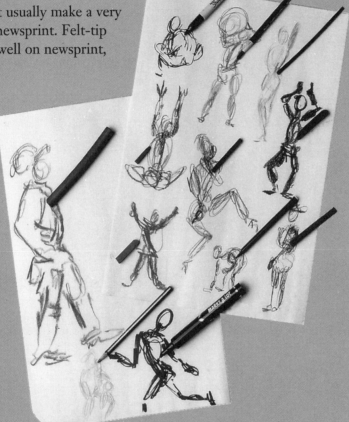

(lower sheet, counter-clockwise) thick, medium-hard vine charcoal; ebony pencil; Marks-A-Lot wide permanent marker
SAFETY NOTE: The Marks-A-Lot wide permanent marker is not recommended for general classroom use. Waterbased markers should be substituted.

(top sheet, clockwise) Sharpie medium-width marker; charcoal pencil; thin, medium-hard vine charcoal; compressed charcoal square; round compressed charcoal stick; fine-tip marker; black conté crayon; burnt sienna pastel; sanguine conté crayon

Design Extension
• Provide students with opportunities to create gesture drawings of animals. Because most animals do not pose on command, gestures are a good technique for catching their movement. Either visit a zoo or farm or bring a rabbit or other pet to class to draw. (When Georgia O'Keeffe was teaching, she once brought a pony into her classroom.)

• Students may create the crayon resist gesture drawings, as described in the activity on page 147, by brushing watercolors over crayon gesture drawings.

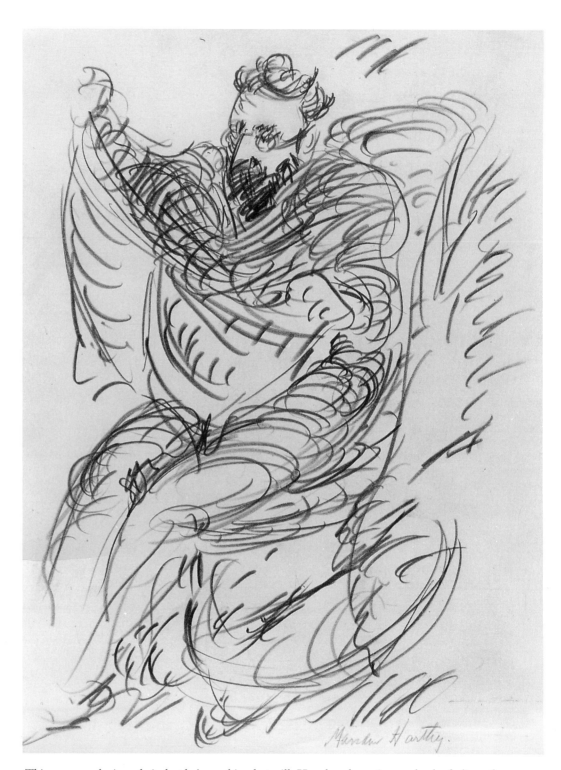

This man may be in a chair, but he's anything but still. How has the artist caught the feeling of energy
that seems to surround this person? Follow a few of the lines from where they begin to where they end.
What shapes do most of them make? Marsden Hartley, *Man in a Chair*, twentieth century. Pencil on
paper, 12" x 8 7/8" (30 x 23 cm). Los Angeles County Museum of Art, Gift of Frank Perls.

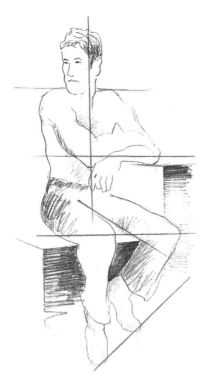

Adding Interest to Gesture Drawings

To build complexity and add interest in a gesture drawing, use line, stroke and tone. Line defines edges. Do you want sharply defined edges or soft edges? Use line to give sensitivity to the edges.

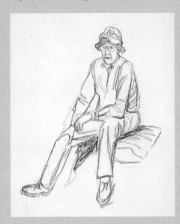

The use of stroke adds strength and weight to the gesture pose. Develop a system of markings to indicate stress and add variety.

Tone can translate large areas of mass. *Tone*, or broad areas of value, captures the volume of a figure or object. In gesture drawing, tones of light and dark can add drama and heighten features.

Developing a marking system of line, stroke and tone will increase your visual vocabulary. This combination of marks will also increase your ability to develop various relationships within a composition. Such a system will be very useful to build beyond the structure of a *contour drawing*.

This diagram shows one way of adjusting proportions when dealing with a figure that is not simply standing facing the viewer. Drawing lines such as these may help you maintain the proper proportions when drawing posed figures.

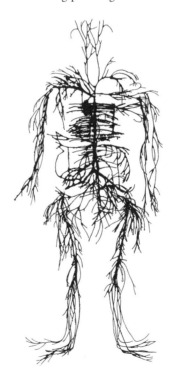

Lesley Dill, *Blue Circulatory System*, 1993. Wire and paper, 72" x 33" x 1" (183 x 84 x 2.5 cm). Courtesy Bernard Toale Gallery.

Contour Drawing

Higher-Order Thinking Skills
Challenge students to locate both gesture and contour drawings of figures and animals in the perspective sketch on page 82.

Extension
Introduce students to the drawings and paintings of Austrian Secessionist artist Egon Schiele. Most of them are based on careful observation of the contours of the human body.

Contour drawing captures the illusion of volume and space. Unlike outlines, which merely define a shape without suggesting depth, contour lines define the edges within a form. These lines create the appearance of three dimensions. Contour lines may be outlined, repeated, overlapped and sometimes broken.

Contour lines are very descriptive. They can vary in weight and thickness and express qualities, such as softness, crispness and boldness. They can also describe textural edges of a form.

Drawing a figure using contour lines demands strong concentration. Draw lines as if you were touching the edges of the subject. Practice will greatly improve the quality of your contour drawing. Here are several methods to help you.

Blind contour Do a contour drawing without looking at the paper. Move your pencil as your eye scans the edges of the figure. Try not to peek at your paper. Don't worry about results. Just focus on drawing what you see.

Emphasizing weight Have a model pose sitting or lying down. Accent the areas of pressure with heavy dark lines. Vary the speed and value of the lines to capture the strength of the pose. Where is the weight the strongest? What edges should be emphasized?

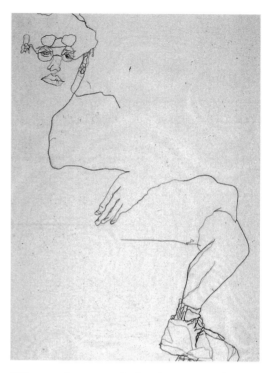

What you leave out of a drawing can reveal almost as much as what you put in. Can you find some lines that create three-dimensionality here? Student work by Julie Haruki, Honolulu, Hawaii.

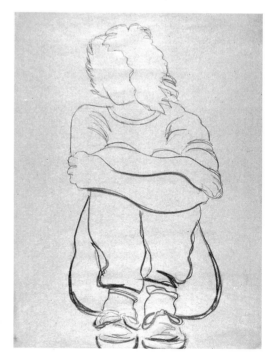

To give visual weight to a contour drawing, darken some of the lines. Consider first what you'd like to emphasize, and why. What is emphasized in this contour drawing?

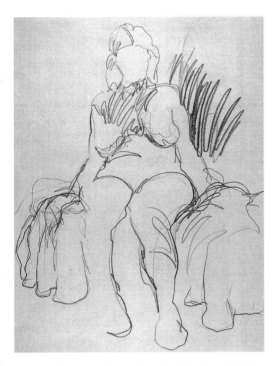

Without faces, without clear details of any kind, contour drawings can still reveal mood and suggest personality.

Inside and out Have a model pose with arms or legs crossed. Draw the pose, using only certain edges inside and outside the figure. Do not draw an outline around the total form. Record only what is necessary to capture the gestural qualities of the pose.

Reverse Do a contour drawing of a figure in a comfortable pose. Draw on one side of the paper. Then have the model take the same pose in the reverse direction. Do a second drawing on the other half of the paper. You can allow some areas of the figures to overlap in both drawings. The reverse images will create interesting compositions and help you develop hand-eye coordination.

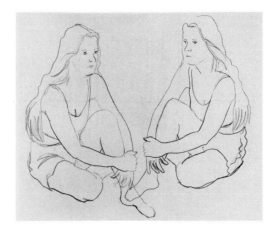

Student work by Alan Levy, Abilene, Texas.

Teaching Tip
Blind contour drawing helps eliminate drawing inhibitions and helps students focus on what they are drawing. Have students tape drawing paper to the desk to prevent it from slipping. Have students try using felt-tip, ballpoint, or other fluid pen. Do not allow them to lift the pen from the paper.

Design Extensions
• Encourage students to paint some of their contour drawings, adding color, shapes, and textures to the background. Studying portraits by Matisse may inspire students to use color in a Fauve or unrealistic style.

• Students may experiment by drawing figures with a brush and ink. Challenge them to capture a figure with as few lines as possible.

Display Duchamp's *Nude Descending a Staircase* to illustrate shifting contours.

Teaching Tips
• Shifting contours can be done with gesture drawing. Suggest that students use different colors for each movement, working from light to dark.

• Start with five-minute drawings and progress to ten- to fifteen-minute drawings. Students can return to earlier drawings to add detail.

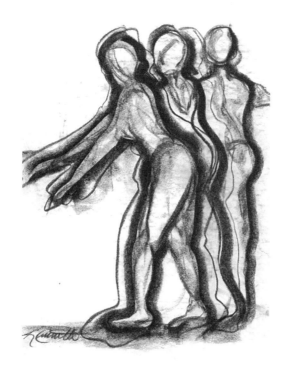

Shifting contours Have a model choose a pose that can be easily shifted to another position. Capture the pose in the first contour drawing. Then have the model change position slightly. Draw a second contour drawing on top of the first. If you like, repeat the process to enhance the sense of movement in the poses.

THINK ABOUT IT
Contour drawing strengthens your ability to focus on a subject. At the same time that you identify the form of your subject, you are analyzing and interpreting it as well.

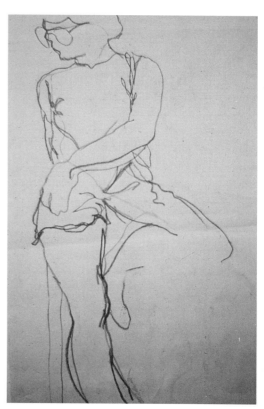

Above left, and above: Cartoonists often show arms and legs making many movements at once, to suggest haste or confusion. As you work on shifting contour drawings like these, think of when you might want to create that sort of movement.

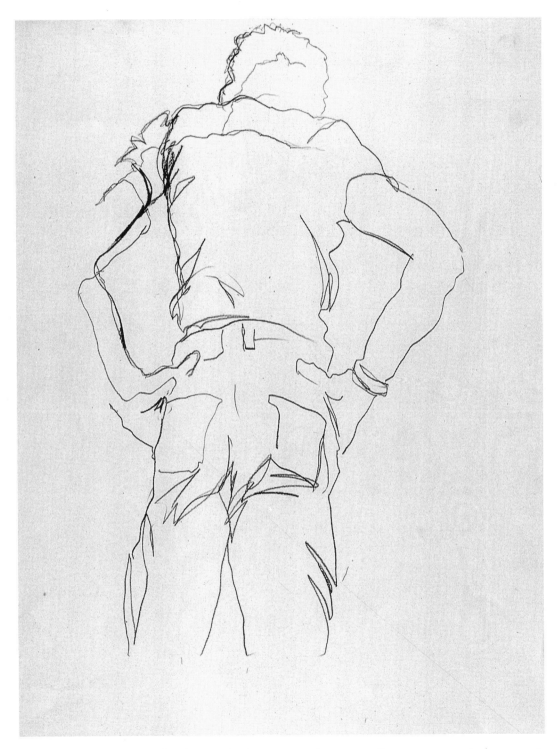

**Higher-Order
Thinking Skills**
Challenge students to
identify other examples
of contour drawings
such as Rembrandt's
St. Jerome on page 99
and Mary Cassatt's
The Caress on page 207.

Design Extension
The class may draw
student models in poses
found in famous works
of art such as the
figures in Michelangelo's
Sistine Chapel Ceiling.
Introduce students
to these pieces before
arranging the pose.

With practice, your contour drawings can begin to capture the essence of a person at a particular moment.

Full Figure Drawing

Learning how to draw the full figure quickly takes time and practice. You must learn how to draw the figure frontally as well as at different angles. There are several ways to approach full figure drawing.

Draw the figure by filling in all of the positive space within the figure with charcoal. Imagine that your charcoal stick is bouncing around the inside edges of the figure. Make marks that reflect the direction of the body mass and the movement of the pose. Draw the whole pose as though you were drawing a silhouette. Don't bother with details.

When you have gained confidence in using positive space to draw the figure, reverse the process and work with negative space. Work with the outside edges of the figure instead of the inside edges. Fill in all the negative space with black strokes and tone. Make the outside edges descriptive.

After you have practiced working with positive and negative space separately, combine these techniques into one drawing. Draw the figure from the hips up by drawing the negative space. Draw the figure from the waist down by filling in the positive space. This method allows you to begin fusing lights and darks within a composition, which will help give the composition unity.

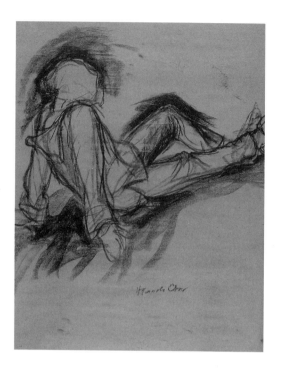

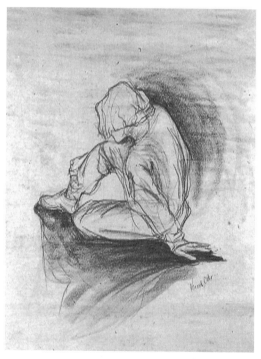

Draw the figure from many different angles. Try to feel the weight of the model's upper body as it presses on her arms. How has that weight affected her shoulders? Her neck? Student work by Hannah Cofer, Knoxville, Tennessee.

Proportion

Proportion is a comparative relationship between the parts of the human form. For example, there is a relationship between the size of the head and the body.

Leonardo da Vinci divided the figure into eight parts. He found that the measurement of a person's head multiplied eight times equals their height. If a person spreads out his or her arms horizontally, the measurement from fingertip to fingertip will equal the person's height.

Another way to establish correct proportions in full figure drawing is to draw a vertical line up through the figure. This line can serve as a reference point. Use the line to show the relationship between parts and the whole figure.

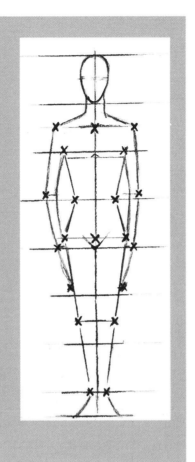

Extensions
• Have students use string for visual measurements. For example, how many head lengths does it take to measure a student's height, etc.?

• Students can feel proportion by:
   —placing the heel of one hand on the chin to measure the face.
   —holding an elbow into the waist. When an arm is dropped in a relaxed fashion, the fingers should touch the leg above the knee.

Higher-Order Thinking Skills
Assign students to measure the proportions of the figures in Longo's photo on page 229, Degas' ballerina on page 207, the Egyptian figures on page 171, the skeleton on page 117, and Ingres' civil engineer on page 17. How many heads tall is each of these figures? How do these compare to Leonardo's findings?

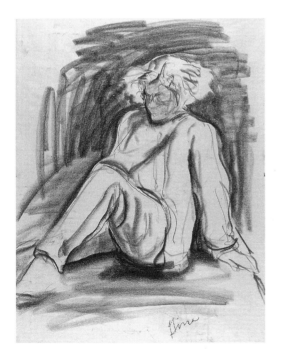

Concentrate at first on the body's forms and overall shapes, not on small details. Leave facial features out at first, or suggest them only with areas of tone. Student work by Gina Miller, Abilene, Texas.

To explore lights and darks within a composition, have a model pose under strong lighting. Use lights to create dynamic shadows inside and outside the figure. Draw the figure by laying in large areas of darks. Work with both positive and negative space. Can you find a relationship between the lights and the darks? How does the figure relate to the whole composition? How does working with positive and negative space help you locate the figure within the composition?

THINK ABOUT IT
Drawing the full figure is a form of problem solving. Each question you ask yourself at the different stages of the drawing process allows you to explore possibilities and solutions.

After you have drawn the figure with large areas of tone, use lines and strokes to emphasize the edges of the figure. Adding thin and thick lines will give detail and strength to the drawing, as well as help you relate the figure to negative space.

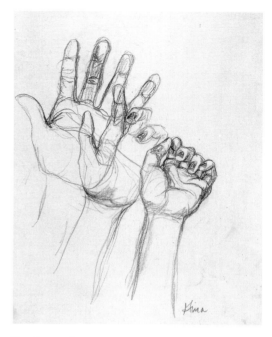

Bend your fingers. Clench your fist. Where do the wrinkles appear? Student work by Gina Miller, Abilene, Texas.

Hands and Feet Concentrate on specific areas of the body, particularly the hands and feet. Hands are complex and challenging to draw. Look at your own hands. Feel the thickness at the base of your hand. What happens when you bend your fingers? Practice drawing hands at various angles and from different viewpoints. You can experiment with using a minimum of lines or overlapping lines. As the edges of the form diminish, so should the weight and strength of the lines.

Work with the feet in the same manner. Explore the variety of curves, muscle padding, and bone structure. Do feet offer some problems in foreshortening? How can you draw a foot that is projecting toward you while keeping the proportions correct? Experiment with contour lines and draw exactly what you see.

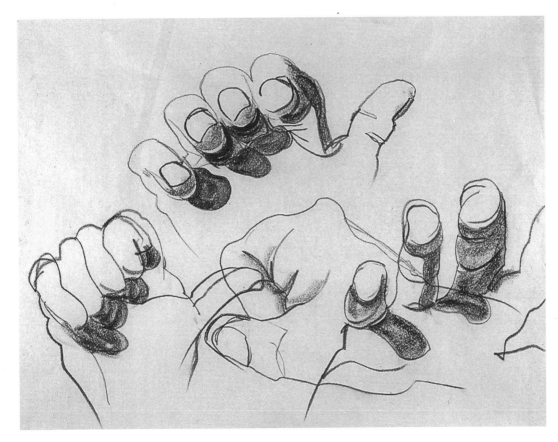

Shine a bright light on your hands. Use tone to create shadow areas.

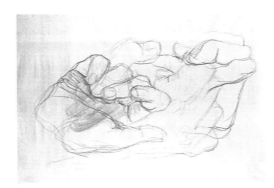

Use overlapping and transparency to explore the hand's many forms.

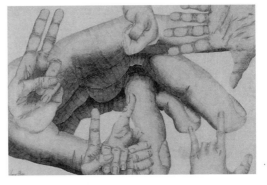

Combining your studies of hands can produce some interesting results. Student work by George Flores, El Paso, Texas.

Teaching Tip
Hands and feet make
good sketchbook and
homework assignments.

Design Extensions
• Tell students to
view hands and feet as
shapes first, like a
mitten or sock, then fill
in details. Challenge
advanced students to
draw bones and joints
in hands and feet.

• Have students draw
each other's eyes,
noses, and mouths with
shadow only, no hard
lines.

• Challenge students to
draw a foreshortened
view of their foot, knee,
and leg by crossing their
legs and drawing what
they see when they look
down over their knee
to their foot. How much
of their shin can they
actually see?

• After students have
been introduced to
Leonardo da Vinci's and
Michelangelo's figurative
studies on pages 200
and 201, suggest that
they create similar
studies in their sketch-
books.

Cooperative Learning
Have students form
teams and ask them to
mix and match each
others' faces in their
drawings. Suggest
that they combine one
person's eyes with
another's nose.

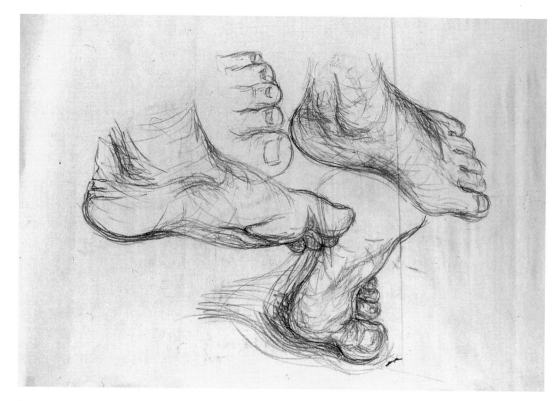

Just as you did with hands, draw feet in as many positions as you can.

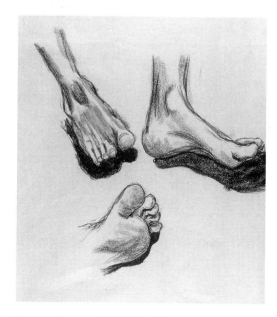

Notice the use of highlights here. Where is the
light coming from?

Feet, Hands, Ears, Eyes, Nose and Mouth

Hands and feet are often considered "difficult" parts to draw. The key to drawing areas like hands and feet is to look for the relationship between the overall structure and its parts. How does each part relate to the whole? First look at each part separately; then examine how each part relates to the other parts. For example, where is the hand in relation to the elbow? How long is the hand in relation to the face? Relating one part to another helps give you an overall sense of direction and unity in your drawing.

Hands and feet and facial features have variations in edges. Observe closely how edges change from sharp to round, smooth to crisp. Varying the edges of the forms will help define the areas and add strength to the drawing.

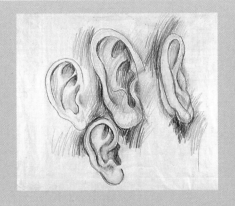

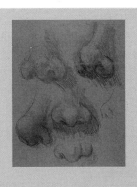

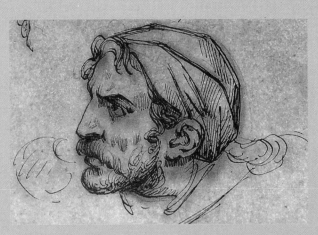

Theodore Gericault, *Three Sailors' Heads* (detail), ca. 1818. Pen and iron gall over pencil on brown wove paper, 8" x 10" (21 x 26 cm). The Baltimore Museum of Art: Fanny B. Thalheimer Bequest Fund.

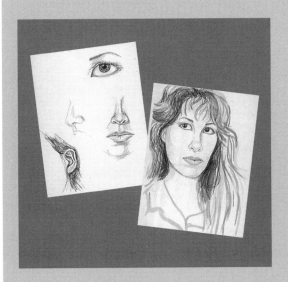

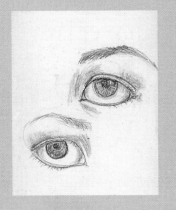

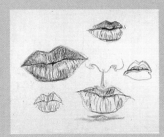

Face A good way to approach the features of the face is to use a mirror and explore your own face. First look for relationships between the parts. Study relationships between areas such as your nose and your eyes. Where is your nose in relation to your eyes? Where is your chin in relation to your forehead?

Try isolating each feature. Draw just your nose or one eye. Can you express more than just an exact likeness of each feature? Can the shape of your mouth convey a feeling?

Gradually expand your skills by drawing your whole face. Try drawing your face at different angles and with different light sources.

THINK ABOUT IT
Drawing a self-portrait is an exercise in reflective thinking. Who are you? What are you thinking and feeling?

Proportions of the Head

The proportions of the human head do not vary from person to person. Although each person looks different from another, the placement of features remains constant.

The eyes are located halfway between the chin and the top of the head.

The human head is essentially an oval. The face can be divided into thirds. A third of the face is located from the nostrils to the chin. Another third is located between the nostrils and the eyebrows. The last third is from the eyebrows to the hairline.

Once you establish the general proportions of the face, you can develop the facial features in greater detail.

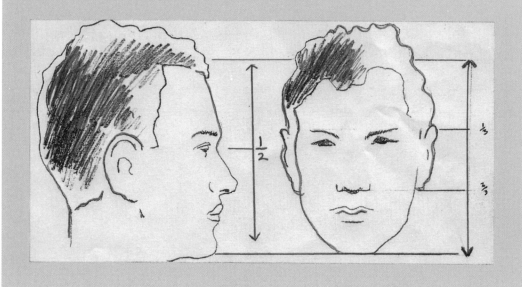

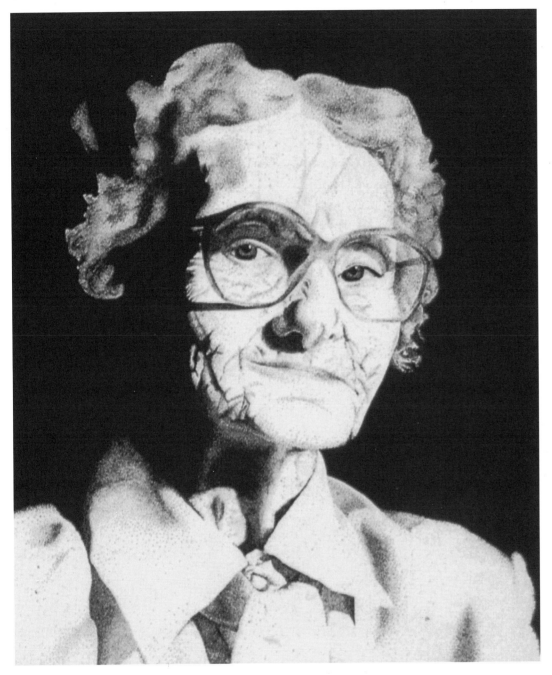

The faces of babies and older people can be especially difficult to draw, because of differences in skin tone and changes in general proportions. Notice how sensitively this artist has used darks and lights to suggest personality as well as likeness. Student work by Kathy Ballsrud, Monticello, Illinois.

Teaching Tips

• In the beginning, urge students to concentrate on proportions, getting eyes and mouth in the correct location. After a few sketches, have them draw the shape of the shadows on the face.

• Point out that the distance between the eyes is about the width of one eye. Notice how the eyebrow lines up with the top of the ear.

• Beginning artists often place the eyes too high within the face. To demonstrate, draw an oval or egg shape on the chalkboard. Place two dots for eyes near the center of the oval. Draw another oval beside this and put the dots higher within the oval, where the forehead would be. Ask students to discuss which drawing looks more realistic.

Design Extension

Tell students that one way to begin drawing a face from life is with two simple contour lines. They should first draw an oval. Next students should draw the curved contour line that runs down the middle of the face from the top of the forehead through the nose to the bottom of the chin. Draw the curved contour line that runs around the head through the eyes. Make a similar sketch for the portrait on page 137.

Portraits

Design Extension
Have students draw portraits with black and white chalks on toned paper. Allow them to use other colors (pastels) to show mood.

Context
Alice Neel, an American painter, was born in Pennsylvania in 1900, studied at Philadelphia College of Art and Design (now Moore College of Art), and worked in New York City. While working for the Federal Art Project of the WPA from 1933 to 1943, she became an advocate for social and cultural reform. She is best known for her expressive portraits of individuals from many walks of life. She died in 1984.

Extension
Introduce students to the facial proportions of toddlers and babies by studying the drawings on page 144 and 146 as well as other photographs of young children. Compare these children's facial proportions to those of adults. Young children have a greater proportion of forehead to the rest of their face. Also their heads are larger in relation to the size of their bodies.

Portraits have been described as windows to people's personalities. Is a successful portrait an exact likeness of a person? Or is it more important to express the qualities that sets the person apart from other people? Portraits can express far more than just a person's likeness, which is why they are so challenging.

In drawing a portrait, the artist must be sensitive to the model's mood and personality and look for ways to communicate them. Is the model relaxed or tense? Can the pose capture that quality?

Alice Neel translated her model's personality and mannerisms into an expressive drawing. How is her drawing a direct visual translation of the model? How is it an emotional response to the model? Because Neel conveys more than just a likeness of the model, her portraits have a strong sense of originality.

Speaking of Art...

In 1530 during a political upheaval in Florence, Michelangelo hid in a small, secret room in the basement of San Lorenzo. It could only be entered by a trapdoor. In 1975, large figure drawings or cartoons by Michelangelo were found on the walls of this crypt. They were drawn with charcoal and red earth pigment. Some of the drawing overlapped, probably because he lacked space or light.

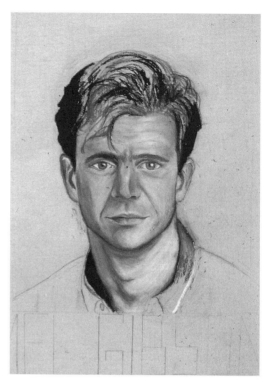

Realistic detail in the face contrasts with looser, darker lines in the hair and shirt. Student work by Juleen Generelli, Worcester, Massachusetts.

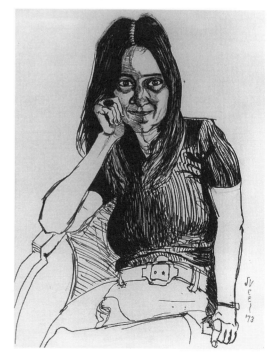

What clues has the artist given you about what this person is like? Alice Neel, *Adrienne Rich*, 1973. Ink with Chinese white on paper, 30 3/8" x 22 7/8" (77 x 58 cm). Courtesy Robert Miller Gallery. Photograph: Zindman/Fremont.

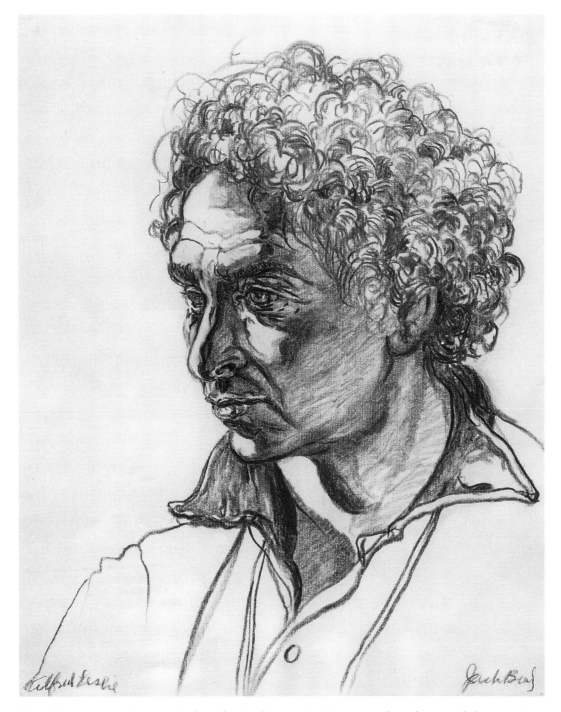

Use of line, stroke and tone is clearly evident in this portrait. Can you see how the many dark areas and strong lines make the work forceful? Jack Beal, *Alfred Leslie*, 1976. Charcoal on paper, 25 1/2" x 19 5/8" (65 x 50 cm). Courtsey Frumkin/Adams Gallery. Photograph: eeva-inkeri.

Teaching Tips
• To emphasize a variety of values in a portrait, students may blacken the entire surface of a piece of drawing paper with soft charcoal, and then rub out highlights and medium tones using a kneaded eraser, tissues, and cotton swabs.

• Discourage the urge to erase that comes with pencil drawings. Students may draw more spontaneously if they use a ballpoint pen or marker.

Context
American artist Jack Beal is best known for his figure paintings. He has studied art at the College of William and Mary, the Art Institute of Chicago, and the University of Chicago.

Higher-Order Thinking Skills
Point out the shape of highlights in Alice Neel's and Jack Beal's portraits. Do you think the artists drew these shapes in the early stages of the drawing? Students often forget to leave areas for highlights in faces, and their portraits look completely gray. One trick is to draw in highlight areas early in the shading process.

Teaching Tips
- Suggest that students:
—work large by using charcoal.
—use Polaroid™ images as reference materials.

- Tell students to notice where the eyelid falls across the top and bottom of the pupil and iris in both wide-open and normally open eyes. Look at the drawings on pages 135–139. Can students see the whites of the eyes either above or below the iris? Look at Pamela Zernia's drawing on page 70. What emotion do the eyes convey?

Context
Refer students to page 36 for more information about Käthe Kollwitz.

Higher-Order Thinking Skills
Ask students to analyze how Kollwitz builds volume in her drawing. (They should note that the areas farther from the viewer have many more lines built up to add volume.)

Inquiry
Both Rembrandt and Dürer created self-portraits throughout their lives. Assign students to find two self-portraits drawn by one of these artists at different times in his life.

Design Extension
Assign students the Mirror and Photograph Self-Portraits activity on page 147.

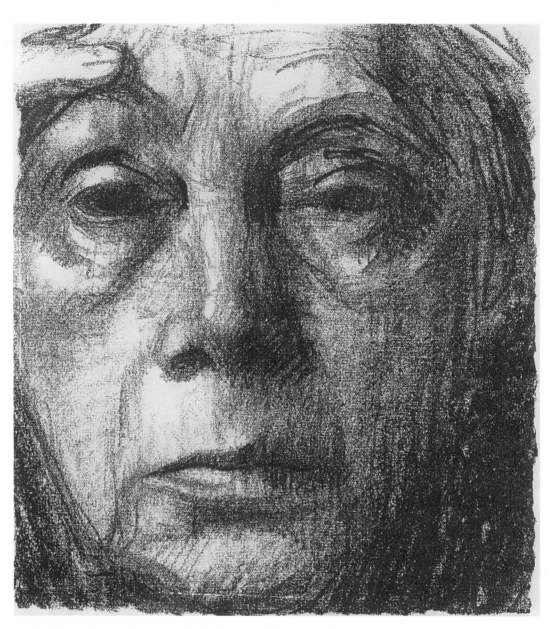

Don't feel you have to show your whole face in a self-portrait. If a close-up seems more appropriate, try it. Käthe Kollwitz, *Self Portrait*, 1934. Lithograph. National Gallery of Art, Washington, DC. Rosenwald Collection.

Self-portraits Self-portraits are a good way to explore portraiture. By using mirrors and photographs, you can draw yourself at your own pace. But more importantly, you can reach down deep inside and translate your feelings and emotions into a drawing. Drawing a self-portrait allows you to draw what you see outwardly while conveying what you feel inwardly. This is a rare opportunity, so be creative and express yourself!

Here are a few suggestions to help you develop a self-portrait.

1. Search for a comfortable pose—one that expresses your personality.

2. Consider the lighting, background and clothing or props you want to include.

3. Set up mirrors so that you can see yourself easily as you draw.

4. Select the proper medium that expresses the subject matter.

5. Use a marking system and colors that reflect the content of the subject matter.

6. Don't be afraid to let your feelings show. Your self-portrait should be a strong image that reflects not only your image but also what lies within.

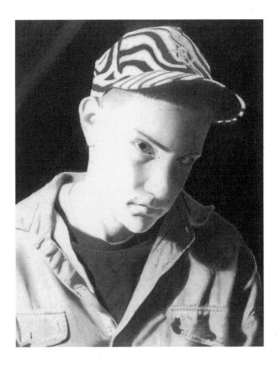

The expression on your face is important in a self-portrait—it sets the tone for the whole work. Here, the angle of the head, slightly pouting mouth and defiant eyes help suggest suspicion or resentment. Student work by Tony Board, Greenwood, Indiana.

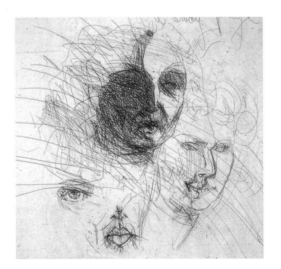

Working in the style of a famous artist is good practice. By trying to recreate the techniques of others, you discover techniques of your own. Pat Steir, *Self After Rembrandt*, 1985. Hardground, 26" x 20" (66 x 51 cm). Courtesy of the artist.

Design Extensions
• Students may vary their self-portraits by drawing their reflections from the rearview mirror of a car, a Christmas ornament, or a piece of jewelry. They should include the surrounding scene in these drawings.

• Students can fragment their self-portraits and reassemble them as a collage. Allow them to experiment with different media for each fragment.

• Assign students to practice making the ugliest faces they can in front of a mirror and then draw this pose. They might want a friend to photograph these poses if they cannot hold them for a long time.

• Encourage students to distort their face with their hand in some way—pulling down one side of the mouth with a finger or resting their chin on their hand and making their cheek wrinkle. They should draw their hand distorting their face as they look in a mirror.

Teaching Tip
Home bathrooms are great places to draw self-portraits; usually they have bright lights and mirrors.

Figurative Compositions

Context

• Paula Moderson-Becker (1876–1907) was a German painter who, together with her husband, lived and worked in Worpswede, an artists' colony near Bremen. Like the other artists in this group, Moderson-Becker painted scenes of peasants and the local landscape, but she developed an individual, earthy style featuring simple images.

• Alberto Giacometti (1901–66) was a Swiss artist best known for his thin, standing figures which seemed to be a metaphor for the human race after World War II. They appear as isolated figures in meaningless voids.

Before you draw a figure, you need to plan your composition. How will you position the figure to create interest? What relationship do you want to establish between the figure and the background environment? Planning the composition is the first step in drawing a figure.

How the figure is placed is a fundamental concern in developing the composition. For example, you don't want to leave large areas of the paper blank. Nor do you want to have half your composition running off the page. Using a system of organizational line drawing is one approach to locating the figure properly. This system is essentially a latticework of gesture lines that are continuous and overlapping. They serve as a framework in which the figure and surrounding shapes are located.

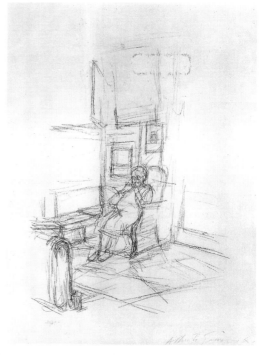

Alberto Giacometti, *The Artist's Mother Sitting, I*, 1964. Lithograph. 20 1/4 x 15 3/8" (51 x 39 cm). © Sotheby Park-Bernet. Art Resource, NY.

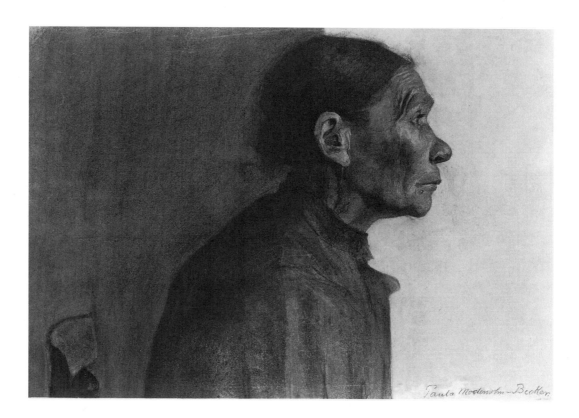

What questions are raised by the division of space in this work? Does the background suggest two sides of the woman's personality? A dark past and a bright future? Paula Modersohn-Becker, *Portrait of a Peasant Woman*, 1900. Charcoal on buff wove paper, 17" x 25" (43.3 x 63.9 cm). The Art Institute of Chicago, Gift of the Donnelly Family, 1978.26.

Gathering Information

Philip Pearlstein once remarked that in developing his figurative work he uses three different systems to gather information. First he records the composition by doing quick sketches that capture the gestural qualities of the pose. Then he freezes the image in a photograph, retaining the lighting and values in the composition. This is an important step in Pearlstein's work because he often uses multiple light sources. Finally he observes and works directly with the model. His three-step systematic approach provides him with unique aspects of visual information.

Design Extension
Encourage the students to try using Philip Pearlstein's three steps in their own compositions.

Context
Philip Pearlstein was born in Pittsburgh in 1924 and graduated from Carnegie Tech in 1949 (with his friend Andy Warhol). He is best known for his realistic paintings of nudes.

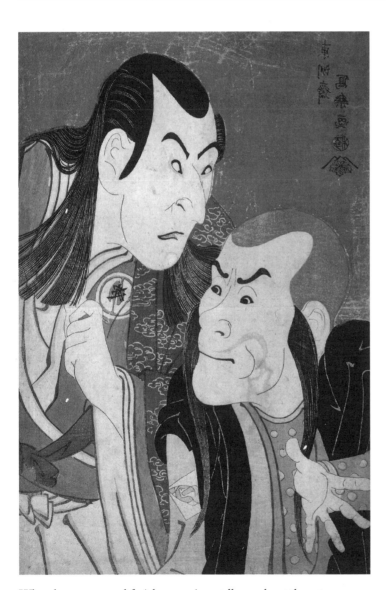

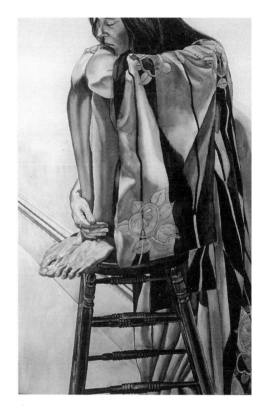

How has composition helped create a focus in this work? Philip Pearlstein, *Model in Plum-Colored Kimono on Stool (both legs up)*, 1978. Watercolor 59 5/8 x 40 1/4 " (151 x 102 cm). Courtesy Frumkin/Adams Gallery. Photograph: eeva-inkeri.

What do gestures and facial expressions tell you about these two people? How has the artist used lines for emphasis and to unify the composition? Sharaku, *Actors*, nineteenth century Musée Chiossone Geneva. Scala/Art Resource, NY.

Extension
As students begin to
consider subjects and
designs for their own
figurative compositions,
encourage them to find
other examples of this
type of drawing. They
should identify the
organizational lines in
these artworks.

Design Extension
Students may draw a
figurative composition
with a brush using
medium and dark values
of ink washes. Remind
them to consider the
figure-ground relation-
ship by creating a range
of values in the back-
ground as well as on
the figure.

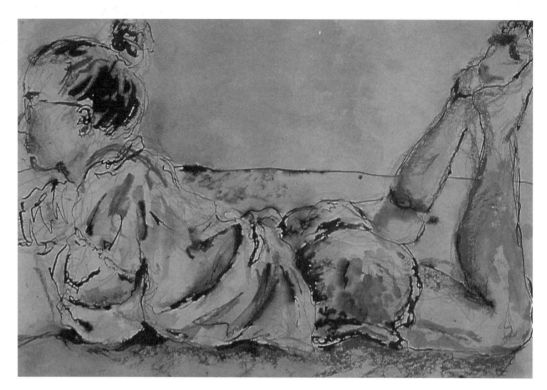

Casual lines echo the casual pose of the model in this ink and chalk composition. Student work by Erica Cho, Ardmore, Pennsylvania.

Using organizational lines allows you to correct mistakes or reevaluate relationships between forms. By gradually building up lines as points of reference, you can develop compositional relationships and images with meaningful proportions.

Alberto Giacometti's drawings often display a latticework of lines that surrounds the figure in space. His drawings are a natural extension of his sculptures.

Here are some suggestions for using a system of organizational lines.

1. Draw vertical and horizontal lines that roughly indicate where the figure and objects will be placed.

2. Develop these lines to establish the height and width of the figure and objects.

3. Draw through the objects to develop the correct proportions.

4. Extend the lines beyond the objects into negative space.

5. Stand back from the work and reevaluate the positioning of the figure and objects in relation to the overall composition. Make any corrections.

Once you have located the forms in space correctly, you can develop the drawing. You do not have to erase the organizational lines.

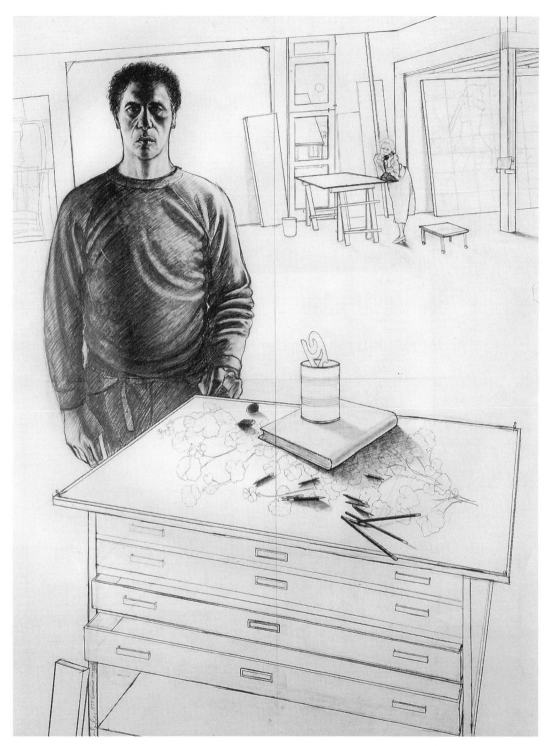

This artist's use of contrast between dark and light areas, and his variation of line width, creates emphasis in certain spots. Can you find them? What is being emphasized? Alfred Leslie, *Artist in the Studio*, 1979. Graphite on paper, 80" x 60" (203 x 152 cm), 4 sheets. Courtesy Frumkin/Adams Gallery. Photograph: eeva-inkeri.

Design Extension
Challenge students to draw two people together as in *Sidney Goodman Holding Maia* or *Attori* on page 141. Refer them to other compositions of two or more figures such as Mary Cassatt's mother and child on page 207; Renoir's dance on page 205; and Frenkel's recess on page 236.

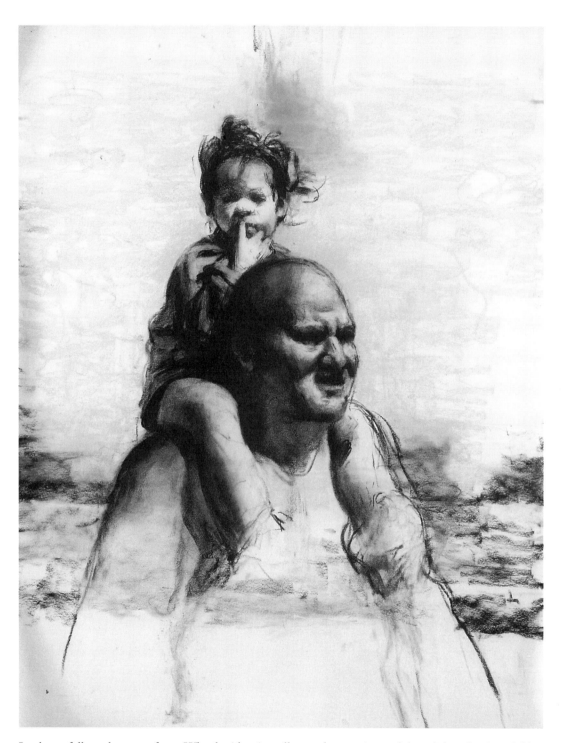

Look carefully at these two faces. What besides size tells you that one is an adult and the other is a child? Sidney Goodman, *Sidney Goodman Holding Maia*, 1991-92. Charcoal and pastel, 44 1/4" x 52" (112 x 132 cm). Courtesy Terry Dintenfass Gallery.

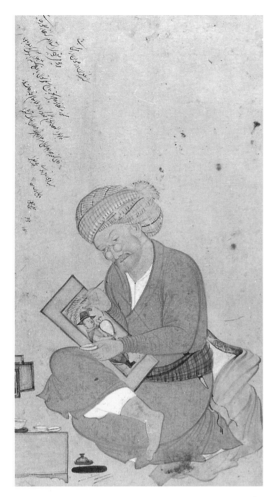

Which parts of this drawing are realistic? Which are more stylized? *Miniature showing Riza-i Abibasi Painting a European*, eighteenth century. Persian. Courtesy Princeton University Libraries.

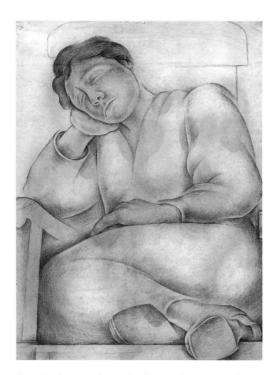

Soft shadows and gentle, flowing lines contribute to the relaxed mood of this drawing. Can you identify where the artist has used foreshortening? Diego Rivera, *Sleeping Woman*, 1921. Crayon, 23" x 18" (58 x 46 cm). Fogg Art Museum, Harvard University. Bequest of Meta and Paul J. Sachs.

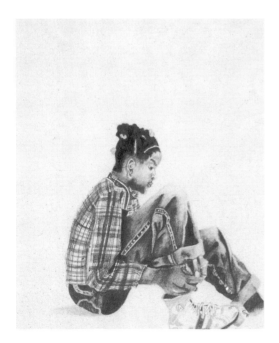

Even the simplest, most familiar scenes can become effective figure drawings. Student work by Christopher Jenkins, Clinton, Mississippi.

Summary

In this chapter, you learned several approaches to drawing the human figure. You explored the structure of the human skeleton and proportions of the human figure. Practice in gesture drawing has developed your ability to capture the movement of a pose and the basic characteristics of a figure. Contour drawing has taught you how to observe closely the edges inside and outside a form. You are learning how to be more expressive and descriptive in your use of line. Drawing the full figure has presented you with challenges in positioning a figure within a composition. And in drawing portraits, you are learning how to convey feelings and emotions.

Drawing the human figure is an ongoing learning process. Figure drawing requires a great deal of time and persistence. Artists like Wayne Thiebaud still spend a number of hours each week studying the figure and developing drawing skills.

The human figure is quite complex and demands a lot of respect in recording it. For any artist, and particularly the beginning drawing student, reaching the point where you are no longer intimidated by drawing the figure is a major accomplishment.

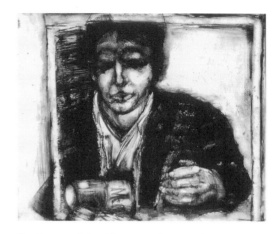

Student work by Chris Pritchett, Milwaukee, Wisconsin.

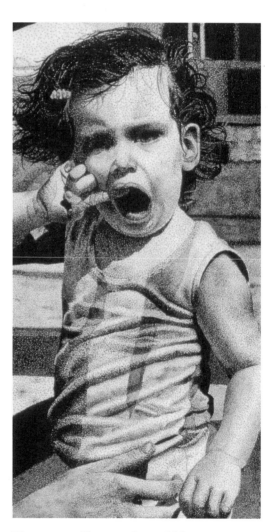

Humor can add personality and life to any portrait. Student work by Michelle Bodie, St, John, Indiana.

Activities

Mirror and Photograph Self-Portraits

Draw two self-portraits. In one, draw yourself by using a mirror. In the other, draw from a photograph of yourself. Compare the two drawings. Which is stiffer or flatter? Which is more lifelike? In which was it easier to show volume? see page 139

A Historical Self-Portrait

Select a portrait painting or drawing from a previous century. Use it to create a self-portrait. Pose in the same position; try to show the same expression; draw the same clothing. Note the style the artist used: is it realistic or somewhat abstract? How is it different from your own style? see page 17

Crayon Resist Gesture Drawings

Use several different colored crayons on manila paper to make gesture drawings of people. Paint over these with a contrasting watercolor. Traditionally black is used for this resist technique, but any color may be used.

Matisse Collages

Make gesture drawings of figures on several colors of construction paper. After studying Matisse's cut paper collages, cut out the gesture drawings. Turn them over so the drawn lines are not showing. Arrange them on construction paper. Try breaking up the background and creating a rhythm with construction paper shapes. Glue it all down.

Wire Gesture Sculpture

Turn a gesture drawing into a wire sculpture. Copy one of your gesture drawings with bendable wire such as aluminum sculpture wire. Begin with about four feet of wire; more may be added to the sculpture. With a staple gun, attach your finished wire figure to a wooden base. Both wire and base may be painted.

Drawing the Figure on a Grid

With your classmates, enlarge an illustration of a figure to larger-than-life proportions. For example, an 8" x 12" illustration could be enlarged to six times its size. Section the enlargement into six-inch squares and number each square on the back.

You and your classmates will each receive one six-inch square and the corresponding two-inch square of the original illustration. Divide your six-inch square into nine smaller squares. Divide the two-inch square into four smaller squares.

Grid a six-inch square of illustration board. Now draw your section of the figure in this grid. Try to match the line, color and value of the original illustration as closely as possible. When you have all finished, join the large squares together on the backs with tape. How successful were you in completing the figure? Share what you learned about scale and the details of human anatomy.

Student work by Stephen Doyle.

A Self-Portrait with Pointillism

Georges Seurat used a method called pointillism, in which he applied small dots of color to a surface so that from a distance they blend together.

Create a self-portrait using the same technique. Begin by drawing a pencil sketch of your head. Take time to measure correct proportions of each part.

When you are satisfied with your sketch, use a fine-point pen to create a pointillist drawing. Use tiny dots to create value, shading and contour.

The Figure and Elements of Design

An easy way to learn to draw the full figure is by drawing the figure from a back view. Drawing a figure from the back minimizes details, stresses shape and contour, and eliminates the face. To make your composition interesting and exciting, emphasize an element or principle of design. Minimize the importance of the figure.

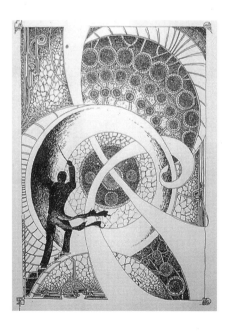

Chapter 6
Stimulating Creativity

Objectives

Students will be able to:

• Use art forms from other cultures as a source of ideas for their artworks. (Art history/ Art production)

• Demonstrate in their own artworks an understanding of how drawing and painting may be fused in a composition. (Art production)

• Understand how photocopied and computer-generated images can be used in artworks. (Art production/Art criticism)

• Experiment with placing an object in an unexpected setting to give life to the object. (Art production/Art criticism)

• Understand that a metaphor may be used as the foundation of an art composition. (Art production)

• Recognize warm, cool, complementary, split complementary, triad, and analogous color schemes. (Art criticism)

• Perceive artists' use of color in artworks. (Aesthetics)

• Demonstrate their understanding of color schemes in their own art. (Art production)

Vocabulary

primary colors
secondary colors
tertiary or intermediate colors
hue
value
intensity
analogous

Chapter Overview

This chapter explores methods that students can use to foster their creativity. The assignments in this chapter are designed to stimulate creativity from different perspectives, including multicultural experiences, graffiti, use of photocopiers and computers, and metaphors. Students are also introduced to color in this chapter.

Lesson 1
pages 148–152   45 minutes

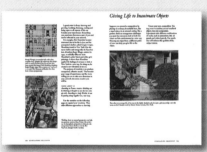

pages 150–151

Teach

Assign students to draw everyday items in an unusual setting or from a different point of view. For objects in unusual settings refer to Linda Murray's *The Urban Forest Lines* on page 188 and the children in gas masks on page 25. For unusual viewpoints of people and objects, see the student work on page 150, Salvador Dali's *Christ in Perspective* and the student work on page 89, and the dustpan on page 24.

Studio Experience

Set out household tools such as an iron, can opener, hammer, blender, hair dryer, pencil sharpener, or staple gun. Brainstorm with the class about unusual settings these could be placed in. List their suggestions on the board.

Now students should draw one of the tools in an unusual setting. Suggest that they lightly sketch their whole composition, including the background, before they begin to work on the details.

Studio Experience

Have students set out household items such as those listed in the above activity and then move them about, looking at them from above and below and at angles from which they are usually not seen. Students can then draw these unusual views of everyday objects.

Students could also search their community and school for unusual views to sketch or photograph and then draw as a finished composition.

Materials (for both activities)

15" x 20" drawing paper or
   illustration board
pencils, markers, or pen and ink

Lessons 2, 3
pages 153–168

each lesson
45 minutes

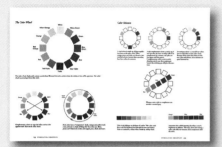

pages 154–155

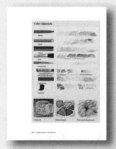

page 158

Teach

• Looking at the color wheels on page 154, review color theory, mixing colors, and making a color wheel. Allow students to create color wheels as you go through the concepts. Provide each student with red, yellow, blue, black, and white pastels or paint and a brush, water, and palette for paint mixing. (If you use watercolors, you do not need white. Water will lighten the colors.)

• Explain subtractive color theory, which asserts that if you mix all the colors of paint together, you get muddy gray. (There is also an additive light theory where all the colors mixed together make white. That theory is used when mixing light on the computer and stage spotlights.)

• Remind students that red, yellow, and blue are the primary hues, the colors that can be mixed to make all the rest of the colors. Begin a color wheel by making a few strokes of these colors. Green, orange, and violet are the secondary colors made by mixing two primaries together. Demonstrate mixing the colors and add a little of each secondary color between their primaries. The tertiary or intermediate colors are created by mixing a secondary color with one of its adjacent primary colors. Demonstrate blending and add red-violet, blue-violet, blue-green, yellow-green, yellow-orange, and red-orange to complete the color wheel.

• Teach students that complementary colors are opposite each other on the color wheel. Ask them to name several complementary color schemes. Have students make a saturation scale using two complements such as the one shown on page 155. Explain that adding a color's complement to it will dull its intensity.

• Direct students to the warm and cool colors on the color wheel at the bottom of page 154. What type of scenes would they paint using a warm color scheme? (deserts, sun) What type of scenes would they paint with cool colors? (water, forests)

• Use the color wheels on page 155 to explain triad color schemes, which have three colors equally distant from each other

on the color wheel. Ask students to name several triads and color and label them on their sheet of paper. Repeat this same process with split complementary and analogous color schemes. A split complementary color scheme is a color plus the two colors on either side of its complement. Analogous means similar; so, analogous colors are next to each other on the color wheel.

• Introduce color value by demonstrating how to grade dark to light values of a color. Have students make their own value chart.

Materials

pastels, colored pencils, watercolors, or tempera paints
12" x 18" manila or drawing paper
easel and poster board or large paper for demonstration
brushes (optional)
water in containers (optional)

Studio Experience

Guide students in selecting a drawing from a previous lesson to add color to or interpret in color. Discuss which colors and types of color schemes on pages 154 and 155 would add emotion, drama, or mood to their drawing. They should select one of these color schemes. When they have completed their work, instruct them to label the type of color scheme they used and explain why they selected that one.

Materials

drawing from previous class
colored media such as colored
  pencils, pastels, crayons,
  markers, watercolors, or
  tempera paints (The weight of
  the paper of the drawing may
  determine which medium is
  used. Paints will wrinkle thin
  paper, but it can be ironed flat.)

Lessons 4, 5, 6
pages 169–173
each lesson
45 minutes

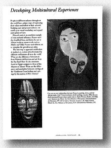

page 169

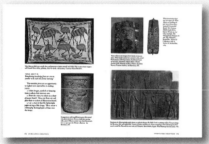

pages 170–171

Teach

• Guide students in discovering
how Picasso utilized African
images in his art. Discuss the similarities between the African mask
and Picasso's painting on page
169. Read the first two paragraphs
on page 169.

• As students compare the
images from different cultures on
pages 170–171, discuss the
questions in the last paragraph on
page 169. If possible, show students other examples of art from
these cultures.

• With the class, read the
steps for making a multicultural
rubbing given on page 170.
Direct students to research a culture's art, perhaps one described
on pages 169–171, one they have
studied in another subject, or a
culture that reflects their heritage.
They can find examples in art
books and the Internet.

Studio Experience

Have students draw their images
for a multicultural rubbing on
poster board. Then, have them cut
out their shapes and experiment
arranging them in various designs
before gluing them to the illustration board.

Demonstrate how to create a
rubbing with crayons, oil pastels,
or pencils. Students should create
several rubbings of their collage
and experiment with different
colors of rubbing materials and
papers.

Materials

pencils
erasers
10" x 14" poster board
10" x 15" illustration board
glue
crayon, oil pastels, and/or ebony
  or charcoal pencils
lightweight papers for rubbings
  such as photocopy paper, rice
  papers, tissue papers, vellum,
  newsprint

Lesson 7
page 174–176
45 minutes

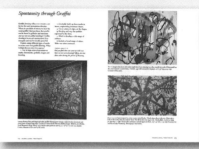

pages 174–175

Teach

• Give students a few minutes
to draw a favorite doodle and then
show them to each other.

• Have students read and discuss the captions for the images on
these pages. After students have
read about Tim Rollins + K.O.S.
on page 176, some of them may
wish to base their graffiti art project on a literary selection.

Studio Experience

Have students read the
directions for a graffiti drawing
on page 174. Demonstrate how
they might start one of these
drawings, by doodling and marking and then adding more images
and values. Stress that this is to
be a very free and unstructured
drawing. Suggest that they use
several different media.

Materials

18" x 24" drawing paper
drawing media such as markers,
  pencils, ink, pens, and pastels

Lessons 8, 9
pages 177–179   each lesson 45 minutes

Teach

• Call students' attention to the importance of the ground in the drawings of the chairs on pages 177 and 178. The artists used shadows and highlights to place the chairs in an environment so they are not floating in space.

• The chart on page 179 introduces students to high-quality papers, which they will likely use only for final projects. To help students understand the difference between hot press and cold press finishes, allow them to feel small scraps of both types of papers and draw on them with various media.

Materials

small pieces of hot and cold press finishes
assortment of drawing media such as ink, conté crayon, and graphite pencil

Studio Experience

Have students read the directions on page 177 and study the drawings on pages 177 and 178. Set up a chair (or chairs) in a spotlight. Demonstrate how to cover the illustration board with a light- to medium-tone pastel and then lightly sketch in the chair. Paint the ground (background) and then paint white highlights on the chair. Add more details with both black and white chalks.

Materials

15" x 20" illustration board
white and black acrylic or tempera paint
light- to medium-tone pastel
black and white chalk or charcoal
brushes
water in containers
erasers
rag

Lesson 10
page 180   45 minutes

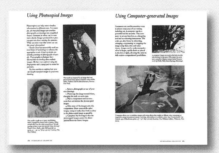

pages 180–181

Teach

• Introduce students to the art of Chuck Close on pages 180 and 225. Call attention to the size of both works. These are huge, extremely realistic portraits. If possible, show more works by Close.

• Tell students to bring an image to class to photocopy. Make several different-sized copies of each student's image or assign the students to make their own copies.

Studio Experience

With the class go over the directions on page 180 for this project. Brainstorm with them some outrageous environments in which to place their images.

Encourage them to carefully plan their composition before they begin drawing. Students will cut out their photocopied images, glue them onto their board or paper, and then draw in the rest of their composition. If students need more time, extend this for another class period or allow them to complete it outside of class.

Lesson 11
pages 181–184   45 minutes

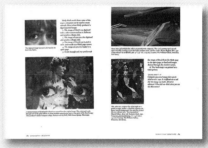

pages 182–183

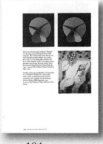

page 184

Teach

As students study each of the images on these pages, discuss how they might have been created. Some, such as the one on page 182, involved manipulating scanned images, while others, such as the work by Harold Cohen on page 183, were actually drawn with the computer.

Studio Experience

• If you have a video camera and DCTV software, try combining and altering images as described on page 182.

• You may also teach students to scan a photograph or drawing and then manipulate it using either the scanner software or a program such as Adobe Photoshop®. If you do not have a scanner, combine and change pieces of clip art. If computers are limited, have students create part of their artwork on the computer, print their image, and then draw and paint on their printout as Barbara Nessim did in *Blind Companions* on page 184.

Materials

computers
printer (If not available, photograph the completed art on the monitor.)
scanning software, or digitized art
computer paper
computer disks for saving art
optional: drawing media such as pencils, pens, and ink

Note: Because graphics programs often use a lot of memory, you may need to use a Zip® disk and Zip® drive or writeable CD. Although these are more expensive than regular floppy disks, they hold much more information, allowing a whole class to store their art on one of them.

Lesson 12
pages 185–189   45 minutes

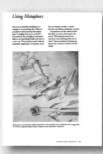

page 185

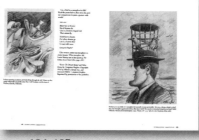

pages 186–187

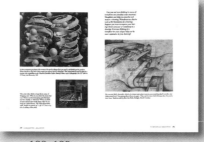

pages 188–189

Teach

After students have read these pages, ask them to define simile and metaphor. Then have each student write an example of a simile and metaphor. Compile a class list of these on the board. Encourage them to think of similes and metaphors in the lyrics of popular songs or poems from their literature course.

Studio Experience

Instruct students to make several thumbnail sketches of similes or metaphors that they might illustrate. After they have decided on their subject, encourage them to consider the composition of their design. Have them enlarge their thumbnail sketch on a larger piece of illustration board or paper.

Materials

drawing media such as pencils, pen and ink, or markers
15" x 20" illustration board or 12" x 18" drawing paper
erasers
paper for planning

Lesson 13
pages 190–191   45 minutes

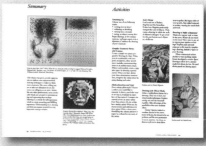

pages 190–191

Reteach

• Review with students the many different ways to stimulate creativity that they studied in this chapter, such as giving life to inanimate objects, using color expressively, gathering ideas from art of other cultures, drawing spontaneously as in graffiti, fusing drawing and painting in a composition, incorporating photocopies and computer-generated images into a drawing, and illustrating metaphors.

• Suggest that students use more than one of these techniques in an activity on page 191. For the Drawing to Make a Statement activity, students might turn inanimate objects into living creatures, illustrate a metaphor, use color expressively, and even include photocopies in their drawing. In the Drawing with Mixed Media activity, students could incorporate several of these creative techniques in a multicultural theme.

Assess

• Direct students to arrange their artworks into a portfolio. Which works do they believe are most creative? Together with each student review the portfolio, looking for growth in creativity in the drawings. Select several for the student to mat or mount to include in a class or school art show. As you assess each portfolio check to see that each student:

—Did create an artwork using art forms from other cultures as a source of ideas. (Art history/ Art production)

—Demonstrates an understanding of how drawing and painting may be fused in a composition. (Art production)

—Understands how photocopied and computer-generated images can be used in artworks. (Art production/Art criticism)

—Experimented with placing an object in an unexpected setting to give life to the object. (Art production/Art criticism)

—Understands that a metaphor may be used as the foundation of an art composition. (Art production)

—Demonstrates an understanding of color schemes in her or his own art. (Art production)

• To determine that students understand warm, cool, complementary, split complementary, triad, and analogous color schemes, ask them to identify examples of these color schemes either in this book or in other materials. This may be done in a class discussion or as a written activity. (Art criticism)

• To demonstrate their perception and appreciation of other artists' use of color in artworks, have students write or report on how Edgar Degas, Charles Burchfield, or the illuminator of the *Hours of the Duchess of Burgundy* used colors to create a mood or heighten the excitement or drama in their artwork. (Aesthetics)

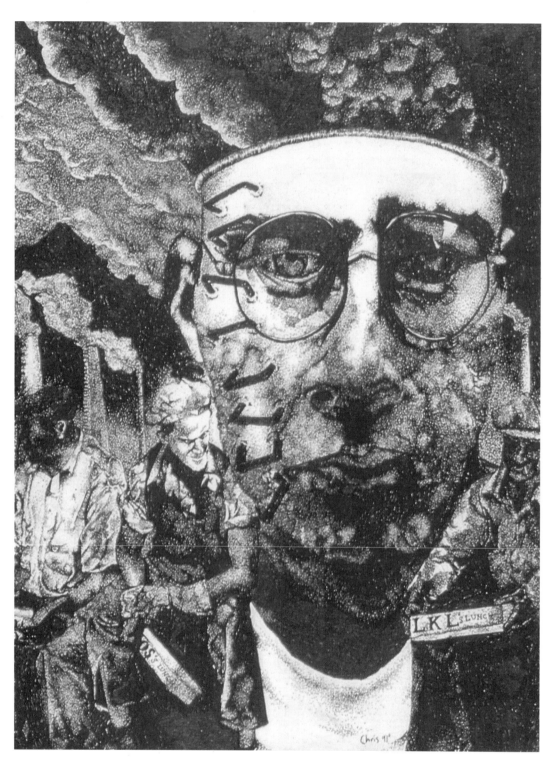

Drawings that make strong statements often combine images in unusual ways. What do you think this combination of images means? Student work by Christopher Ward, Libertyville, Illinois.

6 Stimulating Creativity

Creativity is not something that can be found in a book or learned in a few easy steps. However, you can develop your creativity through a variety of learning experiences.

This chapter investigates various ways to stimulate creativity. Multicultural experiences can help you explore the artwork of different cultures and open you to new ideas. Graffiti drawing can help you develop spontaneity in your drawings. New technology offers another medium for expression. You will learn how to incorporate photocopied and computer-generated images into your compositions.

Interpreting subject matter from a variety of points of view is another way to stimulate your creativity. Placing an inanimate object in a setting in which it does not belong can help you see the object in a different way. Thinking of an object in terms of a metaphor is another way to make an image strong and vivid. Metaphors are dramatic and forceful comparisons that help us see something more clearly and often in a new way.

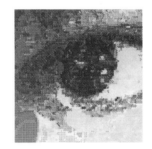

Chapter Warm-up
Draw students' attention to the illustrations on pages 148–152. Why are these artworks creative? Read the Think About It on page 150 and then discuss what is unusual in each of these drawings and paintings. To introduce combining unrelated ideas in unexpected ways, have students do the Loosening Up activity on page 191.

Key Chapter Points

- Art forms from different cultures are a source of new ideas.
- Drawing and painting can be fused in a composition.
- Photocopied and computer-generated images can be used in a composition.
- Placing an object in an unexpected setting can give life to the object.
- A metaphor can be used as the foundation of a composition.

Extension
The following sugges-
tions help students use
play to generate ideas:

• Play different types of
music in the classroom
to generate ideas.

• Let students try using
different media.

• Suggest the use of
doodling to help resolve
an "artist's block."

• Start a free association
word exercise.

• Have students draw
a simple object ten
different ways.

• Look at art from other
cultures.

Context
For a very different style
of art by Piet Mondrian
see page 2.

Mondrian left Paris for
London at the beginning
of World War II. Two
years later he moved to
New York City where he
lived his last four years.
Here he was stimulated
by the bright lights of
Manhattan skyscrapers
at night and the tempo
of the city with its jazz
bands, dance halls, and
general dynamism. Look
for the blinking window
lights of the night time
office buildings in
*Broadway Boogie-
Woogie.*

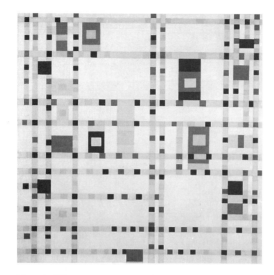

Boogie Woogie is a musical style with a fast,
irregular beat. Imagine the squares in this composition as musical notes. Can you see how they
jump around the image? Piet Mondrian, *Broadway
Boogie Woogie*, 1942. Oil on canvas, 50" x 50" (127
x 127 cm). The Museum of Modern Art, New
York. Given anonymously.

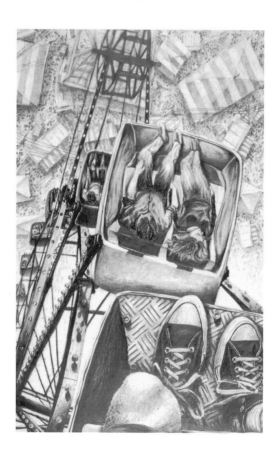

A good artist is always learning and
growing. Looking, listening, reading and
being open to all aspects of life can
broaden your experiences. Everything
you experience becomes a part of you and
can be reflected in your artwork.

For example, Piet Mondrian became
interested late in his life in jazz and the
syncopated rhythm called boogie woogie.
Mondrian found in New York City the
same vitality and energy that he heard in
jazz. *Broadway Boogie Woogie*, painted in
1942, is radically different from
Mondrian's earlier black-and-white grid
paintings. It shows how Mondrian
applied his feelings about jazz to look at
New York in a new way. In doing so, he
created a new direction in his art.

The purpose of creativity is to produce
unexpected, effective results. The broader
your range of experiences and the more
willing you are to take new directions in
your artwork, the more creative you
will be.

THINK ABOUT IT
*According to Picasso, creative thinking can
be thinking a thought no one else has come
up with. According to Andy Warhol, it can
be putting things together in a new way.*

Use the exercises on the following
pages to expand your creativity. They
offer different approaches to drawing.

Thinking about an unusual perspective can help
you generate creative ideas. Notice this artist's
use of atmospheric perspective to help give the
composition focus. Student work by Ben
MacNeil, Raleigh, North Carolina.

Giving Life to Inanimate Objects

Suppose you created a composition by placing an ordinary household item, like a hand mixer, in an unusual setting, like a garden. Such an arrangement challenges you (and the viewer) to look at both the object and the environment in a new way. Drawing an object from a different point of view can help you give life to the object.

Create your own composition. You may want to combine several unrelated objects into one composition. Experiment with different combinations of media, such as watercolors, ink, oil pastels and colored pencils. Use media that will enhance the qualities of the subject matter.

Extensions
• Students should notice how M. C. Escher combined an unusual setting for a bird and a different point of view in *Other World* on page 93.

• Encourage students to find other examples of unusual views of objects and people in this book.

Design Extension
• Challenge students to draw the metamorphosis of an ordinary tool changing into an animal.

• In a series of five steps draw an animal or common object gradually changing into a letter of the alphabet.

Hair takes on a strange life of its own in this highly detailed work. Is it just a girl on a swing—or is the house on fire? Student work by Mason Doran, Livonia, New York.

Extension
The Scale Change activity on page 191 will help students learn more about how the Surrealist artists utilized scale changes to create eerie moods in their art.

Inquiry
Assign students to research the works of a Surreal artist such as Max Ernst, de Chirico, Tanguy, Miro, or Magritte, who used unusual views and exaggerated perspectives to create a mood. Students should also discover how world events influenced these artists. Have students create a poster explaining their findings.

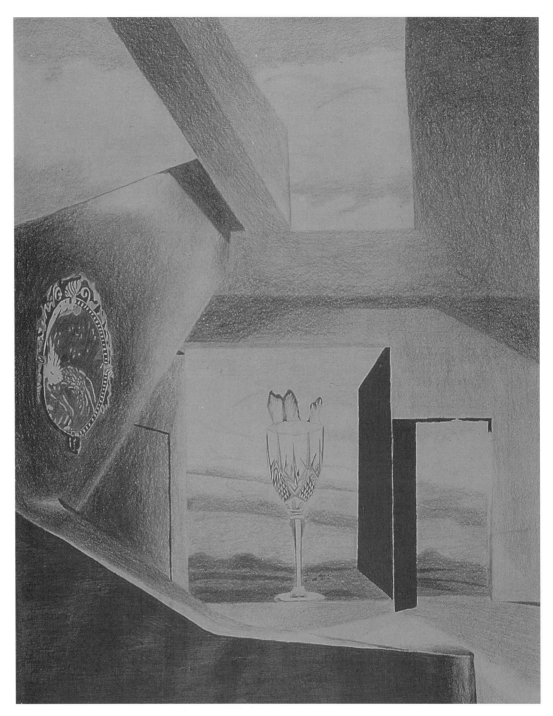

Seeing a crystal goblet by itself in a surreal setting raises immediate questions. Is the goblet a symbol for something else? What is it sitting in, and why? Works that are visual puzzles can make you question your own assumptions and look more closely. Student work by Michael Lowrance, Temple, Texas.

Color

The use of color can give life to a drawing. Color can accent elements and reinforce relationships in a composition. Colors can establish the mood of a work. Exploring color in your work can stimulate your creativity and technical ability. Color gives you the option to emphasize areas, create moods and incorporate a wider range of materials into your work. Colored pencils, pastels, crayons, color inks, and markers are just a few of the materials that you can use to develop color in your drawings.

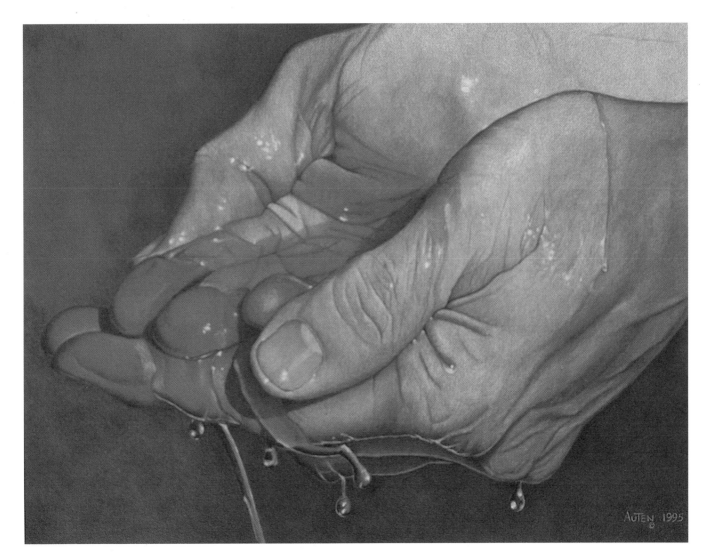

How has the artist's use of color strengthened her development of value in this composition? Bonnie Auten, *The Anointing*, 1995. Colored pencil, 21" x 25" (53.3 x 63.5 cm). Courtesy of the artist.

The Color Wheel

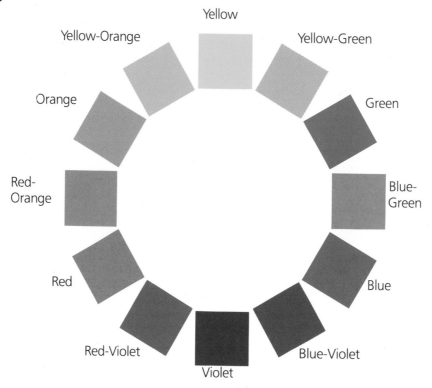

The color wheel. Eighteenth century scientist Isaac Newton first used a circle to show the colors or *hues*, of the spectrum. The color wheel was developed from that circle.

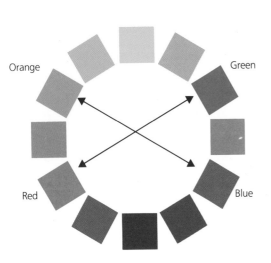

Complementary colors are opposite in hue and are also opposite each other on the color wheel.

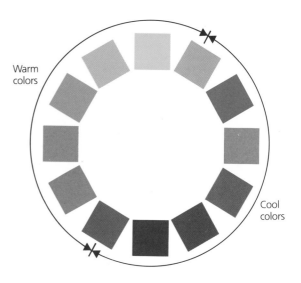

Most colors have a "temperature". Reds, oranges and yellows look warm and make us think of things like fire or the sun. Blues, greens and violets look cooler, and suggest grass, shade and water.

Color Schemes

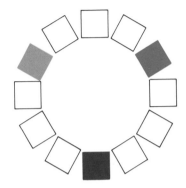

A *triad scheme* is made up of three equidistant hues on the color wheel. Here, orange, green and violet are shown–a harmonious scheme because these secondary hues have colors in common.

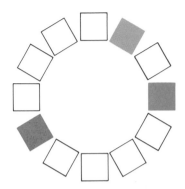

A *split complementary scheme* is made up of one hue plus the hues on either side of its complement: for instance, red, plus yellow-green and blue-green. Complementary colors tend to clash; choosing colors near the complement lessens the clashing, yet still provides contrast.

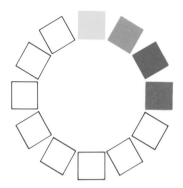

An *analogous scheme* is created from colors next to each other on the color wheel. Because of the colors they share (in this case, blue and yellow), these schemes are quite harmonious.

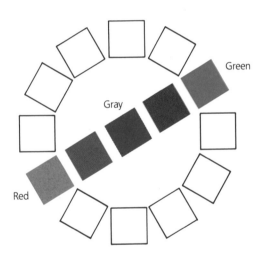

Green

Gray

Red

Mixing a color with its complement can produce a neutral gray.

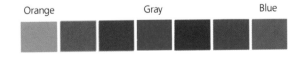

Orange   Gray   Blue

Value is the lightness or darkness of a color. This value scale shows red (fourth block from left) plus its tints and shades. Tints are created by adding white, shades by adding black.

Saturation (also called intensity) describes a color's brightness or dullness. This scale shows how mixing a color with different amounts of its complement dulls the color.

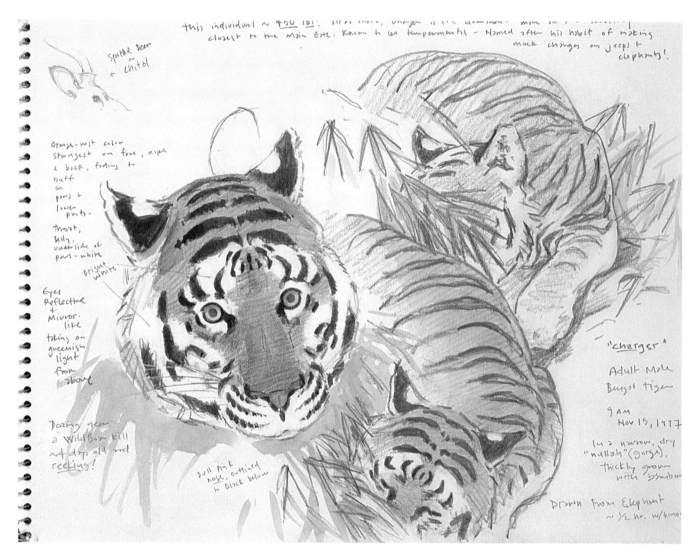

This field sketch was made while the artist sat atop an elephant. More typically, he "gets close" to wildlife by sketching while he looks through a telescope. Barry Van Dusen, *Bengal Tiger, Bandhavgarh National Park, India,* 1997. Pencil and watercolor, 9" x 12" (22.9 x 30.5 cm). Courtesy of the artist.

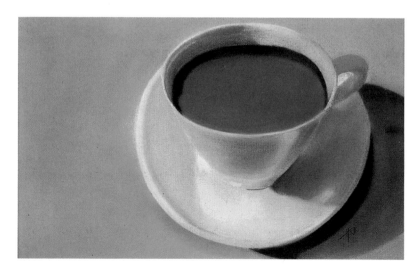

Experiment with your uses of color. Coffee doesn't have to be brown, shadows don't have to be gray. Surprising colors catch the viewer's eye. Student work by Hoang Nguyen, Bondurant, Iowa.

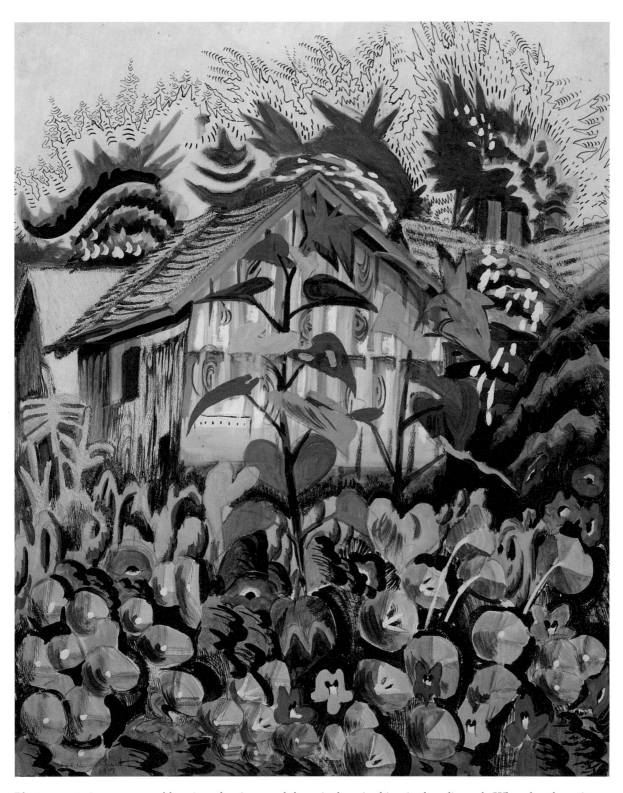

Plants seem to jump, wave and leap into the air around the quiet barn in this mixed media work. Where has the artist used line to emphasize that effect? How do you think he feels about the natural world? Charles Burchfield, *Nasturtiums and the Barn*, 1917. Watercolor, charcoal, gouache, wash, crayon, ink, pencil on paper, 22" x 18" (56 x 46 cm). McNay Art Institute, San Antonio, Texas.

Experiment by drawing the same subject several times, using a different media each time. Combine several of these media in one composition.

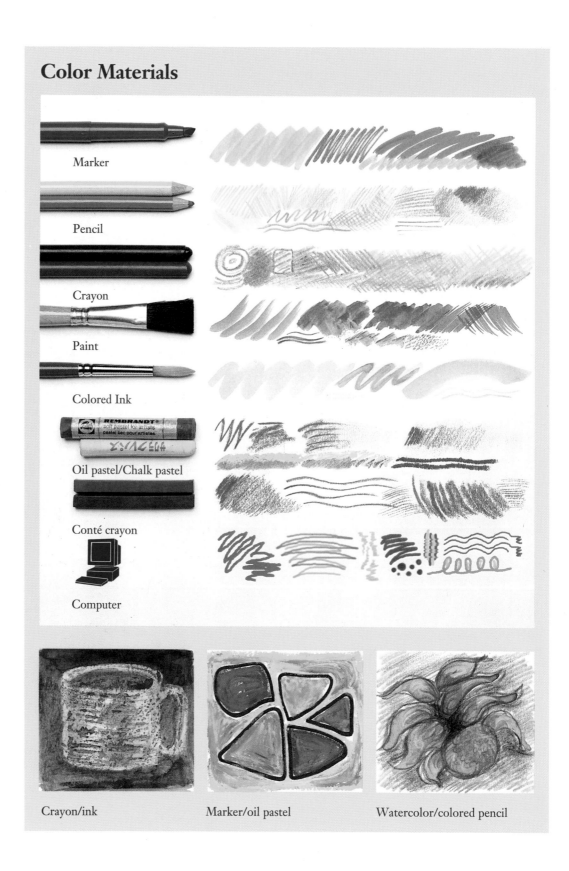

Color Materials

Marker

Pencil

Crayon

Paint

Colored Ink

Oil pastel/Chalk pastel

Conté crayon

Computer

Crayon/ink

Marker/oil pastel

Watercolor/colored pencil

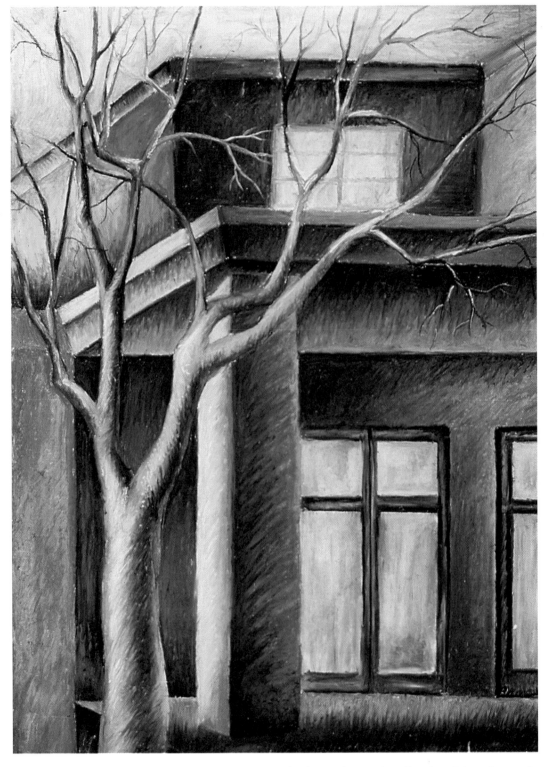

Can you find examples of complementary, warm, cool, and analogous color schemes in these color pages?

You can blend pastel with a finger or tissue to create soft edges and mix colors. In spite of the softness of the medium, pastel colors can be quite vivid. Student work by Natalya Kaliazine, *The Entrance*, 1997. Soft pastels, 24" x 18" (61 x 45.7 cm). Lake Highlands High School, Dallas, Texas.

People associate colors with feelings. For example, we talk of having the blues, or being green with envy. A self-portrait can be an opportunity to use color symbolically to express the kind of person you feel you are. Two of these artworks are self-portraits. What do you think these artists were saying about themselves?

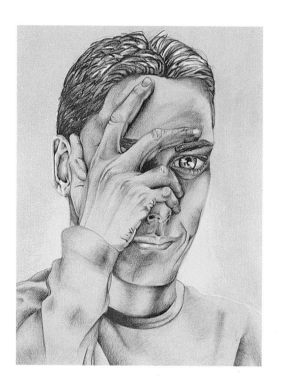

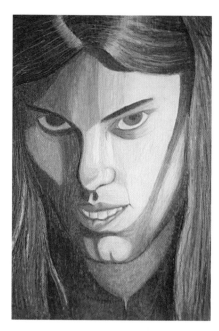

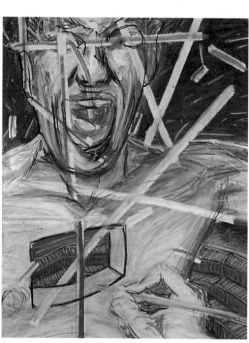

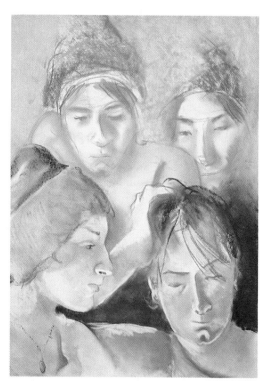

Do you think the use of color enhances these portraits? Why or why not? Student work by (clockwise from upper left): Nicholas Kraszyk, *Me, Myself, and I*, 1999. Pencil, 24" x 16" (61 x 40.6 cm). Oakmont Regional High School, Ashburnham, Massachusetts; Danielle VanVooren, *Ram*, 1998. Oil crayon, 24" x 18" (61 x 45.7 cm). Holy Name CC Junior and Senior High School, Worcester, Massachusetts; Carlee Freeman, *Untitled*, 1998. Pastel, 24" x 18" (61 x 45.7 cm). Asheville High School, Asheville, North Carolina; Jay Carlson, *Self-portrait*, 1998. Pastel, 24" x 18" (61 x 45.7 cm). Plano Senior High School, Plano, Texas.

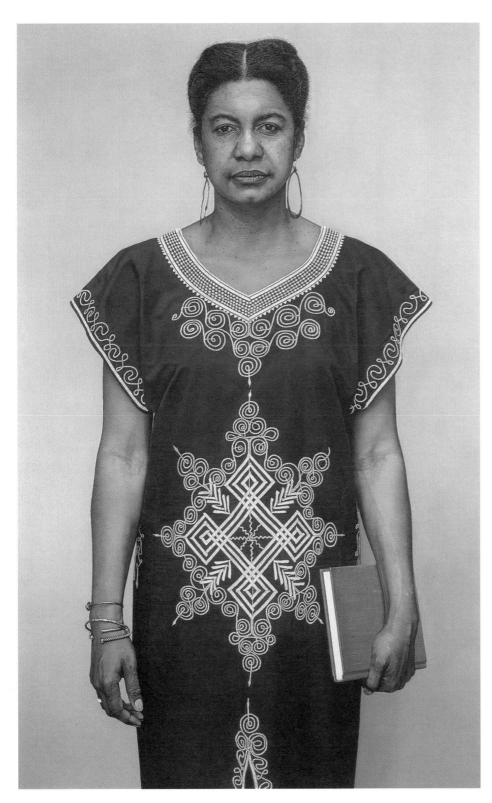

What color are the highlights and shadows in the model's skin? Accurate use and blending of colors is essential in Photo-Realism. How has the artist used the design principle of balance to evoke a particular mood? Jane Lund, *Portrait of a Scholar*, 1994-95. Pastel on paper, 46" x 30" (116.8 x 76 cm). Courtesy of Forum Gallery, New York.

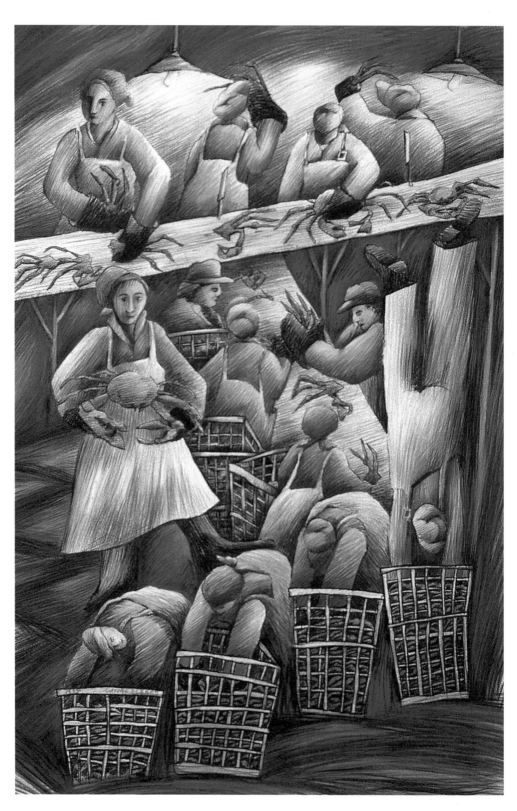

How has this artist created a sense of movement? Has the use of color helped her accomplish this? What gives the work its unity? Compare the technique of the pencil strokes in this work with that of the colored pencil work on page 153. Carolyn Reed, *Cannery Dance VI*, 1997. Colored pencil and charcoal, 26" x 18" (66 x 45.7 cm) Collection of the Alaska State Museum, Juneau, Alaska. Courtesy of the artist.

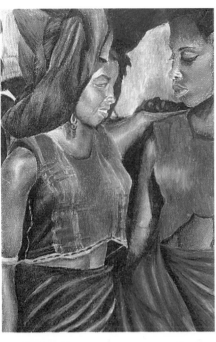

Does the artist's choice of color add to the sense of balance in this drawing? How? Student work by Cecilia Smith, *Tribal Life*, 1999. Colored pencil, 15" x 10" (38.1 x 25.4 cm). Plano Senior High School, Plano, Texas.

Although the pencils used to create this work were not color, the selection of a colored background greatly enhances the final outcome. Student work by Sarah Penniman, *When Cups Break*, 1998. Black and white pencil on toned paper, 11 1/2" x 17 1/2" (29 x 44.5 cm). Oakmont Regional High School, Ashburnham, Massachusetts.

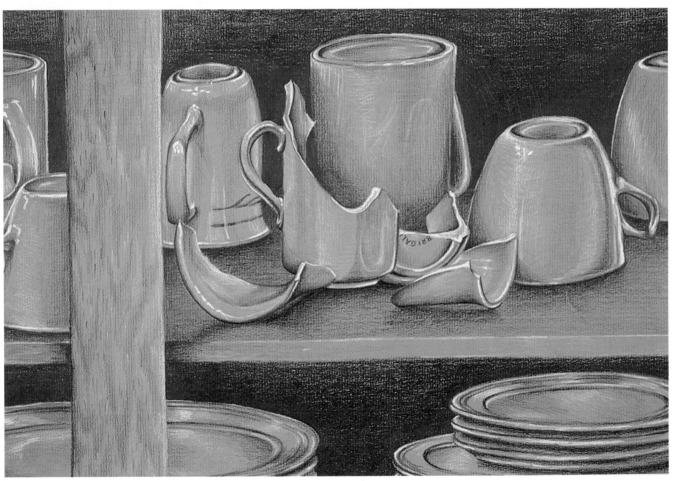

When artists mix pigments to create hues, they are working with subtractive color theory. The colors we see are the wavelengths reflected, not absorbed. A combination of all colors produces black. (Due to the limitations of pigments, it cannot be a true black.)

You can explore additive color theory (mixing light waves) by experimenting with colors on a computer. The primary colors in this system are red, green, and blue. A combination of these pure colors produces white.

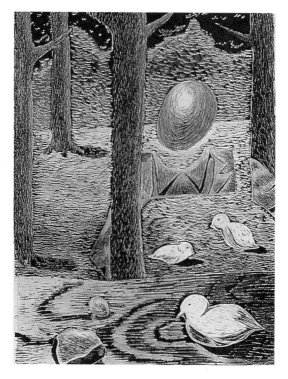

A landscape such as the one shown here can raise intriguing questions. Note how the artist has used color, value, and proportion along with positive and negative space to challenge our sense of depth. Student work by Sharon Huang, *Man in the Woods*, 1998. Colored pencil and scratchboard, 10" x 7 1/2" (25.4 x 19.1 cm). Plano Senior High School, Plano, Texas.

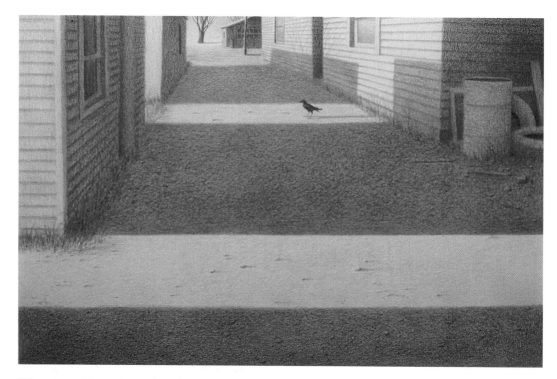

What time of day is shown here? The shadows are sensitively rendered in this work. List the colors found in the shadows. Where are the darkest values? Note how the use of value contributes to the sense of depth. Allan Servoss, *Investigations of a Crow IV*, 1997. Colored pencil, 12" x 30" (31 x 76 cm). Courtesy of the artist.

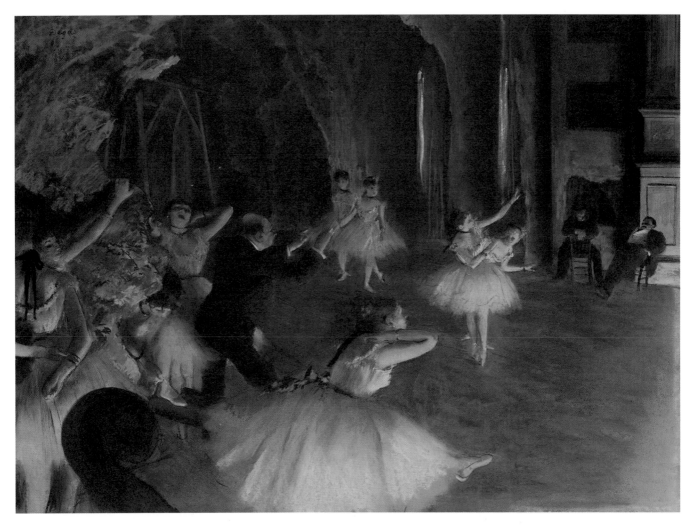

This work, shown in black and white on page 37, is a pastel drawing. How has the artist used light to create drama and interest? Where do you see the most detail? Can you tell the color of the paper the artist worked on? Edgar Hilaire Germain Degas, *The Rehearsal on the Stage*, nineteenth century. Pastel over brush-and-ink drawing on paper, 21" x 28 1/2" (53.3 x 72.3 cm). The Metropolitan Museum of Art, Bequest of Mrs. H. O. Havemeyer, 1929. The H. O. Havemeyer Collection. (29.100.39)

See page 194 for
a detail of the
scene and pages
168 and 200 for
other illuminated
manuscripts.

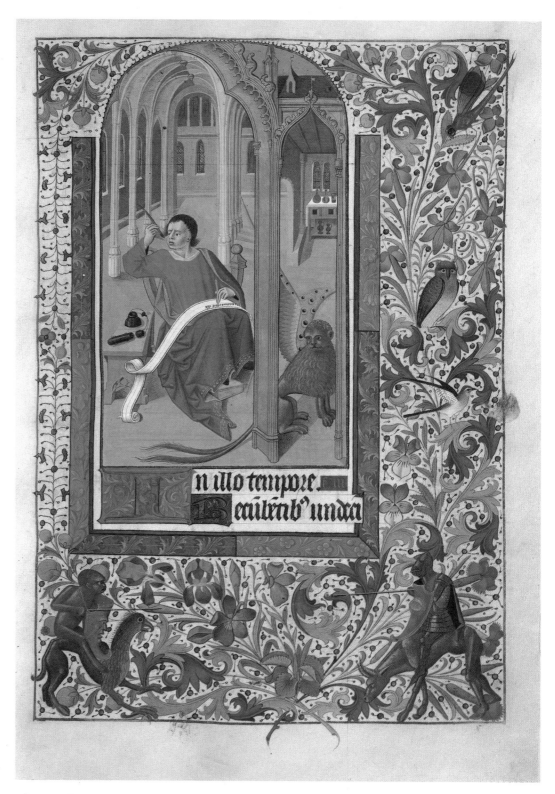

This page from an illuminated manuscript, with its linear perspective, realistic details, and rich, jewel-like colors, is painted in the International style. Look for the jousting scene in the lower margin. How many birds and insects can you find? *Hours of the Duchess of Burgundy*, ca. 1450 (ms. 76/1362), folio with miniature of St. Mark. Chantilly, Musée Condé. Courtesy Giraudon/Art Resource, NY.

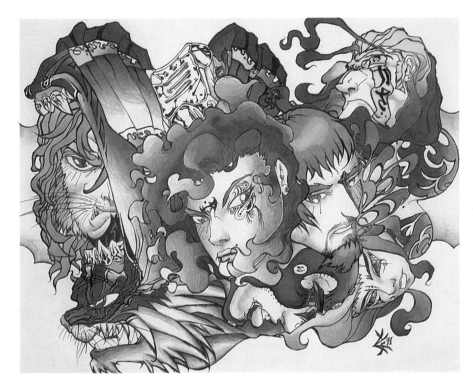

This artist has skillfully used color to render at least seven different faces. Student work by Anthony Austin, *Scarlet Swords*, 1998. Pencil, ink, and colored pencil, 12" x 18" (30.5 x 45.7 cm). Ashland High School, Ashland, Massachusetts.

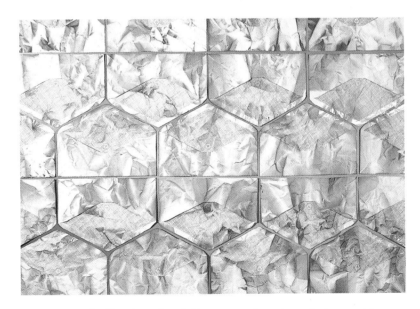

Do you see a familiar shape here? Can you see how the artist has used it to create a repeated pattern? Does color create a mood in the work? Dana Chipman Laman, *Old Mail*, 1991. Mixed media, 28" x 39" (71 x 99 cm). Courtesy of the artist.

You can use colored watercolor washes to indicate wrinkles in crumpled paper. Note that shadows are not just one hue but many. Try using color and value, not line, to show shadows.

This illuminated manuscript includes the intricate ornamental patterns of early medieval art. These curling, colorful shapes produce a feeling of movement. Compare this illuminated manuscript with the later International Style one on page 166. What do you notice about the alphabets?

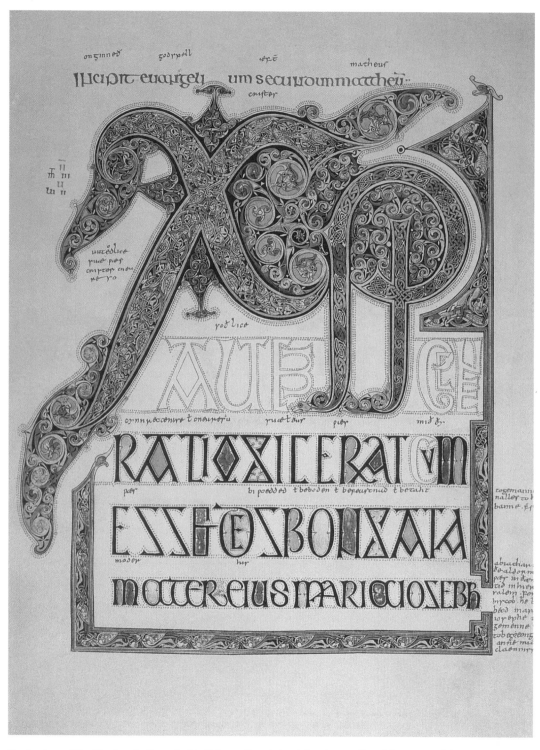

Beginning of St. Matthew's Gospel. *Lindisfarne Gospels* (c. 698 AD), MX. Cott Nero D IV, fol. 29. British Library, London, Great Britain/Art Resource, New York.

Developing Multicultural Experiences

People in different cultures throughout the world have unique ways of expressing their values and beliefs in their artwork. Studying past and present cultures can enrich your visual vocabulary and expand your points of view.

Picasso's work is an excellent example of cross-cultural influence. Picasso used the simplified lines and forms he saw in African masks to create works such as *Mother and Child*. Picasso used African art to stimulate his growth as an artist.

The best way to approach multicultural studies is to review artwork created by different civilizations all over the world. What are the differences between art from Western civilizations and art from the Far East? How do the structures found in Egypt compare to those of the Mayans or Aztecs? What are the differences and similarities between carvings of the Northwest Coast Indians and carvings by the natives of New Guinea?

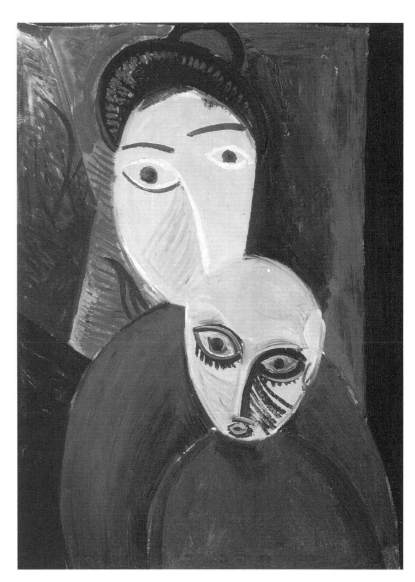

Can you see any relationships between Picasso's painting, above, and the African mask at left? Notice eyebrows, facial markings, mouths. What do you think interested Picasso about masks? Above: Pablo Picasso, *Mother and Child*, 1907. Reunion des Musée des Arts Africains et Oceaniens, Paris. Giraudon/Art Resource, NY. Oil on canvas. Courtesy SPADEM. Left: Mask, Gabon. Musée des Arts Africains et Oceaniens, Paris. Giraudon/Art Resource, NY.

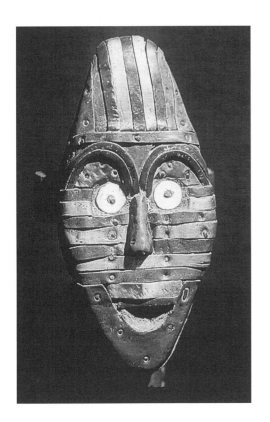

Context
After visiting a museum exhibit of African art, Spanish artist Pablo Picasso began to base the figures in his paintings on African masks and sculpture. To art viewers of the early twentieth century, this derivation of style from outside the Western tradition was shocking.

Design Extensions

• Visit a museum so that students may sketch artworks from other cultures to use as motifs in their multicultural rubbings.

• Ink a brayer very lightly by rolling out ink on a plate and then rolling off excess ink on a scrap piece of paper. Lay a lightweight paper over the collage and roll the lightly inked brayer over the paper to create an impression similar to the rubbings but in ink.

• To print a collagraph from the collage, first coat the collage with acrylic medium. When this has dried, make a print by inking the collage, laying paper over it, and rubbing with either a clean brayer or large spoon or burin or putting it through a press.

Inquiry

Assign each student to research the art of one of the cultures on pages 170–171. What images or motifs often appear in this society's art? They may make a poster about the culture or country, a map indicating its location in the world, and several reproductions of the culture's artwork. Have them label the artworks with the date, media, and meaning of symbols. This activity may be done in cooperative-learning groups.

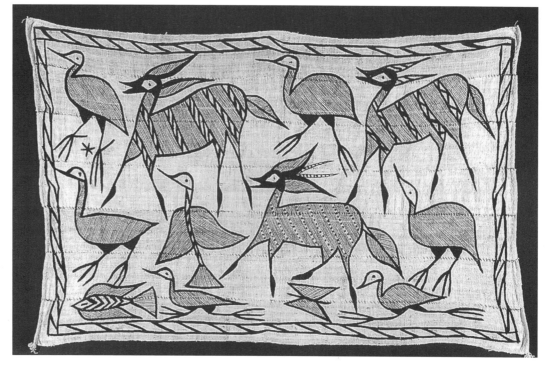

This African cloth uses simple lines and patterns to depict animals and birds. How is movement suggested? French West Africa, painting. Mud on cloth, 20th century. Courtesy Karen Durlach.

THINK ABOUT IT

Transferring knowledge from one area to another is the real test of true learning!

This exercise gives you an opportunity to explore new approaches to making marks.

1. Select images, symbols or lettering from a culture that interests you.

2. Draw the ones you select on a sheet of poster board. Then, cut them out and glue them to a sheet of illustration board.

3. Lay a sheet of durable lightweight paper on top of the image. Then, create a rubbing by drawing layers of lines over the image.

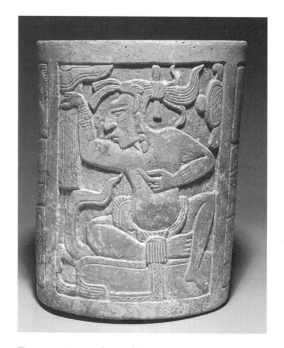

Exaggeration and simplification give this carved vase great presence. Do you think the carving tells a story? Mayan carved vase, late Classic period, ca. 550–950 AD. Private collection. Art Resource, NY.

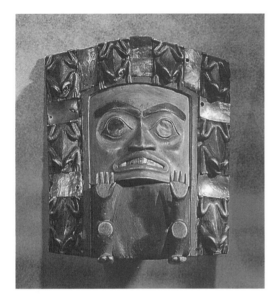

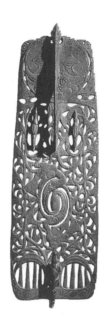

What ceremonies have you been part of? What objects or clothing do you use in those ceremonies? Ceremonial Board, New Guinea, Middle Sepik River, Sawos. Wood, 74 1/4" (189 cm) high. The Metropolitan Museum of Art, The Michael C. Rockefeller Memorial Collection, Gift of Nelson A. Rockefeller, 1969.

Many cultures use images from nature to express ideas. What might nature have meant to this artist? Head plaque with frog totems, Northwest Coast of America, Tsimshian, Skeena River. Wood, abalone shell. Museum of Man, Ottawa. Courtesy Werner Forman Archive. Art Resource, NY.

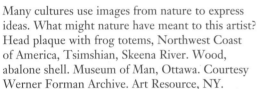

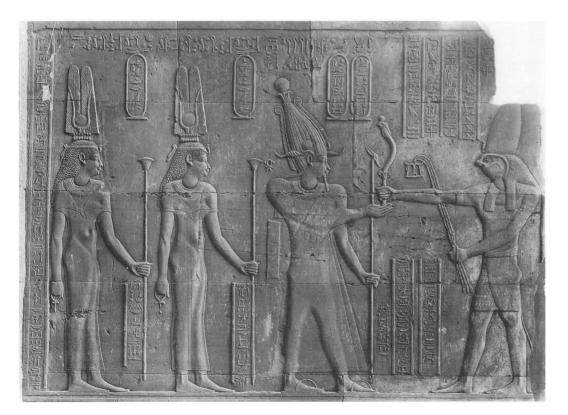

Egyptian art often includes gods shown as animals (notice the bird's head at extreme right). Can you imagine the story this wall relief tells? *Temple of Suchos and Haroeris. Horus consigning to Pharaoh Energetos II his sword, behind the Pharaoh his sister and wife Cleopatra.* Kom Ombo, Egypt. Foto/Marburg/Art Resource, NY.

Interdisciplinary Connection

Social Studies/ Performing Arts—For a deeper understanding of a culture, have students explore the literature, dance, music, food, and geography of a country. Invite other teachers to help create an interdisciplinary unit of study. If possible, invite guest artists from this culture to perform and introduce their art.

Context

• The reasons behind the rigid, unchanging style of Egyptian drawing are explored in Chapter 7. Encourage students to identify similar characteristics between the drawing on page 197 and this relief.

• The ovals between the figures are cartouches enclosing names of the figures written in hieroglyphics. The pharaoh wears his ceremonial beard and the conical crown of Egypt topped by a disk representing the sun god Ra. The two women are holding the ankh sign, symbol of life, in their right hands.

Higher-Order Thinking Skills

Discuss how drawing images and symbols in the style of another culture enriched their understanding of that culture. Encourage students to write brief reflections on the process and what they learned.

Design Extensions
• Refer students to page 32 to review another rubbing activity.

• The rubbings in these examples were made from the sole of a tennis shoe. After students have made rubbings from their own and their friends' shoes, encourage them to create rubbings from other objects in the room.

• Create a resist by brushing watercolors or thinned india ink over rubbings made with crayons and oil pastels.

Context
Frottage is the French term for "rubbings."

Extensions
• To learn more about artists of a culture, students may complete the Multiculturalism and Style activity on page 191.

• The Drawing with Mixed Media activity on page 191 will help students further explore ways to create artwork influenced by another culture.

Rubbings

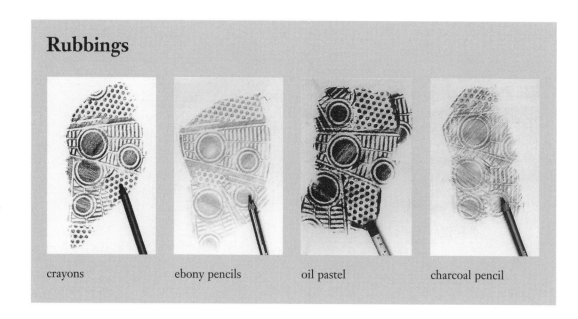

crayons   ebony pencils   oil pastel   charcoal pencil

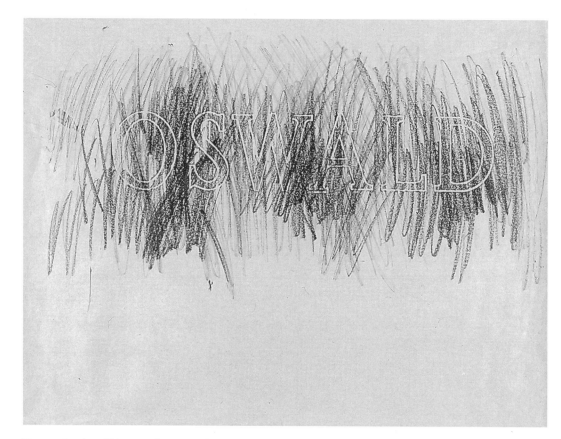

Even a simple rubbing can have visual mystery.

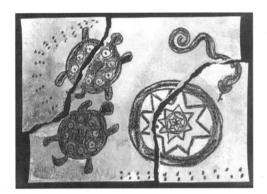

This artist used crayon, salt and watercolor with torn paper to suggest Native American rock art. What symbols has she chosen to use? What might the torn paper mean? Student work by Nikki Kelsey, Temple, Texas.

Context
Did students notice the letters in Ha Young Lee's rubbing? What cultures are alluded to here? (African, but also European if you consider the letter forms)

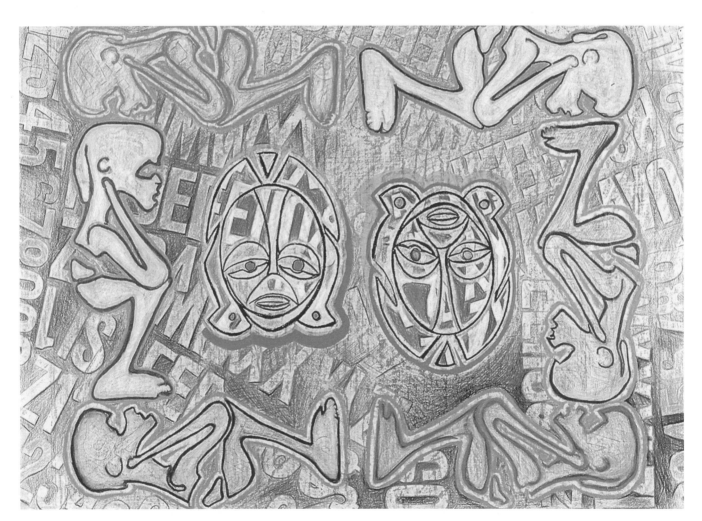

Rubbing techniques and drawn in lines were used to create this energetic composition. Can you see influences from other cultures here? Student work by Ha Young Lee, São Paulo, Brazil.

Spontaneity through Graffiti

Teaching Tip

When reviewing student-generated graffiti, look for spontaneity, richness of surface, creative marking systems, and unique design and image.

Design Extensions

• Have one student draw a doodle on a large sheet of paper and pass the sheet to another student. Continue until all students have drawn on it. Then have students write about the piece they've created.

• Read a short story to the class, one that takes no more than ten minutes. As you read, have students draw along.

• Play music as students create graffiti drawings. Suggest that they try drawing to the music.

• Begin a graffiti wall by stretching large sheets of craft paper on an art studio wall or in the corridor. Encourage people to doodle. To give this wall direction, write a statement for people to respond to in writing and drawings.

Context

Los Four was a group of Los Angeles artists who collaborated on murals that blended elements of graffiti with the Chicano car culture. One of their murals, *Going to the Olympics*, was painted on a Los Angeles freeway retaining wall in 1984.

Graffiti drawing offers you a creative outlet for free and spontaneous drawing. What do you think of when you hear the word graffiti? Did you know that graffiti can be found in galleries and museums and not just on public buildings? Graffiti drawing is loose and unstructured. It is energetic and can be visually powerful.

Explore using different types of media to create your own graffiti drawing. What feelings do you want it to express?

1. Lay in large areas of spontaneous marks, movements, symbols, images and lettering.

2. Gradually build up these marks in layers, emphasizing dominant shapes.

3. Use a variety of edges on the shapes.

4. Develop and vary the qualities expressed by the lines.

5. Work to develop a wide range of surfaces.

6. Include a broad range of values. Make one color dominant.

THINK ABOUT IT
Did you find that you came up with new ideas as you were drawing? Often, the best ideas come during the process of drawing.

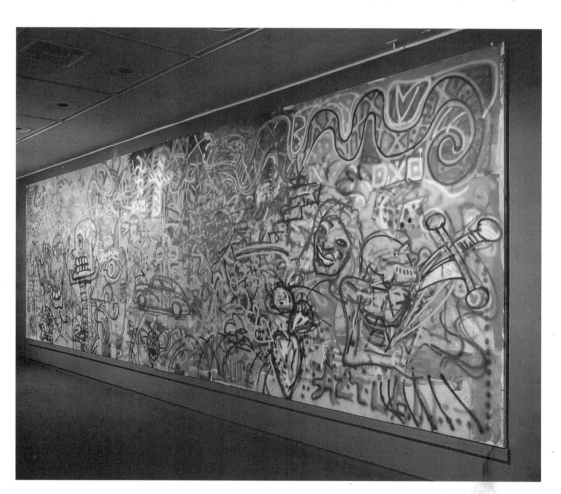

Layers of active lines and shapes give this graffiti drawing great energy—and echo the movement and visual chaos of many large cities. Los Four (Carlos David Almaraz, Gilbert Lujan, Roberto de la Rocha, Frank Romero), *Group Mural*, 1973. Acrylic spray paint on canvas, 9' x 22' (3 x 7.1 m). Los Angeles County Museum of Art, lent by the artists.

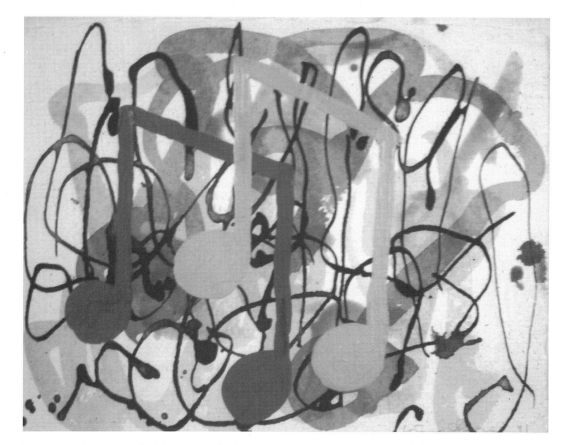

Try to imagine the music this artist might have been listening to as she created this work. What mood has the artist created? Louisa Chase, *Untitled*, 1991. Ink and acrylic on paper, 10" x 13" (25.4 x 33 cm). Courtesy of the artist.

Inquiry
• Research Los Four and Frank Romero to learn more about Chicano murals. (Try the Getty Education Institute which can be accessed via ArtsEdNet at www.artsednet.getty. edu/.)

• Another artist whose early works appeared as subway graffiti was Keith Haring. Ask students to discover some of the causes that he tried to help through his art. (There were many including Special Olympics and drug education.) Haring died of AIDS in 1990 at age 31.

Higher-Order Thinking Skills
Challenge students to identify repeated shapes and elements in this mural. Describe the movement in *Group Mural* on page 174.

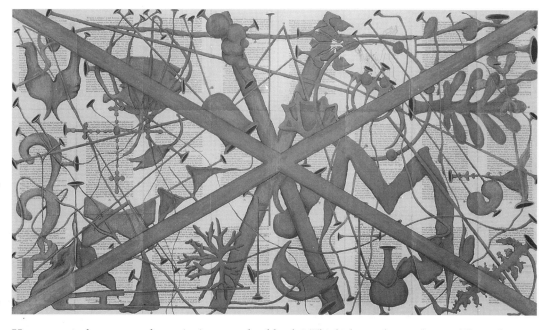

Have you ever been tempted to write in your school books? Think about why or why not. Then take a look at this work, done by students from The Bronx (See also page 176). Tim Rollins + K. O. S., *Study for Amerika X*, 1988. Watercolor and bistre on book pages on linen, 24" x 42" (61 x 107 cm). Courtesy Art and Knowledge Workshop. Photograph: Ken Schles.

Tim Rollins + K. O. S.

In 1981, a young artist named Tim Rollins began to teach art at one of the special education schools in the South Bronx of New York. Rollins often read literary classics to his students. One day Rollins noticed a student was drawing right on the pages of his book. Angry at first, Rollins became astonished as he looked closely at the image the student had drawn. The student had captured the essence of the novel in his drawing. This incident lead to the creation of a new kind of teaching. Rollins called it K. O. S. (Kids of Survival) and the Art and Knowledge Workshop.

What Tim Rollins and his students are creating does not fit into any familiar art category. It is a unique type of collaboration between an artist–teacher and students–artists. The role of the teacher is to select a piece of literature that students will transform into images. K. O. S. students read the text aloud and then work together to decide how to represent it visually. They draw their images on the pages of the text. Then, using a slow process of selection, they select images to place on a piece of canvas as the finished work.

The *Amerika* series was inspired by a famous scene from a novel by Franz Kafka. Students were told to use their imagination. The variety of images that emerged was stupendous. Students represented themselves as golden trumpets, and included letters, body parts, animals and baseball bats in the final panel.

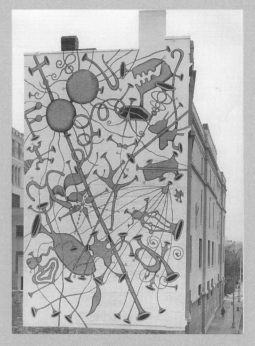

Tim Rollins + K. O. S., *Amerika—For the People of Bathgate*, 1988. Mural, 55' x 36' (18 x 12 m), Central Elementary School 4, Bronx, New York. Executed by Jerry Johnson. Photograph © Peter Bellamy, 1988.

The art produced by K. O. S. has universal appeal. Paintings from the Art and Knowledge Workshop have been exhibited all over the world. The thought-provoking methods used by Tim Rollins have resulted in artwork that is stylistically unique. Through the creation of this art, students from the South Bronx have learned about the world beyond their boundaries and have taught the world about the South Bronx.

Fusion of Drawing and Painting

Have you ever found that you can apply skills that you have learned in one subject area to another? The skills and techniques you have learned in drawing can be applied to paintings. The fusion of drawing and painting can help you plan a composition.

In this exercise, you will be *drawing in* a chair set up at an interesting angle and *painting out* the ground.

1. Prime a sheet of illustration board with a light gray or off-colored pastel.
2. Using graphite pencils and sticks, sketch the chair and the shadows by drawing through the object to find the correct proportions.
3. Layer the lines to explore positive and negative space. Draw the lines in directions that "carve out" the space in the still life.
4. Paint out unnecessary lines and clean up the ground. This layer of paint will clarify the image and give it more life. Using a rag to partially remove some areas of paint will add motion and expression to the chair.
5. To give added strength to the composition, try painting in highlights found in the ground or the chair.
6. Draw in extreme darks and add fine line highlights with white chalk.

Can you give a chair personality? Mystery? Humor? Do you have a favorite chair? Try drawing it for this exercise. Student work by John Chapman, Weatherford, Texas.

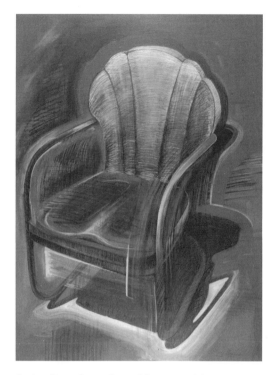

Active lines throughout this composition seem to lift the chair off the ground. What other techniques has the artist used to give the chair life and presence? Author, *Chair*, 1993.

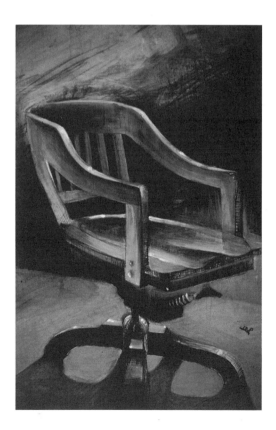

Extension
Explain that the Dutch artist Vincent van Gogh thought that a chair could symbolize its owners' personality. *Vincent's Chair*, with a pipe on the cane seat, is painted in light, sunny colors; he painted *Gauguin's Armchair* with a candle on its seat in darker night tones.

Teaching Tip
This activity synthesizes topics covered in previous chapters. Before students begin, review what students have already learned: drawing through an object to find correct proportions; using shading to suggest volume; creating positive and negative space through tone.

Step-by-step illustrations and instructions for this activity appear on page 178.

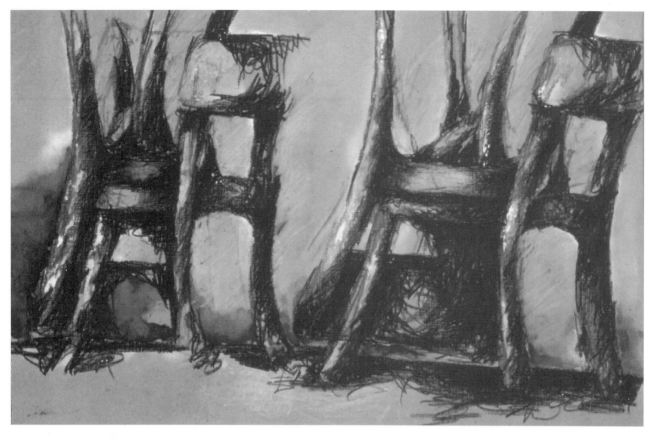

Using many kinds of line, deep shadows and an interesting color of paper can help enliven any composition. And when you really examine them, you may find that chairs aren't as ordinary as you'd thought. Student work by Minn Lee, Charlotte, North Carolina.

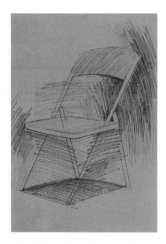

Sketching the planes of space in the chair.

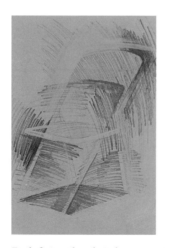

Redefining the chair by painting out unwanted areas.

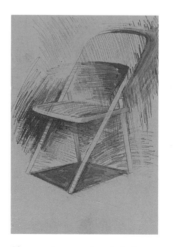

Sharpening up the chair by adding accent lines.

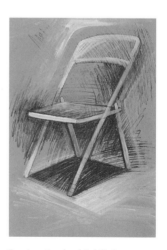

Laying in the highlights.

Papers

Almost any kind of paper can be used for drawing. The least expensive papers are made from wood pulp and produced by machine or molds. High-quality papers are made with a great deal of care and have a high-rag content, which makes them expensive. High-quality papers are easily identified by a watermark or relief stamp of the manufacturer's name. Paper surfaces range from smooth to very coarse with many gradations in between. Smooth paper, also called hot-press or plate-finish, is especially good for pen and pencil drawings. Fine- or medium-grained papers (cold-press or kid-finish) are suitable for graphite pencils or sticks, wax or colored pencils, pastels, colored chalks and wash. The coarsest-grained paper is usually used for watercolor.

While inexpensive papers are excellent for experimenting with media and techniques, they become brittle and yellow with age. High-quality papers are best for works to be included in a portfolio or those expected to last for a long time. Because of their rag content, high-quality papers will not become brittle or yellow with age. They are exciting to use because their surfaces have great tactile appeal.

Materials Used
(left to right)
1. Drawing ink applied with bamboo brush
2. Conté crayon
3. China pencil
4. Graphite pencil, unwrapped
5. Technical-drawing pen

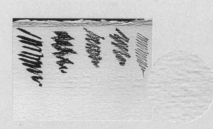

Printmaking paper, 118 lb.

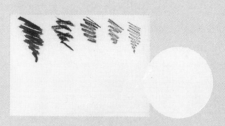

Hot-press illustration board, #172

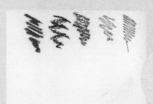

Cold-press illustration board, #80

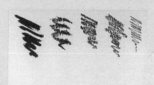

Bristol board, 100 lb., kid-finish

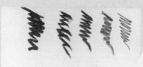

Bristol paper, 1 ply, plate-finish

Higher-Order Thinking Skills
Challenge the students to find art in this book in which the texture of the drawing surface is visible, even affecting the appearance of the art. (Possible examples are on pages 137, 192, 196, 198, and 205.)

Using Photocopied Images

Photocopiers can help artists visualize information in different ways. For example, photocopied images can translate photographs or drawings into simplified shapes. Contrasts in values can be seen more clearly. Images produced by a photocopier can show exciting dot patterns. What are some ways that artists can use this visual information?

Chuck Close has successfully used various forms of technology to enhance his approaches to art. Close's portraits are actually paintings of photographs of people. Photographic techniques have allowed him to develop ultra-realistic images. He has even explored using his fingerprints and a stamp pad to create his portraits.

Try this exercise to explore how you can use photocopied images in your own drawing.

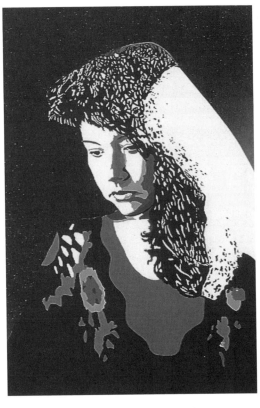

This work was inspired by an image that was photocopied many times to remove some middle values. Student work by Alicia Santana, Queens, New York.

1. Select a photograph or one of your own drawings.

2. Photocopy the image several times, changing the scale on each copy.

3. Plan a composition and environment that can include the photocopied images.

4. Glue some of the images onto the composition. Draw some of the other images, trying to make them look as close to the photocopied image as possible.

5. Complete the drawing so that the photocopied images cannot be distinguished from the drawn images.

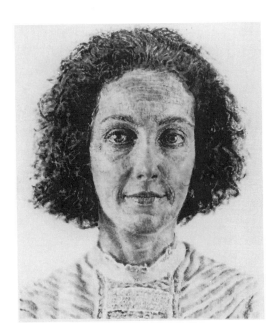

This work is made up of many small kidney shapes stamped or pressed onto a surface. What overall effect has the artist created here? Would you like to have your own portrait done this way? Chuck Close, *Emily*, 1986. Oil-based ink on mylar, 47" x 38 1/4" (119 x 97 cm). Courtesy The Pace Gallery.

Using Computer-generated Images

Computers are used in countless ways in almost every area of our society, including art. A computer can be a powerful tool for an artist. The computer in art can function as a designing tool and as a drawing instrument. The artist can alter forms by distorting, enlarging, compressing or cropping the image using lines, dots and value shapes. Images can be easily manipulated to be larger, upside down or placed to the left or right, allowing the artist to fully explore compositional possibilities.

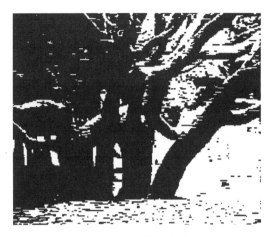

A computer image was used as the basis for this ink drawing of oak trees. Why might the artist have wanted to digitize natural forms? Student work by Holly Hall, Ocean Springs, Mississippi.

Higher-Order Thinking Skills
Have students describe the difference between a computer-generated image and a traditional drawing. Select two images from pages 181–184 for students to compare and contrast. You may want students to write two paragraphs about the similarities and differences between the two images.

Teaching Tip
Emphasize to students one of the computer's main advantages over traditional drawing tools: the ability to save images as they are created. Students can therefore see their own progress and the skills they've developed.

Design Extensions
• Have students photocopy their own hands or faces to make interesting and outrageous images.

• Students may use their fingerprints to create portraits. Have them ink their fingers on ink pads or a folded paper towel saturated with india ink and then press them on paper. Stress that students should try to create of a wide range of values to indicate form rather than drawing lines with their fingerprints.

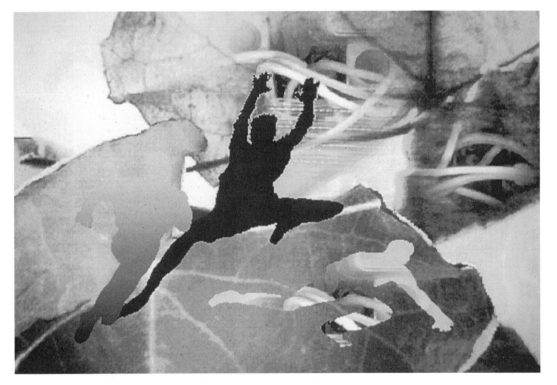

Computers allow you to combine images and create effects that might be difficult, time-consuming or impossible using conventional means. And they offer *millions* of available colors. Joan Truckenbrod, *Take Control*, 1991. Cibachrome print, 25" x 30" (64 x 76 cm). Courtesy The Williams Gallery, Princeton, New Jersey.

Computer Connection
For an easy beginning computer art project, students may combine computer clip art with lines and shapes. Stress the art principles of repetition, pattern, and rhythm by repeating images. Challenge students to emphasize a center of interest with line, value contrasts, and placement in the composition.

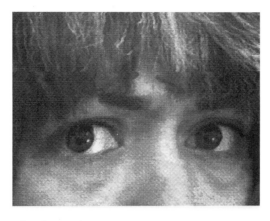

This digitized image was used as the basis for the final work, below.

Holly Hall's work shows some of the ways a computer can be used to create artwork. Here is how Holly produced a digital painted image:

1. The image of David was digitized with a video camera and DCTV Software and saved to a floppy disk.

2. The image of eyes was also digitized and saved to a floppy disk.

3. The image of David was loaded in DCTV paint mode to a blank page screen.

4. The image of eyes was loaded to a spare page.

5. A rub-through tool was used to rub

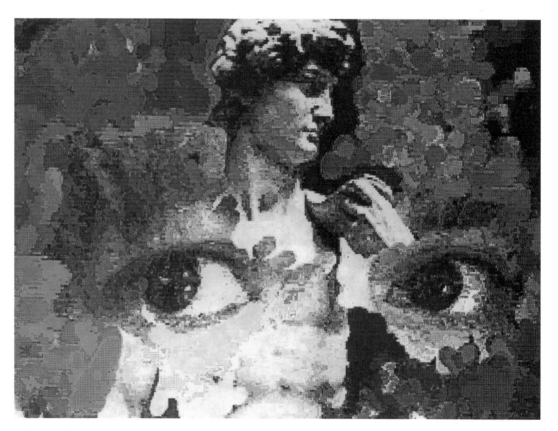

A digitized image of Michelangelo's *David* was inserted into the original image. The artist used a rub-through tool on the paint software to create mottled, textured areas and to erase parts of the *David* image. This produced a kind of computer collage. Student work by Holly Hall, Ocean Springs, Mississippi.

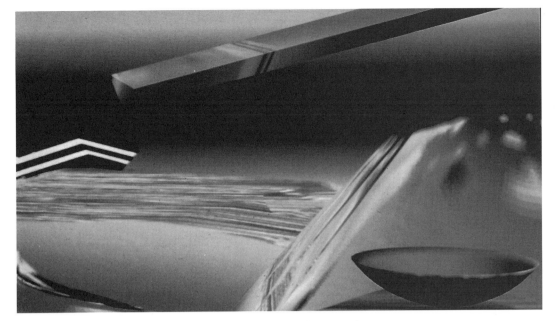

Sharp edges and airbrush-like effects are possible with computers. This work combines hard and soft edges smoothly, creating a scene that looks somehow more real than reality. Wynne Ragland, *#84*, 1992. Topas software on an IBM PC 486, 32" x 47" (81 x 119 cm). Courtesy The Williams Gallery, Princeton, New Jersey.

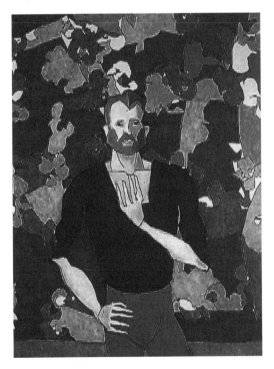

This artist uses computer line as he might use a pencil or magic marker—a hard line separates the figure from its background. The artist has created his own software and a "drawing machine." Harold Cohen, *Aaron with Decorative Panel*, 1992. Computer generated drawing, 72" x 54" (183 x 137 cm). Courtesy The Williams Gallery, Princeton, New Jersey.

the image of David from the blank page to the spare page, so that both images showed through the monitor screen.

6. The final image was printed on a color printer.

THINK ABOUT IT
Computer-generated images force you to think in new ways. It is difficult not to ask how the image was made, altered or enhanced. What did you think when you saw the illustrations?

Barbara Nessim teaches
in the Illustration
Department at Parsons
School of Design in New
York City. She maintains
a continuing interactive
exhibition of her com-
puter art, which she has
developed by inputting
drawings from her
sketchbooks to create a
database.

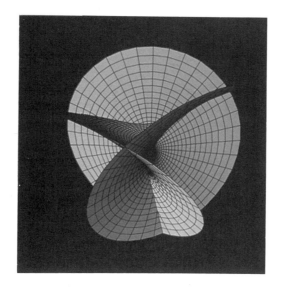 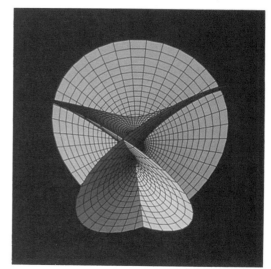

Have you ever made paper sculpture? Origami?
Try drawing a three-dimensional form on the
computer. How will you make areas close to you
come forward, and those farther away recede?
How will you create sharp edges, shadows and
form? This computer work is a stereopair: viewed
through a stereoscope, the image appears three-
dimensional. Steward Dickson, *Enneper's Surface*,
1992. Courtesy The Williams Gallery, Princeton,
New Jersey.

Would you have guessed that this work was made
on a computer? Probably not—many of this
artist's works are handcolored with pastel or
watercolor, and so appear very like paintings.
Barbara Nessim, *Blind Companions*, 1992.
Courtesy The Williams Gallery, Princeton, New
Jersey.

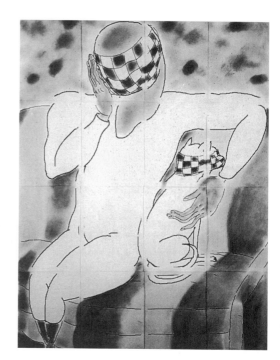

Using Metaphors

One way to describe something is to compare it to something else. What do you picture when you hear the expression, "A mighty fortress is our God"? Comparisons like metaphors and similes help us see something vividly and often in a new way. They surprise us and make an immediate impression. A metaphor states that one thing is another. A simile describes one thing as being like another.

Comparisons are like small puzzles that allow us to say a lot in just a few words. "Wet almond-trees, in the rain,/Like iron sticking grimly out of earth." Can you picture the landscape that D. H. Lawrence created with this simile?

Interdisciplinary Connection
English—Ask an English teacher for examples of poems that contain metaphors and similes. Discuss the imagery in class.

Explain that a writer creates a metaphor that conveys the image through words. Artists, on the other hand, create the image visually. The viewer must put the image into words.

Boots seem to be more than simply footwear here—what metaphor do you think the artist is suggesting? Or is he just exploring shapes in space? Student work by Boris Zakic, Yugoslavia.

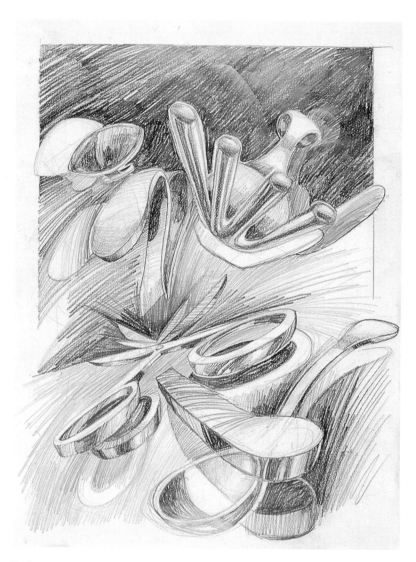

Is there meaning in scissors and forks flying through the air? Where are they going? What will it look like when they land? Student work by Lissa di Pretorio, Lincoln, Nebraska.

Can a bird be a metaphor for life? Read the poem below. How does the poet use comparisons to paint a picture with words?

DREAMS

Hold fast to dreams
For if dreams die
Life is a broken-winged bird
That cannot fly.

Hold fast to dreams
For when dreams go
Life is a barren field
Frozen with snow.

*Langston Hughes**

Like writers, artists use metaphors to create images. What metaphor did Linda Murray use in her painting *The Urban Forest Lines?* (See page 188.)

*From *The Dream Keeper and Other Poems*, by Langston Hughes. Copyright 1932 by Alfred A. Knopf, Inc. and renewed 1960 by Langston Hughes. Reprinted by permission of the publisher.

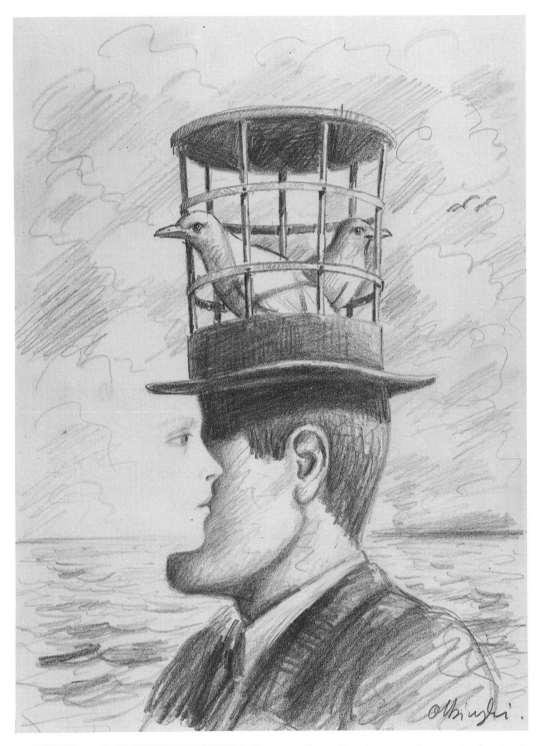

Higher-Order Thinking Skills
Set up this formula for a comparison: How is a _____ like a _____? Write nouns chosen at random on slips of paper. Have each student draw two slips of paper and fit them into the formula. Then have students draw the comparison.

Context
Rafal Olbinski is a Polish artist who immigrated to the United States in 1981. He is an illustrator as well as a painter. His art has appeared regularly in magazines such as *Newsweek, Time,* and *Omni.*

Perhaps you can think of a metaphor for yourself or your personality. Are you a sheep, a cloud, a river? Are your thoughts caged and restless, like these birds? Do you have someone living in your head? Rafal Olbinski, *Memoirs from Easthampton*, 1993. Pencil, 18" x 24" (46 x 61 cm). Courtesy of the artist.

**Higher-Order
Thinking Skills**

• M. C. Escher
(1898–1972) was a
Dutch artist who devel-
oped his unique style
of Surrealism based on
optical illusions. Point
out to students that in
Escher's *Bond of Union*
the man's and woman's
foreheads intertwine to
form a double unity.
They should also notice
how the variation in
shapes and values of the
spheres suggest space.
For another of Escher's
works see page 93. Ask:
How are these pieces
similar?

• Linda Murray, an
artist from Abilene,
Texas, concentrates on
the contradictions
between nature and
technology in *The Urban
Forest Lines*. Notice the
patterns created by the
shadows of the carts.
How does she integrate
and separate the carts
from the rest of the
composition?

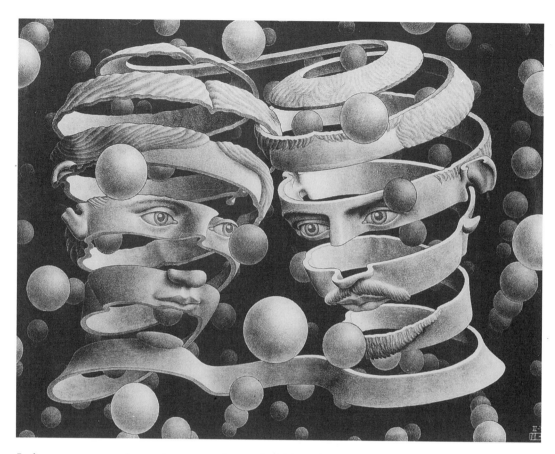

Is there someone you know who seems to be good at things that you aren't, and thinks you're good at things that he or she isn't? How might you express that in a drawing? This artist hints at such an idea in a strange but compelling work. Maurits Cornelius Escher, *Bond of Union*, 1956. Lithograph. 19 x 22" (48.3 x 55.9 cm). Art Resource, NY.

This artist often thinks of city life in terms of shopping carts. Why do you think she thinks that way? What is it about shopping carts that interests her, visually or otherwise? When you think of cities and the lives inside them, what do you think of? Linda Murray, *The Urban Forest Lines*, 1988. Acrylic on canvas, 40" x 48 1/2" (102 x 123 cm). Courtesy of the artist.

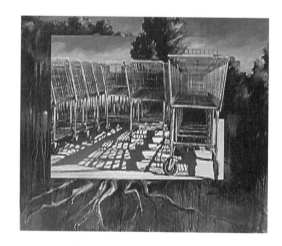

Can you see how thinking in terms of metaphors can stimulate your creativity? Metaphors can help you describe and analyze a drawing. Metaphors can also be used as the foundation of a drawing. Suppose you want to express your feelings about someone or something in a drawing. How can thinking of a metaphor for your subject help you be more expressive in your drawing?

Design Extensions
• Instruct students to write a metaphor describing themselves and then include the images of this metaphor in a self-portrait.

• Refer students to pages 87 and 159 for examples of the Complex Geometric Forms with Cutouts activity on page 191.

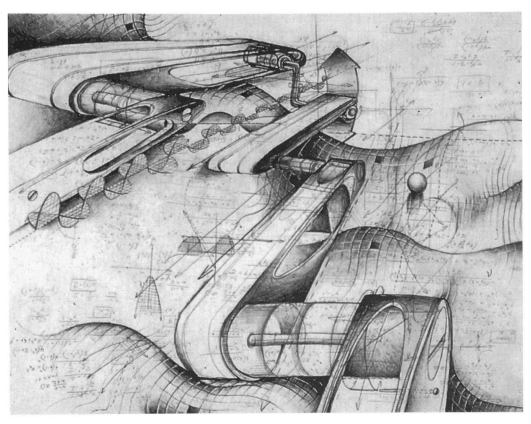

Do you ever think abstractly—that is, do shapes and colors come to your mind that don't look like anything around you? Try putting them down on paper. They can become a kind of image diary for you to draw from. Student work by Ben MacNeill, Raleigh, North Carolina.

Summary

Design Extension
Challenge students to create a "bitmapped" portrait of themselves by drawing their mirrored reflection onto a gridded paper. Encourage them to use values in each square to indicate their form.

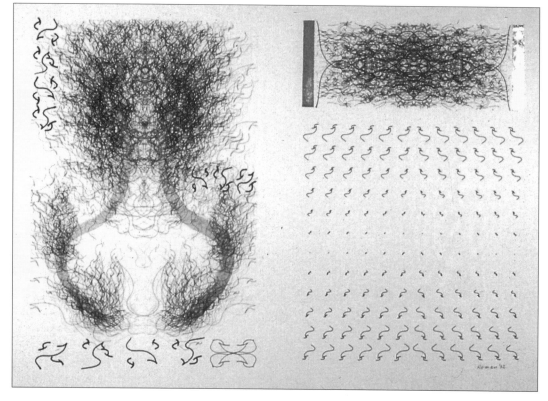

How do these lines "feel"? Why? What do you think the artist is trying to suggest? Roman Verostko, *Diamond Lake Apocalypse*, 1992. Ink plotter on archival paper, 22" x 24" (56 x 61 cm). Courtesy The Williams Gallery, Princeton, New Jersey.

This chapter has given you the opportunity to explore some unconventional drawing techniques to help you think more creatively. The more willing you are to take new directions in art, the more you will grow as an artist. Artists, like any other professionals, must continually break new ground in communicating and expressing their feelings. Drawing is a vehicle for self-expression, which is a truly rewarding and fulfilling experience. Understanding how drawing can help you express yourself is a very important concept to learn.

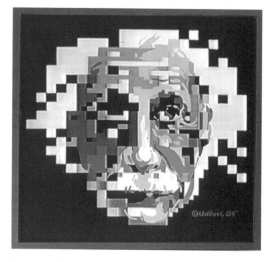

Imagine famous faces digitized: Mona Lisa, Abe Lincoln, John F. Kennedy, Henry VIII. What effect does digitizing have on a face? Look at this image closely. How close can you get before it stops being recognizable? David Udovic, *Einstein*, 1985. Ciba-painting, 8" x 7 1/2" (20 x 19 cm). Courtesy The Williams Gallery, Princeton, New Jersey.

Activities

Loosening Up

Choose one of the following topics:

- turning into an insect
- withering or shrinking
- turning into a monster
- seeing an object coming alive

Begin drawing. At five-minute intervals, exchange papers with a classmate. Continue the drawing of your classmate.

Complex Geometric Forms with Cutouts

Create a simple two-point perspective drawing of a box. When you are comfortable with two-point perspective, draw several more modules, interconnecting them in an architectural design. Within each module, create a negative space by drawing a partial cutout. When you have drawn your three-dimensional construction, complete the composition by using shading and color.

Multiculturalism and Style

Does culture affect style? Choose a culture you would like to research. Is there a particular type of art that is produced by members of that culture? Compare the artwork of two or more artists from that culture. Do the artists have similar styles? What are the characteristics and differences in their styles? Write a short essay, identifying the culture and how it might be reflected in the work of the artists.

Scale Change

Look at the art of Escher, Magritte and the Surrealists. Notice how Magritte particularly changed the scale of objects. Then create a drawing in which the scale of objects is changed. To get a feel for this, put human-sized objects in a dollhouse.

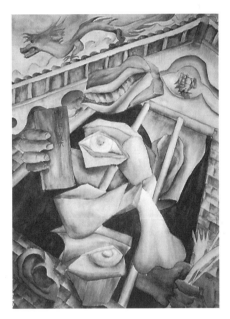

Student work by Danny Nguyen.

Drawing with Mixed Media

Select a multicultural theme for a drawing. Then use at least two mixed media techniques. Explore mixing wet and dry materials together. Take advantage of the possibilities that each medium offers.

Danny Nguyen wanted to combine themes of his native home of Korea, his dream to be an architect and his new permanent home in America. He chose an abstract style to tie these three areas together. He began with colored pencils, then added watercolor washes, weaving the media back and forth.

Drawing to Make a Statement

Think of a current topic or issue in the news. Where do you stand on the issue? How can you use art to express your opinion or feelings? Explore your personal response to the issue by completing a drawing. Include a figure in your drawing.

When commercial airlines decided to ban smoking, Curtis Fesser developed a creative figure drawing to show how a smoker might feel about the ban. He used ebony pencil on drawing paper.

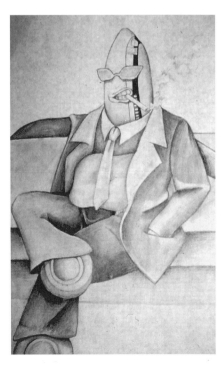

Student work by Curtis Fesser.

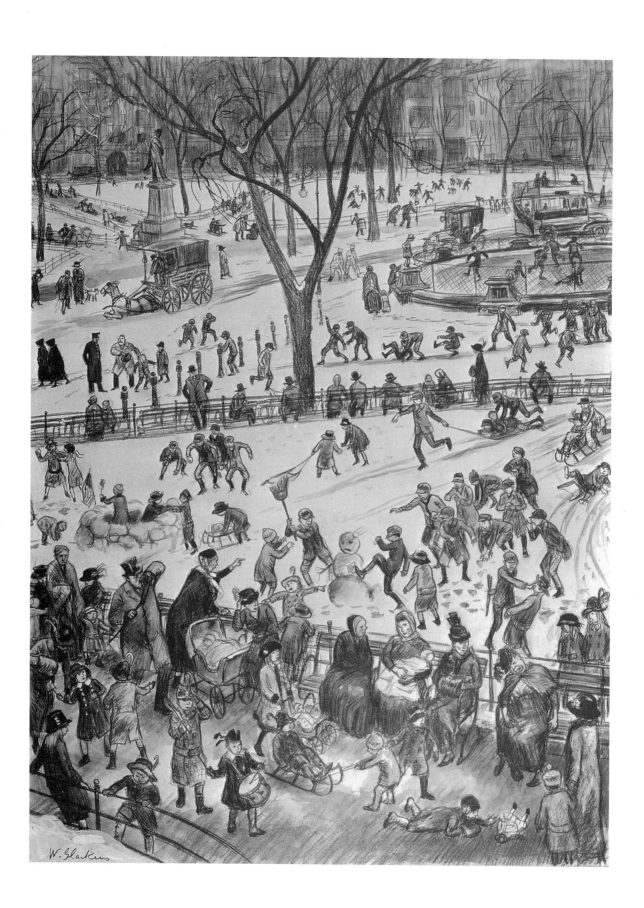

Part 3
Past and Present

Chapter 7
The Past

(See "Chapters 7 and 8" on page T-2 regarding options for teaching this chapter.)

Objectives
Students will be able to:
• Understand that drawing has evolved and changed over the centuries as art styles have changed. (Art history)

• Identify the Egyptian style of drawing figures. (Art history)

• Describe and appreciate how the art of other cultures has influenced European art. (Art history/Art criticism)

• Recognize how Classical Greek and Roman artists created figures with accurate proportions and indicated spatial relations in wall drawings. (Art history)

• Recognize that Renaissance artists drew from life and nature. (Art history)

• Understand that the Impressionists were interested in depicting immediate impressions of their modern life and light in their environment. (Art history)

• Recognize that abstract art uses simplified shapes and geometric forms to represent figures and objects, and may be nonobjective. (Aesthetics)

• Incorporate concepts from various art styles into their own artworks. (Art production)

Vocabulary
Renaissance
Realism
Impressionism
Cubism
abstract
Abstract Expressionism

Chapter Overview
Chapter 7 provides an overview of key periods in Western and non-Western art, beginning with Ice Age art and ending with Abstract Expressionism in the twentieth century. This chapter provides a historical context and framework of development of the drawing process over time. Students should understand that drawing reflects the times and culture in which it was produced.

Lessons 1, 2, 3
pages 195–196   each lesson 45 minutes

Teach
After reading about cave drawings, lead students in imagining where and how they were painted.

Studio Experience
Have students use charcoal to draw animals. If possible, provide live models or toy animals for students to look at as they draw. If you use live animals, which can move frequently, review the quick gesture drawing techniques in Chapter 5.

Students may turn one of their drawings into a low clay relief. On a flat slab of clay, draw an animal with a twig or clay tool. Add dimension to the drawing by depressing some parts of the clay and building out other areas with bits of clay.

If you use ceramic clay, after it is completely dry, bisque fire it. Paint either a dark-value mineral stain or underglaze over the slab and then wipe most of it off with a damp rag, leaving the color in the depressions. Fire again. If you use self-drying clay, stain the depressions with watercolors or thinned tempera or acrylic paint.

Materials
charcoal
18" x 24" newsprint or drawing paper
ceramic or air-drying clay, 1 lb. per student
burlap or canvas
rolling pin
twigs, clay tools
mineral stain or underglaze or paints for clay that won't be fired again

Lessons 4, 5
page 197   each lesson 45 minutes

Teach
After students have read page 197 and studied the illustration, have them look at the Egyptian relief on page 171. Note how in Egyptian art the faces are drawn in profile with frontal eyes; the shoulders face forwards, while the feet are sideways; and the most important figures are largest. Call attention to the hieroglyphic writing in both pieces of art. Ask students to explain what is happening in each of these scenes.

Studio Experience
Have students draw an event using the Egyptian conventions for drawing figures.

Materials
12" x 18" or 18" x 24" drawing
   paper
pencils
erasers
black markers or pen and ink
colored pencils or markers

Lesson 6
page 198   45 minutes

Teach
• As students look at the figures in *Lady playing the cithara*, explain that these may be portraits. As is characteristic of Classical art, they are drawn with accurate anatomical proportions. Discuss possible relationships between the woman and the girl. The woman is playing a cithara, a popular Roman musical instrument with a wooden sound-box and strings.
• Compare the modeled, front facing figures here with the Egyptian profiles on the previous page. In both pieces students will see that the surface is cracked. Both pieces were painted on plaster. The Roman painting was painted on damp plaster in the extremely permanent fresco technique.

Studio Experience
Allow students to experience fresco, the ancient method of painting on damp plaster. To create plaster painting surfaces, mix equal amounts of water and plaster of

Paris and pour into flat Styrofoam™ or paper trays or plates. After it is set (thirty minutes or more), remove the plaster from the mold and draw and paint on it while it is still damp. (You may mix the plaster and pour it into the molds up to a day before class.)

Students may draw their design with a pencil and then paint with tempera paint. They will see how quickly the paint is absorbed into the plaster. (Thin, inexpensive watercolors will be soaked into the plaster, and often not even be visible a day later.) Because the plaster will be soft, some students may be tempted to carve a low relief as they draw.

Note: Plaster of Paris hardens under water so do not put any down the drain.

Materials
plaster of Paris (The amount
   depends on size of molds; 2 lbs.
   should fill about twenty trays.)
plastic mixing bucket
stick or spoon for stirring
water
paper or Styrofoam™ plates or
   trays (flat, with no indentations
   on lower surface)
pencils
tempera paint
brushes

Lessons 7, 8   each lesson
page 199   45 minutes

Teach
Direct students to the art on page 190, the Chinese scroll on page 92, and the Japanese print on

page 141. If possible, show more examples of Asian drawings and fan and screen paintings. Chinese art is noted for its sensitive portrayal of nature. In the scrolls note how space and time are depicted. Several events may happen in one scroll. Follow the horizon lines to see how they connect parts of the composition. Also call attention to the efficiency of line. Often one brushstroke may be used to indicate a leaf or branch.

Studio Experience
Encourage students to plan and design a scroll painting. Suggest scenes that they can see or have sketched or photographed. Look again at the Asian art noting how it is not a literal rendering of a scene but rather an interpretation of it.

After students have planned their composition in small sketches, they may draw it lightly in pencil on a long paper. Then using brushes and ink and ink washes, they can draw in their scene. For washes, dilute india ink in small containers to create several tones.

Materials
paper for planning and practice
pencils
erasers
long sheets of heavy drawing
   paper, about 9" x 24"
watercolor brushes or bamboo
   brushes
india ink
small water containers

Lessons 9, 10
pages 200–203   each lesson 45 minutes

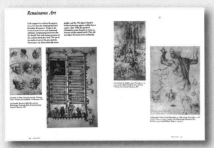

pages 200–201

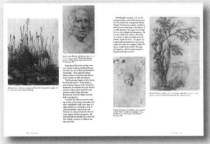

pages 202–203

Teach

• Have students study the illuminated manuscripts on pages 200, 194, 168, and 166. Note the use of decorative letters and how the drawings occupy much of the page. Point out that these books were not printed by a press—each edition was lettered and illuminated individually by hand. Imagine the amount of time needed to produce these. Only the rich and the church could afford them.

• The drawings on these pages were all drawn from life, a new concept in the Renaissance. In the previous Gothic period, figures were drawn according to a formula, not by looking at a real subject. Students should notice how interested artists were in drawing from nature. (Michelangelo and Leonardo da Vinci dissected cadavers in order to draw the human body more realistically.)

• Explain that Renaissance artists kept sketchbooks to record nature and figure drawings. They often used these studies as the basis for their more finished artworks. At least a week prior to beginning the studio activity, instruct students to create a series of studies in their sketchbooks of a subject such as a flower bed, a tree, faces in one of their classes, or parts of a human body. (These studies could be completed in class.)

Studio Experience

Guide students in selecting one or more of their studies to enlarge and draw in a more finished, detailed composition. They may choose to use the combination of drawing and painting as described in the chair drawings on page 177 or use pen and ink techniques pictured on page 58.

Materials

sketchbook drawing
illustration board
pencil
eraser
drawing media—medium-toned, black, and white pastels or black and white drawing pen and india ink or fine-tipped black markers

Lessons 11, 12, 13, 14, 15
pages 204–207   45 minutes each

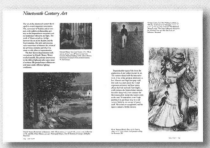

pages 204–205

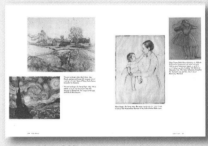

pages 206–207

Teach

• Introduce students to the works of the Impressionists. Manet considered himself to be a Realist. He painted contemporary scenes in Paris and refused to exhibit his art with the Impressionists. But he painted with Monet and eventually adapted his Impressionist style. Monet was interested in capturing the light and the immediate impression of the scene.

• Ask students to compare the mood and energy in the landscapes by Monet and van Gogh. Monet's landscape is calm compared to the swirling strokes in van Gogh's. How many different textures can students pick out in van Gogh's *Father Eloi's Farm?*

• Look at the figures in each work. What is their relationship to each other? In each, note the way the artist has arranged the negative space around the figures. These artists were greatly influenced by Japanese prints, which were cropped to create an asymmetrical composition. Review the Japanese print on page 141.

• Call students' attention to Degas' study of the ballet dancer on page 207. Point out the third leg. Why would he put three legs in this drawing? In Degas' attempt to get the anatomy right on these ballerinas, he went so far as to construct wax models from which to sketch. Refer students back to his pastel on page 165.

• Direct students' attention to Renoir's etching and Cassatt's dry-point. Both of these are intaglio prints—the ink is forced from the recessed grooves in the plate onto paper. In dry-point the grooves are scratched directly into the metal plate while in etching, acid is used to etch the grooves. In both processes ink is rubbed into the grooves and off the surface of the plate. Then the paper is placed on the inked printing plate, and they are put through a printing press which forces the ink from the grooves onto the paper.

Studio Experiences

• Arrange student models in interactive poses for the class to draw. Suggest that the students begin by sketching quick gesture drawings with pencil, and then add lines to these drawings as they work with the negative and positive shapes. Allow students to create at least four or five of these drawings. They might need to review figure drawing techniques in Chapter 5.

• Have students create an intaglio print. First, each student should file a 45-degree bevel on the edges of a rigid acrylic sheet. They should move this transparent sheet over their drawings to discover a composition for their print. Once they have decided on a design, they should tape the acrylic over their drawing and scratch their drawing into the acrylic with a stylus or needle. Stress that they may add more lines later.

Demonstrate how to ink the plate with a brayer by first rolling printing ink out on an inking plate until it is tacky, and then rolling it on the printing plate. Using cheesecloth or a soft rag, wipe off the ink slowly in a wavy motion so that some of the ink is wiped into the scratched lines. Place a damp, not wet, piece of paper on the plate and roll through a printing press.

After students examine their prints, they may wish to add more lines to their prints. Note: To create dark areas students should scratch many small lines as Renoir did in *Dance in the Country*, rather than trying to create large areas of recessed surface. The ink actually clings to the burr of the scratched lines.

Materials
for the drawing:
  pencils
  9" x 12" drawing paper
  erasers
for the dry-point print:
  4" x 6" clear sheet of acrylic, such as Plexiglas (a copper or zinc plate may be used)
  scratching tools such as stylus, needle, scratch knife with pen holder, scriber, or nail
  file
  tape
  water-soluble printing ink
  brayer
  inking plate
  cheesecloth or soft rags
  printing papers—assortment of drawing papers, rice paper, computer papers
  printing press

Lessons 16, 17, 18
pages 208–215   45 minutes each

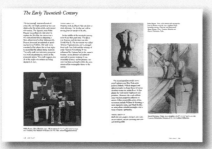

pages 208–209

Teach

• The classical torso by Picasso on page 209 reflects his early traditional art training in Spain. However, when he came to Paris, he was eager to break free of the boundaries of classical art. He and other young artists such as Juan Gris developed Cubism. Have students study the *Three Musicians* on page 208 and look back at Picasso's masks on page 169. Ask: How have the masks changed in the *Three Musicians?* What instruments are they playing? Describe the musicians. The center guitar player is wearing a harlequin or clown costume. The masked figure on the left is playing a clarinet and the bearded monk on the right is singing from sheet music. They are based on figures from the Italian *Commedia dell'Arte.* Can students find the dog? They should notice how the figures have been abstracted, simplified, flattened, and distorted.

• In Juan Gris' *Breakfast* collage on page 210, areas have been flattened, patterns and textures added, and objects drawn from several viewpoints. Ask students to describe the teapot and how it has been altered. Follow lines through the picture, noticing how they seem to begin as part of the table and then continue through other objects and patterns. Where is the artist's name?

• Ask students to compare the movement in Duchamp's *Virgin* and Picasso's *Three Musicians.* Duchamp indicated motion in this Cubist drawing.

• Briefly introduce the art on pages 211–215. Arp was part of the Dada movement, which was a response to the feeling of hopelessness that arose in Europe after World War I.

• Have students study de Chirico's *Metamorphosis* on page 212. De Chirico was a Surrealist, using perspective to create eerie moods. Challenge students to explain the symbolism in this drawing. What is the figure on the left? (a classical Greek figure) What is the seated figure composed of? How has the artist indicated that he is the modern man?

• Klee's drawings often contain machines and humor. Guess what Klee might be saying about Flechtheim in this portrait.

• The whole art world did not go completely abstract during the 1920s and '30s. In the United States many artists including Edward Hopper were depicting their world realistically. Students should look back at Sheeler's drawings of buildings on pages 103 and 39 and Regionalist artist Curry's landscape on page 40.

• At the beginning of World War II many of the European abstract artists fled to America. Influenced by the Europeans, American artists developed Abstract Expressionism with Jackson Pollock and Willem de Kooning as leaders in this movement. As students study Pollock's *Echo,* guide them in imagining the artist holding a basting syringe and walking around this huge canvas on the floor, swinging his arm back and forth as jazz played on the record player.

• Compare the movement in Pollock's painting with the slashing, violent strokes of de Kooning's *Woman.* How did de Kooning feel toward this woman? (This one is quite friendly compared to others.)

• Towards the end of the century some artists began to simplify their works. Mark Rothko developed Color Field paintings while Susan Rothenberg concentrated on a single high-contrast image in her *Untitled Drawing* on page 215.

• If possible, show students examples of other works by artists in this section.

• Divide the class into learning groups of three to four students. Each group will make two lists of the twelve pieces of art on pages 208–215, ranking them from "most realistic to most abstract" and from "most calm and stable to most energy and motion." Stress that they must talk about the art and come to a group consensus about the placement of each work.

Then, ask each group to report their two most realistic works, two least realistic, two most calm and stable, and two with the most energy and motion. Did the groups agree? Have them discuss their judgments.

Studio Experience

Have students create a Cubist drawing and collage similar to Gris' on page 210. Arrange a still life in the center of the room. Students should draw with pencil from one view, then move and continue drawing the same objects from other views. Suggest that they stand up and sit down to give them different viewpoints of the objects.

After they have completed their sketches, suggest that they cut their drawings and glue them to another paper in slightly different positions to create even more distortion. Next, students should add patterns and textures to their shapes. These may be both drawn and also cut from printed papers such as newspapers, wallpapers, telephone books, and ticket stubs.

Materials

12" x 18" drawing paper, one or
  two pieces per student
pencils
markers
colored pencils
glue
scissors
X-acto knives
collage papers such as newspaper,
  wallpaper, receipts, ticket stubs,
  telephone book pages

Lessons 19, 20, 21, 22
pages 194–215   45 minutes each

Reteach

• Hold a dessert party, brunch, or afternoon tea for "famous artists." Assign each student to research an artist from the Renaissance, nineteenth century, or early twentieth century. They should come to the party dressed like this artist, carrying a reproduction of the artist's work, and prepared with three interesting facts about this artist.

Students should introduce themselves to the other guest artists by showing each other an artwork and telling three facts about the artist's life or art.

At the end of the party, review what students learned.

Studio Experience

Have students select two artists from this chapter and draw a subject, once in the style of one artist and again in the style of the second artist.

Materials

drawing and paint media
paper or board appropriate for
  their drawing media

Assess

• To determine that students perceive and understand that drawing has evolved and changed over the centuries into various art styles, have them create a time line showing examples of art in different time periods. (Art history)

• Ask students to explain the Egyptian style of drawing figures. (Art history)

• Have students describe how the art of other cultures has influenced European art. Remind them of the Asian and African art that they studied. (Art history/ Art criticism)

• Ask students to explain how the art on page 198 is typical of Classical art. They should mention that Classic Greek and Roman art features figures with accurate proportions and a sense of spatial relations. (Art history)

• As students review the drawings on pages 202 and 203, ask what these drawings have in common. Remind them that Renaissance artists drew from life and nature. (Art history)

• Challenge students to list some of the characteristics of Impressionism. They should explain that Impressionist artists were interested in depicting immediate impressions of their modern life and light. (Art history)

• Ask how Gris and Picasso altered or abstracted their subjects in their Cubist art. Students should mention they simplified shapes and geometric forms to represent figures and objects. Have students identify two nonobjective and two Abstract Expressionist artworks in this chapter. (Aesthetics)

• Guide students in creating individual portfolios of the artworks that they produced during this chapter. Check their portfolios to ascertain that they did incorporate concepts from various art styles into their own artworks. (Art production)

Chapter Warm-up
Have students read
page 195. Then discuss
the following questions:

• Why look at art from
the past?

• Why would it be
helpful to know about
the time and place a
piece of art was created?

• What does "Art is a
place where minds
shake hands" mean?

Context
The whole illuminated
page that this illustration
comes from is on page
166. Call attention to the
quill that the scribe is
holding and his ink and
writing utensils on the
stool beside him.

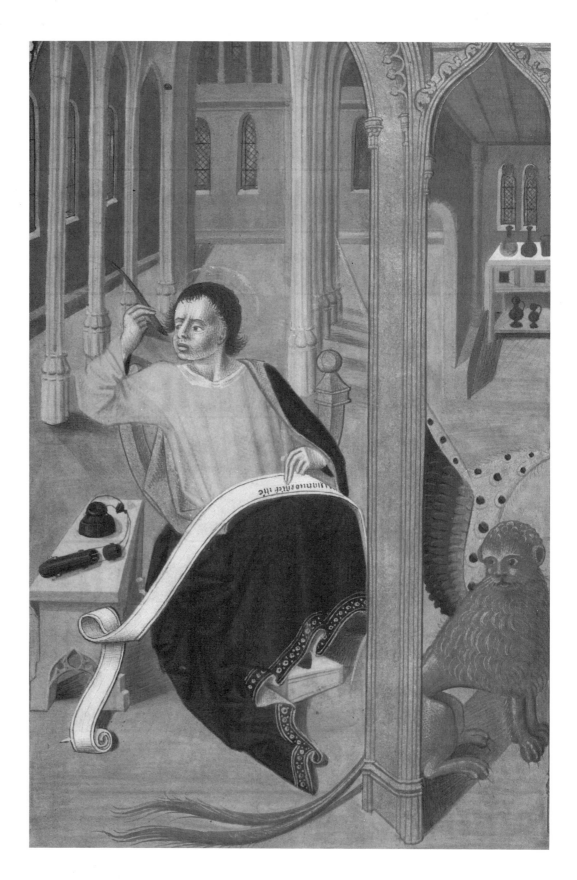

7 The Past

Art is a record of human existence. Art tells a story of the progress of humanity and culture. As a culture or a nation changes, so too does its art. It is important to understand how world events, cultural values and technology have shaped the history of art.

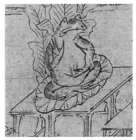

Art history is a vital part of objective art criticism. To truly understand a work of art, you need an understanding of the period and place in which it was produced.

There are many advantages to studying art history. Discovering the value of art history is to discover what other artists themselves have discovered and to experience what they experienced. Art is a place where minds shake hands.

Vocabulary
humanism
idealism
Renaissance
Realism
Impressionism
Abstract
Expressionism

Cooperative Learning
This chapter briefly covers major periods in art. You may want to divide students into small groups and have each group research one of the major cultural periods. Ask each group to list major developments of their period and share their findings with the class.

Key Chapter Points

- Drawing has evolved over the centuries.
- Roman, Greek and Egyptian art have influenced European and American art.
- Egyptian drawings were flat. Figures were drawn according to a strict formula.
- Greek art was expressive. Figures were drawn with accurate proportions and idealized form.

- Asian art emphasized nature in simple yet sensitive works.
- Renaissance artists developed linear perspective and dramatic lighting.
- Impressionism emphasized the effects of light on color.
- Abstract art uses simplified shapes and geometric forms to represent figures and objects. It is often non-objective.

Hours of the Duchess of Burgundy (detail), ca. 1450 (ms. 76/1362), folio with miniature of St. Mark. Musée Conde, Chantilly, France. Giraudon/Art Resource, NY.

Cave Drawings

Context
Even earlier cave murals and carvings of lions, bears, horses, and rhinos have recently been discovered in the Chauvet cave in the Ardéche region of France. Radiocarbon tests date them back more than 30,000 years.

The story of drawing begins deep within the Altamira caves not far from Santilla, Spain. Why does it begin here? Because scholars believe that the prehistoric cave drawings found on the walls of these caves are the first important works of art. The drawings of animals found here are skillfully executed pictures of bison, deer, boar and other animals. The pictures were probably a part of some magical ceremony. The ceilings of some of the caves are so low that viewers must wriggle on their stomachs in order to reach the drawings.

The works are marvelously executed and preserved. The drawings, deep within the cave, have been protected from rain, wind and other elements that would have eroded them. The works of art are believed to have been done between the years of 15,000 to 10,000 BC. However, it is amazing to note that the skill behind these works often surpasses the quality of drawings done thousands of years later. The origin of these drawings still remains a mystery.

THINK ABOUT IT
Like many kinds of art, cave paintings can be examined for their meaning and artistic quality, as well as for what they tell us about the people who drew them.

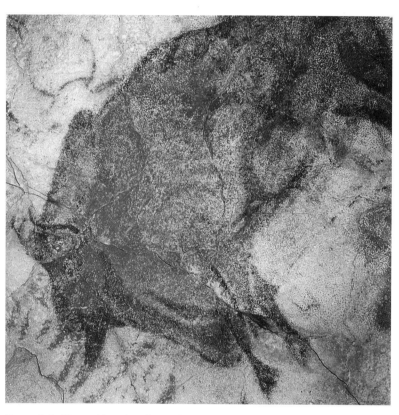

Room of the Bison. Altamira, Spain. SEF/Art Resource, NY.

Speaking of Art...
Although no one really knows why these earliest drawings were made, Joseph Campbell suggests that they may have been used in initiation rites of young hunters. Some of the drawings have pits in them from being struck with spears.

Egyptian Art

The drawings of the Egyptian empire were a part of a mystical religion. The artwork found within the walls of the great pyramids of Egypt was of great religious importance. The Egyptians believed that after death the body of a pharaoh lived within the walls of his tomb or pyramid. Tombs were often robbed and the bodies damaged or destroyed. To make sure that the soul of the deceased had a body to live in, artists painted human figures. The artwork could then become the dwelling place of the spirit or soul of the pharaoh.

Because the images in the drawings served a purpose in maintaining the eternal happiness of the soul of the deceased, they were drawn according to a strict formula. Any departure from the formula could have harmed the soul. The more important figures were larger. Artists drew figures in profile but with the eyes facing front. Artists did not express personal ideas in their drawings. There is little suggestion of depth in the drawings. Nor did Egyptian artists use shading. Their drawings were arranged in panels, as present-day comic books are arranged.

Interdisciplinary Connection
Social Studies—Locate Egypt on a world map. Locate the Nile delta, noting its triangular shape, Upper and Lower Egypt, Giza where the Great Pyramids are, and Thebes, the Valley of the Kings. Have students research the importance of the Nile River in transportation and in providing rich, irrigated fields, and therefore a dependable food supply.

Context
Point out that the artistic rigidity of Egyptian art had to do with the basic conservatism of Egyptian culture. All of its cultural forms changed little over time. As a result of close ties between art and government and religion, the same style of drawings continued for thousands of years.

See an Egyptian relief on page 171.

Inquiry
Assign students to research and report on Egyptian art and architecture including: the Great Pyramids, temples, sculpture, hieroglyphics, wall paintings and reliefs, funerary models, King Tutankhamen's tomb and mummy, and the recent discovery of the tomb of the sons of Ramses II.

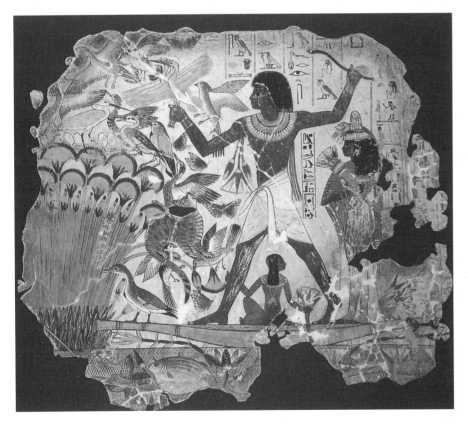

Fowling the Marshes, wall painting, ca. 1400 BC. Reproduced by Courtesy of the Trustees of the British Museum.

Greek and Roman Art

Inquiry
The Greeks advanced the techniques of drawing by depicting figures in natural poses and with correct proportions. Have students research the Classical Period and the influence of Greek philosophy of humanism and idealism on its art. Point out that much of European art and architecture bears the influence of Greek artistic styles.

Context
In 79 A.D. Mt. Vesuvius erupted, covering P. Fannius Synistor's villa at Boscoreale, near Pompeii and Naples in southern Italy. The volcanic ash preserved the home's frescoes of mythological subjects, complex architectural scenes, and the *Lady playing the cithara*. Have students locate Pompeii on a world map.

Interdisciplinary Connection
Earth Science—Research plate tectonics to discover which plate boundary Mt. Vesuvius lies on. Vesuvius is still active and many more people now live on its slopes. Learn more about the geology of the Naples area. What are scientists doing to prevent another disaster like the one that occurred in 79 A.D.?

The art of ancient Greece was utilitarian, but it was also done to replicate beauty and idealized form. The Greek period from about 480 to 323 BC was known as the Classical Period. The art of this period is noted for its beauty, order, symmetry and balance. Greek figurative drawings and sculptures in this period are noted for their accurate proportions, movements and posture. Drawing was expressive and reflected the artist's personal interpretation. The Greeks decorated their pottery with geometric designs and accurate depiction of human figures. Greek depiction and draftsmanship were unrivaled by any previous civilization.

The Romans, who were more concerned about commerce and engineering, made few progressive contributions to art. Roman artworks were often copies of Greek art. Roman artists, like the Greeks, never discovered the value of linear perspective. Therefore, many of their drawings appear flat and lack a sense of depth or space. Roman painters relied upon aerial perspective and architectural structures to suggest depth in their drawings.

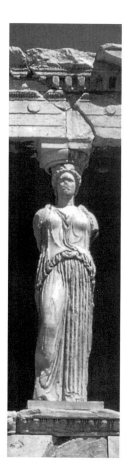

Caryatid from the "Porch of the Maidens," 421–405 BCE, School of Phidias, Erechtheum, Acropolis, Athens.

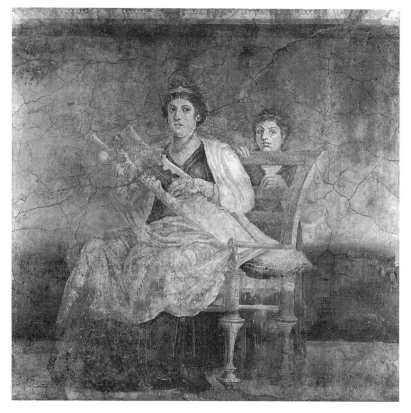

Lady playing the cithara, wall painting, Roman, 100 BC. Courtesy The Metropolitan Museum of Art, Rogers Fund, 1903.

Asian Art

China is thought by many to be the oldest surviving civilization in the world. Its artwork has influenced the art of many other cultures, including Japan, Korea, India and Southeast Asia.

Early Chinese art centered on animals and people in everyday life. Later, its art reflected the spiritual ideas of Buddhism: people became small compared to their natural environment, and more connected to the past and their ancestors.

The rabbit shown here is part of a hanging scroll, painted in ink on silk during the Sung dynasty, sometime after 960 AD. Art was valued at this time in China: people in cities were becoming more wealthy, and they had begun collecting art of the past and present. Notice the contrast of soft and hard edges in the scroll, and the sensitive portrayal of the rabbit. What does it tell you about the artist's feeling about nature?

Japanese art is generally subtle, but simple in form and design, and often concerned with nature. During some periods in history, Japan was isolated from other cultures; at other times China, Korea and Europe provided artistic and cultural

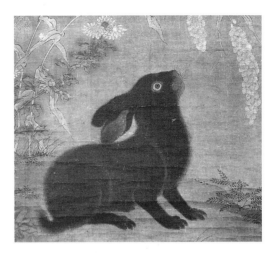

Hanging scroll, Sung, eleventh to thirteenth centuries. Ink and color on silk. National Palace Museum, Taiwan, Republic of China.

influences. The animal caricatures seen below—like the rabbit, part of a scroll—were drawn in ink and were meant to be humorous. They form a kind of Japanese comic strip: their use of satire and cartoon-like style predates Western cartoons and comics by six hundred years! You'll notice that the lines that form benches and tables here go back in space, but do not move any closer together, as they would using one-point perspective.

Design Extension
In all these Asian works notice the chop marks or stamps of the artists. Also, owners would often add their chop marks to a piece of art, creating a record of ownership on the artwork. Students may design their own chop marks by carving a design on a gum eraser, pressing it to a red ink pad, and stamping it on their art.

Context
The Chinese philosopher Confucius taught respect for nature as well as for parents, ancestors, state, and emperor.

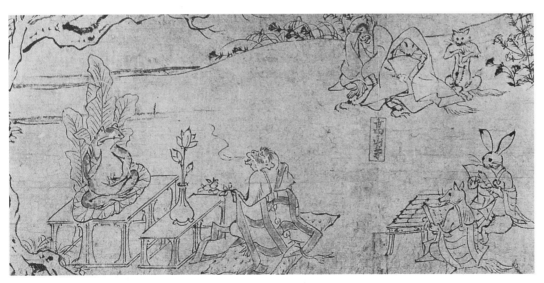

Animal caricatures, detail of a horizontal scroll attributed to Toba Sojo. Later Heian period, ca. late 12th century. Ink on paper, approximately 12" (30 cm) high. Kozan-ji. National Commission for the Protection of Cultural Properties of Japan.

Renaissance Art

Higher-Order Thinking Skills
Ask students what devices Renaissance artists used to create the appearance of depth. They should note the foreshortening in Michelangelo's figure and the linear perspective in van Eyck's *St. Barbara.*

The fall of the Roman Empire meant a new way of life for the people occupying what is now Europe. In the centuries between the Classical world and the modern era there developed an intense focus on the spiritual as the influence of Christianity took hold. We refer to this period as the Middle Ages.

The art of the Middle Ages reflects these changes. Towering cathedrals rose above the cities. Monks and nuns labored to produce exquisitely decorated books called illuminated manuscripts. The art of drawing was developed to a high degree in these manuscripts. Each word was handwritten in a graceful calligraphy. Line and shape were used to create intricate graphic decorations between the lines and in the margins surrounding the text.

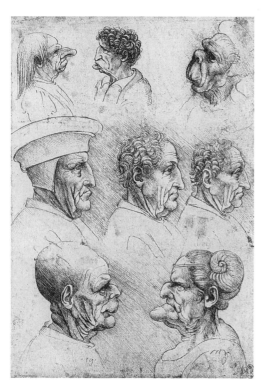

Leonardo da Vinci, *Caricature grottesche*. Windsor Castle, Windsor, Great Britain. Art Resource, NY.

Jean Pucelle, *Breviaro di Belleville*. Bibliotheque Nationale, Paris, France. Courtesy Scala/Art Resource, NY.

Extensions
• For other examples of illuminated manuscripts see pages 194, 168, and 166.

• Students may create their own illumination of a line from a poem or song, using a calligraphy pen. Have them embellish the margins.

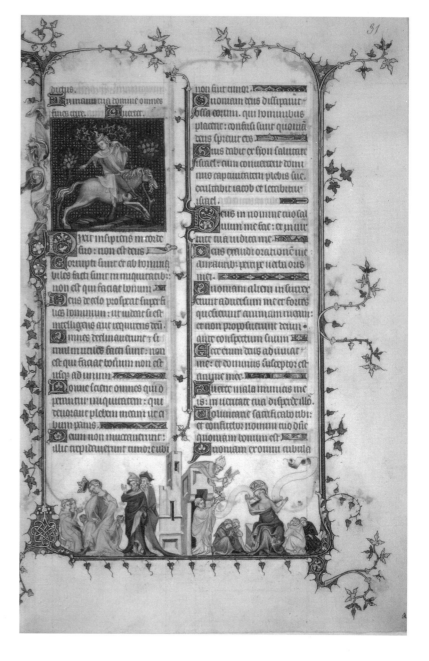

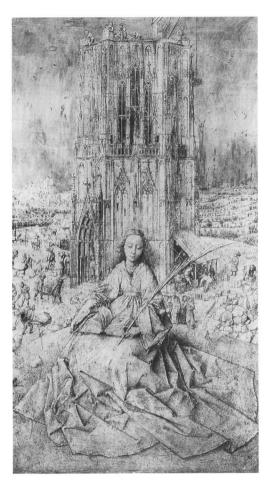

Jan van Eyck, *St. Barbara*, 1437. Drawing, 9 x 19"
(23 x 48 cm). Musée des Beaux Arts, Antwerp.
Courtesy Giraudon/Art Resource, NY.

Context
Jan van Eyck was the
most important Flemish
painter in the fifteenth
century. He was an artist
for Philip the Good,
Duke of Burgundy. He
was an early leader in
developing the use of oil
paints, recording minute
details in glowing colors.

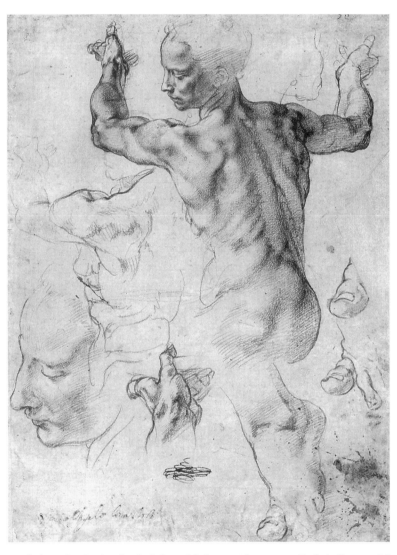

Michelangelo, *Studies for the Libyan Sibyl*, 15–16th century. Red chalk, 11 3/8"
x 8 3/8" (28.9 x 21.3 cm). Courtesy The Metropolitan Museum of Art,
Purchase, 1924, Joseph Pulitzer Bequest. (24.197.2)

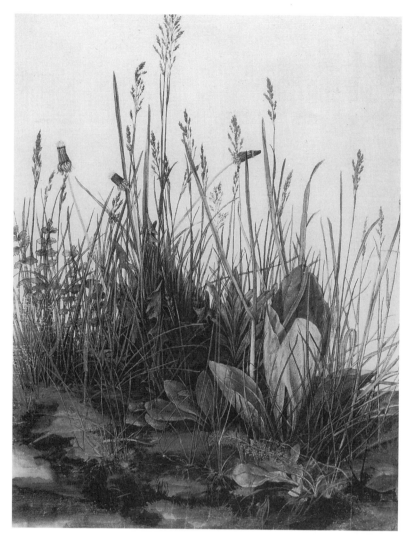

Albrecht Dürer, *The piece of turf*, 1503. Watercolor and gouache on paper, 16"
x 12" (41 x 31.5 cm). Vienna, Albertina.

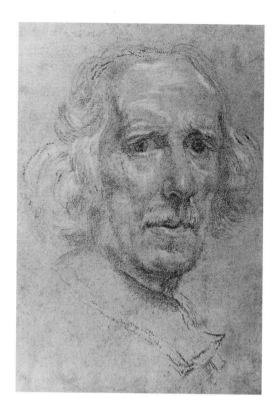

Gian Lorenzo Bernini, *Self-Portrait*, 1665. 16 1/4
x 10 1/2" (41 x 27 cm). The Royal Collection.
Courtesy of Her Majesty Queen Elizabeth II.
Art Resource, NY.

The fifteenth century saw another
change as the modern world began with
the period we call the Renaissance. Artists
began to study Classical themes of the
Greeks for inspiration. In addition, they
also studied anatomy. These studies paid
off in the accuracy of their figure drawings. Renaissance artists developed
pictorial skills in perspective.

Leonardo da Vinci is noted for studying science and anatomy. Leonardo
wanted to scientifically study every facet
of a subject before he attempted to draw
it, which limited his output of artwork.
However, he did systematically discover
many aspects of linear perspective. He
kept detailed sketchbooks and notebooks
that include reminders of subjects that
interested him.

Inquiry
Have students report on the Italian artist Bernini, who
is most famous for his sculptures and fountains in
Rome. Suggest that students consult art history books,
the Internet, and travel guides to Rome.

Context
Dürer was one of the first German artists to travel to
Italy to learn Italian Renaissance techniques of drawing
perspective and human figures. *The piece of turf* shows
the influence of Leonardo with its scientific attention
to minute details of nature.

Michelangelo (see page 201) was the most productive artist of the Renaissance era. He painted the ceiling of the Sistine Chapel. His drawings contain a freshness that had never been seen in the history of art. His figurative drawings and paintings have a sense of depth and perspective. He was one of the first artists to effectively use a series of lights and darks to create realistic depth and form. The figures are twisted and foreshortened at interesting angles that make them appear lifelike. He always worked from detailed drawings and sketches, which he often burned to keep his technique a secret.

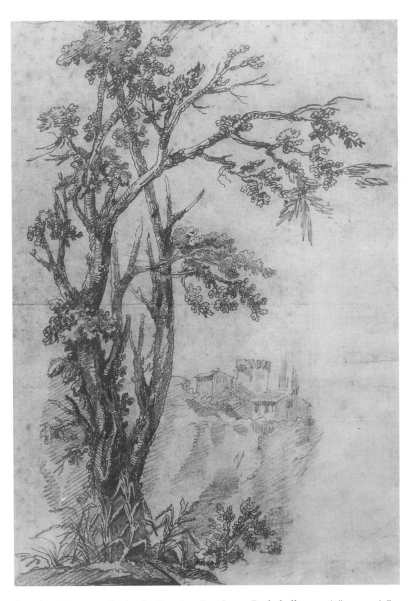

Antoine Watteau, *Study of a Tree in a Landscape*. Red chalk, 17 1/4" x 12 1/4" (43.8 x 31.1 cm). Courtesy Norton Simon, Inc. Museum of Art.

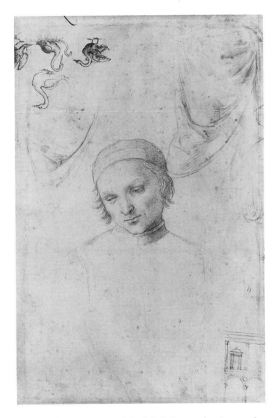

Raphael, *Coronation of St. Nicholas*, early sixteenth century. Charcoal with white highlights. Musée des Beaux-Arts, Lille, France. Giraudon/Art Resource, NY.

Higher-Order Thinking Skills
How did Dürer and Watteau indicate space in these landscapes? Describe the foreground, middle ground, and background of each drawing. What did each artist emphasize most? Where is the most detail?

Nineteenth Century Art

The art of the nineteenth century developed in several important movements. The movement of Realism and its concern with realistic draftsmanship gave way to the Impressionist movement and its fascination with color and light. The work of Manet served as a bridge between the art of the Realists and the Impressionists. His style and concerns were somewhere in between the artists of the previous centuries and what was about to take place in Impressionism.

The best-known Impressionist work was painted by Claude Monet. Monet worked outside. His primary interest was in the shift of light and color upon natural surfaces. He painted many subjects several times under different lighting conditions.

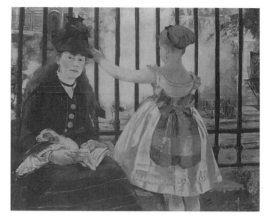

Edouard Manet, *Gare Saint-Lazare*, 1873. Oil on canvas, 36 3/4" x 45 1/8" (93.3 x 114.6 cm). Courtesy National Gallery of Art. Gift of Horace Havemeyer in memory of his mother Louisine W. Havemeyer.

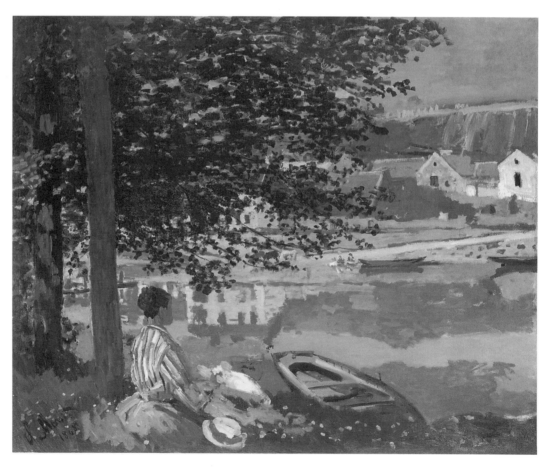

Claude Monet, *On the Seine at Bennecourt*, 1868. Oil on canvas, 32" x 39 5/8" (81.5 x 100.7 cm). Collection of Mr. and Mrs. Potter Palmer, 1922.427. Photograph ©1993, The Art Institute of Chicago, All Rights Reserved.

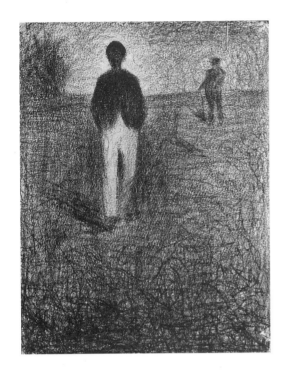

Georges Seurat, *Two Men Walking in a Field*, ca. 1882–84. Conté crayon on laid paper, 12 1/2" x 9 1/2" (31.8 x 24.3 cm). Courtesy The Baltimore Museum of Art. The Cone Collection, formed by Dr. Claribel Cone and Miss Etta Cone of Baltimore, Maryland.

Extension
Show students a reproduction of Renoir's large painting, *Dance at Bougival*, which is very similar to this print. How did Renoir change the painting from the print?

Impressionism opened the doors for exploration of new subject matter in art. The century closed with the innovative work of one of the greatest artists ever to live, Vincent van Gogh (see page 206). His work was more about the overall impression of nature and how nature affects the body and soul. Van Gogh's work contains the Impressionist concern for color along with a new concern for the transcendent energy that nature emits to the soul. To experience a van Gogh painting is to get swept away in a vast current fueled by the energy of nature itself. His colors are exaggerated, and his figures contain a lifelike motion.

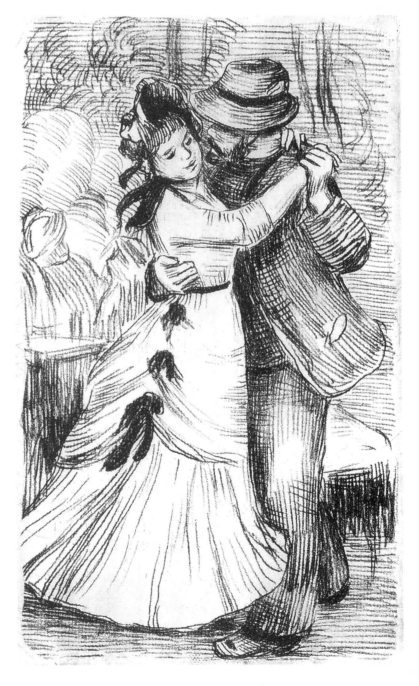

Pierre Auguste Renoir, *Dance at Bougival*, after an 1883 painting of the same title. Soft ground etching. Bibliothèque Nationale, Paris/Art Resource, NY.

Context
After van Gogh cut off part of his ear and Gauguin had left him, he departed from Arles to have himself committed to the sanitarium of Saint-Rémy-de-Provence. There he painted this *Starry Night* from behind the bars in his window.

Examples of van Gogh's art appear on pages 80 and 63. To learn more about his illness see page 96.

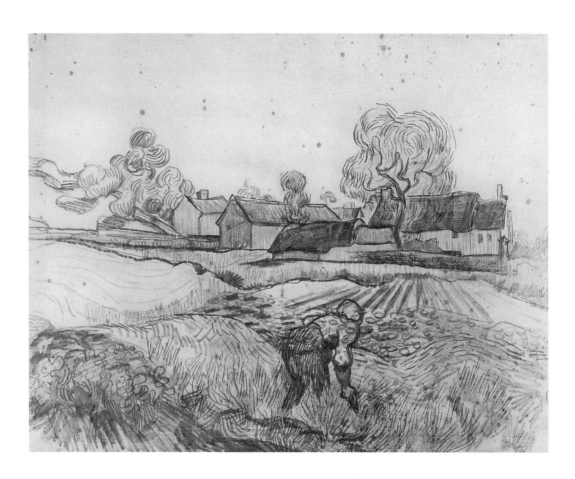

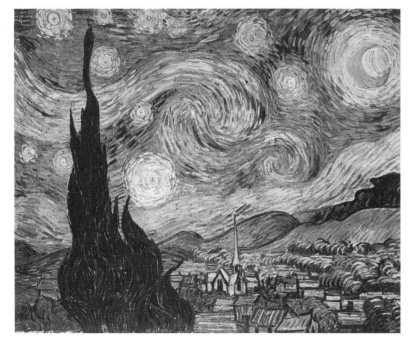

Vincent van Gogh, *Father Eloi's Farm*, 1890. Pencil, reed pen and brown ink on paper, 18 1/2 x 24" (47 x 61 cm). Musée d'Orsay, Paris, France. Giraudon/Art Resource.

Vincent van Gogh, *The Starry Night*, 1889. Oil on canvas, 29" x 36 1/4" (73.7 x 92.1 cm). The Museum of Modern Art, NY. Acquired through the Lillie P. Bliss Bequest.

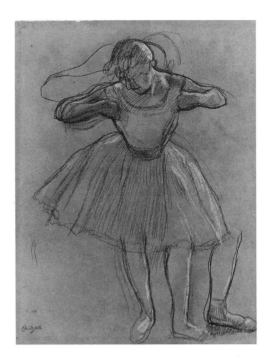

Edgar Degas, *Ballet Dancer Standing*, ca. 1886–90. Black crayon heightened with white and pink chalk on gray-brown wove paper, 11 15/16" x 9 1/2" (30.4 x 24. cm). Courtesy The Baltimore Museum of Art. The Cone Collection, formed by Dr. Claribel Cone and Miss Etta Cone of Baltimore, Maryland.

Context

• For more about Mary Cassatt and her work see page 109.

• See Degas' pastel *The Rehearsal on Stage* on page 165.

• In 1877 Degas invited Mary Cassatt to show her art with the Impressionists. She continued to exhibit with them until their final show in 1886. Degas and Cassatt remained friends throughout their lives. Cassatt even modeled for some of his pictures.

• Although Mary Cassatt never had children herself, the relationship between mothers and children was one of her favorite themes.

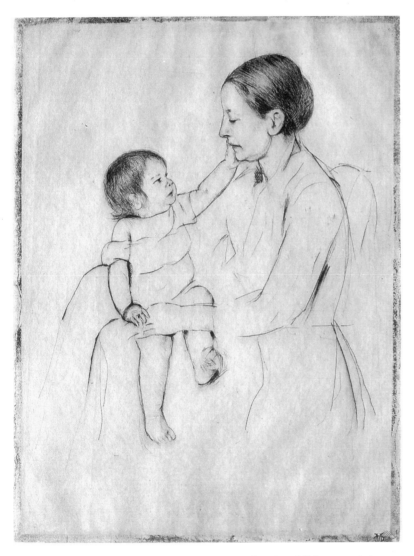

Mary Cassatt, *The Caress*, 1891. Dry-point. 14 1/2 x 10 1/2" (37 x 27 cm). Courtesy The Metropolitan Museum of Art, Gift of Arthur Sachs, 1916.

The Early Twentieth Century

Context

Abstract Expressionism got its title because the artworks were abstract, emphasizing shape, color, and line with no recognizable subject matter, and expressive, stressing strong emotions and individual feelings.

Abstract drawing can be approached from recognizable subject matter that has been simplified and "distilled," or from imagination. Artists can start with shapes, lines, patterns, or textures and build up from there.

Extension

• Read more about Picasso on pages 8 and 11.

• See an African mask and Picasso's *Mother and Child* on page 169.

The increasingly abstracted work of artists like van Gogh opened up new possibilities for the artists of the early twentieth century. The Spanish artist Pablo Picasso was perhaps the first artist to explore the idea that the canvas was a two-dimensional illusion depicting a three-dimensional reality. Subsequently, Picasso pioneered an approach to painting known as Cubism. His early work consisted of flat planes that at best slightly resembled the subject being depicted. The early work was extremely geometric and reduced painting to a series of flat, geometric planes. The work suggests that all of the angles of a subject are being depicted at once.

THINK ABOUT IT

Studying works by Picasso helps you learn to think abstractly. You develop your skill in moving from the specific to the idea.

In the middle of the twentieth century, art took another giant step. The place was America, and the time was after World War II. The movement was called Abstract Expressionism, and it emerged from both New York and the writings of critic Clement Greenburg. It was influenced by Cubism, but in the 1940s it became a more abstract and painterly approach to picture making. It was incredibly abstract, and its primary concern was form and depth within the parameters of the rectangular frame of the canvas.

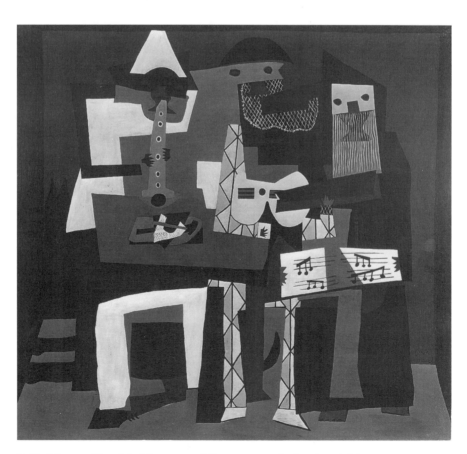

Pablo Picasso, *Three Musicians*, 1921. Oil on canvas, 6' 7" x 7' 3 3/4" (200.7 x 222.9 cm). Courtesy The Museum of Modern Art, NY. Mrs. Simon Guggenheim Fund.

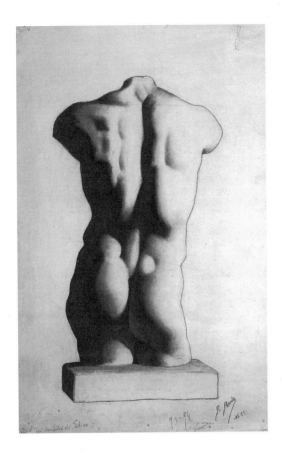

The most legendary of this movement's painters was New York artist
Jackson Pollock. Pollock dripped and
splattered paint on large sheets of canvas
stretched across his studio floor. At first
glance the work seems haphazard and
primitive. However, the work exhibits
many random properties inherent to
nature. Other remarkable artists of this
movement include Willem de Kooning, a
more figurative artist, and Mark Rothko,
an artist whose colorful rectangles emit a
sense of mystic spirituality.

THINK ABOUT IT
*Each time you analyze, interpret and evalu-
ate an artwork, you are exercising your critical thinking skills.*

Pablo Picasso, *Torso in the classical style* (an exercise
done by Picasso when he was a student). Early
twentieth century. Charcoal and black pencil.
Musée Picasso, Paris. Courtesy Réunion des
Musées Nationaux, Paris.

Design Extension
Demonstrate how a
drawing can be
"fractured" and broken
into smaller shapes
made of straight lines
and edges.

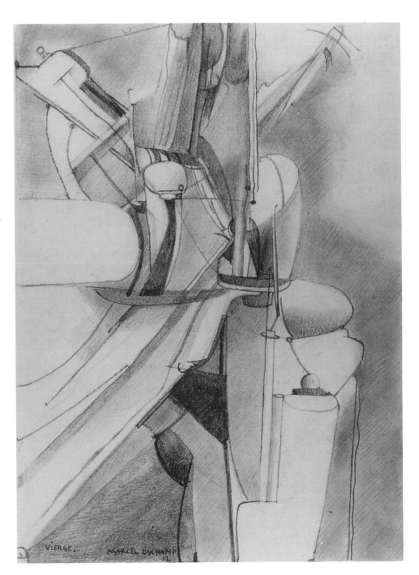

Marcel Duchamp, *Virgin*, 1912. Graphite, 16 7/8" x 8 2/3" (42.8 x 22 cm).
Courtesy Philadelphia Museum of Art: A.E. Gallatin Collection.

Context

• Juan Gris (1887–1927) was a Spanish painter from Madrid who came to Paris in 1906 where he lived with Picasso for a while. Picasso, Braque, and Gris developed Cubism; but while Picasso and Braque's Cubism tended to monochromes, Gris began to concentrate on bright colors. He also produced more Cubist paper collages than the other two artists.

• German-French artist Jean Arp (1887–1966) was a leader in the Dada movement, a reaction against World War I and the bourgeois interests that led to it. Dada is a nonsense word summing up the hopeless feeling about art and life. Artists questioned the meaning of art.

Interdisciplinary Connections

Literature—Dada artists would cut words out of books, drop them on a paper, and glue them where they landed, and that was their poetry. Encourage students to create their own Dada poetry.

Psychology—During the twentieth century artists became influenced by the ideas of Sigmund Freud and Carl Jung and their theories of free expression in psycho-analysis. Encourage students to research their theories about personality and self-expression.

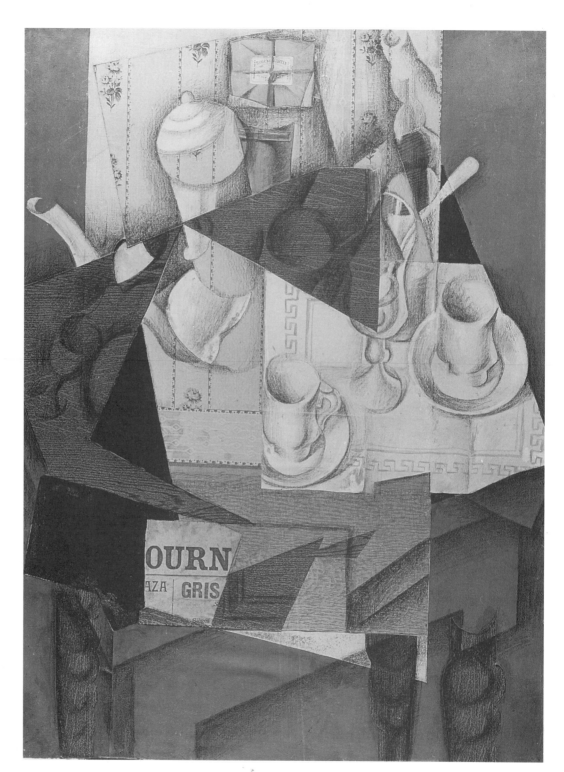

Juan Gris, *Breakfast*, 1914. Pasted paper, crayon and oil on canvas, 31 7/8" x 23 1/2" (80.9 x 59.7 cm). Collection, The Museum of Modern Art, NY. Acquired through the Lillie P. Bliss Bequest.

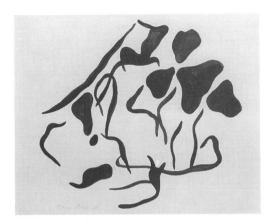

Jean Arp, *Automatic Drawing*, 1916. Brush and ink on gray paper, 16 3/4" x 21 1/4" (42.5 x 54 cm). Collection, The Museum of Modern Art, NY. Given anonymously.

Extension
Display Hopper's *Nighthawks,* the painting of the lonely people in a city cafe. Note how light and shadows were important to Hopper. Call attention to the strong contrasts of light and dark values in *The Locomotive.*

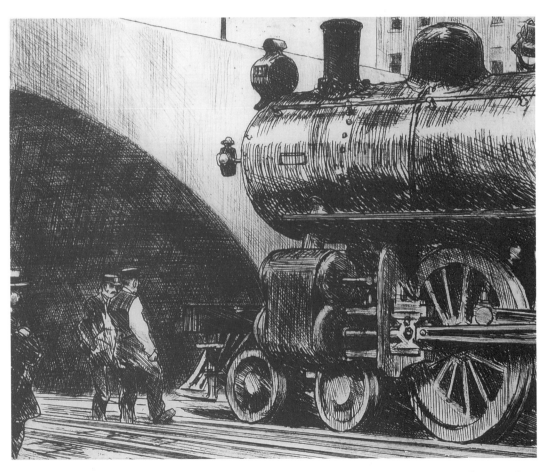

Edward Hopper, *The Locomotive*, 1922. Etching on paper, 7 7/8" x 9 13/16" (20 x 25 cm). Collection of The Whitney Museum of American Art, NY.

De Chirico's drawing
could be used in con-
junction with the Using
Metaphors section on
page 185. What is
de Chirico saying about
mankind in
Metamorphosis?

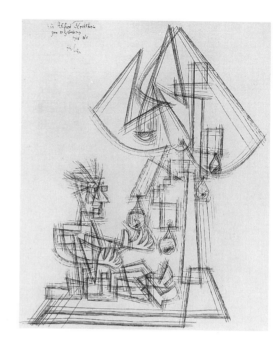

Paul Klee, *Portrait of Flechtheim*, 1928. Pen and
ink, 11 3/8" x 9 1/4" (28.9 x 23.5 cm). Private
collection. Art Resource/NY.

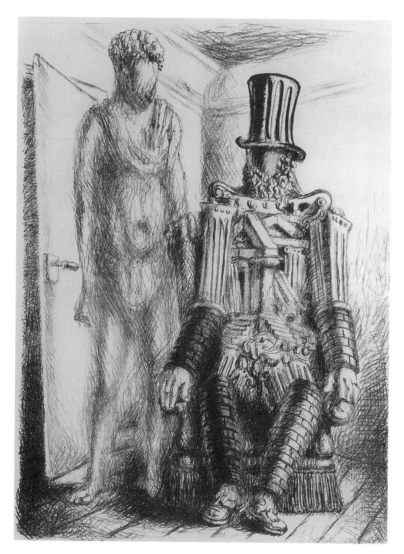

Giorgio de Chirico, *Metamorphosis*, 1929. Lithograph. © Sotheby Parke-
Bernet. Agent: Editorial Photocolor Archives/Art Resource, NY.

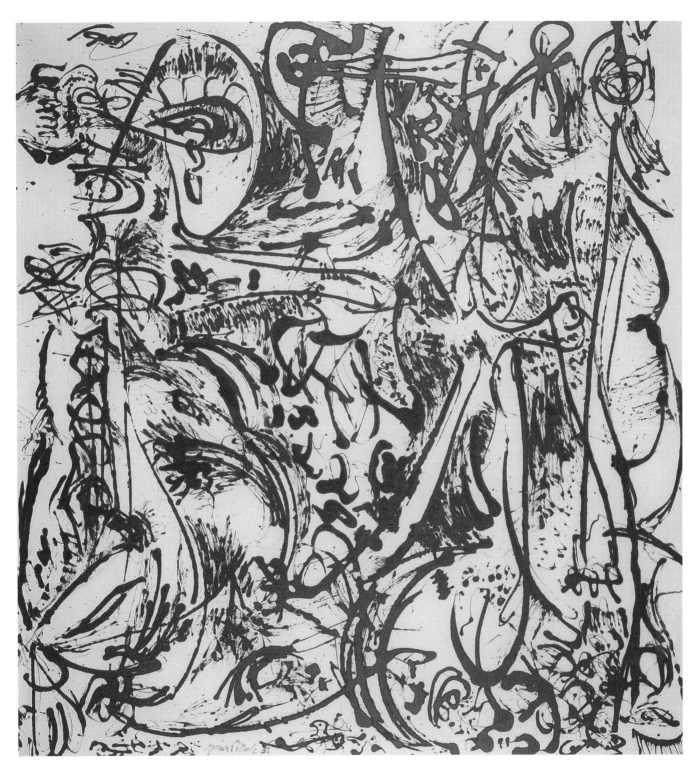

Jackson Pollock, *Echo (Number 25)*, 1951. Enamel on unprimed canvas, 7' 7 7/8" x 7' 2" (233.4 x 218.4 cm). Courtesy The Museum of Modern Art, NY. Acquired through the Lillie P. Bliss Bequest and Mr. and Mrs. David Rockefeller Fund.

Context

Willem de Kooning was born in Rotterdam in 1904. As a child working in his mother's sailors' bar and reading American magazines, he dreamed of becoming a commercial artist. At 22 he stowed away to Manhattan, arriving penniless. At first he worked as a decorator, but by 1935 he had joined the WPA (Works Progress Administration, Federal Art Project). Along with Jackson Pollock he became a leading Abstract Expressionist. He died in 1997 from Alzheimer's disease.

Design Extension

De Kooning's wife said that the turbulence in his portraits came from his image of women and their role and "it was not sweet." Challenge students to paint an emotional portrait emphasizing personality traits with color and brushstrokes.

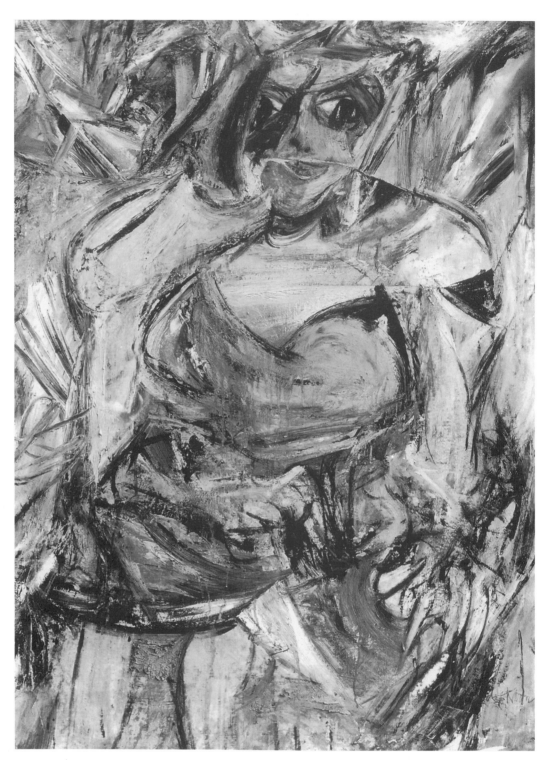

Willem de Kooning, *Woman*, 1952. Oil on canvas, 59" x 43" (149.9 x 109.2 cm). Courtesy The Museum of Modern Art, NY. Gift of Mrs. D. Rockefeller III.

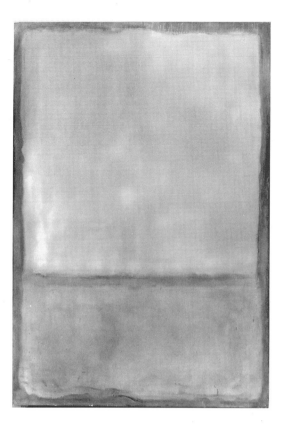

Mark Rothko, *Ochre and Red on Red*, 1954.
92 5/8" x 63 3/4" (235.3 x 161.9 cm). Courtesy
The Phillips Collection, Washington, DC.

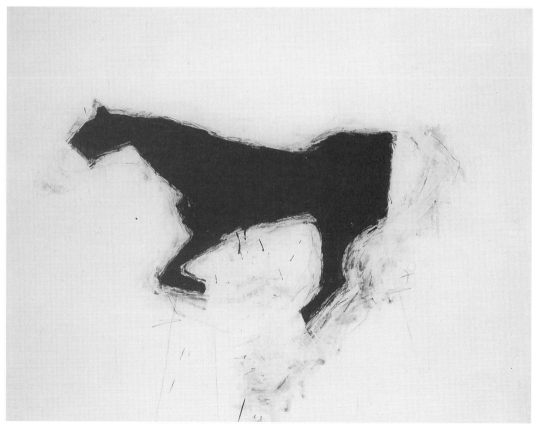

Susan Rothenberg, *Untitled Drawing, No. 44*, 1977. Synthetic polymer paint and tempera on paper, 18 1/2"
x 10 1/8" (98 x 127 cm). The Museum of Modern Art, New York. Gift of Mrs. Gilbert W. Chapman.

Chapter 8
The Present

(See "Chapters 7 and 8" on page T-2 regarding options for teaching this chapter.)

Objectives
Students will be able to:
- Identify Pop Art, Minimalism, Photo-Realism, contemporary abstraction, and Post-Modernism artworks. (Art history)
- Recognize that Pop Art features everyday objects and satirizes popular culture. (Aesthetics/Art criticism)
- Recognize that Minimalism reduces the subject to simplified forms, lines, and colors. (Art criticism)
- Understand that Photo-Realism incorporates the technology of photography. (Aesthetics/Art criticism)
- Understand how Post-Modern artists utilize the art of the past to create contemporary works. (Aesthetics/Art history)
- Create artworks embodying the concepts found in Pop Art, Minimalism, Photo-Realism, contemporary abstraction and Post-Modernism. (Art production)
- Perceive and appreciate the art of various contemporary artists. (Aesthetics)

Vocabulary
Pop Art
Minimalism
Photo-Realism
Post-Modernism
narrative content

Chapter Overview
Chapter 8 explores the various movements and new directions that have taken place in the world of art during the last half of the twentieth century. Students are introduced to the variety of approaches and materials being utilized today. Students should gain insight into the complexities found in the drawings reflecting our society.

Lessons 1, 2, 3 each lesson
pages 216–219   45 minutes

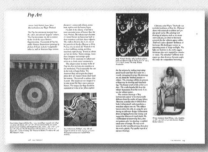

pages 218–219

Teach
After students have read pages 218 and 219, ask them what is similar about the subject matter in the works by Johns, Lichtenstein, and Warhol. (The subjects are all ordinary icons of our culture.) Point out the huge size of these works, which ensures that the viewer cannot overlook them.

Studio Experience
Encourage students to list mass-produced objects or subjects that they see every day but pay little attention to. These might be soda bottles, coins, candy wrappers, or faces that are constantly in the news. Brainstorm a list of items, writing the suggestions on the board. Guide students in selecting one of these as a subject, drawing it small, and then enlarging it on an 18" x 24" piece of paper. Students may wish to add color with markers or colored pencils.

Another option is to repeat the object instead of enlarging it, as Warhol did in *Marilyn*.

Materials
9" x 12" paper
18" x 24" drawing paper
pencils
erasers
markers
colored pencils

Lesson 4
pages 220–223   45 minutes

Teach
- Study the art on these pages. Ask what they have in common. Students should notice that images have been pared down to simple geometric forms. Compare Richard Serra's sketch to his sculpture. Is this how students imagined his sketch would look as a sculpture?

• Notice the size of each piece of art. Help students envision their scale and how they fill the viewer's field of vision with color. If possible, show students other examples of Minimalist art, such as sculptures by Donald Judd.

Studio Experience

In this activity students will create three drawings of one subject, such as a significant object from their childhood. Each drawing will become more simple and less objective than the previous drawing. Demonstrate how to sketch an object realistically, then draw it again very abstractly, and finally just draw a shape or two. Allow students to try this type of simplification for one or two objects.

Materials

drawing media such as pastels, oil pastels, or colored markers
9" x 12" drawing paper, 3 to 6 pieces per student
objects to draw such as tools, fruit, plants, cars, and toys

Lessons 5, 6
pages 224–225   each lesson
                       45 minutes

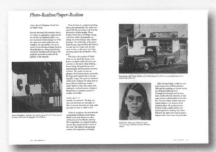

pages 224–225

Teach

After students have read these pages, call their attention to the size of the images, especially the size of Close's portrait. At this enlargement every hair and pore is visible. Remind students that as these artists began to pursue their art careers, Abstract Expressionism was the accepted art of the contemporary art scene.

Studio Experience

Assign students to photograph a location with which they are very familiar. This may be done in groups during class or as an out-of-class assignment. (Polaroid cameras provide instant prints but color 35 mm film with one-hour developing is often less expensive.)

Show students how to use a viewfinder to discover a composition within their photograph. Move a viewfinder over the photograph. When you find an interesting composition, tape the viewfinder to the photo or mark the edges of the composition with a grease pencil or marker. Enlarge the composition using a grid or a photocopier.

Students will draw their composition on their illustration board and then shade it with graphite pencil or colored pencils. Because this type of drawing is a slow process, students may want to work on it outside of class.

Materials

15" x 20" illustration board
graphite or colored pencils
erasers
viewfinders

Lesson 7
pages 226–227   45 minutes

Teach

• As students study the art on these pages, encourage them to imagine the artists creating these large works.

• Which painting indicates the most depth? Discuss how the artist created this depth.

• Ask how these are different from the abstract art in Chapter 7. How do these differ from Minimalist art on the previous pages? Which appeals to the students—abstract, Minimalism, or Photo-Realism? Why?

Studio Experience

Encourage students to experiment with creating depth or space in an abstract pastel or oil pastel drawing. Remind them that cool, pale, and dull colors tend to recede while bright, warm colors seem to come forward in a composition. Allow students to experiment, drawing some small studies with strokes of colors on a variety of colored backgrounds. If they use oil pastels, students may wish to incorporate some rubbings into their designs to vary the texture.

After students have experimented on a small scale, they can work on their larger paper.

Materials

pastels or oil pastels
18" x 24" drawing or pastel paper
fixative for pastels

Lessons 8, 9, 10
pages 228–233   45 minutes each

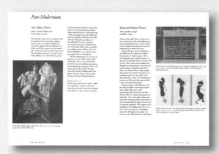

pages 228–229

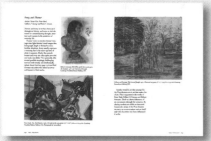

pages 230–231

Teach
• Briefly review the styles of art that immediately preceded Post-Modernism, from Abstract Expressionism to Minimalism. These were the "accepted" styles of art when Post-Modern artists introduced their new subjects and viewpoints. Contrast the art on pages 228–233 with art in the first part of this chapter.

—How is Mariani's *April* different from the Pop Art on pages 218–219 and the Photo-Realism images on pages 224–225?

—Try to verbalize the messages of Kruger's *Untitled (Questions)* and Longo's *Untitled* on page 229. Why did the artists leave these untitled?

—What is funny or ironic in the three pieces on pages 230 and 231? Notice how the drawing technique contributes to the sense of humor. What do Arneson's *Elvis* and Mariani's *April* have in common? (Like many Post-Modern pieces, they both make reference to classical arts.)

—What is happening in Coe's *No Job* on page 232? Write a word to describe the mood. Share these with the class. How do the shapes and their placement establish this mood?

• Discuss the definition and purpose of a narrative in painting. On page 233, notice how lettering contributes to the whole compositional design of Rivers's *Dreyfus*. What has been repeated?

Studio Experience
Have some fun with art from the past. Have students select a piece of art from Chapter 7 and redraw it in pencil in their own way by adding contemporary objects or changing a face to that of a current popular personality. They may add ink and/or color to their drawings. Students should write an explanation of their completed drawing and display it beside the drawing.

Materials
12" x 18" drawing paper or illustration board
choice of drawing media such as colored pencils, markers, ink, or oil pastels
pencils
erasers

Lessons 11, 12, 13
pages 234–239   45 minutes each

Teach
Divide the class into six cooperative-learning groups. Encourage each group to become the "experts" on one of the six artists in this lesson. Each group should determine the subject of their piece of art and what message or mood the artist was trying to convey. Then make new groups that include an "expert" from each of the six original groups. Each expert will present an artist to this new group.

Studio Experience
Ask: "If there were one thing in the world that you could change or make better, what would that be?" Instruct the students to write a paragraph describing some issue, cause, or problem that concerns them. How can they solve this problem?

Guide students in planning a mixed media artwork about their issue. They should draw their design, possibly including news clippings or photocopies in their artwork. They may add oil pastels or paint to their art.

Materials

15" x 20" illustration board
pencils
erasers
collage items such as newspapers
　and magazines
oil pastels
tempera or acrylic paints
brushes
water in containers

Lesson 14
pages 216–239　　45 minutes

Reteach

Review the various art styles
studied in this chapter. Have students make a chart with the
headings Pop Art, Minimalism,
Photo-Realism, contemporary
abstraction, and Post-Modernism.
Under each heading list artists
and famous artworks. Instruct
them to also write a characteristic
of each of these art styles.

Assess

• Check the charts that the
students compiled to ascertain
that they can identify Pop Art,
Minimalism, Photo-Realism,
contemporary abstraction, and
Post-Modernism. (Art history)

• In their charts students should
include these characteristics:

　—Pop Art often features
　everyday objects and satirizes
　popular culture.
　—Minimalism reduces a sub-
　ject to simplified forms, lines,
　and colors.
　—Photo-Realism incorporates
　the technology of photography.

—Post-Modern artists utilize
the art of the past to create
contemporary works.
(Aesthetics/Art history/Art
criticism)

• Lead a class discussion about
the six artists interviewed at the
end of this chapter. What are
these artists expressing in their
works? Have students compare
and contrast one of these artists
with an artist from another
period, such as the Renaissance or
the nineteenth century. What was
each artist trying to achieve?
Why would an artist from another
century appreciate the art by the
contemporary artist? (Aesthetics)

• Guide students in organizing
their art from this chapter into a
portfolio. Review these pieces to
determine that they did create
artworks embodying the concepts
found in Pop Art, Minimalism,
Photo-Realism, contemporary
abstraction, and Post-Modernism.
Together with the students select
work to mat or mount and
preserve in their course portfolio.
(Art production)

• Display the students'
works in a school or community
art show. Each piece should be
labeled with the artist's name,
title of the art, medium, and age,
grade, or course level. Students
should also include a statement
about the work and a description
of the assignment so that viewers
will understand what skills and
concepts were being learned.

Chapter Warm-up

Encourage students to look through this chapter for art that appeals to them. Remind them that each of the movements discussed in this chapter either grew out of a previous art style or was a reaction against a dominant art style. Ask them to select a piece that they would hang in their home and another piece to put in a public place such as the foyer of their school. Why did they select each of these pieces?

Context

• *Autumn Rhythm* is one of Jackson Pollock's drip paintings, which he created by slinging paint from a stick dipped into a bucket of paint. Have students compare the texture, movement, and width of lines in this painting with those squirted from a baster in *Echo* on page 213.

• Pollock was raised in a poor family in Wyoming, but by the time he was in high school, he and his family had moved to California. In 1930 he drove across the country to New York where he eventually studied with Thomas Hart Benton at the New York Art Students League. Pollock was an alcoholic, in and out of mental hospitals. During psychiatric counseling he was introduced to Jung's ideas of free expression, which influenced his painting. In 1956 while driving drunk, Jackson and a passenger were killed in an automobile accident.

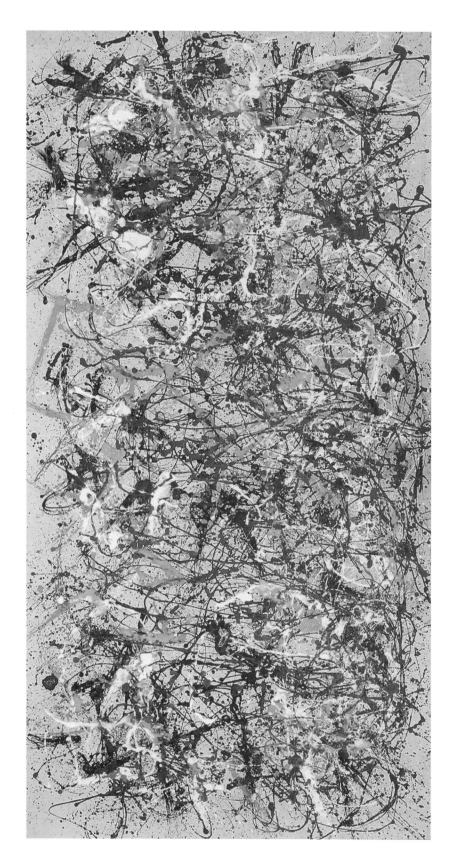

8 The Present

Each new movement in art is built upon the art created in previous decades. The art of today has been heavily influenced by the art of the past thirty years. Contemporary art serves as a point of departure for developing artists. As a developing artist yourself, you should use works of art as an artistic resource to learn about new techniques, trends and media.

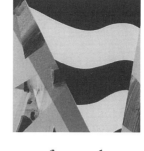

There is another important reason for exploring contemporary art history. Much contemporary art is concerned with social issues. Art has always had a relevancy to the times in which people live, but this is particularly true of contemporary art. In our time, art has become an important means of communication.

This chapter covers eight movements and trends in contemporary art. As you read about each one, consider the relevancy of the art to your own life. How have these artists influenced your definition of art?

Vocabulary
Pop Art
Minimalism
Photo-Realism
Abstraction
Post-Modernism
narrative content

Higher-Order Thinking Skills
Ask students to consider the definitions of art they gave in Chapter 1. Select a drawing from this chapter for discussion. Does the work meet the criteria for a work of art? Do students need to change their definitions of art? Point out that it is difficult today to give a simple, clear definition of what art is.

Key Chapter Points

- Artists in the twentieth century have developed new art movements and forms of expression.
- Pop Art features everyday objects and satirizes popular culture.
- Minimalism reduces the subject to simplified geometric forms and lines.
- Photo-Realism incorporates the technology of photography.
- Abstraction is nonrepresentational art.
- Post-Modernism is an era of openness to new subject matter and techniques.

Jackson Pollock, *Autumn Rhythm*, #30, 1950. Oil on canvas, 105" x 207" (266.7 x 525.8 cm). Courtesy The Metropolitan Museum of Art, George A. Hearn Fund, 1957. (57.92)

Pop Art

Higher-Order Thinking Skills

The art on these pages was created in opposition to Abstract Expressionism such as Pollock's painting on page 216. Ask: How are these works different from Abstract Expressionism?

Artists: Andy Warhol, Jasper Johns, Roy Lichtenstein and Wayne Thiebaud

The Pop Art movement emerged from the 1960s and satirized "popular" culture. The Pop movement was also a reaction to the art of the 1950s Abstract Expressionism. The content of Pop Art, unlike Abstract Expressionist paintings by Jackson Pollock, included recognizable subjects, such as American flags, cartoon characters, commercial objects, comic book replicas and the human figure.

No artist in the history of art had a more unceasing sense of humor than did Andy Warhol. His tedious reproductions of cultural heroes are humorous both in their monotony and their sheer vulgarity. The work is effective, but to see one of his portraits of Marilyn Monroe or Elvis Presley is to see them all. Warhol's work is about molding, casting, and then, senselessly reproducing. Trends in culture and art are similar. Trends emerge, reproduce, disappear and emerge again. Warhol's work comments on culture and serves as an ironic social commentary.

The subject matter in many works of Pop Art often includes the mundane or the overlooked. This is especially the case in the work of Jasper Johns. The American flags and targets that Jasper Johns drew are removed from their familiar contexts. The artwork is seldom what it seems. The targets are not designed to be shot at and the flag is not a patriotic banner. The targets and flags should be examined as works of art. Johns exploits

Jasper Johns, *Target with Four Faces*, 1955. Assemblage: encaustic and collage on canvas with objects, 26" x 26" (66 x 66 cm) surmounted by four tinted plaster faces in wood box with hinged front. Box, closed, 3 3/4" x 26" x 3 1/2" (9.5 x 66 x 8.9 cm). Overall dimensions with box open, 33 5/8" x 26" x 3" (85.3 x 66 x 7.6 cm). Courtesy The Museum of Modern Art. Gift of Mr. and Mrs. Robert C. Scull.

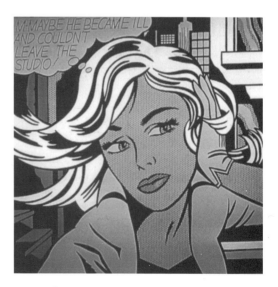

Roy Lichtenstein, *M–Maybe*, 1965. Oil and magna on canvas, 60" x 60" (152.4 x 152.4 cm). Photograph courtesy Leo Castelli Photo Archives.

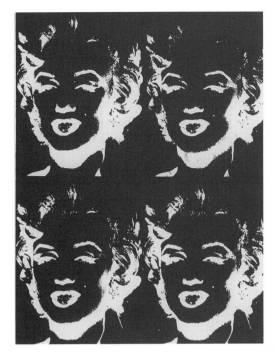

Andy Warhol, *Marilyn*, 1964. Synthetic polymer paint and silkscreen ink on canvas. 36" x 28" (91.4 x 71.1 cm). Courtesy The Andy Warhol Foundation.

California artist Wayne Thiebaud is an unrivaled draftsman of Pop Art. Thiebaud draws with extremely confident and precise pencil marks. His paintings and drawings of subjects, such as ice cream cones and pies, are often so lusciously executed that the subjects appear edible. Thiebaud is also a dynamic draftsman of landscape. His landscapes contain an interesting sense of design and light. The light and shadows in the works suggest landscapes that were inspired by a sunrise or sunset. The suburban California landscapes are often drawn at dynamic angles that make the composition interesting.

the flat subjects by making interesting pencil marks and lines that make for a visually intriguing drawing. His drawings are not about the finished product or subject. The drawings exhibit the process of discovery by drawing and then looking. The human touch of the artist is evident. The works breathe life from the subject that comes from the work of art, not the subject matter.

The cartoon drawings of Roy Lichtenstein appear to be dramatically different from the works of Jasper Johns. However, a similar idea is behind them both. Lichtenstein's work transforms a mundane subject into art. The subject matter exists, but only as a prop for producing an elaborate design. Lichtenstein draws intriguing forms that overlap and suggest the illusion of visual depth. His combinations of interesting lines, dots and patterns give his drawings a sophisticated sense of design. He uses a rich sense of color (usually primary) that gives the work a plastic, Pop quality typical of cartoon drawings.

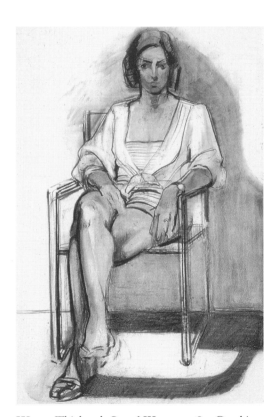

Wayne Thiebaud, *Seated Woman*, 1985. Graphite, 23 1/8" x 29" (58.7 x 73.7 cm). Courtesy Rutgers Barclay Galleries.

Minimalism

Design Extension
Guide students in creating a minimal drawing and then a sculpture based on their drawing.

Higher-Order Thinking Skills
• Write "Less is more" on the board. Ask students how they think this dictum by the Bauhaus architect Mies van der Rohe applies to Minimalist art. Research examples of International Style architecture from the mid-twentieth century and compare it to the art in this lesson.

• Challenge students to find pieces of art in Chapter 7 that are most like the Minimalist art on pages 220–223.

Artists: Richard Serra, Dan Flavin and Agnes Martin

Minimalism is an art movement that began in the 1960s. In this movement, artwork was reduced to minimal colors and simple geometric forms, lines and textures. Sculpture, a medium of pure, reduced form, was very appropriate for this movement. Important Minimalist sculptors include Donald Judd, Dan Flavin and Richard Serra.

However, this movement also produced outstanding draftspeople. One of these is Agnes Martin. Martin employs the reductive use of form. Any subject other than form is removed from her work. The work of the Minimalist painters and sculptors was criticized as being an end to art because Minimalism was an art of pure form. Critics suggested that this implied that art had taken its full course. Painting and sculpture had progressed from realism to abstraction, from abstraction to nonrepresentational abstraction, and finally, to minimalism. In a sense, art had played itself to an end.

Museums and galleries played a crucial role in the acceptance of Minimalist artworks. A series of boxlike sculptures by Donald Judd are only boxes—until they are placed in a museum. In that context, they become art.

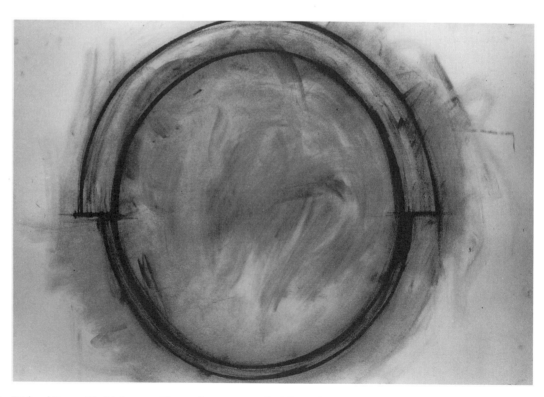

Richard Serra, *Untitled*, 1971. Charcoal on paper, 26 1/2" x 40" (67.3 x 101.6 cm). Courtesy of the artist. Photograph by Eric Pollitzer.

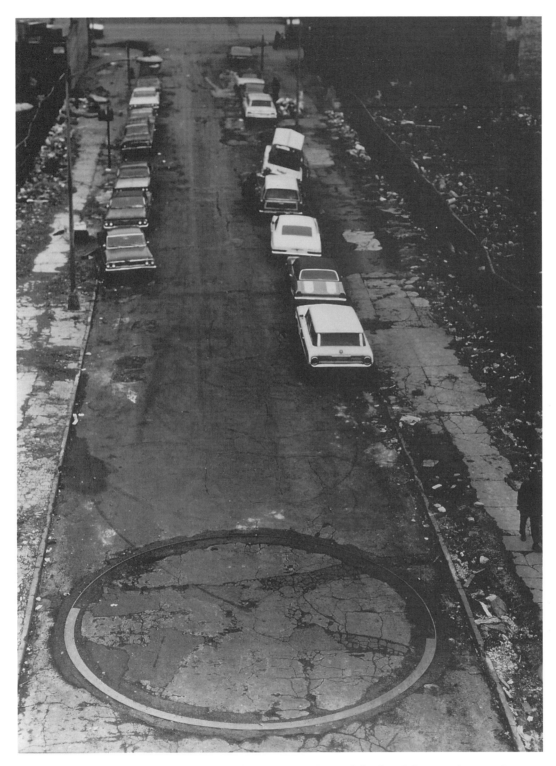

Richard Serra, *To Encircle Base Plate Hexagram, Right Angles Inverted*. Steel, 26' diameter (792.5 cm), 8" rim (20.3 cm). Installed 183rd and Webster Street, Bronx, NY. Collection of Ronald Greenberg, St. Louis.

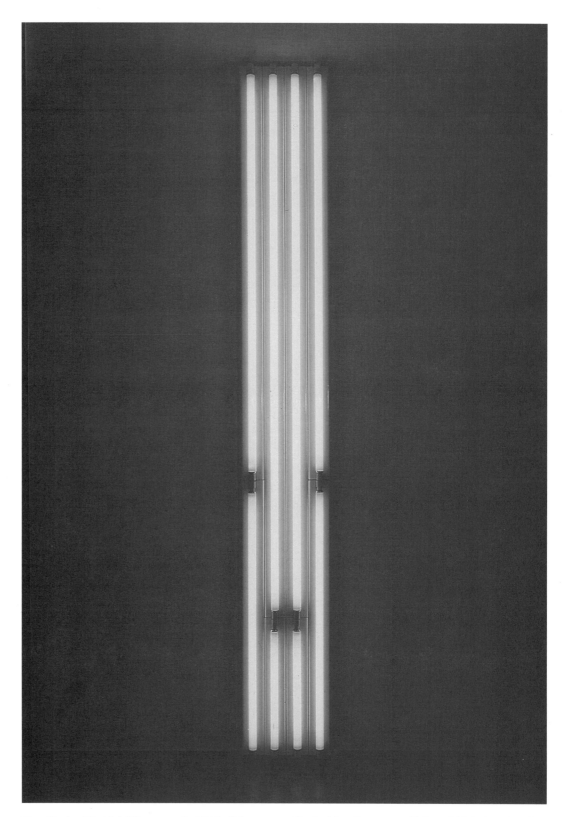

Dan Flavin, *Untitled (Monument for V. Tatlin)*, 1975–1. Cool white, fluorescent light 10' high (304.8 cm).
Photograph courtesy Leo Castelli Photo Archives.

Context
Canadian-born artist
Agnes Martin lives and
works in Taos, New
Mexico. For over thirty
years she has painted on
huge square canvases.
She is known for her
delicately colored striped
acrylic paintings.

Inquiry
Encourage students to
learn more about
Minimalist artists. Assign
them to research the
hard-edge paintings of
Ellsworth Kelly and
Kenneth Noland and the
thin poured colors of
Morris Louis.

Agnes Martin, *Untitled #8*, 1975. Acrylic, pencil and Shiva gesso on canvas, 6' x 6' (182.9 x 182.9 cm).
Courtesy The Pace Gallery. Photograph by Albert Mozell.

Photo-Realism/Super-Realism

Context
• The large sizes of many works by Photo-Realists are astonishing when seen firsthand. Project slides of these works on a wall to create an image about the same size as the original.

• Refer students to pages 106 and 107 to see other works by Robert Cottingham.

Artists: Robert Cottingham, Chuck Close and Ralph Goings

Pop Art introduced the common objects of a culture as appropriate subject matter for art. Pop Art exploited reality, but a new movement would emerge out of the late 1960s that would exploit the commonplace one step further. The movement is Photo-Realism or Super-Realism. Photo-Realism is a fitting name for the movement. Painting and drawing in this particular movement contains all the qualities of photography.

Photo-Realism is a method of painting almost photographically. The artists associated with this movement work from the information of photographs. Photo-Realists Chuck Close and Ralph Goings work from smaller photographs and enlarge the works to large-scale, realistic paintings. The technology of the photograph became reproduced by the brush of an artist and on a larger scale. In what sense are these works more "real" than anything supplied by the Realism of the past?

The large-scale portraits of Chuck Close are not about the beauty of the human condition; rather, his work concentrates on the harsh reality of being a human being. His portraits are never commissioned and the portraits never lie or flatter. The works are close-up glimpses of the human psyche exposed by the large-scale reproduction of the photographic image. The works are technical studies of his medium. He paints them in many different techniques, usually a square block at a time. His earlier work employed a minimal amount of pigment that produces a maximum amount of realistic visual effect.

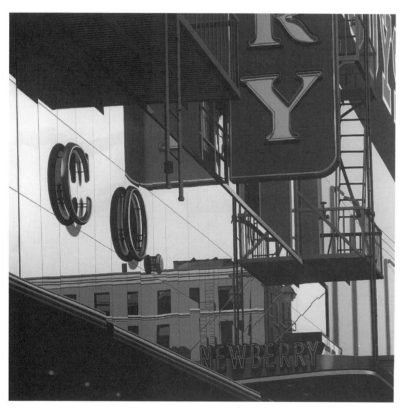

Robert Cottingham, *Newberry*, 1974. Oil on canvas, 78" x 78" (198 x 198 cm). Courtesy of the artist. Photograph by Eric Pollitzer.

THINK ABOUT IT
Consider this statement: "We shape our tools, and afterwards our tools shape us." How do the tools that artists use today reflect and shape the times in which we live?

Robert Cottingham, the most formally accomplished draftsman of the Photo-Realist movement, focuses on urban architecture and its reflective surfaces. His compositions are cropped in such a manner that design becomes a focus of the work. The angles in the paintings enhance the composition and design.

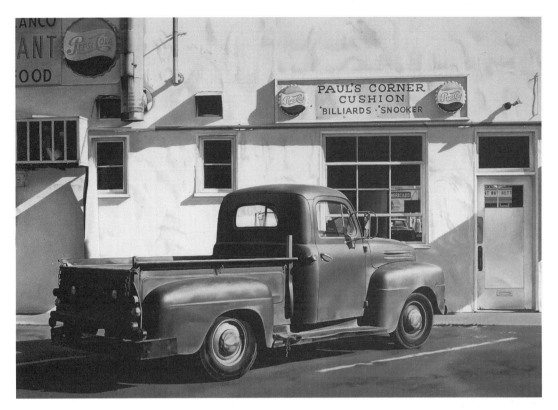

Ralph Goings, *Paul's Corner Cushion*, 1970. Oil on canvas, 48" x 68" (122 x 173 cm). Courtesy O. K. Harris Works of Art, NY.

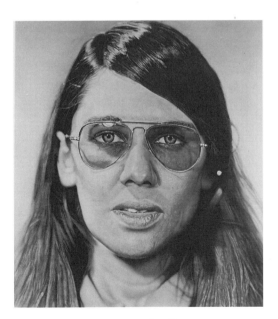

Chuck Close, *Susan*, 1971. Acrylic on canvas, 100" x 90" (254 x 228.6 cm). Courtesy The Pace Gallery.

Ralph Goings brings a different twist to the tediousness of Photo-Realism. Although his paintings are formal studies not altogether different from Cottingham's, Goings's work focuses more on the suburban elements of landscape and the rigid discipline of the still life. One of Goings's favorite and most typical subjects is the interior of the American diner. He prefers to draw ketchup bottles, napkin holders and scenes typical of a working-class diner. However, he approaches such mundane subjects with a keen sense for perfection.

Higher-Order Thinking Skills

The statement for discussion in Think About It is a paraphrase of a comment by the nineteenth-century writer John Ruskin, who said, "We shape our buildings, and afterwards our buildings shape us." What tools such as the Internet, photographic technology, electronic music, computer images, and MTV videos are shaping our times? Have students discuss this question in small groups.

Extension

Compare the realistic portraits by Chuck Close with portraits by Rembrandt. How does Photo-Realism differ from the Realism of the nineteenth century? How have TV and photographs influenced how we see and draw people and objects?

Context

• See another portrait by Chuck Close on page 180.

• Chuck Close said he was uncomfortable with the idea of being a Realist because he was as interested in artificiality as in Realism.

Contemporary Abstraction

Higher-Order Thinking Skills
Have students select one of the abstract works on these pages and write a short interpretation. What do they think the artist was trying to say? Can the work be interpreted in more than one way?

Interdisciplinary Connections
Music—Ask a music teacher for some music by contemporary composers, such as Philip Glass. Play the music as students look at the artwork in this chapter.

Theater—Either read or watch a video of the play *Art* by Yasmina Reza, which equates Minimalism, abstraction, and realistic art with personalities. The play is about a man who buys a white painting and the reaction of his friends to this purchase.

Context
To learn more about Ted Rose see "The Author" on page iv.

Artists: Ted Rose, Howard Hodgkin and James Havard

Abstraction became less relevant with the emergence of Pop Art and Photo-Realism. However, there are many innovative abstract artists producing relevant artwork today.

In looking at abstract or nonrepresentational painting, examine the surface of the painting and the painting's sense of illusionistic space or depth. Good design is not enough to make an abstract painting successful. Without space and depth, an abstract painting is "static" or motionless.

The paintings of Ted Rose utilize tones of color and texture to suggest illusionistic depth. Rose prefers to have the brightest colors and the richest textures appear to be in front of the simple backgrounds, which have muted gray tones of color. Rose also employs the use of collaged shapes in his paintings to enhance the sense of depth and design.

Howard Hodgkin employs the illusionist device of overlapping segments of troweled paint. The warm (yellow and red) colors appear to float over the rest of the cooler colors. Often in Hodgkin's paintings, the brushwork and troweled paint overlap onto the ornate frame to

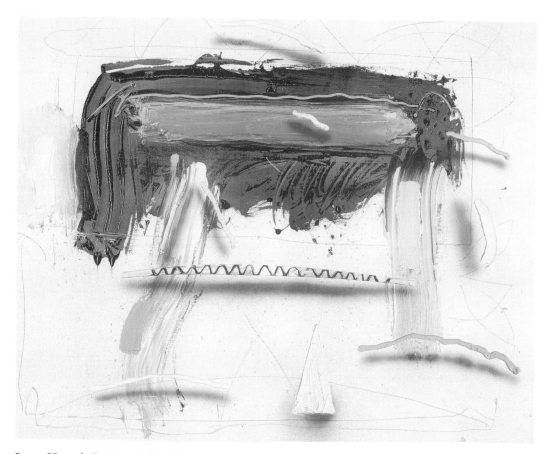

James Havard, *Zuni*, 1976. Acrylic on canvas, 48" x 60" (121.9 x 152.4 cm). Photograph courtesy Louis K. Meisel Gallery, NY.

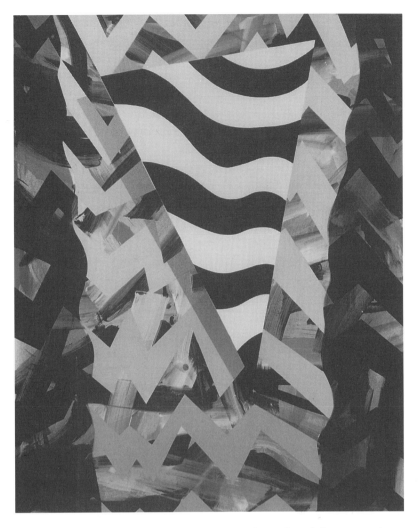

Ted Rose, *New York Wedge*, 1990. Acrylic transfer, 38" x 48" (97 x 122cm).

Cooperative Learning
Divide the class into groups of four to five students. Each group is a committee that has been assigned to buy a new piece of art for the town hall. The art will be purchased with community money. As a group they must select a piece of art from pages 216–227. At a local community meeting they must justify their purchase of this piece of art.

make the picture less confined and more interesting.

James Havard, an abstract-illusionist painter, often employs line and shadow to give his works the illusion of three-dimensional space. The images in his paintings appear interesting because they seem to float above the picture plane.

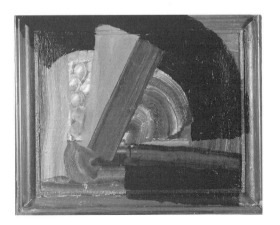

Howard Hodgkin, *Down in the Valley*, 1985–88. Oil on wood, 29" x 36" (73.67 x 91.4 cm). Courtesy Knoedler & Company, NY.

Post-Modernism

Higher-Order Thinking Skills
Have students search for the surprises in Mariani's art. What is the almost classical figure holding in his hand? (a Calder mobile) How about the hand on the floor? Follow the angles of the hands and legs, noticing how they create a sense of movement.

New Subject Matter

Artists: Martin Maddox and Carlo Maria Mariani

The period of time that encompasses the last quarter of the twentieth century is known as the era of Post-Modernism. The term suggests that the Modern era of the early three-quarters of the twentieth century has ended and that the end of the twentieth century is no longer a part of the Modern era. The Modern period has been characterized by its many different styles and artistic movements. What started with the Cubist paintings of Picasso progressed to the drips and splatters of Jackson Pollock and ended with the Minimalist sculptures of Donald Judd. However, with the increasing irrelevancy of Modernism and Abstraction there came a need for new subject matter. Hence, the art of the Post-Modern era is open to many new approaches to creating art.

The Post-Modernist era is an era of openness to new subject matter and techniques. The era has witnessed a rebirth in classical architecture and neo-classical figurative paintings. This is evident in the works of Post-Modern artists like Martin Maddox and Carlo Maria Mariani. Their works contain Classical and Neo-Classical themes.

THINK ABOUT IT
Synthesizing means fitting together different combinations to form a whole. By using ideas and styles from other centuries, artists find new ways to express meaning.

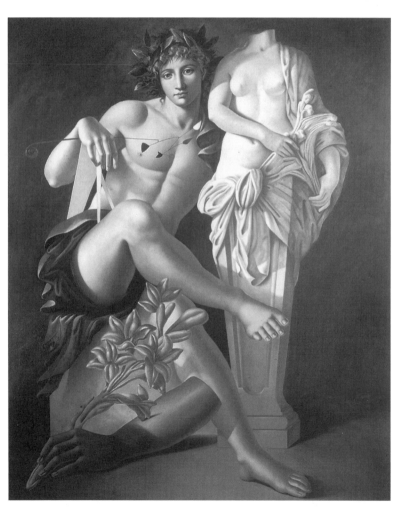

Carlo Maria Mariani, *April*, 1988. Oil on canvas, 90 1/2" x 70 3/4" (229.9 x 179.7 cm). Courtesy of the artist.

Social and Political Themes

*Artists: Barbara Kruger
and Robert Longo*

Artists in the 1980s like no other era in
art produced art with overt references to
social and political issues. Artists of this
era have approached political and social
commentary in numerous ways.

Barbara Kruger creates installations
and billboards for social and political
commentary. A visual image is often
accompanied with a simple sentence or
group of words that relate the image with
an idea. The work is commanding and
designed to communicate a message that
can be easily and quickly understood.
The work often evokes a sense of guilt
that probes the viewer's conscience for a
prolonged period of time. Her work
often contains a sense of screaming help-
lessness, as if the art is the only truthful
source of social commentary.

Robert Longo's work effectively uti-
lizes the discipline of drawing to reproduce reality and create social
commentary. His series of work titled
Men in Cities is a social commentary on
urban life. The works depict urban professionals dancing in urban nightclubs. At
close examination, the figures seem to be
in awkward positions. They appear to be
stumbling or freefalling and out of control. The work captures a disturbing
sense that the figures are caught in a
senseless and self-destructive social ritual.

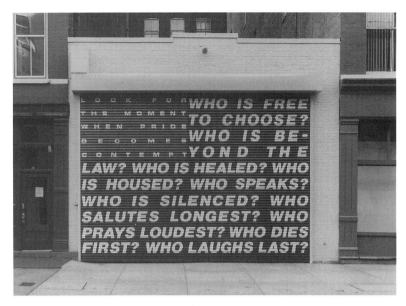

Barbara Kruger, *Untitled (Questions)*, 1990. Enamel on aluminum, 186" x 254"
(472.4 x 645.2 cm). Courtesy Mary Boone Gallery, NY. Photograph by
Zindman/Fremont.

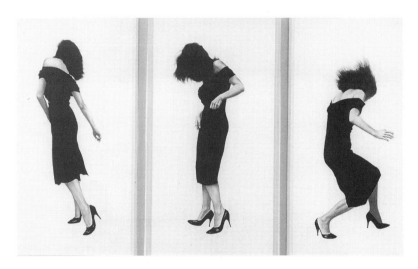

Robert Longo, *Untitled*, 1980. Oil, paintstick and graphite on paper, 3 panels,
each 60" x 40" (152 x 102 cm). Photograph courtesy Metro Pictures, New
York. Collection of Charles Saatchi.

**Higher-Order
Thinking Skills**
Barbara Kruger said "I
want to speak and hear
impertinent questions
and rude comments."
How did she accomplish
this in her billboard-
style, mock advertising
graphic?

Irony and Humor

Artists: Susan Coe, Peter Saul, Gilbert & George and Robert Arneson

Humor and irony in art have been used throughout history, and serve as vital elements for communicating thought, emotion and reaction to the problems of everyday life.

Humor tends to translate human messages into light-hearted visual images that help people laugh at themselves or at familiar situations. Irony usually expresses a meaning that is the exact opposite of what is expected. Works that contain humor and irony are often quite powerful and make you think. They generally offer several possible meanings, challenging viewers both visually and intellectually. Artists Susan Coe (see page 232) and Red Grooms are artists who often use irony and humor in their works.

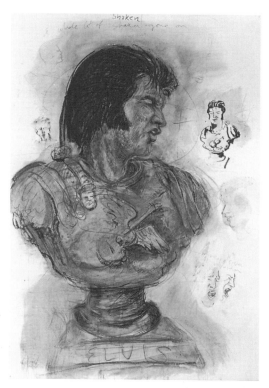

Robert Arneson, *Elvis (#1)*, 1978. Ink, conté, pencil on paper, 40" x 31" (101.6 x 78.7 cm). Courtesy Frumkin/Adams Gallery, NY.

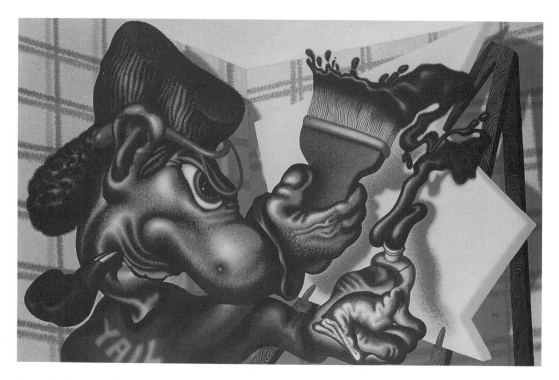

Peter Saul, *New York Painter*, 1987. Oil and acrylic on canvas, 72" x 108" (182.9 x 274.3 cm). Courtesy Frumkin/Adams Gallery, NY. Photograph by eeva–inkeri.

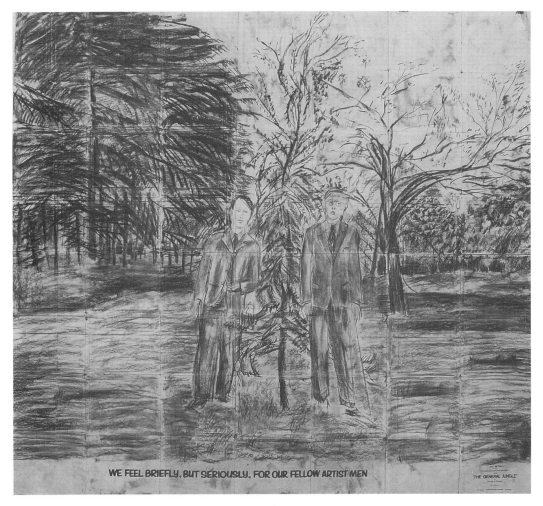

WE FEEL BRIEFLY, BUT SERIOUSLY, FOR OUR FELLOW ARTIST MEN

"THE GENERAL JUNGLE"

Gilbert and George, *The General Jungle*, 1971. Charcoal on paper, 8' x 7' (243.8 x 213.4 cm). Courtesy Sonnabend Gallery, NY.

Design Extension
Students may be willing to explore their dreams in their artwork. Suggest that they write down some dream sequences and then illustrate them. Written dreams intermixed with images, symbols, and illustrations can often provide a rich format for compositional subject matter in drawings.

Another trend in art that emerged in the Post-Modern era is art that makes fun of art. This is apparent in the works of Peter Saul, Gilbert & George and Robert Arneson. Their art shows influences of art movements through the centuries. By placing modern art within an historical framework, artists of the Post-Modern era carry on a conversation with art itself and with the artists who have influenced it so far.

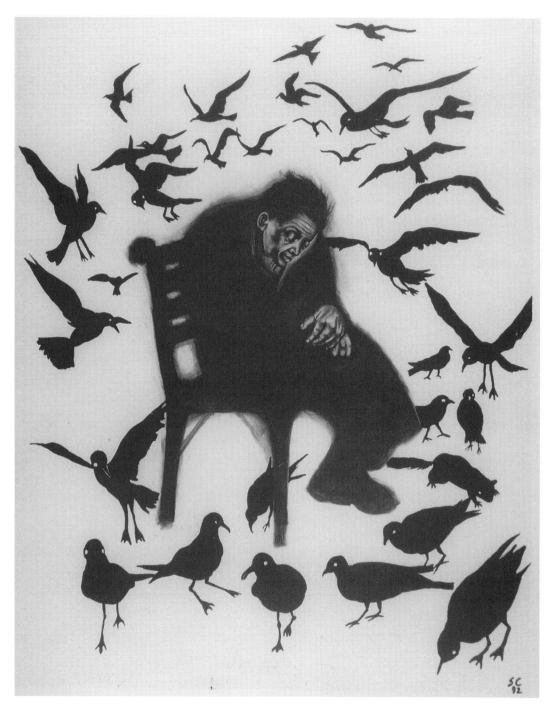

Sue Coe, *No Job*, 1992. Graphite, crayon, gouache and ink on Strathmore Bristol board, 29 1/8" x 23 1/8" (74 x 58.7 cm). Courtesy The Galerie St. Etienne.

Narrative Content

Artists: Eric Fischl, Ed Ruscha and Larry Rivers

Narrative painting emerged during the 1980s. The narrative that accompanies the image serves as an in-depth explanation for the work itself. These works suggest that visual images alone are not enough to communicate visual perceptions. Post-Modernism, at this point, is concerned with the role of both language and the visual image to communicate.

However, not all narrative work requires words. The artwork of Eric Fischl is narrative, but it needs no words to tell the story. Fischl's work is a twofold narrative. On one level, Fischl is describing real-life situations in suburbia, but on another level, Fischl is exorcising his own and our self-consciousness about being ordinary and vulnerable human beings. He uses nudity in most of his paintings to force the viewer to recognize his or her sense of self-consciousness.

Ruscha employs the illusive device of cliché to set the mood in his paintings. The work itself contains a commercial graphics quality that becomes a part of making the work a visual and literal cliché.

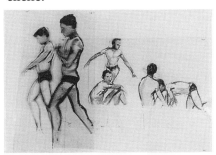

Eric Fischl, *Study for Cargo Cults*, 1984. Oil/mylar, 56 x 70" (142 x 179 cm). Courtesy Mary Boone Gallery, New York.

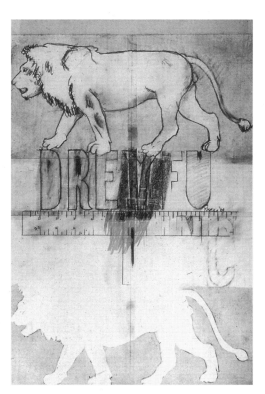

Larry Rivers, *Dreyfus*, late twentieth century. Graphite on paper. Courtesy of the artist.

Perhaps one of the most talented and accomplished narrative artists creating innovative work today is New York artist Larry Rivers. Rivers's work often contains autobiographical references, and is honest and confessional. His work often contains mixed media, collage, found objects and is often done in relief. A characteristic of Rivers's work that sets his work apart from others' is his austere sense of gesture. His paintings seldom contain the elements of figurative realism, but his sense of gesture is poignant and precise.

Extension
Have students collect examples of Pop Art, Minimalism, Photo-Realism, abstraction, and Post-Modernism in magazine, newspaper, and poster advertisements. They can also watch for them in television commercials. If possible, display the advertisement and a reproduction of an artwork in the same style so that students can see both the commercial and fine arts directions.

Design Extension
Teach students to join lettering with a shape like Larry Rivers did in *Dreyfus*. They may use type books, computer fonts, or stencils as letter shapes. Remind them that type fonts carry connotations that are often reflected in their name. Some seem young and jazzy while others are more serious. Encourage students to experiment fitting a shape with the lettering to form a unified design.

Six Artists Speak

Extensions

• This section features six contemporary artists talking about their work. Students can discuss the statements and the artworks in relation to one another: How well does the statement seem to "match" the artwork? Do artists see their work as others see it? How well do they communicate their ideas through their art? This can lead to discussions of students' own works, as well as writing exercises in which students explain what their art means to them, and how they feel they express their ideas through drawing and other forms of art.

• Discussions of ethnicity in art, specialized drawing techniques, and choice of subject matter might also be prompted by these statements and artworks.

W. Perry Barton

For me, there is something about the relationship between paper and the way it responds to the touch of the brush and charcoal stick that keeps pulling me back to drawing. In my drawings, the images are figurative, which immediately invokes a narrative and familiarity. I try to keep both these elements in an uneasy balance. I believe that the viewer must be engaged to complete the picture. So each story is incomplete and eventually totally different. The nature of black and white is quite helpful here. If the figure is familiar, the familiarity is kept at bay by the black-and-whiteness of it.

And yes, there is also humor in my drawings. Art can be funny and serious at the same time. So here we have figurative–narrative–kept at a distance–funny–serious drawing.

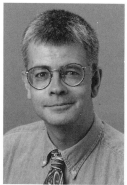

W. Perry Barton. Photography by Kalman Zabarsky.

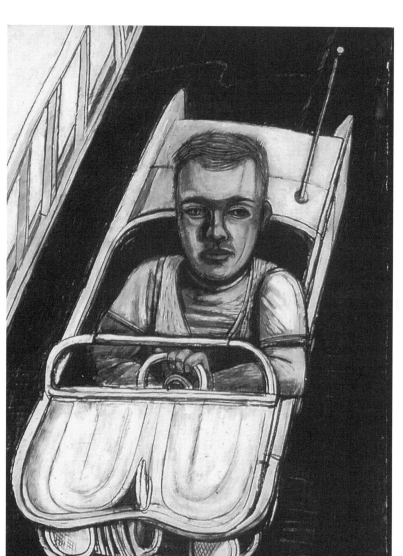

W. Perry Barton, *Cruising Through Toy Town*, 1990. Charcoal and acrylic on paper, 42" x 58" (106.7 x 147.3 cm). Courtesy of the artist.

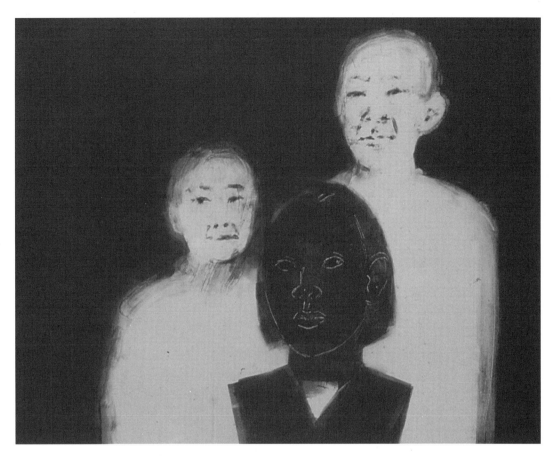

Joanna L. Kao, *Two Generations*, 1992. Monotype, 22" x 27" (55.9 x 68.6 cm). Courtesy of the artist.

Extension
For other examples of family images, see pages 33, 144, 198, and 207. After studying these, students may draw their own family, indicating their heritage, personality, interests, or relationships.

Joanna L. Kao

My art is concerned with cultural and racial identity. The child of Chinese immigrants, I knew only one other Chinese person in school, my sister. I felt disconnected from the world because I looked different from everyone else. Yet even within our family, cultural and generational gaps separated us from our parents.

When I finally traveled to China as an adult with my parents, I found I was an outsider there too. I took pride in my Chinese heritage, which connected me to my parents, but I did not know the language or culture that accompanied this heritage.

Art is one of the means by which I can explore how I am different and where I fit in. I have been working on a series of monotype prints concerned with images from the histories of my parents and from my childhood. Through these images, I seek to explore the interactions that have shaped my family and myself.

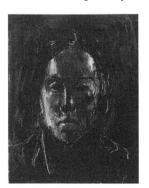

Self-portrait, 1992. Monotype. 18 x 14" (46 x 36 cm). Courtesy of the artist.

Extension

• Refer students to another work by Frenkel on page 15.

• Ask students to compare this drawing to Glackens's *Washington Square* on page 192. Contrast the size of the figures and how each artist indicated depth. What was each artist most interested in showing? Draw a group of people playing. Indicate their environment or location. Refer to Figurative Compositions on page 140.

Yetti Frenkel

Ordinary characters from everyday life, like the people one might see on the subway, in school yards or at shopping malls, populate my paintings. I am fascinated by the unspoken dialogue between people, the language of posture and expression, and by the small moments of drama in daily life. The challenge by a bully, the weariness of a commuter, the joyous abandon in an unguarded moment—these moments are the main focus of my work. My work is political in that it portrays contemporary problems and attitudes; if I have a social agenda, it is to create a feeling of empathy in the viewer and a feeling of connectedness to the community.

My most recent exhibit was shown at the Lynn Historical Society in Lynn, Massachusetts. This exhibit portrayed the children of the city of Lynn and was the culmination of two years of painting and drawing people from the community.

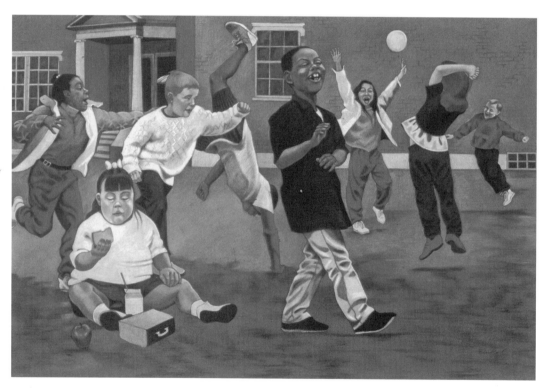

Yetti Frenkel, *Recess*, 1991. Conté, 40" x 60" (101.6 x 152.4 cm). Courtesy of the artist.

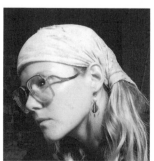

Yetti Frenkel.

Susan Avishai

In my series of colored pencil drawings, my subject is fabric affected by form, which I use as a metaphor for any covering that can both hide and reveal what is underneath. By eliminating the head and hands, I focus more on the elements of picture-making rather than storytelling. Human expression is still implied by the stance of the figure, the choice of clothing, the "body language," but it is no longer predominant. I'd like to feel I could convey the smell of freshly ironed cotton or the coarseness of linen. I have turned up the volume by adding color. It feels heady and full of possibilities; I'm like a cook discovering spices.

Scale is important in my new work. I have come in close to the subject, presenting it right up to the picture plane and often eliminating the background altogether. The size lets the viewer become more bound up in the image.

Extension
Students may want to compare the work on this page to another Avishai work on page 6.

Design Extension
Allow students to draw a close-up of a piece of fabric such as a denim jacket or letter sweater. Encourage them to concentrate on the texture and the form.

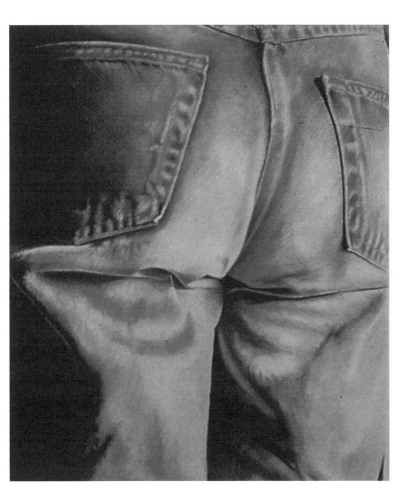

Susan Avishai, *Study in Blue*, 1990. Colored pencil, 12" x 13 1/2" (30.5 x 34.3 cm). Courtesy of the artist.

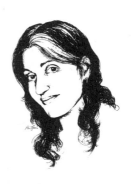

Self-portrait, 1994. Pen and ink. 6 x 7 3/8" (18 x 19 cm). Courtesy of the artist.

Extension
Other works by Riesing
can be seen on pages
100, 102, and 103.

Design Extension
Experiment with
Riesing's method of
darkening the page with
powdered charcoal or
by rubbing soft charcoal
over the page and then
wiping out the light
areas.

Tom Riesing

Most of my recent work has used the Alcoa Highway Bridge as its main subject matter. As a form, the bridge fits nicely with the way I think about the interaction of structure and space. I like the way this bridge both frames and mimics the landscape and how it changes as you move around it. It can go from dense and impenetrable to open and ethereal, or from towering (even heroic) when seen from below to almost inconsequential when seen from above.

These drawings are done on paper treated with powdered charcoal. The image is produced exclusively by erasing the black surface. This erasing technique allows me to work reductively and create light at the same time. The powdered charcoal I use is not very dark; I have a very narrow range of value to work with. In the finished piece, there is a lot less shown than is actually perceived by the viewer.

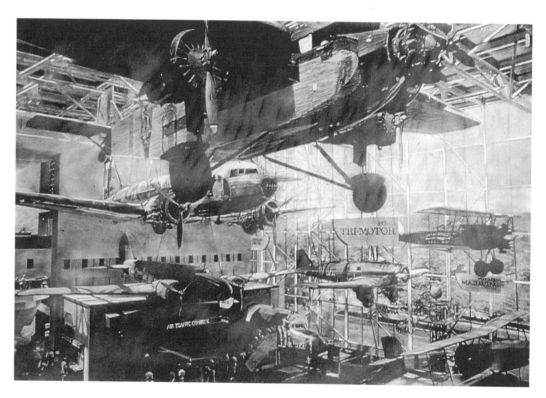

Thomas Riesing, *Ford Tri–Motor*, 1989. Charcoal on paper, 42 1/2" x 62" (108 x 157.5 cm). Courtesy of the artist.

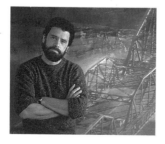

Tom Riesing. Photography by Robin Hood Photography, Nashville, TN.

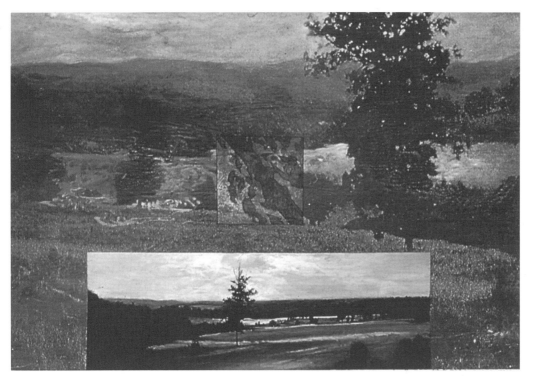

Marcia Goldenstein, *Reversal*, 1991. Acrylic, watercolor, xerox and pencil. 30 x 21" (76 x 53 cm). Courtesy of the artist.

Marcia Goldenstein

My mixed media pieces are motivated by the rich tradition of landscape painting. The variety of materials enables me to analyze both the historical significance of landscape painting and my personal response to unique places. Having grown up on the Great Plains in Nebraska, I found my understanding of landscape challenged when I moved to East Tennessee. The emphasis of the landscape shifted from sky to foliage; from horizontal to diagonal; from distant panorama to more intimate spaces.

There are so many ways in which a sense of place can be experienced—through panoramas, intimate close-ups, maps, photographs and historical references. In my works, the shifts in focus, perspective, scale and visual language are overlaid and combined to create a composite of various levels of reality and personal responses to a particular time and place.

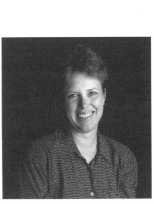

Marcia B. Goldenstein.
Photography by Mary Entrekin.

Glossary

abstraction Simplification and/or alteration of forms, derived from actual observation or experience to present the essence of the objects, people or places.

aesthetics Artistic qualities of forms, and what's beautiful in a work of art.

aggressive line A line that is strongly emphasized.

ambiguous space The spatial relationships between the positive and negative space are not clearly defined.

analogous colors Colors that are adjacent to one another on the color wheel.

analytical line A line that establishes objects in relation to one another and to the space they occupy.

anatomy The study of the parts of the human body.

atmospheric perspective or **aerial perspective** A means to achieve the illusion of space, based on the observation that the value and value contrasts of objects decrease as the objects recede into the distance.

avant garde Term used to describe the work that is in the newest form of visual expression.

background The area of a picture that appears farthest away in a three-dimensional illusion.

balance Principle of art that arranges elements in a work of art so that they seem to be "weighted" evenly throughout.

base line The imaginary line on which an object lies.

biomorphic shape Irregular shape that resembles the curves found in live organisms.

blind contour Line drawing in which the artist never looks at the paper. This method helps the artist develop a feel for space and form. It also improves eye-hand coordination.

broad strokes Wide drawn markings achieved by using the sides of drawing media, such as charcoal, graphite, pastels, etc.

caricature Drawing that exaggerates prominent features or characteristics of the subject.

cartoon A comic drawing that simplifies or exaggerates a person or event.

cast shadows The shadow cast by a form onto a nearby surface.

chiaroscuro In drawing or painting, the use of strong contrast between light and dark, and the gradual transition of values, producing the effect of modeling.

chromatic Relating to colors.

collage A work of art in which materials, such as paper, cloth or found materials, are glued onto a surface.

color An element of art that refers to the character of a surface, derived from the response of vision to the light reflected from that surface.

color tonality A particular selection and arrangement of color schemes, involving hue, value and intensity relationships.

color triad A group of three colors spaced equally apart on the color wheel.

color wheel The circular arrangements of hues based on a color theory.

complementary colors Hues that are directly opposite each other on the color wheel. Intense color effects are achieved through the placement of complementary colors next to each other.

composition The organization or arrangement of visual elements, such as lines, spaces, tones and colors, in a work of art.

constricted line An aggressively stated line that creates a feeling of tension.

content The essential meaning, significance or aesthetic value of an art form, that includes emotional, intellectual, symbolic, thematic and narrative connotations.

contrast Extreme differences in colors, values, textures and other elements.

contour The outer edges of any three-dimensional form that is defined by line.

contour drawing A line drawing that defines the outer and inner shapes of forms.

contour line In drawing, the line of varying thickness, tone and speed, that follows and emphasizes the contour of three-dimensional forms.

convergence In the system of linear perspective, the point at which parallel lines meet, or converge, as they recede.

cropping Masking unnecessary areas of a picture to create an interesting composition.

cross-contour lines Contour lines that intersect one another at oblique angles. Cross-contour line emphasizes the volume of an object.

cross-hatching The overlapping of hatched or parallel lines to create value.

Cubism A style of art that uses two-dimensional geometric shapes to depict three-dimensional organic forms.

curvilinear Stresses the use of curved lines.

Dada An anti-art movement that resulted from the social, political and psychological effects of World War I.

design The overall conception of a work of art.

diminution The phenomenon of objects farther away appearing smaller in linear perspective.

distortion To deform or change something from its normal shape to another, less realistic shape.

diptych A work of art in two sections or parts.

dominance Effect created by making certain elements appear more important than others in a composition.

drawing style A particular way of drawing that defines the artist's own style or a specific period of time.

elements of design The basic components used by the artist to create works of art. Shape, value, texture, line and color are elements of design.

elevation A drawing that contains images on a vertical plane without depth or perspective.

ellipse A circle seen from an oblique angle, creating an elongated shape.

elongated Stretched out in length.

emotionalism Theory of art that judges the expressive qualities of a work of art.

emphasis Principle of art by which the artist combines contrasting sizes, shapes, colors or other elements to place greater attention on certain areas in a work of art.

exaggeration Enlargements or distortions of elements in a work of art.

Expressionism A movement in art of the early twentieth century that began in Germany. Also used to describe all art that communicates strong emotional and personal feelings.

eye level An imaginary horizontal line that is even with the height of your eyes.

Fauvism An art movement that began in France about 1905, that featured a strong, emotional use of color and decorative qualities.

figure The human form or any recognizable object or nonrepresentational shape.

fixative A chemical that is sprayed over a two-dimensional work of art to prevent smearing and to make art media, such as charcoal, graphite or pastels, adhere to the paper.

found objects Any natural or human-made objects found and used by an artist in a work of art.

foreground Area of a picture that appears nearest to the viewer.

foreshortening A technique used to show the proportions of an object in a space, and distinguish the foreground and background of a picture plane.

form A three-dimensional shape that encloses space.

formalism A theory that judges a work of art by its organization of the elements of art.

format The overall shape and size of the surface of a work of art and the position it occupies in relation to the viewer.

Futurism A twentieth century submovement within Cubism. The imagery is based on an interest in time, motion and rhythm, in response to the machinery and human activities of modern times.

gallery An enterprise where art is exhibited and sold.

gestural drawing A quick drawing that captures the gestures and movements of the body.

graphic artist An artist who designs, illustrates and creates any kind of art for printed reproduction.

ground Any surface on which a picture is drawn or painted, such as canvas, paper, cardboard, etc.

hard copy Printed computer image.

hard edge Crisp, clean edges achieved through the use of flat, even values or colors.

harmony Principle of art that stresses the related qualities of all parts of a composition.

hatching A technique in which lines or strokes are placed parallel to each other; used to create gray tones.

highlight The area on a form that reflects the most light.

horizon line The line at which sky and earth meet.

hue The characteristic or quality identified by the name of a color.

implied line Line that is suggested by a change in color or value.

Impressionism Late nineteenth-century movement in which artists recorded the immediate effect produced by light.

incised line A line cut into a surface with a sharp tool.

intensity The saturation, strength or purity of a color. A brilliant color is of high intensity; a dull color, of low intensity.

intermediate color Color created by mixing a primary color with a secondary color. See tertiary.

interpenetration The movement created by shapes or objects breaking through each other.

layering A technique in which art media are used over one another.

line An element of art that is a continuous mark made by a tool as it is drawn across a surface.

linear perspective Technique used to create the illusion of depth on a two-dimensional plane.

local color The natural color of an object as it appears to the naked eye.

logo A design that symbolizes or represents a company or individual.

lyrical line A decorative line that is gracefully ornate.

manipulation To model; to shape.

manuscript illumination The decorative drawings and paintings of handwritten books in the Middle Ages.

mass The illusion of weight or density of an object.

mechanical drawing A drawing made by using compasses or other drafting tools.

media Materials or tools used to create a work of art.

middleground The intermediate zone of space, between foreground and background, in a work of art.

mixed media A combination of media, such as ink and watercolor, to create a work of art.

modeling The use of light and dark values to create form.

monochromatic A color scheme of one color plus black and white.

motif The repetition of visual elements, or combination of elements, that dominate and help unify a work of art.

movement Principle of art that uses elements to create the illusion of action.

multiple perspective Different illusions of space used in one drawing.

museum A place where art is collected for public viewing.

narrative art A form of art that tells a story.

negative space The area surrounding positive shapes.

neutrals White, gray or black. Neutrals result when there is no reflection of any single wavelength of light, but rather all of them at once.

nonobjective Artwork without recognizable natural objects. The images are products of the artist's imagination.

one-point perspective Perspective in which all parallel lines converge at a single point on the horizon line.

opaque The quality of a material that does not let light pass through.

optical color Color seen when modified by the quality of available light.

organic Free, irregular form that resembles living things.

organizational line Line that gives structure to a drawing.

outline Line of uniform thickness around the outer edge of a form, to show its overall shape.

overlapping Placing one object in front of another, to create depth in a work of art.

pattern An arranged repetition of forms or design, or a combination of both.

perspective A technique used to create the illusion of three-dimensional space and objects on the two-dimensional surface of a picture plane.

perspective drawing A drawing on a two-dimensional surface that gives the illusion of three-dimensional space and objects.

picture plane The actual two-dimensional surface on which a drawing is made.

pigment Finely powdered coloring material used in paints and drawing media.

portfolio A collection of an artist's work for presentation.

portrait A picture that features a person or group.

positive-negative reversal The perception of shapes in a work of art that alternate between positive and negative identities.

positive shape The shape of an object that is the subject in a work of art.

primary colors Red, blue and yellow; colors that cannot be created by mixing together other pigments.

primitive art Visual art that uses imagery of folk art, and is characterized by an emphasis on form and expression. Often appears child-like.

principles of art The means by which the visual elements are organized and integrated into a unified arrangement. They include balance, harmony, emphasis, movement, rhythm, unity and variety.

proportion Relationship of elements to one another and to the whole artwork in terms of their properties of quantity, size and degree of emphasis.

realism The representation of actual places, people or objects according to their appearance in visible nature. The nineteenth-century Realism was a style of art that interpreted the subject matter of every-day life, and the meanings beneath surface appearances.

relief The raised parts of a surface background.

repetition The use of the same visual elements over and over in a composition. Repetition may produce the dominance of one visual idea, harmony, unity or a rhythmic movement.

representational drawing A drawing of objects, people or places that looks very much like what one sees.

rhythm Principle of art that uses repetition of visual elements in a work of art, to create a feeling of movement.

rubbing A technique of reproducing textures by placing paper over the textured surface, and rubbing the paper with a drawing medium.

saturation Intensity of a color.

scale The relative size or weight of an object compared to a constant size or weight.

secondary color The colors that result from the mixture of two primary colors; orange, green and purple are secondary colors.

shading Using art media to create darkened areas (shadows) that give the illusion of space and depth.

shallow space A space with limited depth.

shape An element of art that is two-dimensional, and encloses space. Shape can be divided into two categories: geometric shape and organic shape.

simulated (visual) texture The imitation of a texture implied in an artwork.

simultaneous contrast Intensified contrast that results whenever two different color tones or two contrasting values come into contact.

sketch A quick drawing that may be a reference for later work.

sketchbook A drawing notebook in which artists record things they see or imagine.

space An element of art that is the area around and within an object.

spatial gesture The implication of gestural movement by an imagined connection of objects distributed in space.

spectrum The complete range of color presented in a beam of light.

still life An arrangement of non-moving objects that are subject matter for a work of art.

stippling A technique that uses patterns of dots to create values and value gradation.

structure The constructive elements of a work of art; the foundation of a composition.

style The unique character contained in a work of art, period of time or geographical location. Style also means an artist's expressive use of media to give works individual character.

subjective Personal or individual viewpoint through which the artist is free to change, or modify characteristics of a natural form, emphasizing personal emotions.

subjective colors Colors selected by the artist that have no connection with object reality.

subject matter Things represented in a work of art.

subject meaning The content derived from subject matter in a work of art.

symbol An image that stands for something more than its own literal meaning.

symmetrical balance Balance created through the duplication of an image, or of an element on either side of a composition divided in half.

tactile A quality perceived through the sense of touch.

technique The method, skill or system of working with tools and materials.

tertiary colors Colors created by mixing primary and secondary colors. See intermediate color.

texture An element of art that refers to the tactile quality of a surface.

three-dimensional shape A shape that has height, width and depth.

thumbnail sketches Small, quick sketches that record ideas and information for a final work of art.

tone In visual arts, the lightness and darkness of a color.

tooth The texture of a sheet of paper.

translucent Quality of any material that allows some light to pass through.

trompe-l'oeil The French term for trick-the-eye. It is an illusionistic technique in which nature is copied so realistically that the subject can be mistaken for a natural form.

two-dimensional shape An area defined by length and width.

unity A principle of design that relates to a work of art whose many different parts seem to connect well to one another.

value An element of art that refers to the relative darkness or lightness of an area.

value gradation The gradual change from dark to light areas. It creates the illusion of three dimensions on a flat surface.

Bibliography

value scale The range from white through gray to black, modified gradually.

vanishing point In linear perspective, the point on the horizon line at which all the receding parallel lines converge.

variety The use of many different elements in a composition.

viewfinder A device that works as a "window" through which subject matter is pictured. It gives the artist an idea of proportion, layout, and is excellent for cropping.

visual elements The means by which artists convey their ideas and feelings. Visual elements are color, line, shape, texture and value.

visual environment All the natural or human-made things that surround you.

volume The quality of a three-dimensional object that occupies a certain amount of space.

wash The application of ink or paint thinned with water to the drawing surface.

wash drawing Drawing in which washes of thinned ink or paint are used.

working drawings The study drawings for a final work of art.

Angelo, Sandra. *Exploring Colored Pencil.* Worcester, MA: Davis Publications, Inc., 1999.

Betti, Claudia, and Teel Sale. *Drawing: A Contemporary Approach.* Orlando: Harcourt Brace Jovanovich, 1998.

Blake, Wendon. *Figure Drawing Step by Step.* Mineola, NY: Dover Publications, 1998.

———. (drawings by Ferdinand Petri). *Starting to Draw.* New York: Watson-Guptill Publications, 1981.

Borgeson, Bet. *Basic Colored Pencil Techniques.* Cincinnati: North Light Books, 1997.

———. *The Colored Pencil.* New York: Watson-Guptill Publications, 1995.

Brommer, Gerald F. and Joseph Gatto. *Careers in Art: An Illustrated Guide.* Worcester, MA: Davis Publications, Inc., 1999.

Brommer, Gerald F. *Exploring Drawing.* Worcester, MA: Davis Publications, Inc., 1988.

Calle, Paul. *The Pencil.* Cincinnati: Writer's Digest Books, 1985.

Doyle, Michael. *Color Drawing: A Marker-Colored Pencil Approach.* New York: John Wiley and Sons, 1997.

Edwards, Betty. *Drawing on the Right Side of the Brain.* Los Angeles: J. P. Tarcher, Inc., 1989.

———. *Drawing on the Artist Within.* New York: Simon and Schuster, 1987.

Enstice, Wayne, and Melody Peters. *Drawing: Space, Form and Expression.* Englewood Cliffs, NJ: Prentice-Hall, Inc., 1995.

Gatto, Joseph. *Drawing Media and Techniques.* Worcester, MA: Davis Publications, Inc., 1986.

Goldstein, Nathan. *The Art of Responsive Drawing.* Englewood Cliffs, NJ: Prentice-Hall, Inc., 1998.

———. *Figure Drawing.* Englewood Cliffs, NJ: Prentice-Hall, Inc., 1999.

Graves, Douglas R. *Drawing Portraits.* New York: Watson-Guptill Publishers, 1983.

———. *Life Drawing in Charcoal.* Mineola, NY: Dover Publications, 1994.

Hanks, Kurt, and Belliston, Larry. *Draw! A Visual Approach to Thinking, Learning and Communicating.* Los Altos, California: William Kaufmann, Inc., 1990.

———. *Rapid Viz: A New Method for the Rapid Visualization of Ideas.* Menlo Park, CA: Crisp Publications, Inc., 1992.

Harrison, Hazel. *How to Paint and Draw: A Complete Course on Practical and Creative Techniques.* Brookline, MA: Hermes House, 1998.

———. *Pastels: Art School: Step-By-Step.* New York: Anness Publishing, Ltd., 1998.

Kaupelis, Robert. *Learning to Draw: A Creative Approach to Drawing.* New York: Watson-Guptill Publications, 1989.

Lohan, Frank J. *The Drawing Handbook.* New York: NTC Publishing Group, 1993.

Larson, Karl V. *See & Draw.* Worcester, MA: Davis Publications, Inc., 1993.

Martin, Judy. *The Encyclopedia of Colored Pencil Techniques.* Philadelphia: Running Press, 1997.

Mayer, Ralph. *The Artist's Handbook of Materials and Techniques.* New York: The Viking Penguin Press, Inc., 1991.

Mendelowitz, Daniel M., and Duane A. Wakeham. *A Guide to Drawing.* 5th ed. Orlando: Harcourt Brace, 1997.

Mugnaini, Joseph. *Expressive Drawing: A Schematic Approach.* Worcester, MA: Davis Publications, Inc., 1988.

Parramón, Jose Maria. *The Basics of Artistic Drawing.* Hauppauge, NY: Barrons Educational Series, Inc., 1994.

Petrie, Ferdinand. *Drawing Landscapes in Pencil.* New York: Watson-Guptill Publishers, 1992.

Roukes, Nicholas. *Art Synectics.* Worcester, MA: Davis Publications, Inc., 1984.

———. *Design Synectics.* Worcester, MA: Davis Publications, Inc,. 1988.

Sarnoff, Bob. *Cartoons and Comics: Ideas and Techniques.* Worcester, MA: Davis Publications, Inc., 1989.

Shadrin, Richard L. *Design and Drawing: An Applied Approach.* Worcester, MA: Davis Publications, Inc., 1993.

Sheaks, Barclay. *Drawing Figures and Faces.* Worcester, MA: Davis Publications, Inc., 1987.

Smagula, Howard J. *Creative Drawing.* Carmel, IN: Brown and Benchmark, 1993.

Winter, Roger. *On Drawing.* San Diego: Collegiate Press, 1991.

Index

Acknowledgments

There are many whom I wish to thank for their part in this book.

First there is my family, Kathy, Mason and Anna, who have given freely of their time and provided constant support. I would like to thank my parents, Wally and Billie Rose, who have been a constant source of encouragement to me.

I would also like to thank my students for their time, labor and encouragement. These students include Todd Walker for his work on chapters seven and eight, Gina Miller, for her research throughout the book, and Ha Young Lee, for her assistance on writing the glossary. Sarah Romeo provided much needed assistance throughout the book as my secretary.

This book certainly would not have been possible without the foundation that was laid over the years by such professors as Lee Forest, Jim McMurray, Carl Sublett, Tom Riesing, Jim Myford and Pat Pinson.

I would like to thank the following people for their encouragement and helpful suggestions; Don Umphrey, Arthur Williams, and Talle Johnson.

The driving force for the vision and development of the text belonged to Wyatt Wade and Claire Golding of Davis Publications. I would like to thank the following people who work for or are associated with Davis Publications; Nancy Burnett, Holly Hanson, Douglass Scott, Ewa Jurkowska and Janet Stone.

My sincere appreciation goes to all my students over the years who have provided me with a source of inspiration and a wealth of learning experiences.

— *Ted Rose*

Davis Publications, Inc. would like to thank Susan Ebersole and Diane McNutt of Scholastic, Inc. for their invaluable assistance in obtaining student work. Scholastic awards photographs appear on pages 13, 25, 32, 33, 35, 41, 43, 44, 50, 53, 70, 84, 85, 93, 100, 101, 104, 105, 124, 135, 139, 142, 145, 146, 148, 150, 151, 156, 178, and 189.

We would also like to thank Sally Bales and Donald Dodd for contributing student work.